Frommer's®

Toronto

...ition

by Pamela Cuthbert

WILEY

John Wiley & Sons Canada, Ltd.

ABOUT THE AUTHOR

Pamela Cuthbert is an award-winning food writer and editor published in *Macleans*, *Saveur*, *The Economist*, *Common Dreams*, and elsewhere. A past editor with *Time Out Toronto*, she has also contributed to other books, including *The Edible City* and the *Slow Food Almanac*. She lives in her hometown, Toronto, with her husband and young son.

Published by:

JOHN WILEY & SONS CANADA, LTD.

6045 Freemont Blvd.
Mississauga, ON L5R 4J3

ISBN 978-1-118-11595-4 (pbk); 978-1-118-14549-4 (ebk); 978-1-118-14547-0 (ebk); 978-1-118-14548-7 (ebk)

Editor: Gene Shannon
Developmental Editor: Melissa Klurman
Production Editor: Elizabeth McCurdy
Cartographer: Lohnes + Wright
Photo Editor: Richard Fox
Production by Wiley Indianapolis Composition Services
Front cover photo: Clock Tower of the Old City Hall and a modern building in downtown Toronto at dusk.
© HP Canada / Alamy Images
Back cover photo: New York Islanders' Zenon Konopka (28) is tripped by Toronto Maple Leafs goalie James Reimer. © Christopher Pasatieri / PhotoShot

SPECIAL SALES

For reseller information, including discounts and premium sales, please call our sales department: Tel. 416/646-7992. For press review copies, author interviews, or other publicity information, please contact our marketing department: Tel. 416/646-4584; Fax: 416/236-4448.

Manufactured in the United States of America

1   2   3   4   5 RRD 16   15   14   13   12

CONTENTS

10 SIDE TRIPS FROM TORONTO 204

11 PLANNING YOUR TRIP TO TORONTO 248

LIST OF MAPS

ACKNOWLEDGMENTS

Many thanks to my terrific editor Gene Shannon and to the Frommer's team who together made this assignment a pleasure. A heartfelt thanks to my husband, Paul French, whose keen observations of Toronto's many idiosyncrasies fuelled new discoveries. And a special thanks to my son Dylan who shows me around *his* town: a place that is bright and fascinating in its own right.

HOW TO CONTACT US

In researching this book, we discovered many wonderful places—hotels, restaurants, shops, and more. We're sure you'll find others. Please tell us about them, so we can share the information with your fellow travelers in upcoming editions. If you were disappointed with a recommendation, we'd love to know that, too. Please write to:

Frommer's Toronto, 18th Edition
John Wiley & Sons Canada, Ltd. • 6045 Freemont Blvd. • Mississauga, ON L5R 4J3

ADVISORY & DISCLAIMER

Travel information can change quickly and unexpectedly, and we strongly advise you to confirm important details locally before traveling, including information on visas, health and safety, traffic and transport, accommodation, shopping and eating out. We also encourage you to stay alert while traveling and to remain aware of your surroundings. Avoid civil disturbances, and keep a close eye on cameras, purses, wallets and other valuables.

While we have endeavored to ensure that the information contained within this guide is accurate and up-to-date at the time of publication, we make no representations or warranties with respect to the accuracy or completeness of the contents of this work and specifically disclaim all warranties, including without limitation warranties of fitness for a particular purpose. We accept no responsibility or liability for any inaccuracy or errors or omissions, or for any inconvenience, loss, damage, costs or expenses of any nature whatsoever incurred or suffered by anyone as a result of any advice or information contained in this guide.

The inclusion of a company, organization or Website in this guide as a service provider and/or potential source of further information does not mean that we endorse them or the information they provide. Be aware that information provided through some Websites may be unreliable and can change without notice. Neither the publisher or author shall be liable for any damages arising herefrom.

FROMMER'S STAR RATINGS, ICONS & ABBREVIATIONS

Every hotel, restaurant, and attraction listing in this guide has been ranked for quality, value, service, amenities, and special features using a **star-rating system.** In country, state, and regional guides, we also rate towns and regions to help you narrow down your choices and budget your time accordingly. Hotels and restaurants are rated on a scale of zero (recommended) to three stars (exceptional). Attractions, shopping, nightlife, towns, and regions are rated according to the following scale: zero stars (recommended), one star (highly recommended), two stars (very highly recommended), and three stars (must-see).

In addition to the star-rating system, we also use **seven feature icons** that point you to the great deals, in-the-know advice, and unique experiences that separate travelers from tourists. Throughout the book, look for:

special finds—those places only insiders know about

fun facts—details that make travelers more informed and their trips more fun

kids—best bets for kids and advice for the whole family

special moments—those experiences that memories are made of

overrated—places or experiences not worth your time or money

insider tips—great ways to save time and money

great values—where to get the best deals

The following abbreviations are used for credit cards:

AE	American Express	DISC	Discover	V	Visa
DC	Diners Club	MC	MasterCard		

TRAVEL RESOURCES AT FROMMERS.COM

Frommer's travel resources don't end with this guide. Frommer's website, **www.frommers. com**, has travel information on more than 4,000 destinations. We update features regularly, giving you access to the most current trip-planning information and the best airfare, lodging, and car-rental bargains. You can also listen to podcasts, connect with other Frommers. com members through our active-reader forums, share your travel photos, read blogs from guidebook editors and fellow travelers, and much more.

THE BEST OF TORONTO

Toronto, Canada's largest city, is easy to like. An orderly metropolis of 5.7 million, it's a good place for shopping, dining, kicking back, and exploring attractions such as the CN Tower, Toronto Islands, AGO, and ROM. People here are friendly, and it's the influence of the city's 200-plus ethnicities that together make Toronto vibrant. And it all happens in the heart of the city, which means it's possible to drop in for a few days and "do the town" without running yourself ragged.

THINGS TO DO   Hop on a Red Rocket, the city's streetcars, and tour West Queen West's galleries, restaurants, and boutiques, or take a stroll through the historic Distillery District and then venture to pretty Sugar Beach for a taste of the East End. Hop on a ferry, and in just minutes it takes you to the giant park that is the Toronto Islands, or catch a thrilling show at the Air Canada Centre. Or you can reach for the sky and ride to the top of the CN Tower, one of the world's tallest freestanding structures.

RELAXATION   An abundance of parks grace the city's core. The Toronto Islands, a short ferry ride across the city's harbor, are car-free and perfect for cycling, rollerblading, or simply strolling. And the views back to the city are stunning. Green spaces such as Trinity Bellwoods and Queen's Park are ideal for picnics and afternoon idylls. On the east end of town, the Beach residential neighborhood, along with Kew Gardens and the boardwalk, are good for a lazy afternoon lakeside.

RESTAURANTS AND DINING   Locals have a hunger for local fare from the surrounding region's agricultural riches and wines from Niagara's wine country. If you'd like a taste of Toronto terroir, any number of restaurants, new or established, will satisfy your appetite. And this celebration of Ontario's bounty equally inspires all cuisines and cultures, from Canadiana to Italian, Indian to fusion, burgers to bistros at restaurants such as Woodlot, Canoe, Porchetta, Aravind, Allen's, TOCA . . . the list goes on.

NIGHTLIFE AND ENTERTAINMENT   Toronto, like most major cities, brings in big-ticket touring musicals and other blockbuster shows. However, the city's independent troupes, such as the brilliant Soulpepper, the venerable Canadian Stage, and the Factory Theatre, mount consistently well-received productions. Additionally, the Shaw Festival or Stratford Theatre Festival offer fine performing arts, plus a pretty road trip.

Metropolitan Toronto

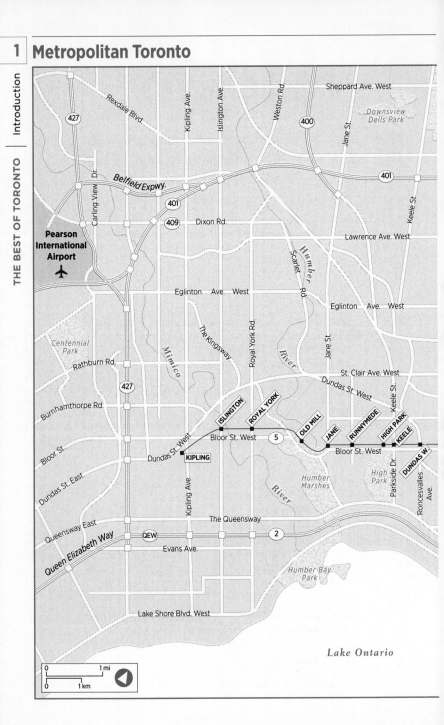

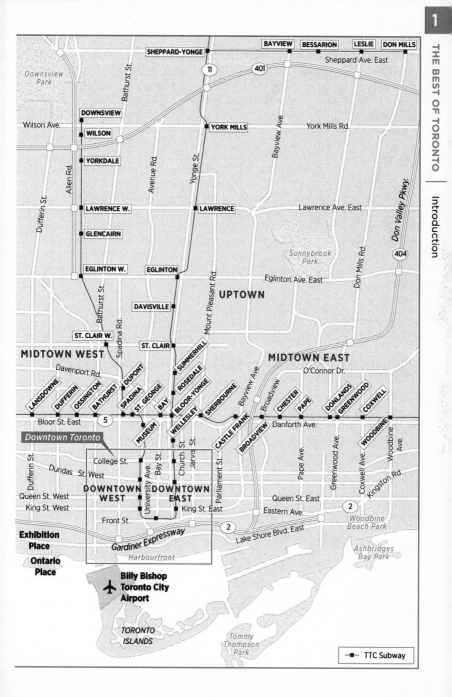

THE most MEMORABLE TRAVEL EXPERIENCES

o **Taking in the Thomson Collection at the Art Gallery of Ontario:** Locals are thrilled with local boy Frank Gehry's renovation of the AGO. His design has brilliantly revised (and expanded) the space, but the very best thing about the newly reopened AGO is the 2,000 works of art (great paintings, miniature sculptures, model ships) donated by local media magnate Ken Thomson. See p. 99.

o **Checking Out Local Theater and Music:** Sure, Toronto mounts its fair share of blockbusters. But the fine, and often more rewarding, offerings from Soulpepper, Opera Atelier, the Canadian Stage Company, Tafelmusik, and the Lorraine Kimsa Theatre for Young People are innovative and generally excellent. And seeing the Canadian Opera Company onstage at the Four Seasons Centre for the Performing Arts is breathtaking. See "The Performing Arts," in chapter 9.

o **Exploring the Distillery District:** Not only is this carefully restored area a remarkably intact example of 19th-century industrial architecture, largely thanks to its recent past as a stage set for movies and other productions, it's also a hive of activity. In addition to art galleries, shops, restaurants, and the city's finest chocolate emporium, SOMA, you can hear live music or visit the farmers' market. See p. 103.

o **Visiting the Toronto Islands:** Toronto is blessed with a chain of leafy islands just a brief ferry ride away that are mostly residential and offer a pretty, quiet, car-free spot for a stroll or a bike ride. The main attraction, Centre Island, is wide open parkland with an old-fashioned theme park, complete with pony rides and cotton candy (needless to say, it's great for kids). From the islands, you'll have a perfect view of Toronto's ever-evolving skyline. Pack a picnic, paddle a canoe, go bare if you dare at the sandy nudist beach, or take in the amusement park for a vacation within your vacation. See p. 108.

o **Skydiving at the CN Tower:** Okay, it's not *really* skydiving . . . but it's close. From the ground, it looks simply mad, but the EdgeWalk, which opened in summer 2011, is a thrill-seekers' dream. You're locked into a harness that is attached to a pulley system and then circumnavigate the elevated, narrow (1.5m/5-ft.) ledge that circles the perimeter of the tower's main pod. Not for vertigo sufferers! See p. 102.

THE best SPLURGE HOTELS

o **The Ritz Carlton:** It's Ottawa's first Ritz, and the brand's reputation for elegance and five-star service does not disappoint. From the moment you enter the dramatic lobby, the ambition to impress is all around. Sip a sophisticated cocktail in one of the lounges, save room for a sublime meal at the Canadiana-themed restaurant TOCA by Tom Brodi, and luxuriate in spacious rooms or corner suites. There's an excellent on-site spa with an adjoining lap pool and polished gym, too. See p. 54.

o **Hôtel Le Germain Maple Leaf Square:** Last year, the small Le Germain chain opened a second Toronto location, Le Germain Maple Leaf Square, directly opposite the Air Canada Centre. The brand's attention to detail is obvious throughout the property, and rooms are inviting and bright, fitted with sumptuous beds with Frette linens, and feature waterfall-like showerheads and other luxuries. See p. 56.

STAY ON trend

Toronto Trending (http://trending.see torontonow.com) is an online tool that provides a look at what's on, where to eat and stay, cultural highlights, and more, along with live satellite feeds, maps, and other tools.

o **Thompson Toronto:** The hip, luxury brand that started in New York City has landed in Toronto. Smartly situated in the King West district, this super-hot new hotel opened in summer 2010. Sixteen floors of fine modern design are complemented by floor-to-ceiling windows, a rooftop pool, a private screening room, a sushi bar, an all-night diner, an outpost of New York City's Scarpetta restaurant, and excellent service. See p. 56.

THE best MODERATELY PRICED HOTELS

o **Delta Chelsea:** This is a longtime favorite with budget-minded families. Perks include a playroom with live bunnies and fish, a video arcade, and a waterslide. It also offers children's programs, a day-care center, and kid-friendly restaurants. Many rooms have fridges or kitchenettes. See p. 57.
o **Hotel Victoria:** In a landmark downtown building near the Hockey Hall of Fame, the Victoria retains glamorous touches of an earlier age, including crown moldings and marble columns in the lobby. Standard rooms are on the small side but are nicely put together; deluxe rooms are larger and have coffeemakers and mini-fridges. A recent major renovation has only sweetened the deal: New guest rooms offer LCD TVs and new furnishings. See p. 59.
o **The Gladstone Hotel:** This groovy hotel is moderately priced overall. And its locale along West Queen West; the many bars, lounges, and restaurants on-site and nearby; along with the friendly service make for a good, fun stay. See p. 57.

THE most MEMORABLE DINING EXPERIENCES

o **The Black Hoof:** Nose-to-tail eating is taken to extremes—and to truly tasty heights—at this brilliant restaurant-bar. Co-owner/chef Grant van Gameren's hand-crafted charcuterie is the main draw (the tongue sandwich receives raves), but the pastas and entrees are equally inspired, as are the cocktails created by co-owner Jen Agg. See p. 76.
o **Canoe:** The panorama from the 54th floor of this iconic bank tower in the heart of the Financial District is stunning, but as the many regulars can attest, the food is so good you might forget all about the view. It's Canadian cuisine, such as Nunavut caribou and Québec foie gras, handled with delicacy and expert technique. The daytime vibe is corporate; evening is more romantic. See p. 70.

- **Gilead Bistro:** Local top chef Jamie Kennedy is behind the stove at this small, beautiful *boîte*. In other words, the food is sublime. Come for a light breakfast, a simple yet lovely lunch, or a real treat: a memorable dinner. Whatever time of day or evening, local seasonal ingredients are the stars. Great value, too. Finding your way can be tricky: It's situated in a tiny alley in Corktown. See p. 81.

- **Guu Izakaya:** There are plenty of good sushi spots and Japanese restaurants to choose from in town, but there's little doubt of the fun and fine food to be had at this chaotic pub/restaurant with a great selection of small-plate dishes. A second location on Bloor Street West, Guu Sakabar, opened in spring 2011 and has helped to lessen the notoriously long lines. See p. 82.

- **The Local Kitchen:** Parkdale's favorite spot is part authentic Italian trattoria, part contemporary Toronto. The crowded, convivial room is idiosyncratic, the service pro yet friendly, and the food delicious. Chef Fabio Bondi arrives pre-dawn each morning to make stunning fresh pastas such as smoked gnocchi with creamy *taleggio*. See p. 77.

- **Scaramouche:** Chef Keith Froggett and maitre d' Carl Corte have been quietly perfecting one of the city's finest restaurants for over 25 years. The formal dining room, which is best for special occasions, is complemented by the adjoining casual pasta bar and grill. Located in a tony apartment building in midtown, there are beautiful views over the city. See p. 92.

- **Woodlot Restaurant and Bakery:** It's a bit of the farm in the city, a coy conceit that works to great effect. There's a wood-burning oven where breads, pies, and even meats and fish are cooked by chef/co-owner David Haman and his team. Menus (one meat, one vegetarian) feature savory pies, excellent soups, fresh pasta—all prepared with heart. Desserts and breads are not to be missed. See p. 76.

THE best THINGS TO DO FOR FREE (OR ALMOST)

- **Seeing Great Museums When They're Discounted—or Free:** Admissions to the Royal Ontario Museum and the Art Gallery of Ontario have jumped since their massive renovations. However, you can pay less—or nothing—if you know when to go. See "Saving on Admission Costs," on p. 108.

- **Listening to a Concert at the Toronto Music Garden:** Cellist Yo-Yo Ma co-designed this serene space that's intended to evoke Bach's "First Suite for Unaccompanied Cello." It's easy on the eyes, but the best time to come here is for a summertime concert. Pure bliss. See p. 123.

- **Wandering through Riverdale Farm:** In case you need more proof that Toronto is a very green city, it has a working farm in its midst. Cows, sheep, pigs, goats, and other critters call it home. See p. 128.

- **Strolling the Lakeside Boardwalk:** You can choose from a number of starting points, but don't miss the quirky parks, open-air concert venues, and wintertime skating rink near Harbourfront. Or venture east to the long boardwalk in the neighborhood called The Beach, where you'll share the lake views with locals and their many dogs and youngsters. See p. 114.

o **Visiting Harbourfront Centre and the Power Plant Gallery:** The collection of studios, stages, open-air exhibits (especially in summer), and the Power Plant Gallery itself together offer an always-interesting, ever-changing attraction. You might call it a living museum. Watch for the many free special events. See p. 103.

THE best MUSEUMS AND GALLERIES

o **Art Gallery of Ontario:** Still fresh a few years after a top-to-bottom renovation—and reinvention—by Toronto-born Frank Gehry, The AGO is a wonder (the fabulous, circular, floating staircase is especially impressive). There's a lot to see here; the collection numbers 79,450 pieces and growing. Don't miss the Thomson Collection; central to the AGO, it spans 20 rooms and includes an unparalleled collection of great Canadian art. See p. 99.

o **Royal Ontario Museum:** Good for the whole family, especially with the massive dinosaur collection and creepy bat cave, the impressive exhibits also include Chinese temple art, Roman statues, and Middle Eastern mosaics. See p. 107.

o **Ontario Science Centre:** You don't have to be a tyke to appreciate the impressive interactive displays here that take in the realm of science disciplines, from biology to technology, and make them fun and interactive. See p. 106.

o **Stephen Bulger Gallery:** If you're interested in fine-art photography, especially in the documentary tradition, this is the place to go in Toronto. The Gallery displays Canadian and international photography, both by established artists and up-and-comers, from Ruth Orkin to Pete Doherty. See p. 166.

THE best PLACES TO HANG WITH THE LOCALS

o **Ossington Avenue:** This once-downtrodden strip is now packed with good places to eat, drink, and catch live music. Dine at the excellent restaurants or grab a great pizza, sip a cocktail at an intimate club, take in some live music, and then stroll the streets that frame the area and get a look at how the locals live—in Victorian-era homes side-by-side with family-owned shops. Utterly charming. See p. 40.

o **The Drake Hotel:** Set in the middle of the Art & Design District, this hotel fosters a sense of community by hosting music events, literary readings, and other festivities. If you hate feeling like a tourist, this place is for you. See p. 54.

o **The Rogers Centre or the Air Canada Centre:** The Rogers Centre is home base for the Toronto Blue Jays baseball team. The Air Canada Centre is where the Maple Leafs (hockey) and the Raptors (basketball) play. Torontonians come out to support them in droves. See p. 120.

o **Comedy Clubs:** Maybe it's something in the water: Toronto has produced more than its share of top-notch comedians, including the shagadelic Mike Myers, Jim Carrey, Dan Aykroyd, and the late John Candy. Checking out local talent or international stand-up stars at one of the many comedy clubs is a favorite pastime for Torontonians. See p. 195.

o **Treasure Hunting for Vintage Clothing in Kensington Market:** How can one small area have a dozen vintage-clothing vendors? And how do they keep prices low and the quality high? Haphazard Kensington Market is a big draw for local bargain hunters. See "Walking Tour 1: Chinatown & Kensington Market," in chapter 7, and "Hunting for Vintage," in chapter 8.

TORONTO IN DEPTH

Toronto is Canada's biggest city and the country's economic epicenter, with a population of 5.7 million in the greater metropolitan area, and it's booming. Each year, the population expands with about 140,000 new arrivals, most of them coming not from maternity wards, but from around the globe, further augmenting Toronto's extraordinary multicultural makeup. Tourist attractions rate, too, if that's your thing, but the city's sheer cultural diversity, which has been compared with London's, is what ultimately gives pulse to the place. Ethnicity infuses great dining spots, theater, music, and other cultural festivals and bargain-busting shopping strips, such as Little India and multiple Chinatowns.

There's a lot that's new about this place, which has its pros and cons. Although bike lanes, roads, and other systems of infrastructure struggle to keep up—the forest of cranes is testament to an ongoing building boom—there's plenty of energy in new culture, environmental initiatives, innovative architecture, food and drink, and even science and technology.

TORONTO TODAY

A patchwork of neighborhoods, Toronto is remarkable for its vibrant downtown core where Torontonians eat, play, sleep, and work. If you're coming in from Pearson International Airport, the city might seem sprawling—and the Greater Toronto Area including its former boroughs, *is* big at 7,124 square km (2,750 sq miles)—but once you're grounded downtown, everything is here: shoulder-to-shoulder condo towers, office buildings, theaters, parks, schools, restaurants and cafes, bars and nightclubs, taverns, and places of worship.

The city draws on its vast international pedigree to give it shape and definition: The polyglot Toronto *is* the Toronto story. And lately, it's changing at a rapid pace. For the most part, that's welcome news for citizens and visitors alike. The city, which held onto its reputation as "Toronto the Good" with faded nostalgia, has finally awakened to the realization that it might be Toronto the Rude, Toronto the Tough, Toronto the Cool, or, as one recent immigrant has named it, Toronto the Great.

In late 2010, the people voted in a new mayor, a return to the right for the first time this century. Mayor Rob Ford promises cutbacks, lower taxes, and smaller government; the city is deeply in debt. Ford, often lampooned for his substantial girth, is out to "clean up" this town, and the consensus is his legacy will likely entail reduced government services. Then again, he keeps surprising his constituents: The anti-cyclist is planning new bike lanes, just one of a string of unexpected developments.

The signs of growth are all around. The skyline downtown is a forest of cranes, as condo towers stretch upwards to 75 stories. There are marvelous new parks, new heights to property values (topped by a $28-million penthouse sold at the Four Seasons tower), electric cars and other green initiatives, a widespread alternative foods movement, and better waterfront playgrounds.

Meanwhile, the city by the lake is taking strides to reclaim its final frontier along the waterfront. After years of political dithering while developers erected a concrete curtain of condos that deprived downtown of lake views and cooling on-shore breezes, some visible progress is taking shape to replace the city's derelict shipping and industrial past at the water's edge. The impetus that finally spurred development was the city's winning the hosting bid for the Pan Am Games in 2015. This Olympics-lite requires scads of housing for athletes, which is rising around the mouth of the Don River just to the east of downtown.

New developments underway include a revitalization of Union Station, the city's main train station, that will brighten the historic building with a glass-canopy roof and expand services; the elimination of three lanes of traffic at Queen's Quay in front of Harbourfront to make room for bike and pedestrian lanes, as well as some new landscaping; the whimsical retreat called Sugar Beach opposite the Redpath Sugar refinery at the water's edge; Sherbourne Common, another new waterfront park; and last but not least, saving the iconic Maple Leaf Gardens, an historic hockey shrine, from demolition and developing it into a new athletic facility for nearby Ryerson University (as well as a major supermarket: from pucks to plums?) set to open in the winter of 2012.

There are shuttered storefronts, too, as the retail world continues to lurch in fits and starts. Traffic is congested at best—chaotic at worst—in the city's core, especially on weekdays. There are parts of town, some of them downtown, where guns and gangs rule. The city's reputation was dealt a serious blow with the now-notorious G20 riots and police brutality of 2010; it's still a contentious topic for Torontonians.

So, for better or for worse, Toronto is not simply "good" anymore. A local reporter has compared it to a teenager (it's a young city, turning 178 in 2012). The comparison is apt: Toronto is out for fun, exuberant, a bit rambunctious, and sometimes a challenge to manage. The reward is that it's more interesting than merely nice.

LOOKING BACK AT TORONTO
Early Settlement in "Muddy York"

Native Canadians had long lived here—at the entrance to the Toronto Trail, a short route between the lower and upper Great Lakes—when in 1615, French fur trader Étienne Brûlé became the first European to travel the trail. It wasn't until 1720 that the French established the first trading post, known as Fort Toronto, to intercept the furs that were being taken across Lake Ontario to New York State by English rivals. Fort Rouillé, built on the site of today's Canadian National Exhibition (CNE) grounds, replaced the trading post in 1751. When the 1763 Treaty of Paris ended the Anglo-French War after the fall of Québec, French rule in North America effectively ended, and the city's French antecedents were all but forgotten.

In the wake of the American Revolution, the Loyalists fled north, and the British decided it was time to carve a capital city out of the northern wilderness. In 1791,

> ## Muddy York
>
> Just how muddy was the early settle-
> ment of Muddy York? It was a subject
> of continuous complaint by early set-
> tlers. One apocryphal story tells of a
> man who saw a hat lying in the middle
> of a street and went to pick it up. When
> he did, he found the head of a live man
> submerged in the muck below.

the British established Upper Canada (modern-day Ontario) as a province. Its first lieutenant governor, John Graves Simcoe, made Toronto its capital and renamed it "York" in honor of Frederick, Duke of York (one of George III's sons). Simcoe ordered a garrison built and laid it out in a 10-block rectangle around King, Front, George, and Berkeley streets. Beyond stretched a series of 40-hectare (100-acre) lots from Queen to Bloor, which were granted to mollify government officials who resented having to move to the mosquito-plagued, marshy outpost. York was notorious for its always-muddy streets, earning it the nickname "Muddy York."

By 1796, the hamlet had grown, and the first parliament buildings were erected. Simcoe also surveyed Yonge Street, which would eventually become the longest street in the world. The first Parliament meeting confirmed York as the capital of Upper Canada.

The War of 1812 & Its Aftermath

When America declared war on Britain in the War of 1812, President Madison assumed it would be simple to invade and hold Canada. The opposite proved to be true. In April 1813, 14 ships carrying 1,700 American troops invaded York (population 625), looting and destroying the parliament buildings, the Fort York garrison, and much of the settlement. It was a Pyrrhic victory because the Americans suffered heavy losses and failed to take any more Canadian territory. In retaliation, British and Canadian troops marched on Washington, D.C., in 1814 and burned all government buildings, including the American president's residence. (The Americans later white-washed it to hide the charred wood—hence, the White House.)

Perhaps unsurprisingly, given the events of the war, York's ruling oligarchy shared a conservative pro-British outlook. Called the Family Compact, the group consisted of William Jarvis, a New England Loyalist who became provincial secretary; John Beverley Robinson, son of a Virginia Loyalist, who became attorney general at age 22 and, later, chief justice of Upper Canada; and Scottish-educated Dr. John Strachan, a schoolmaster who became an Anglican rector and, eventually, the most powerful figure in York. Anglo-Irish Dr. William Warren Baldwin, doctor, lawyer, architect, judge, and parliamentarian, laid out Spadina Avenue as a thoroughfare leading to his country house; the Boultons were prominent lawyers, judges, and politicians—Judge D'Arcy Boulton built a mansion, the Grange, which later became the core of the art museum and still stands today.

The Early 1800s Rebellion & Immigration

In 1834, the city was incorporated, and York became Toronto, a city bounded by Parliament Street to the east, Bathurst Street to the west, the lakefront to the south, and 366m (1,201 ft.) north of the current Queen Street (then called Lot) on the northern edge. Outside this area—west to Dufferin Street, east to the Don River, and

The Toronto Rebellion

William Lyon Mackenzie, Toronto's first mayor, founded the *Colonial Advocate* to crusade against the narrow-minded Family Compact, calling for reform and challenging their power to such an extent that some of them broke into his office and dumped his presses into the lake. By 1837, Mackenzie, undaunted, was calling for open rebellion. The city's financial turmoil in the wake of some bank failures made his wish come true. On December 5, 1837, 700 rebels gathered at Montgomery's Tavern outside the city (near modern-day Eglinton Ave.). Led by Mackenzie on a white mare, they marched on the city. But Sheriff Jarvis was waiting for them, and his militia crushed the rebellion. Mackenzie fled to the United States, but two other rebellion leaders were hanged (their graves are in the Toronto Necropolis). Mackenzie was later pardoned, returned to Toronto in 1849, and was elected to the Upper Canada legislature.

north to Bloor Street—laid the "liberties," out of which the city would later carve new wards. North of Bloor, local brewer Joseph Bloor and Sheriff William Jarvis were already drawing up plans for the village of Yorkville. In 1843, the University of Toronto opened; this was an intellectual achievement but also an aesthetic one, as the university added new and beautiful architecture.

As increasing numbers of immigrants arrived, demands arose for democracy and reform. Among the reformers were such leaders as Francis Collins, who launched the radical paper *Canadian Freeman* in 1825; lawyer William Draper; and, most famous of all, fiery William Lyon Mackenzie, who was elected Toronto's first mayor in 1834.

Immigration was changing Toronto more than anything else. During the 1820s, 1830s, and 1840s, immigrants—Irish Protestants and Catholics, Scots, Presbyterians, Methodists, and other nonconformists—arrived in droves. Slavery was outlawed throughout the British Empire in 1834; by the 1850s, roughly 3% of Toronto's population was black. But the biggest change was the arrival of the Irish. In early 1847, Toronto's population stood at 20,000. That summer 38,000 Irish immigrants fleeing the Great Famine landed in Toronto, forever changing the city.

Canadian Confederation & the Late Victorian Era

During the 1850s, the building of the railroads accelerated Toronto's booming economy. By 1860, it was the trading hub for lumber and grain imports and exports. Merchant empires were founded, railroad magnates emerged, and institutions such as the Bank of Toronto were established. The foundations of an industrial city were laid: Toronto gained a waterworks, gas, and public transportation.

Despite its wealth, Toronto lagged behind Montréal, which had twice Toronto's population in 1861. But under the Confederation of 1867, the city was guaranteed an advantage: As the capital of the newly created Ontario province, Toronto, in effect, controlled the minerals and timber of the north.

By 1891, Toronto's population was 181,000. The business of the city was business, and amassing wealth was the pastime of such figures as Henry Pellatt, stockbroker, president of the Electrical Development Company, and builder of Casa Loma; E. B. Osler; George Albertus Cox; and A. R. Ames.

The boom spurred new commercial and residential construction. Projects included the first steel-frame building, the Board of Trade Building (1889) at Yonge and Front streets; George Gooderham's Romanesque-style mansion (1890) at St. George and Bloor streets (now the York Club); the provincial parliament buildings in Queen's Park (1886–92); and the city hall (1899) at Queen and Bay streets. Public transit improved, and by 1891, the city had 109km (68 miles) of tracks for horse-drawn cars. Electric lights, telephones, and electric streetcars appeared in the 1890s.

From Boomtown to the Great Depression

Toronto's Great Fire of 1904 demolished 5.6 hectares (14 acres) of downtown, and the damage was an estimated C$10 million (in 1904 dollars). Miraculously, no one died in the fire, the cause of which was never discovered. Less impressively, insurance companies raised all premiums for businesses in the torched area by 75%, retroactive to the night of the fire, April 19th.

Between 1901 and 1921, Toronto's population more than doubled to 521,893. The economy continued to expand, fueled by the lumber, mining, wholesale, and agricultural machinery industries, and after 1911, by hydroelectric power. Much of the new wealth went into construction, and three impressive buildings from this era can still be seen today: the Horticultural Building at the Exhibition Grounds (1907), the King Edward Hotel (1903), and Union Station (1914–19).

The booming economy and its factories attracted a wave of new immigrants—mostly Italians and Jews from Russia and Eastern Europe—who settled in the city's emerging ethnic enclaves. By 1912, Kensington Market was well established, and the garment center and Jewish community were firmly ensconced around King Street and Spadina Avenue. Little Italy clustered around College and Grace Streets. By 1911, more than 30,000 Torontonians were foreign-born, and the slow march to change the English character of the city had begun.

Increased industrialization brought social problems, largely concentrated in Cabbagetown and the Ward, a large area that stretched west of Yonge Street and north of Queen Street. Here, poor people lived in crowded, wretched conditions: Housing was inadequate; health conditions were poor; and rag picking, or sweatshop labor, was the only employment.

As it became larger and wealthier, Toronto also became an intellectual and cultural magnet. Artists such as Charles Jefferys, J. H. MacDonald, Arthur Lismer, Tom Thomson, Lawren Harris, Frederick Varley, and A. Y. Jackson, most associated with the Group of Seven, set up studios in Toronto. Their first group show opened in 1920.

"Toronto the Good"

Toronto's reputation for conservatism was well deserved. While the city was blessed with many beautiful churches, its nickname, "Toronto the Good," had less to do with religion and more to do with legislation against fun. This was, after all, the city that, in 1912, banned tobogganing on Sunday. As late as 1936, 30 men were arrested at the lakeshore resort of Sunnyside because they exposed their chests—even though the temperature was 105°F (41°C)! In 1947, cocktail lounges were approved, but it wasn't until 1950 that playing sports on Sunday became legal. Leopold Infeld, a University of Toronto physicist who worked with Einstein, famously said: "I dreaded the Sundays and prayed to God that if he chose for me to die in Toronto he would let it be on a Saturday afternoon to save me from one more Toronto Sunday."

TORONTO IN DEPTH | Looking Back at Toronto

Toronto also became the English-language publishing center of the nation, and such national magazines as *Maclean's* (1896) and *Saturday Night* (1887) were launched. The Art Gallery of Ontario, the Royal Ontario Museum, the Toronto Symphony Orchestra, and the Royal Alexandra Theatre all opened before 1914.

Women advanced, too, at the turn of the 20th century. In 1880, Emily Jennings Stowe became the first Canadian woman authorized to practice medicine. In 1886, the University of Toronto began to accept women. The women's suffrage movement gained strength, led by Dr. Stowe, Flora McDonald Denison, and the Women's Christian Temperance Union.

When Britain entered World War I, Canada was immediately pulled into it, as well. Toronto became Canada's chief aviation center; factories, shipyards, and power facilities expanded to meet the needs of war; and women entered the workforce in great numbers.

> **Impressions**
>
> *In the eyes of the rest of the country, Toronto is a kind of combination Sodom and Mecca.*
> —Pierre Berton, 1961

The 1920s roared along, fueled by a mining boom that saw Bay Street turned into a veritable gold-rush alley. Then the Great Depression followed, and the only distraction from its bleakness was the opening of Maple Leaf Gardens in 1931. Besides being an ice-hockey center, it was host to large protest rallies during the Depression; later, it welcomed anyone, from the Jehovah's Witnesses to the Ringling Bros. Circus and the Metropolitan Opera.

As in the United States, hostility toward new immigrants was rife during the '20s. It reached a peak in 1923, when the Chinese Exclusion Act was passed, banning Chinese immigration. In the 1930s, antagonism toward Jews intensified. In August 1933, the display of a swastika at Christie Pits Park caused a battle between Nazis and Jews. As if things weren't bad enough, a polio epidemic broke out in 1936.

World War II & Aftermath

Unlike World War I, Canada wasn't automatically bound to enter World War II by Britain's declaration of war. However, the Canadian Parliament voted to declare war on Germany on September 10, 1939, a move that was widely supported by Canadians.

The Second World War brought new life to Toronto—literally. Toronto men rushed to volunteer to serve while women took their place in the factories. At the same time, 8,000 British children were sent to Toronto by their parents, to keep them safe from the war. Once again, the city became a major aviation center.

After World War II, prosperous Toronto continued to expand, especially into the suburbs. By the 1950s, the urban area had grown so large, disputes between city and suburbs were so frequent, and the need for social and other services was so great, that an effective administrative solution was needed. In 1953, the Metro Council, composed of equal numbers of representatives from the city and the suburbs, was established.

Mid- & Late 20th Century

Toronto became a major city in the 1950s, with the Metro Council providing a structure for planning and growth. The Yonge subway opened, and a network of highways was constructed. It linked the city to the affluent suburbs. Don Mills, the first post-war planned community town, was built between 1952 and 1962; Yorkdale Centre, a mammoth shopping center, followed in 1964. American companies began locating branch plants in the area, fueling much of the growth.

The city also began to loosen up. While the old social elite continued to dominate the boardrooms, politics, at least, had become more accessible and fluid. In 1954, Nathan Phillips became the first Jewish mayor. In 1947, the Chinese Exclusion Act of 1923 was repealed. And after 1950, Germans and Italians were allowed to enter once again. Then, under pressure from the United Nations, Poles, Ukrainians, Central European and Russian Jews, Yugoslavs, Estonians, Latvians, and other East Europeans poured in. Most arrived at Union Station, having journeyed from the ports of Halifax, Québec City, and Montréal. At the beginning of the 1950s, the foreign-born were 31% of the population; by 1961, they were 42%, and the number of people claiming British descent had fallen from 73% to 59%. The 1960s brought an even richer mix of people—Portuguese, Greeks, West Indians, South Asians, refugees from Chile, Vietnam, and elsewhere—changing the city's character forever.

In the 1960s, the focus shifted from the suburbs to the city. People moved back downtown, renovating the handsome brick Victorians so characteristic of today's downtown. Yorkville emerged briefly as the hippie capital—the Haight-Ashbury of Canada. Gordon Lightfoot and Joni Mitchell sang in the coffeehouses, and a group called the Toronto Anti-Draft Programme helped many Americans fleeing the Vietnam draft settle in Toronto.

During the 1970s, the provincial government also helped develop attractions that would polish Toronto's patina and lure visitors: Ontario Place in 1971, Harbourfront in 1972, and the Metro Zoo and the Ontario Science Centre in 1974. The CN Tower is another development from that era, and for more than 3 decades, it was the tallest free-standing structure in the world (now surpassed by the Burj Dubai tower). Unfortunately, in spite of strong efforts by preservationists, Toronto lost many historic buildings in the 1960s and '70s.

The 1980s were an interesting time in Toronto. On the one hand, the city fell into the habit of conspicuous consumption that seemed to define the era. Yorkville was transformed from hippie coffeehouse central into a hive of chic boutiques. But, on a more positive note, previously neglected neighborhoods such as the Annex and Cabbagetown were revitalized, the grand mansions brought back to life by new waves of residents. In fairness to the oft-mocked 1980s, this was a time when people began to appreciate Toronto's historic architecture, working to restore it rather than tear it down as they had in the 1970s. The Elgin and Winter Garden theaters were fully renovated and reopened, as was the Pantages Theatre (now called the Canon). In 1986, Toronto's Mirvish family (of "Honest Ed's" fame) created Mirvish Productions, which (along with the now-defunct Livent group) ushered in a renaissance on the Toronto theater scene. There was also important new construction in the city: Roy Thomson Hall opened in 1982, and SkyDome (now called the Rogers Centre) debuted in 1989.

In the 1990s, the Greater Toronto Area (GTA) really began to boom, fueled in part by rising immigration to the city. In 1998, the megacity merger forced the former city of Toronto into a union with five previously independent boroughs, causing cuts in public services as the provincial government off-loaded transit and welfare costs to the city.

In the 1970s, Toronto became the fastest-growing city in North America. For years, it had competed with Montréal for first-city status, but it was the election of the separatist Parti Québécois, in 1976, that boosted Toronto over the top. Montréal's loss was Toronto's gain, as English-speaking families and large companies chose Toronto over French-speaking Québec. The city overtook Montréal as a financial center, boasting more corporate headquarters. Its stock market was more important, and it remained the country's prime publishing center.

The 21st Century

The new century began with a renewal of the city's cultural inventory. At long last, the city got a purpose-built opera house, the **Four Seasons Centre for the Performing Arts,** which opened in 2006 (see p. 188). Also, the **Royal Ontario Museum** (see p. 107), **the Art Gallery of Ontario** (see p. 99), **the Ontario Science Centre** (see p. 106), the **Royal Conservatory of Music** (see p. 194), the **National Ballet School,** and the **Gardiner Museum of Ceramic Art** (see p. 110) all underwent extensive renovations.

By 2008, Toronto had become North America's largest condo market, with towers going up all over the city. The trend continues unabated, and Toronto's future seems destined to become a city of high-rise living. In 2011, the market reached a new extreme: C$28 million for a penthouse suite in the new Four Seasons hotel/condo tower, which was still under construction.

Also on the rise are efforts (long overdue) to reclaim the waterfront; developments are bursting, complete with hotels, stadiums and theaters, bars, restaurants, and parks. Some of the parks are especially attractive, like the whimsical Sugar Beach, at the foot of Jarvis Street (a reference to the Redpath sugar refinery, one of the last remaining industrial uses on the waterfront). There is no access to the lake from this beach, but a new boardwalk heads east to this burgeoning new East Bayfront neighborhood. The 1.5-hectare (3¾-acre) Sherbourne Common is a welcome addition of green space on the site of a former industrial area, plus it claims to be the first park in Canada with a neighborhood-wide storm-water treatment facility as an integral part of its design. And Don River Park, when completed in 2012, should draw people to the previously uninviting Don River in re-naturalized 7.3 hectares (18 acres) with bike trails, plenty of open green space, and a pavilion for entertainment.

As the city grows, heritage-minded preservationists are stepping up to do their part. Three recent additions bridge past and present. Artscape Wychwood Barns is an artist's colony and local food resource center fashioned from streetcar repair barns from the 1920s. The Toronto Railway Heritage Centre, just a fly-ball away from the Rogers Centre, is set in an old railroad roundhouse. And Evergreen Brick Works has transformed a quarry into a center for sustainable living.

Toronto continues to be very much a work in progress. As the skyline becomes more crowded, there's a noticeable increase in street life and energy as all those rising condos fill up. This dynamic metropolis beckons with an embrace of diverse and cosmopolitan cultures that give shape to an ever-changing city.

TORONTO'S ARCHITECTURE

In a rush to grow up, the city shamefully demolished much of its past in the name of so-called progress. Visitors and locals alike, however, get to witness a Toronto reinventing itself today with bold new initiatives to reclaim the waterfront from industrial decay, to remake failed social housing experiments from the post-war era, to dazzle with whimsy, and to accommodate cultural growth and house all who want to make Toronto their home.

That said, the city's architectural history is still in evidence and is made up of a wealth of architectural styles, from Gothic Revival churches to Romanesque civic buildings to the modernist bank towers in the Financial District. While it lacks any unique and defining Toronto style, the city's push for sustainable architecture that is environmentally aware will characterize the future of its buildings.

The Settling of York (1793–1837)

Early architecture in what was York and, after 1834, Toronto took its stylistic cues from England. The most notable style of the era was:

GEORGIAN These buildings are characterized by their formal, symmetrical design and by their classically inspired details, such as columns and pediments. There are few examples in Toronto, but an outstanding one is **Campbell House** at 160 Queen St. W. (p. 119). Built for Sir William Campbell in 1822 (he was a Loyalist and a chief justice of Upper Canada), it is currently a museum.

Early Victorian (1837–60)

The Victorian era in Toronto was a creative time in which a many architectural styles were employed. There was a strong tendency to look at the styles of the past and reinterpret them for the present. The chief ones were:

GOTHIC REVIVAL This fanciful style was part of a literary and aesthetic movement in England in the 1830s and '40s, and became very popular in Toronto. Gothic Revival design was asymmetrical, with pointed arches and windows, extensive ornamentation, and steeply pitched roofs; towers were often incorporated into the design. **St. James' Cathedral** (p. 117), built between 1850 and 1874, is a perfect example of the style with its 30m-tall (100-ft.) bell tower and its Romantic-inspired stained glass windows. **St. Michael's Cathedral** (p. 118); the **Toronto Necropolis** (p. 124), a cemetery that was established in 1850; and **Hart House** (p. 111), at the University of Toronto, are further examples.

RENAISSANCE REVIVAL Buildings designed in this style tended to be large, impressive, and formal, with symmetrical arrangements of the facade, quoins (cornerstones that give an impression of strength and solidity), columns separating windows, and large blocks of masonry on the lowest floor. Toronto's **St. Lawrence Hall** (next to the St. Lawrence Market, p. 122), built in 1850, is a textbook example of Renaissance Revival. Improving the sightlines of this building is a key element in the new design for the north building at St. Lawrence Market, which will open in 2013.

Late Victorian (1860–1901)

Later in the Victorian period, Toronto was still being influenced by Britain, but the city was also becoming more original in its design:

RICHARDSONIAN ROMANESQUE Arguably old Toronto's most beloved architectural style. Toronto's Richardson Romanesque buildings were influenced by the American architect Henry Hobson Richardson. The style is immediately identifiable by its massive scale, rounded archways, belt courses (continuous rows of bricks in a wall), decorative arcading, and large towers. The **Ontario Legislature** at Queen's Park (p. 117), built in 1893, is a Richardsonian Romanesque masterpiece, as is **Old Toronto City Hall** (p. 116).

BAY-AND-GABLE Closely related to Gothic Revival architecture, this is a style that is considered unique to Toronto. It applies some of the more decorative elements of Gothic Revival to single-family homes. Lots in 19th-century Toronto were oddly long and narrow (6.1×4m/20×13 ft.), and the Bay-and-Gable style, with its sharply peaked roofs, large bay windows (often filled with stained glass), and extensive decorative gabling managed to fit into these lots perfectly (most stand three stories tall). There are excellent examples of Bay-and-Gable in **Cabbagetown** (see Walking Tour 4, on p. 148), as well as in the **Annex** and in **Little Italy.**

Early & Mid-20th Century (1901–70)

Toronto erected its first skyscraper in 1894—the Beard Building—but it has been demolished. In the first decades of the 20th century, the city became less interested in looking back at the past and more intrigued by the future. When the decision was made to create a new city hall in the 1950s, Torontonians voted down a classically designed city hall, eventually favoring a modern building based on International Style (see below):

EARLY SKYSCRAPER The **Royal Bank Building** at the corner of King and Yonge streets was the tallest building in the British Commonwealth when it was completed in 1914.

BEAUX ARTS Taking its name from the École des Beaux-Arts in Paris, this style was an idealization of classical Greek and Roman architecture. Toronto's most beloved example of Beaux Arts style is **Union Station** (p. 42), which was built between 1914 and 1921.

> ### Impressions
>
> *You build your stations like we build our cathedrals.*
>
> —The Prince of Wales, speaking at the opening of Toronto's Union Station in 1927

INTERNATIONAL STYLE In the 1930s, this was modern architecture. These stark, rectangular buildings, which were generally surfaced with glass, were influenced by the Germany Bauhaus School. They were simple (at least, to the naked eye) in design. The **Toronto-Dominion Bank Tower,** at 66 Wellington St. W., was designed by Mies van der Rohe, perhaps the most famous of the Modernist architects. Built in 1967, it is distinctive for its black steel structure and black-glazed glass.

Late 20th Century & Beyond (1970–Present)

Toronto architecture in the past 4 decades has veered from the postmodern to the eclectic. It's hard to group works together in a cohesive style, though they do share elements of whimsy and improbability. In the 1970s, a postmodern approach, in which classical or historical references were incorporated into the design of a building,

BE AN archi-tourist

From blogs to talks to walks, there are many ways to stay on top of the city's ever-changing skyline:

o The **Toronto Society of Architects** offers walking tours on architectural themes from June through September. Tours have included "Toronto's Cultural Renaissance: Buildings of the 21st Century" and "Skyscrapers of the Financial District." For details and schedules, visit www. torontosocietyofarchitects.ca.

o **Doors Open Toronto** is a popular, free celebration of buildings in and around the city. Each year, during the last weekend in May, more than 150 architecturally significant buildings—many of them otherwise not accessible to the public—open their doors to the public. For details, visit www.toronto.ca/doorsopen.

o **Jane's Walk** is named for the late Toronto-based writer and urban activist Jane Jacobs and allows impassioned residents to lead tours of their neighborhoods each May. What began in 2007 as a local commemoration is now an international phenomenon, with Jane's Walks in 68 cities around the world. For more, see www.janeswalk.net.

o The **Design Exchange** (see p. 110) has year-round programming on architecture themes with exhibits, talks, and film screenings, and its blog gives great insight into local trends. See www.dx.org.

o The **Pug Awards** were launched in 2004 as a way to raise awareness of architectural and design issues in Toronto. The public votes via the Web for the best and worst new buildings of the year. The exposure has shamed developers and lauded unsung works. The Pugs are raising the bar, and hopes, for a better-built tomorrow. There's also a lecture series, "Pug Talks," held throughout the year. For more, see www.pugawards.com.

became popular. There was a great deal of leeway in terms of the overall shape of a building, rather than using a simple rectangle. The **Toronto Reference Library** (p. 119) and the **Bata Shoe Museum** (p. 109), both designed by Toronto architect Raymond Moriyama, are two visually stunning counterpoints within walking distance of each other.

Toronto is basking in the afterglow of a cultural Renaissance that saw major additions by leading architects to its key arts institutions over the past few years. The transformation elevated discussion of the public realm by adding controversy to the mix with some less-than-universally-accepted remakes of the city's beloved attractions.

Prime among them is David Libeskind's crystal addition to the **Royal Ontario Museum** on Bloor Street. Love it or loathe it, it got people talking. Local boy Frank Gehry finally added his imprimatur to the cityscape with a favorable remake of the **Art Gallery of Ontario.** There is no Bilbao-effect here: just a tasteful rendering of the space to accommodate the AGO's wonderful art collection. Another local, Jack Diamond, designed Canada's first purpose-built opera house, the **Four Seasons Centre for the Performing Arts,** whose exterior lights up University Avenue with its glass facade and whose interior provides wonderful sightlines and acoustics. And the newest addition, the **Bell Lightbox,** provides even more wattage to the Toronto International Film Festival with a gallery and year-round screening rooms on King Street West.

The **Sharp Centre for Design** (p. 118), which opened in 2004, still shocks many visitors. Best described as a checkerboard on colorful stilts, it was designed by English architect Will Alsop for the Ontario College of Art and Design and captures a sense of possibility and playfulness in contemporary architecture. (Alsop is also creating a subway station in the suburbs for an extension of the University Ave. line.)

Currently, one of the most cherished buildings in the city is getting a makeover, rather than the wrecking ball: **Maple Leaf Gardens.** This hockey shrine on Carlton Street has sat empty for a decade since the Leafs decamped to the Air Canada Centre. Its future was in doubt but was secured when a grocery chain and Ryerson University teamed up to preserve it. Scheduled to reopen in 2012, the mixed-use facility will become Ryerson's hockey rink and will also offer groceries at street level. The designers say they will retain as much character as possible of the legendary.

The biggest trend in architecture in the city right now is one not always visible to the naked eye: Sustainable design. LEED (Leadership in Energy and Environmental Design) buildings incorporate energy-saving systems such as green roofs, lake water to cool buildings instead of conventional air conditioning, and new window glazing and shading techniques to prevent heat build-up. Some buildings on the vanguard of these principals include the **Evergreen Brick Works, One Cole** condominium in the renewed Regent Park, and new campus buildings at the **University of Toronto.**

Even City Hall, the modernist marvel with a space ship–looking pod embraced by two curving towers, is being refashioned for these "green-minded" times with a wonderful garden on the elevated podium above the entrance.

TORONTO IN POPULAR CULTURE

Toronto has had a reputation of always being the bridesmaid and never the bride when it comes to its portrayal in the movies. As a stand-in for large American cities, it has fueled a busy film-production industry but done little to attract the curious since its streets and skyline always depict some other place. That is still the case overall, but the city claimed a starring role in Atom Egoyan's well-received film *Chloe* (2009). Toronto was itself, for once, and plays a key role.

As a city on the page, however, Toronto can claim a rich legacy. It's home to many of the country's most prolific and acclaimed writers, which might be the reason for its literary stardom.

Margaret Atwood's *The Robber Bride* (Emblem Editions) pays homage to Toronto with a story that covers three decades of life in the city. Some of her other novels— *The Edible Woman, Cat's Eye,* and *The Blind Assassin* (all published by Emblem Editions)—also use Toronto as a backdrop. *In the Skin of a Lion,* by Michael Ondaatje, the celebrated author of *The English Patient* (both published by Knopf Canada), is a moving love story that brings the city's landmarks to life. Carol Shields, who died in 2003, set her final novel, *Unless* (Harper Perennial), in Toronto's streets. Michael Redhill's *Consolation* (Doubleday, Canada) bounces back and forth between contemporary Toronto and the city in the 19th century.

Another notable novel is *Cabbagetown,* by Hugh Garner, the story of the fight to survive in a Toronto slum in the 1930s. (Cabbagetown was famous as the largest Anglo-Saxon slum in North America.)

"A few houses on almost every street were as verminous and tumbledown as any in the city, but next door or across the street was the same type of house, clean and in good repair, reflecting the decency or pride of the occupants, or reflecting the fact that the tenant was buying it. In 1929, most Cabbagetowners rented their homes, from the ingrained habit of generations or because they refused to tie themselves down to the district. This was a neighborhood almost without tenements, and the streets were lined with single-family houses, many of whose upper stories accommodated a second family.

The citizens of Cabbagetown believed in God, the Royal Family, the Conservative Party, and private enterprise. They were suspicious and a little condescending towards all heathen religions, higher education, 'foreigners,' and social reformers. They were generally unskilled working people, among whom were scattered, like raisins in a ten-cent cake, representatives of the State—such as postmen, civic employees, streetcar conductors, and even a policeman or two."

—From *Cabbagetown,* by Hugh Garner, 1950

For those more interested in possible futures than the past, there's an Afro-futurist/sci-fi novel called *Brown Girl in the Ring,* by Nalo Hopkinson (Warner Books). Some other books to consider: *Noise* (Porcupine's Quill) and *How Insensitive* (Doubleday Canada), by Russell Smith; *Headhunter,* by Timothy Findley (HarperCollins Canada); *Then Again,* by Elyse Friedman (Random House Canada); *Lost Girls,* by Andrew Pyper (Harper Collins Canada); and *The Origin of Waves,* by Austin Clarke (McClelland & Stewart). Clarke has also written three novels that are collectively known as the Toronto Trilogy: *The Meeting Point, Storm of Fortune,* and *The Bigger Light* (all published by Knopf Canada). The literary legend Robertson Davies was working on the third novel in his own Toronto Trilogy when he died in 1995. The first two books, *Murther and Walking Spirits* and *The Cunning Man* (both published by Penguin Books), were published in 1991 and 1994, respectively.

If you like the look of Old City Hall, pick up the novel *Old City Hall,* by Robert Rotenberg (Picador). Published in 2009, the story—written by a veteran criminal lawyer—explores Toronto's noir side.

Insightful books on architecture include *Emerald City: Toronto Revisited,* by John Bentley Mays (Viking), and as handy reference to recent buildings, *A Guidebook to Contemporary Architecture in Toronto,* by Margaret and Phil Goodfellow (Douglas & McIntyre), covers the bases.

EATING & DRINKING IN TORONTO

Toronto is a good place to eat. In keeping with the city's overall character—generally agreeable, occasionally inventive, sometimes brilliant—you can expect to find plenty of decent food here, as well as some truly memorable fare (fine or rustic).

The prevailing multicultural makeup ensures a rich banquet: There are authentic Thai, Ethiopian, and French bistros; an emerging Canadiana cuisine; excellent Indian;

"I DIDN'T KNOW SUPERMAN WAS FROM TORONTO . . ."

Torontonians show up in films, television, music, and literature that's famous the world over, and their scientific, architectural, and political accomplishments have had a global impact. How many people on this list did you know were from Toronto?

o **Margaret Atwood** (b. 1939): Canada's most famous literary luminary—her books have been translated into more than 20 languages, and there's a university in Sweden that teaches a course just in the use of comedy in her novels—Atwood is best known for her futuristic novel *The Handmaid's Tale*, which was made into a Hollywood film. Her body of work includes *The Edible Woman, The Robber Bride, Alias Grace,* and *Oryx and Crake* (all published by Emblem Editions).

o **Jim Balsillie** (b. 1961) and **Mike Lazaridis** (b. 1961): Co-founders of Research in Motion, the firm in nearby Waterloo, Ontario, that invented the now-ubiquitous BlackBerry, the wireless hand-held device. They are both billionaires.

o **Sir Frederick Banting** (1891– 1941): Banting was the co-discoverer of insulin at the University of Toronto; in 1923, he was awarded the Nobel Prize for his life-saving research. He also distinguished himself as a captain in the Army Medical Corps in World War I and, later in life, as an artist.

o **John Candy** (1950–94): The well-loved funnyman and Toronto native got his start in comedy with the local Second City troupe, playing a succession of crazy characters on "SCTV." In Hollywood, he made a succession of popular films that included *Only the Lonely, Uncle Buck,* and *Planes, Trains and Automobiles.* He was also a co-owner of the Toronto Argonauts football team.

o **Jim Carrey** (b. 1962): Before striking it rich in Hollywood with movies such as *The Mask, Ace Ventura: Pet Detective, Dumb and Dumber, The Truman Show,* and *Eternal Sunshine of the Spotless Mind,* Carrey lit up the stage at Toronto comedy clubs.

o **Michael Cera** (b. 1988): This fast-rising Hollywood actor was born and raised in the suburb of Brampton, Ontario. His films include *Superbad, Juno,* and *Scott Pilgrim vs. the World,* and he appeared in the cult-hit television series *Arrested Development.*

o **David Cronenberg** (b. 1943): This director knows how to shock audiences—witness his 1996 film *Crash,* which explored violent injury fetishes and won the Jury Prize at the Cannes Film Festival. His eerie body of work includes *The Fly, The Dead Zone, Dead Ringers, Naked Lunch,* and *A History of Violence.*

o **Frank Gehry** (b. 1929): Arguably the world's most famous living architect, Gehry put Bilbao, Spain, on the map with the swooping titanium shape of its Guggenheim Museum. In a more subdued way, Gehry refashioned the Art Gallery of Ontario to fit within the context of its residential neighborhood, where he grew up.

o **Norman Jewison** (b. 1926): This multiple award-winning director found fame south of the border making films that include *Fiddler on the Roof, The Cincinnati Kid, Jesus Christ Superstar, Agnes of God,* and *Moonstruck.* In 1986, the Toronto native established the Canadian Centre for Film Studies in his hometown.

o **k-os** (b. 1972): His real name is Kevin Brereton, but he's better known as k-os in his work as a rapper, singer, songwriter, and producer. He frequently references places and events in Toronto in his songs.

o **K'naan** (b. 1978; aka Keinan Abdi Warsame): This Somalia-born poet, rapper, and singer gained global exposure for writing *Wavin' Flag,* Coca Cola's anthem for the 2010 FIFA World Cup of Soccer, and continues to win over fans with songs about the immigrant experience in Canada.

o **Marshall McLuhan** (1911–80): The man who is best known for coining the phrases "the medium is the message" and "the global village" was a professor of English and the director of the Centre for Culture and Technology at the University of Toronto. His seminal works include *The Gutenberg Galaxy* (University of Toronto Press), *Understanding Media* (MIT Press), and *War and Peace in the Global Village* (Ginkgo Press).

o **Lorne Michaels** (b. 1944): Ever wonder why *Saturday Night Live* has featured so many Canadian performers? That may have had something to do with the fact that the show's creator was born and raised in Toronto. Michaels has also produced SNL alumni movies such as *Wayne's World* and *Baby Mama,* and TV shows including *30 Rock.*

o **Mike Myers** (b. 1963): Myers became a celebrity when he starred on *Saturday Night Live* from 1989 to 1994, playing a series of characters that included metal-head rocker Wayne Campbell and German aesthete Dieter. On the big screen, Myers has struck gold writing and starring in such films as *Wayne's World* and

Austin Powers (and their respective sequels).

o **Michael Ondaatje** (b. 1943): Ondaatje is perhaps best known for his novel *The English Patient* (Knopf Canada), which was adapted into an Oscar-winning film. Born in Sri Lanka, he earned his B.A. from the University of Toronto and taught English literature at Toronto's York University from 1971 to 1988. His acclaimed body of work includes *Running in the Family, In the Skin of a Lion,* and *Anil's Ghost* (all published by Knopf Canada).

o **Christopher Plummer** (b. 1929): He's usually remembered as the dashing Baron Von Trapp in *The Sound of Music,* but this versatile actor has played every role imaginable in a film career that has spanned more than 50 years. Born in Toronto, the Shakespearean-trained Plummer has returned to his roots many times at the nearby Stratford Festival.

o **Joe Shuster** (1914–92): Poor Joe Shuster—if only he and his Superman co-creator Jerome Siegel had known what a success their cartoon character would be one day, they wouldn't have sold the rights to D.C. Comics for a pittance in 1940. Shuster had been a newspaper boy for the *Toronto Star,* and in the early Superman strips, Clark Kent worked for the *Daily Star* (later rechristened the *Daily Planet*). Toronto purportedly served as the model for the city of Metropolis.

o **Neil Young** (b. 1945): Maybe Neil shouldn't be on this list—the genius singer/songwriter is likely the only famous person Toronto has produced that people actually realize is *from* Toronto.

ICE WINE & COOL CHARDONNAY

Ontario vintners' greatest successes so far have been mainly with white wines (although cool-climate red varietals like Pinot Noir are on the rise). Often delicious and complex, they can compete on an international scale. Varietals include fine Rieslings, Gewürztraminers, Chardonnays, late-harvest vintages, and interesting blends. Lately, international wine critics are praising "cool Chardonnays" from Ontario (as well as British Columbia). The top ones are from smaller wineries, and a summer-time festival highlights the top of the crop: **www.coolchardonnay.org**.

In winter, there are festivals that celebrate an Ontario specialty: ice wine. A highly sweet, and sometimes heavenly, creation, it's the wine that launched the local industry more than 20 years ago when it was honored abroad. Ice wine is

a tricky business: The grapes are left on the vine until the arrival of the first frost and then immediately harvested. (While the frost sends grapes' sweetness through the roof, it can also ruin the fruit if it's exposed too long.) Pickers often work through the night, but the hard work can pay off, as it did for Inniskillin in 1991, when the Ontario winery won the Grand Prix d'Honneur for its 1989 Vidal ice wine.

To learn more about Ontario wine before your visit, check out the Ontario Wine Council at **www.winesofontario. org**. And be sure to buy VQA (the acronym for the Vintners' Quality Alliance), which guarantees wines made from 100% Ontario-grown grapes. ("Cellared in Canada" means it was bottled here, but not grown or made here.)

Portuguese grills; halal and kosher; Japanese beyond sushi; oodles of good Italian; and more. It's hard to find a taste that Toronto can't satisfy, from greasy diners to organic vegan "bars," molecular gastronomy to pub grub. The one thing you won't find is an entrenched culinary tradition; food culture is very much of the here-and-now, which has its pros and cons. On the whole, this work-in-progress makes for a good deal of gusto and on occasion some appetizing originality the city can call its own.

More good news: In comparison to other big cities, it all adds up to a fairly affordable feast. The bad news is that high taxes on food and alcohol put a dent in the budget, even if menu prices are generally fair.

While restaurants of all descriptions are found across the city, certain neighborhoods are renowned for their specialties: Little Italy for its trattorie, Chinatown for its Chinese and Vietnamese eateries, and the Danforth for its Greek tavernas. King Street West, in the past several years, has become a magnet for gourmet restaurants, offering a bevy of bistros and *boîtes*. One thing that's particularly wonderful about Toronto's dining scene is that it's entirely possible to have a great meal at a bargain price. Restaurants such as **Torito Tapas Bar** (p. 81), **Guu Izakaya** (p. 82), **Woodlot** (p. 76), and **Gilead Café** (p. 81) let you dine well without breaking the bank.

Here's one more indulgence, if you have the time for a day trip. Just south and west of Toronto is the Niagara region, the biggest wine country in Canada. Follow its Wine Route to discover the reason local vintners such as Inniskillin and Henry of Pelham, and *garagistes* ("garage" winemakers) such as Daniel Lenko, are winning international competitions. Niagara's wineries use imported European vines, and because the region lies on the same latitude as France's Burgundy region, this meeting of Old and

New World results in bottles of Riesling, Sauvignon Blanc, Chardonnay, Pinot Noir, and Cabernet Sauvignon that are consistently excellent.

On second thought, even if you don't have the time for a day trip, you can try many of these wines at the local restaurants. Along with a celebration of local ingredients, the nearby grape is to be found in the city's best spots.

WHEN TO GO

Toronto is a city with four distinctive seasons. Autumn is a particularly good time to visit: The climate is brisk but temperate, the skies are sunny, the trees are a riot of color, and the cultural scene is in full swing. Another great time to see the city—if you don't mind a dusting of snow—is early winter in December, with holiday festivities for everyone. Spring is pretty, although rainy and cool days can make for a moody stay. Midsummer can be oppressive with heat, but there are plenty of parks and other places to cool down, like Ontario Place's busy water park and the Toronto Islands. Really, the only time the city can seem unwelcoming is on a windy February day when the temperature hits –22°F (–30°C). In fact, bone-chilling days are less frequent as the planet warms: You could call it a boost for Torontonians and the city's visitors—at least, for now.

Never mind what the calendar says; these are Toronto's true seasons: **Spring** runs from late March to late May (though occasionally there's snow in Apr); **summer,** June to early September; **fall,** mid-September to mid-November; and **winter,** late November to sometime in March. The highest recorded temperature is 105°F (41°C); the lowest, –27°F (–33°C). The average date of first frost is October 29; the average date of last frost is April 20. The windblasts from Lake Ontario can be fierce, even in June. Even in summer, bring a light jacket.

Toronto's Average Temperatures °F (°C)

	JAN	FEB	MAR	APR	MAY	JUNE	JULY	AUG	SEPT	OCT	NOV	DEC
HIGH	28 (-2)	29 (-2)	39 (4)	52 (11)	65 (18)	73 (23)	79 (26)	77 (25)	68 (20)	56 (13)	44 (7)	33 (1)
LOW	15 (-9)	15 (-9)	24 (-4)	35 (2)	45 (7)	54 (12)	60 (16)	58 (14)	50 (10)	39 (4)	31 (-1)	20 (-7)

Holidays

Toronto celebrates the following holidays: New Year's Day (Jan 1), Family Day (third Mon of Feb), Good Friday and Easter Monday (Mar or Apr), Victoria Day (Mon following the third weekend in May), Canada Day (July 1), Simcoe Day (first Mon in Aug), Labour Day (first Mon in Sept), Thanksgiving (second Mon in Oct), Remembrance Day (Nov 11), Christmas Day (Dec 25), and Boxing Day (Dec 26).

Don't Forget the Sunscreen

Because of Canada's image of a land of harsh winters, many travelers don't realize that summer can be scorching. "The UV index goes quite high, between 7 and 10, in Toronto," says Dr. Patricia Agin of the Coppertone Solar Research Center in Memphis. A UV index reading of 7 can mean sunburn, so don't forget to pack your sunscreen and a hat, especially if you're planning to enjoy Toronto's many parks and outdoor attractions.

On Good Friday and Easter Monday, schools and government offices close; most corporations close on one or the other, and a few close on both. Only banks and government offices close on Remembrance Day (Nov 11).

Calendar of Events

January, February, March, and April are dominated by trade shows, such as the International Boat and Automobile shows, Metro Home Show, Outdoor Adventure Sport Show, and more. For information, call **Tourism Toronto** (✆ **800/499-2514** or 416/203-2600; www.torontotourism.com).

For an exhaustive list of events beyond those listed here, check http://events.frommers.com, where you'll find a searchable, up-to-the-minute roster of what's happening in cities all over the world.

JANUARY

Toronto WinterCity Festival, citywide. Formerly known as WinterFest, this 2-week celebration blankets the city with fun, mostly outdoor, events. It features ice-skating shows, snow play, performances, art shows, and more. For information, visit **www.toronto.ca/special_events**. Late January through early February.

Winterlicious, citywide. Baby, it's cold outside, but Toronto's restaurants really know how to heat things up. Roughly 150 of the city's finest eateries offer prix-fixe lunch (C$15–C$25) and dinner (C$25–C$45) menus. See **www.toronto.ca/special_events** for a complete listing. Late January through early February.

FEBRUARY

Chinese New Year Celebrations, various sites in the city. In 2012, the Year of the Dragon is celebrated. Festivities include traditional and contemporary performances of Chinese opera, dancing, music, and more. For **Harbourfront** celebration information, call ✆ **416/973-4000** or visit **www.harbourfrontcentre.com**; for the **Rogers Centre,** call ✆ **877/666-3838** or check **www.rogerscentre.com**. The 2012 new year starts on January 23.

International Readings at Harbourfront, Harbourfront. This weekly series invites authors from around the globe to read from their most recent works. Participants have included David Sedaris, Pico Iyer, and Jhumpa Lahiri. For information, call Harbourfront at ✆ **416/973-4000** or go to **www.readings.org**. February through June.

MARCH

Canada Blooms, Metro Toronto Convention Centre. At this time of year, any glimpse of greenery is welcome. Canada Blooms treats visitors to 2.5 hectares (6¼ acres) of indoor garden and flower displays, seminars with green-thumb experts, and competitions. For information, call ✆ **416/593-0223** or visit **www.canadablooms.com**. Second or third week of March.

St. Patrick's Day Parade, downtown. Toronto's own version of the classic Irish celebration. For information, call ✆ **416/487-1566** or visit **www.topatrick.com**. March 17.

Toronto Festival of Storytelling, Harbourfront. Now in its 33rd year, this event celebrates international folklore, with storytellers imparting legends and fables from around the world. For information, call ✆ **416/973-4000** or check **www.torontofestivalofstorytelling.ca**. Late March to early April; check for dates.

One-of-a-Kind Craft Show & Sale, Exhibition Place. More than 400 crafts artists from across Canada display their unique wares at this show. For information, visit **www.oneofakindshow.com**. Late March to early April; check for dates.

APRIL

Blue Jays Season Opener, Rogers Centre. Turn out to root for your home-away-from-home team. For tickets, call ✆ **888/OK-GO-JAY** (888/654-6529) or 416/341-1234, or visit **http://toronto.bluejays.mlb.com**. Mid-April.

The Shaw Festival, Niagara-on-the-Lake, Ontario. This festival presents the plays of George Bernard Shaw and his contemporaries, as well as modern Canadian works. Call ℭ **800/511-7429** or 905/468-2172, or visit **www.shawfest.com**. Mid-April through first weekend of November.

Hot Docs Film Festival, citywide. North America's largest documentary festival has grown from a modest celebration to an 11-day extravaganza with over 170 films from more than 40 countries. Call ℭ **416/203-2155** or visit **www.hotdocs.ca**. Late April to early May.

Total Health Show, Metro Convention Centre. Founded in 1975, this 3-day event organizes panels and events with medical professionals, authors, alternative practitioners, organic farmers, and local chefs to talk about public and personal health issues. For information, call ℭ **416/924-9800** or visit **www.totalhealthshow.com**. Mid-April.

MAY

CONTACT Photography Festival, citywide. This annual month-long event shows the work of more than 500 Canadian and international photographers. For information, call ℭ **416/539-9595** or visit **www.contactphoto.com**. May 1 to 31.

Salut Toronto Food + Wine Festival, Yorkville. Formerly known as Santé, this week-long event celebrates international wines, as well as Ontario vintages, great cocktails, and the best in food. For information, visit **www.salutwinefestival.com**. Early May.

The Stratford Festival, Stratford, Ontario. Featuring a wide range of contemporary and classic plays, this festival always includes several works by Shakespeare. Call ℭ **800/567-1600** or check out **www.stratfordfestival.ca**. Early May through mid-November.

ALOUD: A Celebration for Young Readers, Harbourfront. A 3-day literary fun fest for kids. For information, call Harbourfront at ℭ **416/973-4000** or go to **www.readings.org**. Mid-May.

Inside Out Lesbian and Gay Film Festival, citywide. Toronto has no shortage of film festivals, but Inside Out, now in its 22nd year, is unique. This 11-day event has nurtured plenty of new talent and supported many established artists. Call ℭ **416/977-6847** or check out **www.insideout.ca**. Mid-May.

Doors Open Toronto, citywide. Hugely popular, this weekend event invites city residents and visitors alike to tour some of Toronto's architectural marvels. Some of the more than 150 participating buildings aren't normally open to the public, and all are free of charge. Visit **www.toronto.ca/doorsopen**. Late May.

JUNE

Luminato, citywide. First launched in 2007, this 9-day festival of "arts + creativity" has quickly become a highlight of the city's calendar. Featuring music, dance, theater, art, and educational programs, it really does offer something for the whole family. For information, visit **www.luminato.com**. Early to mid-June.

North by Northeast Festival, citywide. Known in the music biz as NXNE, this hot 3-day event features rock and indie bands at multiple venues around town. For information, visit **www.nxne.com**. Mid-June.

Waterfront Blues, Woodbine Park in the Beaches. This used to be the Distillery District's blues fest. Toronto shows that it's got soul in this 3-day festival of Canada's best blues musicians. The event is free; no tickets are required. For information, visit **www.waterfrontblues.ca**. First or second weekend in June.

Telus Toronto International Dragon Boat Festival, Centre Island. More than 160 teams of dragon-boaters compete in the 2-day event, which commemorates the death of the Chinese philosopher and poet Qu Yuan. For information, visit **www.dragonboats.com**. Third weekend in June.

Pride Week & Pride Parade, citywide. Celebrating Toronto's gay and lesbian community, Pride Week features events, performances, symposiums, and parties. It culminates in an extravagant Sunday parade, one of the biggest in North America. For information, call ☎ **416/92-PRIDE** (416/927-7433) or 416/927-7433, or visit **www.pridetoronto.com**. Late June.

TD Canada Trust Toronto Jazz Festival, citywide. This 10-day festival showcases international artists playing every jazz style—blues, gospel, Latin, African, traditional—at venues around town. For information, call ☎ **416/928-2033** or check out **www.tojazz. com**. Late June.

The Fringe: Toronto's Theatre Festival, citywide. More than 90 troupes participate in this 12-day festival of contemporary and experimental theater. Shows last no more than an hour. For information, call ☎ **416/966-1062** or visit **www.fringe toronto.com**. Late June to early July.

JULY

Canada Day Celebrations, citywide. July 1, 2012, marks the nation's 145th birthday. Street parties, fireworks, and other special events commemorate the day. For information, contact **Tourism Toronto** (☎ **800/363-1990** or 416/203-2600; **www.seetorontonow.com**). July 1.

Canada Dry Festival of Fire, Ontario Place. Formerly known as the Symphony of Fire, this fireworks extravaganza lights up Toronto's waterfront, with the pyrotechnics synchronized to music. For information, call ☎ **416/314-9900** or visit **www.ontario place.com**. Early July.

Summerlicious, citywide. It's just like January's Winterlicious event, except that you can dine alfresco. The prix-fixe menus (C$15–C$30 lunch, C$25–C$45 dinner) are some of the best deals around. See **www. toronto.ca/special_events** for a complete list. First 2 weeks of July.

Honda Indy, the Exhibition Place Street circuit. Formerly known as the Molson Indy, this is one of Canada's major races on the IndyCar circuit. Away from the track, you'll find live music and beer gardens. For information, call ☎ **416/922-7477** or visit **www.hondaindytoronto.com**. Second weekend in July.

Just for Laughs, citywide. This offshoot of the successful Montréal-based comedy festival brings to town the world's top comics, alongside emerging talent. Visit **www.hahaha.com/toronto** for more information. Early to mid-July.

RBC Canadian Open, Glen Abbey Golf Club, Oakville. Formerly called the PGA Tour Canadian Open, Canada's national golf tournament has featured the likes of Greg Norman and Tiger Woods. Visit **www. rbccanadianopen.com** for more information. Mid- to late July.

Beaches International Jazz Festival, Queen Street East, between Woodbine and Beech avenues. Both local and international jazz artists turn out for this annual festival, which plays out over 9 days. All of the performances are free. For information, visit **www.beachesjazz.com**. Late July.

Caribbean Carnival, citywide. Toronto's version of Carnival transforms the city. It's complete with traditional foods from the Caribbean and Latin America, ferry cruises, picnics, children's events, concerts, and arts-and-crafts exhibits. Visit **http://toronto caribbeancarnival.com**. Late July through early August.

AUGUST

Beerlicious, Fort York. More than 70 major Ontario breweries and microbreweries turn out for this celebration of suds. There's also a wide selection of food from local restaurants, as well as live blues, swing, and jazz music. **Note:** Fort York is normally a great spot for kids, but no one under 19 is allowed at this event. For info, call ☎ **416/698-7206** or visit **www.beer festival.ca**. First weekend in August.

Canadian National Exhibition, Exhibition Place. It's an old-style touring amusement fair. One of the world's largest exhibitions, this 18-day extravaganza features midway rides, display buildings, free shows, and grandstand performers. The 3-day Canadian International Air Show (first staged in 1878) is a bonus. Call ☎ **416/393-6300** or visit **www.theex.com** for information. Mid-August through Labour Day.

Rogers Cup, Rexall Centre at York University. This international tennis championship is an important stop on the pro tennis tour. In 2012, the men play in Toronto and the women in Montréal. In 2013, they'll swap. For information, call ✆ **877/283-6647** or visit **www.lovemeansnothing.ca**. Mid-August.

SEPTEMBER

Toronto International Film Festival, citywide. The stars come out for the second-largest film festival in the world. More than 250 films from 70 countries are shown over 10 days. For information, call ✆ **416/968-FILM** (416/968-3456) or surf over to **www.tiff.net**. Mid-September.

Word on the Street, Queen's Park. This open-air event celebrates the written word with readings, discounted books and magazines, and children's events. Other major Canadian cities hold similar events on the same weekend. For information, call ✆ **416/504-7241** or visit **www.thewordon thestreet.ca**. Last weekend in September.

The Clothing Show, Exhibition Place. More than 300 booths, featuring everything from indie design to vintage couture, all under one roof. For information, call ✆ **416/516-9859** or visit **www.theclothingshow.com**. Last weekend of September.

OCTOBER

Oktoberfest, Kitchener–Waterloo, about 1 hour from Toronto. This famed 9-day drink-fest features cultural events, plus a pageant and parade. For information, call ✆ **888/294-4267** or 519/570-4267, or visit **www.oktoberfest.ca**. Mid-October.

International Festival of Authors, Harbourfront. Founded in 1980, this renowned 10-day literary festival is arguably the most prestigious in Canada. It draws the absolute top writers from around the world and at home, and has also proven to be an important stage for discovering new talent. Among the literary luminaries who have appeared are Salman Rushdie, Margaret Drabble, Thomas Kenneally, Joyce Carol Oates, A. S. Byatt, and Margaret

Atwood. For information, call Harbourfront at ✆ **416/973-4000** or visit **www. readings.org**. Last 10 days of October.

Toronto Maple Leafs Opening Night, Air Canada Centre. Torontonians love their hockey team, and opening night is always a big event. For tickets, call ✆ **416/872-5000** or visit **http://mapleleafs.nhl.com**. October.

NOVEMBER

Royal Agricultural Winter Fair and Royal Horse Show, Exhibition Place. The 12-day show is the largest indoor agricultural and equestrian competition in the world. Displays include giant vegetables and fruits, homey crafts, farm machinery, livestock, and more. A member of the British royal family traditionally attends the horse show; in 2010, it was a highlight when Prince Charles and Camilla cut the ribbon. In 2011, it was the less famous Governor General of Canada, David Johnston. Call ✆ **416/263-3400** or check **www.royalfair. org** for information. Mid-November.

Santa Claus Parade, downtown. A favorite with kids since 1905, it features marching bands, floats, clowns, and jolly St. Nick. American visitors are usually surprised that the parade's in November, but it's better than watching Santa try to slide through slush. For information, contact **Tourism Toronto** (✆ **800/363-1990** or 416/203-2600; **www.thesantaclaus parade.com**). Third Sunday of November.

Cavalcade of Lights, Nathan Phillips Square. This holiday celebration brings to life the skating rink at City Hall with a fantastic light show, performances, parties, and fireworks. Visit **www.toronto.ca** for more information. Late November through late December.

Canadian Aboriginal Festival, Hamilton. More than 1,500 Native American dancers, drummers, and singers attend this weekend celebration. There are literary readings, an arts-and-crafts market, lacrosse-playing, and traditional foods. Call ✆ **519/751-0040** or visit **www.canab. com**. Last weekend in November.

DECEMBER

First Night Toronto and New Year's Eve at City Hall. First Night is an alcohol-free family New Year's Eve celebration. There are a variety of musical, theatrical, and dance performances at downtown venues.

In Nathan Phillips Square and in Mel Lastman Square in North York, concerts begin at around 10pm to usher in the countdown to the New Year. Visit **www.toronto.ca** for more information. December 31.

RESPONSIBLE TRAVEL

By North American standards, Toronto is an exceptionally green city. It boasts good eco-initiatives such as composting and recycling programs, a powerful local-foods movement, and more. The city's wealth of parkland, even in the downtown core, is a standout. And although there is nothing on the scale of, say, Central Park, there are green spaces scattered throughout, from tiny plots in the Financial District to neighborhood gems like Riverdale, Allan Gardens, Trinity Bellwoods, Dufferin Grove, and High Park. (The green spaces are well maintained, but you may notice a fair number of weeds because cosmetic use of pesticides is banned in the city.)

Cycling is a popular mode of transit, and the city has ambitious plans to expand the number of dedicated bicycle lanes as part of a proposed 1,000km-plus (621-mile) Bikeway Network. There are biking trails through most of the city's parks and more than 29km (18 miles) of street bike routes. Favorite pathways include the **Martin Goodman Trail** (from the Beaches neighborhood to the Humber River along the waterfront); the **Lower Don Valley** bike trail (from the east end of the city north to Riverdale Park); **High Park** (with winding trails over 160 hectares/395 acres); and the best of them all for bi-pedal fans: the **Toronto Islands,** where bikes rule and cars are forbidden. Bike lanes, which are clearly marked, include routes along College/Carlton streets, the Bloor Street Viaduct leading to Danforth Avenue, Beverly/St.

jump UP!

One of the undisputed highlights of summer in Toronto is the annual **Scotiabank Caribbean** Festival (formerly known as Caribana). Created in 1967 as a community heritage celebration to tie in with Canada's centennial, Caribana has become North America's largest street festival, drawing more than a million visitors from North America, Britain, and the Caribbean each year. Originally based on Trinidad's Carnival, the festival now draws on numerous cultures—Jamaican, Guyanese, Brazilian, and Bahamian, to name a few—for its music, food, and events.

During the 2 weeks that it runs, you will see the influence of Caribana around town. It starts with a bang—think steel drums—at Nathan Phillips Square with a free concert featuring calypso, salsa, and soca music. In the days that follow, there are boat cruises, dances, and concerts; the King and Queen Extravaganza, which showcases some of the most amazing costumes you'll ever hope to see; and an arts festival. The highlight is the closing weekend Parade, which brings together masquerade and steel-drum bands, dancers, and floats in a memorable feast for all the senses. This is one party you just can't miss.

George streets, Jarvis Street, and Davenport Road. For cycling maps, rentals, and more information, visit www.toronto.ca/cycling.

TOURS
Architectural & Cultural Tours

Toronto is a city for walking, and there's no shortage of options for those willing to pound the pavement. The **Royal Ontario Museum** has a **ROMwalks** program (© 416/586-5513) throughout the summer that offers guided tours of architectural highlights and neighborhoods from the Entertainment District to the Danforth. During the summer, **Heritage Toronto** (© 416/338-0684; www.heritagetoronto.org) offers walking tours of several neighborhoods, including Cabbagetown and Rosedale. If you're in town on the first weekend of May, check out Jane Walks (www.janeswalk. net), in honor of the late Jane Jacobs, the city's beloved author, thinker, and believer in "cities planned for and by people."

Bike Tours

Year-round, **A Taste of the World Neighbourhood Bicycle Tours and Walks ★** (© 416/923-6813; www.torontowalksbikes.com) leads visitors through the nooks and crannies of such places as Chinatown, Yorkville, and Rosedale. It's particularly well known for its "haunted" tours, including one about the ghosts of Yorkville (remember, that chic neighborhood stands atop a former cemetery).

Another option is the **Toronto Bicycling Network** (© 416/766-1985; www. tbn.ca). The association organizes tours and provides information about routes you can explore in and around the city.

Chefs & Gourmets

Bonnie Stern is a local legend, and the **Bonnie Stern Cooking School** is a wonderful place to pick up some of her culinary secrets (she teaches many of the classes herself). The school is located at 6 Erskine Ave. (3 blocks north of the Eglinton subway station); call © 416/484-4810 or visit **www.bonniestern.com** for information. The school offers classes in everything from challah baking to Moroccan cooking.

The Fairmont Royal York runs a popular Shop with a Chef package that includes a tour of St. Lawrence market and a delicious meal led by the eco-minded executive chef David Garcelon. Winery tours in the Niagara Region are popular and plenty. For more information, go to **www.tourismniagara.com/wine_country.html**.

Ecology & Wildlife

If you're interested in exploring the Toronto region's natural wonders, contact **Toronto and Region Conservation** at © 416/661-6600 or visit **www.trcaparks. ca**. The organization offers tours that include bird-watching and wildlife-viewing.

Harbor Tours

Mariposa Cruise Line (© 800/976-2442 or 416/203-0178; www.mariposa cruises.com) operates 1-hour narrated tours of the waterfront and the Toronto Islands

IT'S easy BEING GREEN

We can all help conserve fuel and energy when we travel. Here are a few simple ways you can help preserve your favorite destinations:

o Each time you take a flight or drive a car, greenhouse gases release into the atmosphere. You can help neutralize this danger to the planet through "carbon offsetting"—paying someone to invest your money in programs that reduce greenhouse gas emissions by the same amount you've added. Before buying carbon offset credits, just make sure that you're using a reputable company such as **Carbonfund** (www.carbonfund.org), **TerraPass** (www.terrapass.org), or **Carbon Neutral** (www.carbonneutral.org). **Air Canada** partnered with **Zerofootprint**, a not-for-profit organization, to offset flight emissions when you book on **www.air canada.com**. In February 2010, they tallied the program's savings: Since 2007, the offsets were 15,108 tons of carbon dioxide, or the equivalent of removing 3,740 cars from the road.

o Whenever possible, choose non-stop flights; they generally require less fuel than indirect flights that stop and take off again. Try to fly during the day—some scientists estimate that nighttime flights are twice as harmful to the environment. And pack light—each 6.8kg (15 lb.) of luggage on a 8,047km (5,000-mile) flight adds up to 23kg (51 lb.) of carbon dioxide emitted.

o Call the **Green Tourism Association of Toronto** for inspiration and advice about eco-friendly travel (© **416/392-1288**).

o Rely on public transportation to get around Toronto: The Toronto Transit Commission (**TTC**) is safe and clean, and it makes it easy to get to downtown, midtown, and uptown sights. Or rent a bike: Check out **Bikeshare** (© **416/504-2918**; http://communitybicyclenetwork.org/bike_rentals).

o If renting a car is necessary for a side trip (such as to Niagara-on-the-Lake), ask for a hybrid or rent the most fuel-efficient car

from mid-May to September. Tours leave from the Queen's Quay Terminal at 207 Queens Quay W.

The *Kajama*, a three-masted, 50m (164-ft.) schooner, offers 90-minute cruises. The schedule varies, but in July and August, three tours a day take place on weekdays and weekends. For more information, call the **Great Lakes Schooner Company** (249 Queens Quay W., Ste. 111; © **800/267-3866** or 416/260-6355; www. greatlakesschooner.com).

Escorted General-Interest Tours

Do you really need a package tour to visit Toronto? Generally speaking, no—it's easy to arrange accommodations and show tickets yourself. However, if you're determined to see a particular show (or the Canadian Opera Company, whose performances often sell out), a package is a good idea. Package tours are simply a way to buy the airfare, available. You'll use less gas and save money.

- Take a look at **"The City of Toronto Green Guide"** online at www.toronto.ca/environment/. And pick up a copy of *Green Living Magazine* for good resources, also online at **www. greenlivingonline.com**.
- Where you stay during your travels can have a major environmental impact. To determine the green credentials of a property, ask about trash disposal and recycling, water conservation, and energy use; also whether sustainable materials were used in the construction of the property. The website **www. greenhotels.com** recommends green-rated member hotels around the world that fulfill the company's stringent environmental requirements. Also consult **www.environmentallyfriendly hotels.com** for more green accommodation ratings.
- At hotels, request that your sheets and towels not be changed daily. (Many hotels already do this.) Turn off the lights and air-conditioner when you leave your room.
- Last, but definitely not least, eat at locally owned and operated restaurants that use local, seasonal, and (wherever possible) organic produce. Ditto for meats: Look for pasture-raised and non-industrial suppliers. Not only do these choices contribute to the local economy, they cut down on greenhouse gas emissions. Check out the city's farmers markets and, when shopping at supermarkets, look for the Local Food Plus (www.localfoodplus.ca) label, which identifies local producers that aim for sustainable practices. Toronto has too many restaurants that support the local foods movement to list here, but some suggestions include Gilead Bistro & Café (see p. 81), Trattoria Giancarlo (see p. 75), Cowbell (see p. 74), The Local Kitchen (see p. 77), and Scaramouche (see p. 92).

accommodations, and other elements of your trip (such as car rentals, airport transfers, and sometimes even activities) at the same time and often at discounted prices.

One good source of package deals is **Tourism Toronto** itself, which lists deals on its website (www.seetorontonow.com). Several of Toronto's hotels (including the **Park Hyatt, the Fairmont Royal York,** and the **Delta Chelsea**) offer special packages; see chapter 5. Several big **online travel agencies**—Expedia, Travelocity, Orbitz, and Lastminute.com—also do a brisk business in packages.

Maxxim Vacations (© **800/567-6666;** www.maxximvacations.com) is a Canadian company that has a long track record with Toronto package tours. One advantage with their packages is that you can guarantee you get to see the show (or shows) you have your heart set on while in town.

Travel packages are also listed in the travel section of your local weekend newspaper and sometimes in midweek editions. Or check ads in national travel magazines such as *Arthur Frommer's Budget Travel Magazine, Travel + Leisure, National Geographic Traveler,* and *Condé Nast Traveler.*

Escorted tours are structured group tours, with a group leader. The price usually includes everything from airfare to hotels, meals, tours, admission costs, and local transportation.

There are some great special-interest tours you can take part in while you're in town (see above), and the city is easy to navigate and explore without a group. However, if you do want an escorted tour, there are several options, including **Great Adventure Tours** (© **800/638-3945;** www.greatadventuretours.com), which explores Toronto and Niagara, and **SWT Tours** (© **212/988-1359;** www.poshnosh. com), which specializes in theater tours.

For more information on escorted general-interest tours, including questions to ask before booking your trip, see Frommers.com.

SUGGESTED TORONTO ITINERARIES

Toronto is a patchwork of neighborhoods with a remarkably vibrant downtown core. (Once you're in the heart of the city, you can head in just about any direction and end up somewhere with plenty to see, eat, and do.) Where most North American urbanites might know the heart of their metropolis as a workplace, a practical daytime shopping network, or an occasional night-time destination, more than 200,000 Torontonians eat, play, sleep—and work—in the downtown core. If you're coming in from Pearson International Airport, the city might seem sprawling, but once you're grounded downtown, everything is here: shoulder-to-shoulder shops, theaters, parks, galleries, restaurants and cafes, bars and night-clubs, and places of worship. Residential neighborhoods are found in pockets and increasingly with new developments in the downtown core.

Where most of the world is still proceeding with post-recessionary caution, the building here keeps booming. The skyline is littered with cranes, and the majority of the building activity is new condo towers and high-end hotels. The Trump Tower will be the city's second tallest skyscraper at 57 stories, First Canadian Place is 72, while the new Four Seasons hotel stands out for setting a record in condo sales with a penthouse that sold for C$28 million in 2011.

The city's diverse cultural makeup is evidenced all around town. Foods reflect the multicultural fabric, from Little Italy's residential laneways lined with garages where wine and tomato sauces are made in late summer to outdoor BBQs charring spiced corn-on-the-cob along Little India's strip. There are cultural centers of every stripe, music to suit any taste, galleries galore, and interesting shops of interest all around.

Start anywhere in the downtown core, walk in any direction for no more than 15 minutes, and you'll see eclectic modern buildings side by side with neo-Gothic and Art Deco architecture, or catch a fair glimpse of the city's ethnic spectrum. Sometimes, you'll walk right into a pleasing patch of greenery.

This is a happy coincidence because the layout and organization of the city mean you *will* almost certainly get lost at least once during your stay. Streets have names, not numbers, and they have a crazy-making habit of changing their monikers as they go along. In Midtown, the must-see

Following the lead of such cities as New York and Sydney, Toronto is training some of its citizens to act as tour guides in popular neighborhoods. Tours take an hour or more, and they're free of charge. Call ✆ 416/338-2786 or head to www.toronto.ca/tapto for more information. Every effort is made to match visitors and greeters by interest, so if you are particularly curious about architecture, history, food, or culture, make sure to mention that when you book your tour.

Avenue Road, for example, turns into Queen's Park Crescent, then into University Avenue as you head south, and into Oriole Parkway if you go north. My best advice: Relax and enjoy the ride.

ORIENTATION

City Layout

Toronto is laid out in a grid . . . with a few interesting exceptions. **Yonge Street** (pronounced *young*) is the main north-south artery, stretching from Lake Ontario in the south well beyond Hwy. 401 in the north. Yonge Street divides western cross streets from eastern cross streets. The main east-west artery is **Bloor Street,** which cuts through the heart of downtown.

"Downtown" usually refers to the area from Eglinton Avenue south to the lake, between Spadina Avenue in the west and Jarvis Street in the east. Because this is such a large area, it's been divided here into five sections. **Downtown West** runs from the lake north to College Street; the eastern boundary is Yonge Street. **Downtown East** goes from the lake north to Carlton Street (once College St. reaches Yonge St., it becomes Carlton St.); the western boundary is Yonge Street. **Midtown** extends from College Street north to Davenport Road; the eastern boundary is Jarvis Street. **The Danforth/the East End** runs east to Danforth Avenue; the western boundary is Broadview Avenue. **Uptown** is the area north of Davenport Road.

In Downtown West, you'll find many of the lakeshore attractions: Harbourfront, Ontario Place, Fort York, Exhibition Place, and the Toronto Islands. It also boasts the CN Tower, City Hall, the Four Seasons Centre for the Performing Arts, the Rogers Centre (formerly known as SkyDome), Chinatown, the Art Gallery of Ontario, and the Eaton Centre. Downtown East includes the Distillery District, the St. Lawrence Market, the Sony Centre (formerly the Hummingbird Centre), the St. Lawrence Centre for the Arts, and St. James's Cathedral. Midtown contains the Royal Ontario Museum, the Gardiner Museum, the University of Toronto, Markham Village, and chic Yorkville, a prime area for shopping and dining. The Danforth/the East End features Riverdale Farm, the historic Necropolis, and Greektown. Uptown has traditionally been a residential area, but it's now a fast-growing entertainment area, too. Its attractions include the Sunnybrook park system and the Ontario Science Centre.

North Toronto is another developing area, with theaters such as the Toronto Centre for the Arts, galleries, and some excellent dining. It's not yet a prime tourist destination, but it is on the rise and gets a few mentions throughout this guide.

Note: Some of the primary attractions lie outside the downtown core or even the city limits. The Toronto Zoo, Paramount Canada's Wonderland, and the McMichael Canadian Art Collection are all full- or half-day trips.

FINDING AN ADDRESS This isn't as easy as it should be. Your best bet is to call ahead and ask for directions, including landmarks and subway stations. Even the locals need to do this.

The Neighborhoods in Brief

DOWNTOWN WEST

The Toronto Islands These three islands in Lake Ontario—Ward's, Algonquin, and Centre—are home to a handful of residents and no cars. They're a spring and summer haven where Torontonians go to in-line skate, bicycle, boat, and picnic. However, it's also a good place to visit in winter if you're up for a bracing walk. Centre Island, the most visited, holds the children's theme park Centreville. Catch the ferry at the foot of Bay Street by Queen's Quay. You can rent bicycles on the island.

Harbourfront/Lakefront The landfill where the railroad yards and dock facilities once stood is now a glorious playground opening onto the lake. This is home to the Harbourfront Centre, one of the most vibrant literary, artistic, and cultural venues in Canada.

Financial District Toronto's major banks and insurance companies have their headquarters here, from Front Street north to Queen Street, between Yonge and York streets. Toronto's first skyscrapers rose here; fortunately, some of the older structures have been preserved. Ultramodern BCE Place incorporated the facade of an historic bank building into its design.

Entertainment District Also known as the Theatre District, this area, dense with big-name venues, stretches from Front Street north to Queen Street and from Bay Street west to Bathurst Street. King Street West is home to most of the important venues, including the Royal Alexandra Theatre, the Princess of Wales Theatre, and Roy Thomson Hall. Just north is the Four Seasons Centre for the Performing Arts (the new home of the Canadian Opera

underground TORONTO

In cold weather, it's a good idea to quickly familiarize yourself with the labyrinthine walkways beneath the pavement. This miles-long network is an excellent way to get around the downtown core when the weather is grim. You can eat, sleep, dance, shop, and go to the theater without ever donning a coat.

You can walk from the Dundas subway station south through the Eaton Centre until you hit Queen Street; turn west to the Sheraton Centre and then head south. You'll pass through the Richmond-Adelaide Centre, First Canadian Place, and Toronto Dominion Centre, and go all the way (through the dramatic Royal Bank Plaza) to Union Station. En route, branches lead off to the stock exchange, Sun Life Centre, and Metro Hall. Additional walkways link Simcoe Plaza to 200 Wellington West and to the CBC Broadcast Centre. Other walkways run around Bloor Street and Yonge Street, and elsewhere in the city. Check the "Underground Toronto" map on p. 38 or look for the large, clear underground PATH maps throughout the concourse.

This underground city even has its own attractions. First Canadian Place, in particular, is known for free lunch-hour lectures, opera and dance performances, and art exhibits.

Underground Toronto

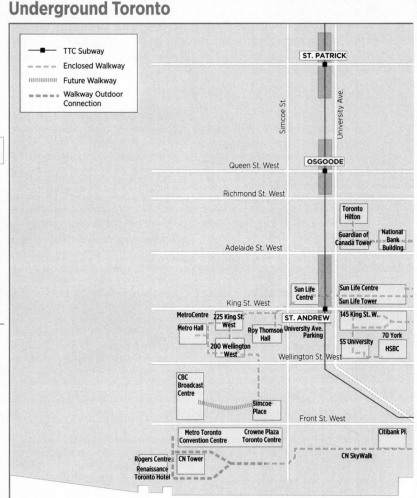

Legend:
- ━■━ TTC Subway
- - - - - Enclosed Walkway
- ⁝⁝⁝⁝⁝⁝ Future Walkway
- ▬ ▬ ▬ Walkway Outdoor Connection

ST. PATRICK

Simcoe St.

University Ave.

Queen St. West

OSGOODE

Richmond St. West

Toronto Hilton

Adelaide St. West

Guardian of Canada Tower

National Bank Building

Sun Life Centre

Sun Life Centre
Sun Life Tower

King St. West

MetroCentre

225 King St. West

ST. ANDREW

145 King St. W.

Metro Hall

Roy Thomson Hall

University Ave. Parking

70 York

200 Wellington West

55 University

HSBC

Wellington St. West

CBC Broadcast Centre

Simcoe Place

Front St. West

Metro Toronto Convention Centre

Crowne Plaza Toronto Centre

Citibank Pl.

Rogers Centre

CN Tower

CN SkyWalk

Renaissance Toronto Hotel

Company and the National Ballet of Canada), and south are the Convention Centre, the CN Tower, and the Rogers Centre.

Chinatown Dundas Street West from University Avenue to Spadina Avenue and north to College Street are the boundaries of Chinatown. As the Chinese community has grown, it has extended along Dundas Street and north along Spadina Avenue. Here, you'll see a fascinating mixture of old and new. Hole-in-the-wall restaurants share the sidewalks with glitzy shopping centers built with Hong Kong money.

Kensington Market Just west of Spadina Avenue and north of Dundas Street West is one of Toronto's most colorful neighborhoods. Successive waves of immigration—Eastern European Jews, Portuguese, Caribbean, and more—have left their mark. Filled with tiny but wonderful food shops, restaurants, and vintage clothing stores, it's easy to while away an afternoon here

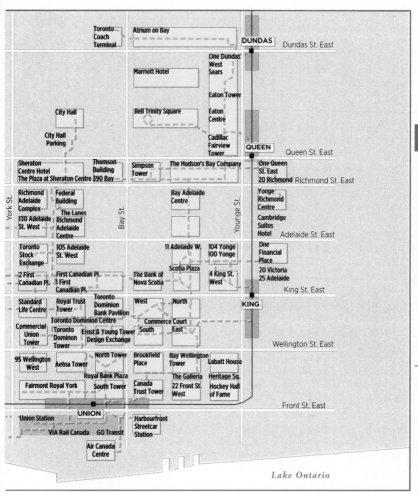

Map labels:

Toronto Coach Terminal · Atrium on Bay · DUNDAS · Dundas St. East

One Dundas West Sears · Marriott Hotel · Eaton Tower · City Hall · Bell Trinity Square · Eaton Centre · City Hall Parking · Cadillac Fairview Tower · QUEEN · Queen St. East

Sheraton Centre Hotel · Thomson Building · Simpson Tower · The Hudson's Bay Company · One Queen St. East · The Plaza at Sheraton Centre · 390 Bay · 20 Richmond · Richmond St. East

Richmond Adelaide Complex · Federal Building · Bay Adelaide Centre · Yonge Richmond Centre · The Lanes · 130 Adelaide St. West · Richmond Adelaide Centre · York St. · Bay St. · Younge St. · Cambridge Suites Hotel · Adelaide St. East

Toronto Stock Exchange · 105 Adelaide St. West · 11 Adelaide W. · 104 Yonge 100 Yonge · One Financial Place · 2 First Canadian Pl. · First Canadian Pl. 1 First Canadian Pl · Scotia Plaza · The Bank of Nova Scotia · 4 King St. West · 20 Victoria · 25 Adelaide · King St. East

Standard Life Centre · Royal Trust Tower · Toronto Dominion Bank Pavilion · West · North · KING · Toronto Dominion Centre · Commerce Court · Commercial Union Tower · Toronto Dominon Tower · Ernst & Young Tower Design Exchange · South · East · Wellington St. East

95 Wellington West · North Tower · Brookfield Place · Bay Wellington Tower · Labatt House · Aetna Tower · Royal Bank Plaza · The Galleria · Heritage Sq. · Fairmont Royal York · South Tower · Canada Trust Tower · 22 Front St. West · Hockey Hall of Fame · Front St. East

UNION · Union Station · Harbourfront Streetcar Station · VIA Rail Canada · GO Transit · Air Canada Centre · Lake Ontario

(especially on the car-free summer Sundays, when the area becomes a pedestrian-only zone).

Queen Street West This stretch from University Avenue to Bathurst Street offers an eclectic mix of mainstream shops, funky boutiques, secondhand bookshops, and vintage-clothing emporiums. It's also packed with eateries: bistros, cafes, and gourmet food shops line the street. Despite

the intrusion of mega-retailers, many independently owned boutiques still flourish.

Art & Design District In the past, Queen Street West (see above) was considered edgy. Now, that description is more accurately applied to West Queen West, which starts at Bathurst Avenue and runs west to Gladstone Avenue and beyond. This neighborhood is one of the coolest in the city, full of fine art galleries; one-of-a-kind boutiques selling clothing, housewares, and antiques; and some truly great restaurants.

Ossington Avenue   Ossington remains a hot hub of Toronto's nightlife scene with great restaurants, bars, and cafes that round out a thriving day-time culture. Combine a tour of the strip with a walk en route along Dundas Street West to see some of the hippest and newest spots the city has to offer.

Little Italy   This charming, lively area filled with open-air cafes, trattorie, and shops, serves the longstanding Italian and Portuguese communities along College Street, between Palmerston Boulevard and Shaw Street. The crowds can't stay away, which has driven up traffic, especially on weekend evenings, and helped to expand the neighborhood offerings to include sushi spots and trendy bars and restaurants.

DOWNTOWN EAST

Old Town/St. Lawrence Market   During the 19th century, this area, east of Yonge Street, between the Esplanade and Adelaide Street, was the focal point of the community. Today, the market's still going strong, and attractions such as the glorious St. James Cathedral continue to draw visitors. It's also an area on the rise with fine restaurants and stellar shops.

The Beaches   Communal, youthful, safe, and comfortable—these adjectives describe this neighborhood that's just 30 minutes from downtown at the end of the Queen Street East streetcar line. A summer resort in the mid-1800s, the Beaches' boardwalk and sandy beach ensure that it remains casual and family-oriented to this day. In 2006, there was a local poll to rename this area "The Beach" (a term preferred by many residents), but "The Beaches" is still the way the neighborhood is known.

Leslieville   Once a down-on-its-luck stretch of Queen Street East, between Carlaw Avenue and Leslie Street, and a former industrial area, the strip has now been gentrified. There are upstart boutiques, vintage and antique stores, cafes, bars, and excellent bistros. Its borders are

expanding, too—you'll see "Leslieville" signs after you cross Broadview Avenue.

Little India   Gerrard Street East, between Greenwood Avenue and Main Street, is well known for its festival-like atmosphere. It's partly because of the multicolored lights that light up the street at night, but the vibrant street life is visible at any time of day. The blocks are filled with Indian restaurants, grocers, and shops that specialize in saris, beautiful textiles, and treasure-chests of trinkets.

MIDTOWN

Queen's Park and the University   Home to the Ontario Legislature and many of the colleges and buildings that make up the handsome campus of the University of Toronto, this leafy neighborhood extends from College Street to Bloor Street, between Spadina Avenue and Bay Street. Expect to find good bistros en route.

Yorkville   Originally a village outside the city limits, this area immediately north and west of Bloor and Yonge streets became Toronto's Haight-Ashbury in the 1960s. For the past few decades, the vibe has been haute, not hippie. The pretty streets are lined with designer boutiques, galleries, cafes, and restaurants.

The Annex   This largely residential neighborhood is a mix of small parks, handsome homes, and a strip along Bloor Street West that offers some good shopping for books and knick knacks, plus a few attractive restaurants and pubs, and one unique attraction, the Bata Shoe Museum. The Annex stretches from Bedford Road to Bathurst Street and from Harbord Street to Dupont Avenue. Revered urban-planning guru the late Jane Jacobs called this area home.

Koreatown   The bustling blocks along Bloor Street West, between Bathurst and Christie streets, are filled with Korean restaurants; alternative-medicine practitioners, such as herbalists and acupuncturists; and shops filled with made-in-Korea merchandise.

THE DANFORTH/THE EAST END

Rosedale   Meandering these quiet, tree-lined avenues offers a tour of some of

Toronto's grandest homes. This residential area, composed of snaking streets that make it easy to get lost, runs from Yonge and Bloor streets northeast to Castle Frank and the Moore Park Ravine. It's named after the residence of Sheriff William Jarvis, who is largely credited with ending the 1837 Upper Canada Rebellion.

Church Street/the Gay Village Between Gerrard Street and Bloor Street East, along Church Street, lies the heart of Toronto's original gay and lesbian community. The "ghetto" has since evolved, and gay Torontonians now live and play all around town. Still, there remains a concentration of restaurants, cafes, and shops that offer a gay focus. Church Street is where 19th-century Toronto's grandest churches were built.

Cabbagetown Writer Hugh Garner described this as the largest Anglo-Saxon slum in North America, long before it became a gentrified neighborhood of restored, often pretty and pricey, Victorian and Edwardian homes. The boundaries run from east of Parliament Street to the Don Valley and between Gerrard and Bloor streets. The name is an historic reference: The original Irish immigrants who settled here in the late 1800s grew row upon row of cabbages on their front lawns. Riverdale, Toronto's only inner-city farm, is at the eastern edge of the district.

Greektown Across the Don Valley Viaduct, Bloor Street becomes the Danforth, which marks the beginning of Greektown. It's lined with old-style Greek tavernas and hip Mediterranean bars and restaurants that are crowded from early evening into the night. The densest wining-and-dining area starts at Broadview Avenue and runs about 8 blocks east.

UPTOWN

Christie and St. Clair Until not long ago, this was a modest residential neighborhood where Torontonians would venture for some great Italian gelato or for a street party during the World Cup. Now, the area and beyond are proving a popular place to visit for good cafes, some fine Jamaican fare, and the Green Barns development, a mix of artists studios, farmers market, community gardens, and events space. The area runs west from Christie Street to Dufferin Street.

Eglinton Avenue The neighborhood surrounding the intersection of Yonge Street and Eglinton Avenue is jokingly known as "Young and Eligible." It's a bustling area filled with restaurants—from neighborhood favorites to fine-dining destinations—as well as live-music pubs and nightclubs. To the east, it intersects with the 243-hectare (600-acre) Sunnybrook park system and with the Ontario Science Centre.

THE BEST OF TORONTO IN 1 DAY

You'd better put on your walking shoes because seeing the best of Toronto in a day means covering a lot of territory. This itinerary explores the city's most famous attractions, including the ones everyone back home will ask you about (like the CN Tower). It's a downtown walk that will take you from the city's highest point to highlights along the waterfront, from the commercial core to a handful of lofty public buildings. Take comfort: There is plenty of refreshing green space along the way. *Start: From Union Station, walk west along Front Street to Bremner Boulevard to the CN Tower.*

1 CN Tower ★

Today, you're starting at the top. Even if the famous tower isn't the tallest in the world anymore, don't overlook Toronto's most celebrated icon (plus, the glass elevator makes the ride up even more of a thrill). Beginning your tour here will give you a perspective on Toronto, its neighborhoods and general layout, even if it all seems on a model scale from the great heights. If it's a clear day, you might be able to see all the way to Niagara Falls. But even if it isn't clear out, you can check out the stomach-churning glass floor. Lie flat, I dare you, or just jump up and down on it for a vertiginous thrill. See p. 102.

2 Rogers Centre ★

This is the domed stadium formerly known as SkyDome. The formal tour is for sports fans only; otherwise, just idly appreciate the massive statues of cheering (and jeering) spectators on the facade. If you want to see the Toronto Blue Jays play ball (or the Toronto Argonauts play football, Canadian style), come back later in the day. See p. 121.

3 Toronto Music Garden ★★★

I know that getting to the waterfront is no joy, but it's entirely worth it when you reach the tranquil Toronto Music Garden. A lovely green space, it's also reached by a comfortable street-car ride and is flanked by new boardwalks and some additional, albeit less green, parks. The Music Garden was designed by world-renowned cellist Yo-Yo Ma and landscape architect Julie Moir Messervy to invoke Bach's First Suite for Unaccompanied Cello. It may sound highfalutin, but when you're wandering around the grounds, it's simply serene. See p. 123.

4 Harbourfront Centre ★★

This is the kind of place where you could easily spend a day, so you may need to tear yourself away to stay on track. There are glassblowers, potters, jewelry makers, and other artisans to watch at their work in the Craft Studio; the Artists' Gardens, a series of diverse landscapes created by local talent, is another highlight. Depending on how active you feel, this is also your chance to get out on the water: The Harbourfront Canoe and Kayak School will let you rent a boat and offers instruction. There are also an excellent theater and concerts a-plenty. See p. 103.

5 Air Canada Centre ★

One nice thing about walking back to the downtown core this way is that you can cross through the Air Canada Centre, which is a lot more pleasant than the other busy and often traffic-congested options. This sports complex is home to both the Raptors basketball team and the Maple Leafs hockey team, but it also hosts blockbuster music concerts; you'll see photographs of some of the acts as you walk through the passageway. See p. 120.

6 Air Canada Centre 🍽

When you think sports center, fine food probably isn't the first thing that comes to mind. But this complex prides itself on a range of tempting goods, including three fine-dining rooms, a wine cellar of more than 600 labels, and one of the country's top sommeliers. The vast kitchen feeds the teams, too. For a casual bite, there are dozens of concessions on-site, including beer and customized hot dogs at Burkie's Dog House. The Air Canada Club is the most luxurious of the three restaurants (✆ 416-815-5983). See p. 120.

7 Union Station ★

This is one of the city's underappreciated wonders. Toronto's temple to trains is a Beaux Arts beauty, and it's worthwhile to walk through the main hall, even if you're not hopping aboard a train. Pop in to admire the tile ceiling designed by

Suggested Toronto Itineraries (Days 1 & 2)

DAY ONE

1 CN Tower
2 Rogers Centre
3 Toronto Music Garden
4 Harbourfront Centre
5 Air Canada Centre
6 Air Canada Centre ☕
7 Union Station
8 New City Hall
9 Four Seasons Centre for the Performing Arts
9a Roy Thomson Hall

DAY TWO

1 Yorkville
2 Royal Ontario Museum
3 George R. Gardiner Museum of Ceramic Art
4 Gardiner Museum Cafe ☕
5 Victoria College
6 Queen's Park & the Ontario Legislature
7 Casa Loma
8 Spadina Museum

Post Office ✉
TTC Subway Ⓣ

0   1/4 mi
0   0.25 km

architect Rafael Guastavino. Until the age of mass air travel, Union Station was often the first place new immigrants saw upon arrival in their new home of Toronto.

8 New City Hall ★

It's an iconic piece in Toronto's history, plus a popular gathering place throughout the year. In warm weather, the reflecting pool and fountains create a piazza, and when the mercury drops, it's fun to visit the skating rink, complete with festive lights and music. Framing the whole scene, quite perfectly, is the modernist masterpiece of the city hall building itself; walk up toward and around it, and you'll see the Henry Moore sculpture *The Archer*. A walkway circumventing the towers is now open and offers great views to the streetscape below, as well as a tour around the pretty new "rooftop" gardens (which sit atop the podium roof, not the tall towers). See p. 116.

9 Four Seasons Centre for the Performing Arts ★★★ or Roy Thomson Hall ★★★

Toronto's stunning opera house, the Four Seasons Centre, designed by local firm Diamond and Schmitt, is home to the Canadian Opera Company and the National Ballet of Canada. The acoustics have been described as quite perfect. Both companies are phenomenally popular, and you absolutely need to purchase tickets in advance. Roy Thomson Hall is the base of the Toronto Symphony Orchestra; Torontonians tend to book ahead and buy seasons tickets, but it's possible to get last-minute discounted "rush" seats for concerts here. There are free daytime concerts scheduled fairly frequently; visit the website before you arrive to see if your visit coincides with one of these special events. (Line-ups are long: You need to arrive well in advance.)

THE BEST OF TORONTO IN 2 DAYS

After you've taken in some of Toronto's best-known landmarks by following the tour above, it's best to choose between one of two itineraries, each one worth a day. The first focuses on Yorkville, the Royal Ontario Museum (ROM), and other nearby attractions (with a whimsical castle to boot). The second heads downtown. **Note:** This tour includes the city's top museum—the ROM—which could easily command a day on its own, so budget a few extra hours for this tour if you plan to explore the museum at the same time you sample the rest of the itinerary. **Start:** *Bay Station.*

1 Yorkville ★★

Filled with chic boutiques and elegant galleries (and high-priced condo developments, such as the new Four Seasons), this neighborhood, which is part residential, mostly commercial, has long departed from its groovy 1960s vibe when it was home to the city's hippies; a century before that, it was a cemetery. Progress? See p. 114.

2 Royal Ontario Museum (ROM) ★★★

Toronto's most famous museum embarked upon a Daniel Libeskind–designed renovation a few years ago. Ambitiously titled Renaissance ROM, it was intended to expand the viewing area, largely through the addition of six crystal galleries that jut out over Bloor Street West. Where you spend your time here will depend on whether you have kids in tow: The collection of dinosaur bones is truly awesome; the Biodiversity Wall a breathtaking collection of species rare and beautiful, and the Bat Cave is a must. Adults may be more interested in the stellar Chinese galleries, which include a Ming tomb. The Libeskind remains a divisive addition to the city's new architectural destinations. See p. 107.

3 George R. Gardiner Museum of Ceramic Art ★★
Just across the street from the ROM, the Gardiner (which was beautifully renovated in 2006), is an understated gem. The singular collection of ceramics and carefully curated exhibits are a rare find. For those who want to get their hands dirty, there are hands-on workshops, too. See p. 110.

4 Gardiner Museum Café 🍽
A great bet for lunch or a snack is the Gardiner Museum cafe (conveniently located across the street from ROM), which is overseen by local celebrity chef Jamie Kennedy (𝓒 416/362-1957). Don't miss the splendid soups, famous frites, and delicious sandwiches.

5 Victoria College ★
This historic college is federated with the University of Toronto but maintains its own digs just east of the rest of the campus. It has a pretty college quad, bordered by imposing Romanesque architecture (there's some blocky 1960s stuff, too). It was also home to the famous scholar Northrop Frye.

6 Queen's Park & the Ontario Legislature
This sweeping, pretty midtown park is also home to the less beautiful provincial legislative building. (A *New Yorker* humor writer once dubbed it "Early Penitentiary.") It's possible to take a tour on most days, or just enjoy the setting and, if you're in luck, one of the many peaceful protests that take place on the lawn. See p. 117.

7 Casa Loma ★
Casa Loma is a kitschy castle on a hill that offers an inspiring view of the sweep of the city (you'll see a lot more of Toronto than you did from the CN Tower the day before yesterday). But while you can admire the view for free, it's worth visiting the castle, too. The elegant rooms and period furniture are appropriately grand, though most interesting is perhaps climbing the towers (one Norman, one Scottish, both great). See p. 115.

8 Spadina Museum: Historic House & Gardens ★
This mansion with spectacular seasonal gardens reopened in 2010 after an extensive and expensive renovation. The result is worth a visit: Now a museum run by the City of Toronto, it's a year-round destination to get a sense of domestic life in Toronto in the 1920s and '30s. The garden is also themed: It's a Victorian-Edwardian masterpiece. See p. 120.

THE BEST OF TORONTO IN 3 DAYS

If you can, do Days 1 and 2, and then add this tour on your third day. It focuses on downtown west and includes the city's top art gallery—the AGO—which is worth a full day alone. **Start:** *College Station and a streetcar west to Augusta Avenue.*

1 Kensington Market ★★

A bustling street market of fishmongers, vintage retailers, coffee shops, and music stores, Kensington Market pulses to its own beat. It's a multiethnic mélange that was once a Jewish neighborhood—the original synagogue still remains—and has been gradually layered with successive waves of immigrants from Portugal, the Caribbean, and the Middle East. If you want to bring home great vintage finds, do some shopping in this area (check out Tom's Place, Fresh Baked Goods, and Courage My Love, all in chapter 8). Life starts later in the morning here and stays up well into the night. See p. 122.

2 La Tortilleria 🍽

On the edge of the market is this tiny spot comprising just a few stools inside and, weather permitting, tables out front, that serves good corn tortillas made daily. Tacos and bottled drinks from Mexico round out the tiny menu. There are other locations around town, some of them supplying Mexican groceries, as well (𝒞 647/723/8760).

3 Chinatown ★★

Toronto has a large Chinese population dispersed throughout the city, but this was home to the first great wave of Chinese immigrants. It's changed since its early days, particularly because of the infusion of Hong Kong money. It's such a large and significant area that it's a shame no official entryway exists. The recent addition of gilded statues of dragons and the like on poles in the middle of Spadina Avenue is a nice touch, however. See p. 113.

4 Art Gallery of Ontario ★★★

Newly renovated—by local boy Frank Gehry, who grew up around the corner—and now blessed with the brilliant Thomson Collection, the AGO is arguably Toronto's best gallery. Visit for the stellar collection of paintings by Canadian legends and European masters, the best collection of Henry Moore sculpture in the world, the photography gallery, and much more. See p. 99.

5 Art Gallery of Ontario 🍽

The AGO has two dining options: lovely FRANK (𝒞 416/979-6688), an upscale restaurant that serves creative, fine food, and the AGO Café (𝒞 416/979-6648), a low-key space in the basement that offers sandwiches, salads, baked goods, and other treats. Both are good options; your choice should depend on mood, time, and budget.

6 Sharp Centre for Design ★★

Although Toronto has long suffered an out-of-date reputation for being strait-laced, when people do wacky things here, the new additions are quickly absorbed into the accepted cityscape. This brilliant bit of design from Will Alsop is a cube on stilts that requires a first-hand view to really appreciate its beauty. It's home to the Ontario College of Art and Design (OCAD) and is closed to the public except on special occasions, such as an annual art fair. See p. 118.

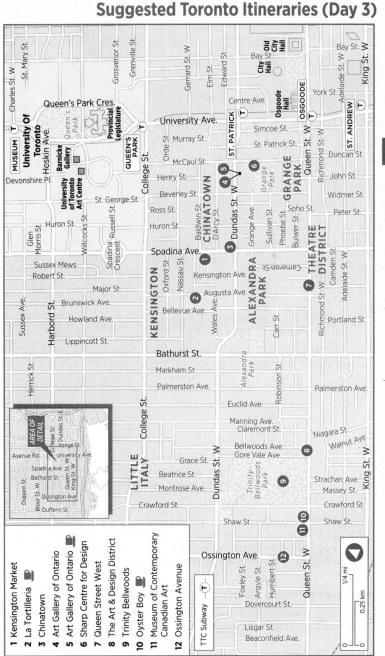

1 Kensington Market
2 La Tortilleria
3 Chinatown
4 Art Gallery of Ontario
5 Art Gallery of Ontario
6 Sharp Centre for Design
7 Queen Street West
8 The Art & Design District
9 Trinity Bellwoods
10 Oyster Boy
11 Museum of Contemporary
   Canadian Art
12 Ossington Avenue

7 Queen Street West ★

Once considered the edge of the city's hipsterdom, this strip is now a mix of chains such as The Gap and enduringly cool boutiques (Fashion Crimes, Peach Berserk, and the like; see chapter 8). It's still a great place to park at a cafe, bar, or pub, and watch the parade go by—there's always plenty of street life to take in.

8 The Art & Design District ★★★

This is one of Toronto's most interesting neighborhoods. Still a bit gritty in spots (which means it hasn't been sanitized), it's filled with exceptional, small-scale art galleries and independent boutiques run by local designers. Mid- to late afternoon is the perfect time to check it out because everything is open (some of the shops are closed all morning) and the streets are full of life. Great restaurants with lively patios and some exciting live-music spots make it an appealing destination after dark, as well. See p. 113.

9 Trinity Bellwoods ★

This site used to be the home of the precursor to the University of Toronto. The buildings have been torn down, but the impressive stone-and-wrought-iron gates that face Queen Street West still remain, and there are Victorian lampposts along the main paths. There are benches where you can rest and take in the scene, but it's more fun to wander. As you do, watch out for the legendary albino squirrels who reside in the park. See p. 123.

10 Oyster Boy 🍺

Torontonians love oysters and other seafood, and this is one of the city's seafood institutions. It's known for its exceptionally fresh oysters, an excellent selection chosen by owner Adam Colquhoun, and a friendly pub-like atmosphere. The fish-and-chips are great, too. 872 Queen St. W. ✆ 416/534-3432.

11 Museum of Contemporary Canadian Art ★★

You've already seen the iconic art of the AGO; now's your chance to see what's happening in today's art scene. MOCCA is a gallery that has a reputation for its (sometimes freaky) temporary exhibits. Edgy, good stuff. See p. 112.

12 Ossington Avenue ★★

For years, this has been a sleepy part of town, part of Toronto's Little Portugal neighborhood, where many of the houses have religious icons painted near the front door. But now, Ossington Avenue is the epicenter of Toronto nightlife. Drop in at Watusi (p. 200) for 1960s retro-cool cocktails and ambience, or at Sweaty Betty's (p. 200) for a no-fuss vibe and a great patio.

THE BEST OF TORONTO IN 4 DAYS

Spend your first 3 days following the earlier tours, then top it off with this exploration of the best that Toronto's east end has to offer. This tour will take you through some of the oldest areas, which keep evolving in new ways, and to one of the city's most dynamic, reinvented destinations that combines environmental rehabilitation with great food, superb events, and lush parkland. *Start: Dupont Station, and then walk 2 blocks north.*

Suggested Toronto Itineraries (Day 4)

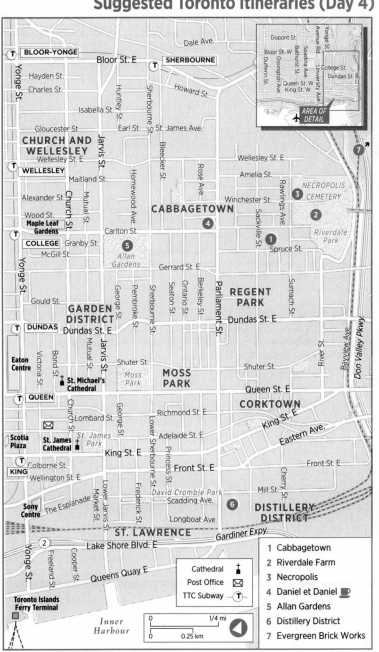

1 Cabbagetown
2 Riverdale Farm
3 Necropolis
4 Daniel et Daniel
5 Allan Gardens
6 Distillery District
7 Evergreen Brick Works

1 Cabbagetown ★★

You can't walk these residential streets without getting a powerful sense of Toronto's history. Once considered a slum, Cabbagetown is now filled with beautifully restored Victorian and Queen Anne–style houses. Even the first housing project in Canada, Spruce Court (at the intersection of Sumach and Spruce sts.), looks like a charming collection of cottages. For a complete tour, see p. 148.

2 Riverdale Farm ★★

For some, this farm is a sacred space. Whenever you visit, you'll find kids here, many of whom live in the area, learning about farm life, interacting with chickens and rare-breed piglets, and cuddling bunnies. Sound bucolic? It's a serene spot and well worth a visit, especially with young ones in tow. See p. 128.

3 Necropolis ★

This Victorian cemetery is not only picturesque, but also filled with monuments to famous people who played key roles in Toronto's history. And the Gothic Revival chapel, tiny though it is, is considered a great example of this style. See p. 124.

4 Daniel et Daniel 🍵

If you go to an event in Toronto and discover that Daniel et Daniel is catering it, you know that you're in excellent hands. At the shop, in addition to the divine pastries and chocolates, you can order salads and prepared meals for takeout. 248 Carlton St. ☎ 416/968-9275. See p. 148.

5 Allan Gardens ★

This was Toronto's first civic park, and the Edwardian Palm House conservatory is still a glamorous relic of the past. But it was only recently, when the University of Toronto's old greenhouses were relocated here and reborn as a conservatory for children, that Allan Gardens became a place to hang out again, free in the daytime of much of the seedier activity it had become known for. See p. 122.

6 Distillery District ★★★

Once the home of the largest distillery in Canada, today, it's a multifaceted complex that has something for everyone. The redbrick architecture—a signature of Toronto's red-clay brickworks—is a Victorian wonder, but the art galleries, restaurants, and boutiques are all completely modern. You might want to stay well into the evening: Performing-arts troupes such as Soulpepper are based here, and if you're visiting in nice weather, there's probably an open-air art fair, market, or festival underway. There's great chocolate, too, at Soma. See p. 103.

7 Evergreen Brick Works ★★★

This is the perfect place to finish your tour. Once the home of the city's founding brick factory, it has lately been reinvented by the dynamic, Canadian Evergreen foundation (national in scope: its business is to "green" cities) to include a farmers market that runs year-round on Saturday mornings, a cafe and restaurant featuring local goods under the Café Belong moniker, marshlands, a beautiful park, and thoughtful exhibits that take advantage of the unique setting of the age-old kilns where Toronto's signature red bricks were once formed. A taste of past and present, the Brick Works is proving to be one of the city's most attractive locales for brilliant events. There are programs for families, parties for grown-ups, and much more. See p. 124.

WHERE TO STAY

Toronto's hotel landscape offers plenty of choice, from idiosyncratic inns to island B&Bs, conventional hotels to deluxe palaces. With more than 38,000 rooms to choose from, it's easy to tailor your stay to your needs.

Prices tend to be fair, especially when you consider that this is a major metropolis. Although there are plenty of spots to stay near the airport locations, most of the activity is downtown.

THE best HOTEL BETS

o **Best Service:** The original **Hôtel Le Germain,** located in the heart of the entertainment district, gets the vote for top boutique with unparalleled service. Staff here are attentive, but not cloying, and are known for going to unusual lengths to accommodate special requests, like tours outside of town and dietary needs. The Canadian-owned small chain has opened a second location, **Hôtel Le Germain Maple Leaf Square,** that remains true to the superior standard of thoughtful service, with a location perfect for sports fans and anyone attending an event at the Air Canada Centre. See p. 56.

o **Best Historic Hotels:** There are a few top contenders, but kudos go to the **Fairmont Royal York,** which has managed to seamlessly blend the timeless glory of a 1929 Canadian Pacific Railway–built hotel with a forward-thinking eco-consciousness. Menus are rich with sustainable choices, and the roof garden, where the hotel grows its own mint for mojitos, is home to several honeybee hives for the hotel's signature honey. (See p. 54.) **The Gladstone,** the city's longest-operating hotel, deserves a nod not only as a property with a past—the Victorian facade, birdcage elevator, and more are well preserved—but as a dynamic destination in itself. The rooms feature art by local artists, including some ambitious installations that transform spaces; the bars hop with an eclectic range of music; and the restaurants excel in casual, delicious fare. See p. 57.

o **Best for a Romantic Getaway:** If your idea of romance is pampering and luxury, the **Windsor Arms** hotel offers an unusual level of intimacy with just 28 rooms (26 of which are suites), along with fine service, top-notch in-room and on-site dining, and a pretty indoor swimming pool (all a stone's throw from some of the city's top jewelers, should the mood strike). See p. 63.

PRICE CATEGORIES

| Very Expensive | $300 and up | Moderate | $100–$200 |
| Expensive | $200–$300 | Inexpensive | Under $100 |

o **Best for a Stylish Stay: Thompson Toronto,** the first international venture of the New York–based hotel mini-empire, has a super-cool vibe matched by smart service. A rooftop pool, top restaurant (Scarpetta), terrace, and more all add to the very hip experience. See p. 56.

o **Best for Business:** It's a tie. For short trips, the **Hilton Toronto** offers a convenient location, a good range of amenities, and a suitable restaurant, Tundra, for business lunches and dinners. But for a longer-term stay, the **Cambridge Suites Hotel** gives you plenty of space, kitchenettes, and a staff that will even shop for you. See p. 53 and p. 60.

o **Best Budget Hotel:** Given the location and amenities, it's hard to beat the prices at **Hotel Victoria,** especially now that extensive renovations are complete. The hotel is close to the Eaton Centre, some theaters, and the Financial District. See p. 59.

o **Best Hotel Restaurant: TOCA by Tom Brodi,** at the dazzling new Ritz Carlton, is a hit, receiving raves for fine menus that celebrate the best of Canadian ingredients. Think: East Coast lobster, BC scallops, and aged beef and tender lamb from Ontario.. The **Drake** restaurant is a personal favorite, with its tasty and generous dishes, great brunches, busy bar, and buzzing patio. The overall joie de vivre and fine fare are largely the work of Chef Anthony Rose and his crew. See p. 75 and p. 76.

o **Best Splurge:** The **Ritz Carlton** is Ontario's first Ritz, and the brand's reputation for elegance and five-star service does not disappoint. From the moment you enter the dramatic lobby, the ambition to impress is all around. Sip a sophisticated cocktail in one of the lounges, save room for a sublime meal at the Canadiana-themed restaurant TOCA by Tom Brodi, and luxuriate in the spacious rooms. There's an excellent on-site spa with an adjoining lap pool and polished gym, too. To gild the lily, upgrade your reservation to Club status, and you'll get access to the 20th-floor lounges, which include a generous breakfast, honor bar, and other treats. See p. 54.

o **Best for Families:** The **Delta Chelsea's** location is convenient to many of the city's top attractions and it has a four-story indoor waterslide, super swimming pool, children's center, and babysitting. Weekend packages often include tickets to the city's top attractions and theaters. See p. 57.

DOWNTOWN WEST

This area encompasses a handful of neighborhoods, most of the city's more interesting hotels, and many top attractions, such as the CN Tower, AGO, and Air Canada Centre.

Best for: A central location, plus the city's highest concentration of attractions. In a nutshell, it's all here. If you're on a shopping spree, big department stores and jewel-box boutiques are all around. If art, music, or theater is on the agenda, you'll find each at your doorstep. Ditto for great restaurants, trendy clubs, and top-drawer sports venues.

Drawbacks: With all that activity, this is a busy and often noisy part of town.

Very Expensive

Hilton Toronto ★   Across the street from the Four Seasons Centre for the Performing Arts, the 32-story Hilton has big rooms and business-minded luxuries. Because of its proximity to the Financial District, the Hilton is a dependable choice for business travelers. The standard rooms are spacious and equipped with generous work spaces. Upgrading to an executive room adds personal concierge service and access to a private lounge that serves complimentary breakfast and evening snacks.

145 Richmond St. W. (at University Ave.), Toronto, ON M5H 2L2. www.toronto.hilton.com. ℂ **800/445-8667** or 416/869-3456. Fax 416/869-1478. 601 units. From C$319 double. Children 18 & under stay free in parent's room. Multi-night packages available. AE, DC, MC, V. Parking C$30. Subway: Osgoode. Pets accepted (C$75 per pet). **Amenities:** 3 restaurants; bar; babysitting; children's programs; concierge; health club; Jacuzzi; indoor & outdoor lap pools; room service; sauna. *In room:* A/C, TV, hair dryer, Internet ($12 per day), minibar.

The Metropolitan Hotel ★★   A sophisticated choice and a bit artier than other upscale business digs, this property (located just off Dundas St. W. behind City Hall) caters to business and leisure travelers who avoid big chains. Rooms are spacious and styled in a serene color palette of beige and beechwood that evokes a spa. **Lai Wah**

4

WHERE TO STAY | Downtown West

WHAT YOU'LL REALLY PAY

The prices quoted here are for a hotel's rack rate, the maximum that it charges; it is, however, seriously unlikely that you'll end up paying that rate unless you arrive at peak times. These include the weeks during the Toronto International Film Festival (early to mid-Sept; check dates); the first weekend of August, due to the crowds for Scotiabank Caribbean Festival; and Pride in early June. Online and agencies offer discounts for early and last-minute bookings. Toronto is a major convention town, so keep informed of business events and large group bookings (www.seetorontonow. com). You can typically find discounts of up to 20% for rooms when booking through websites such as hotels.com or Expedia. During slow times, it's not impossible to obtain a room at an expensive property for the same rate as a more moderate one.

Lodgings are grouped by both price and location. Most are in the neighborhoods defined in chapter 3 as Downtown West, Downtown East, and Midtown. If you're having trouble finding a hotel, call **Tourism Toronto** (ℂ **800/499-2514** or 416/203-2600) or visit **www.seetorontonow.com** for advice. Keep in mind that some special deals are available only through a hotel's website. The **Fairmont Royal York** (p. 54) almost always has an online deal; the **Park Hyatt Toronto** (p. 64) often does, too.

A note about Internet and Wi-Fi: Most accommodations in this chapter offer in-room or in-lobby Internet or Wi-Fi access. Some charge for it, some don't. For hotels that charge for Internet or Wi-Fi, the price ranges from C$15 to C$21 per day. When included in the room price, I've listed the services as "free."

Heen (p. 70) serves some of the best dim sum in the city, and room-service meals are also of a high standard.

108 Chestnut St. (just S of Dundas St. W.), Toronto, ON M5G 1R3. www.metropolitan.com. ✆ **800/668-6600** or 416/977-5000. Fax 416/977-9513. 427 units. From C$300 double. Children 17 & under stay free in parent's room. AE, DC, DISC, MC, V. Parking C$21. Subway: St. Patrick. **Amenities:** 2 restaurants; bar; babysitting; concierge; health club; Jacuzzi; indoor pool; room service; sauna. *In room:* A/C, TV/DVD player, CD player, hair dryer, minibar, Wi-Fi ($12 per day).

Ritz Carlton Toronto ★★★ This very luxe property, which opened in 2011, delivers on the brand's reputation for attentive service, refined style, and excellent amenities. A sleek and slender tower, it's located smack dab in the middle of the entertainment district and across the road from the Roy Thomson Hall. The understated stylish rooms are spacious and appointed with dreamy linens, an additional TV screen in the bathroom mirror, soaking tubs and rainwater showers, and floor-to-ceiling windows, some of which offer lake views straight across to the pretty Toronto Islands. The lobby and other public spaces are showy: The ground-floor bar attracts locals who work in the surrounding towers, plus plenty of wedding and other special-occasion affairs. The spa is pretty, as is the adjoining lap pool, a good place to build up an appetite for the excellent TOCA by Tom Brodi restaurant, where the service, wine, and Canadian-themed gourmet fare are all top notch.

181 Wellington St. W. (1 block W of University Ave.), Toronto, ON M5V 3G7. www.ritzcarlton.com. ✆ **416/585-2500.** Fax 416/585-2503. 267 units. From C$325 double. Children 18 & under stay free in parent's room. AE, DC, MC, V. Parking C$42. Subway: Osgoode. Pets under 30 lb. accepted (C$150 per pet). **Amenities:** 2 restaurants; bar; concierge; health club; indoor lap pools; room service; spa. *In room:* A/C, TV, hair dryer, Internet ($10 per day), minibar.

Expensive

The Drake Hotel ★ 📇 The Drake is better known for its bars and restaurants than the tiny (from 14–36 sq. m/151–388 sq. ft.) guest rooms above. The rooms are, however, cleverly designed and have good amenities (CD/DVD players and lovely linens, for example) and offer an ideal place to rest your head after a long night's indulgence in the hotel's public rooms. The Drake is something of a trend-setter and attracts a stylish and fashionable crowd to its restaurant, bar, rooftop lounge, cafe, and the Underground, a live performance venue that draws top names. Little wonder the hotel's current expansion is focused on a new BBQ joint and another lounge, not more guest rooms. An artist-in-residence program keeps the wall art changing. This is one hotel where you're more likely to meet city residents than visitors.

1150 Queen St. W. (at Beaconsfield Ave.), Toronto, ON M6J 1J3. www.thedrakehotel.ca. ✆ **800/372-5386** or 416/531-5042. Fax 416/531-9493. 19 units. From C$219 double. AE, MC, V. Subway: Osgoode, then streetcar W to Beaconsfield Ave. **Amenities:** 2 restaurants; cafe; 2 bars; access to local health club. *In room:* A/C, TV/DVD player, CD player, hair dryer, Internet (free), MP3 docking station.

Fairmont Royal York ★★ Built by the Canadian Pacific Railroad in 1929 and located across from Union Station, this massive hotel has 1,365 guest rooms and suites, and 35 meeting and banquet rooms. Just sitting on a plush couch in the magnificent old-fashioned lobby and watching the crowd is an event. Still, you have to decide whether you want to stay with countless business travelers, tour groups, and conventioneers. Service is efficient, if impersonal. The hotel pays attention to accessibility, and some guest rooms are specially designed for wheelchair users, the hearing impaired, and the visually impaired. The hotel is also a leader in eco-friendly initiatives. The restaurants are a good bet and eco-minded, noted for their sustainable

Where to Stay in Downtown West

Baldwin Village Inn **2**
Delta Chelsea **5**
The Drake Hotel **6**
Fairmont Royal York **14**
The Gladstone Hotel **7**
Hilton Toronto **8**
Hôtel Le Germain **10**
Hotel Le Germain Maple
  Leaf Square **16**
Hotel Victoria **15**
Hyatt Regency Toronto **11**
The Metropolitan Hotel **3**
Planet Traveller Youth Hostel **1**
Rtiz Carlton **12**
The Strathcona **13**
Thompson Toronto **9**
Toronto Marriott Downtown
  Eaton Centre **4**

4

WHERE TO STAY | Downtown West

55

seafood program and admired for beehives on the roof that supply honey for the kitchens and, ultimately, for your toast. *Tip:* Watch the website for special offers.

100 Front St. W. (at York St.), Toronto, ON M5J 1E3. www.fairmont.com/royalyork. ℂ **800/441-1414.** Fax 416/368-9040. 1,365 units. From C$205 double. Packages available. AE, DC, DISC, MC, V. Parking C$40. Subway: Union. Pets accepted ($25 per night). **Amenities:** 5 restaurants; 2 bars/lounges; babysitting; concierge; health club; Jacuzzi; sky-lit indoor pool; room service; sauna; spa. *In room:* A/C, TV, hair dryer, Internet ($15 per day), minibar.

Hôtel Le Germain ★★   This Quebec-based company adds a continental touch that blends effortlessly with an edgy elegance. Elevators are "wrapped" in words of English and French poetry. The library lounge has a fireplace, a wall of objets d'art, and cozy white couches. The breakfast room on the second floor is like an expansive landing, and the tables are communal. The guest rooms are beautifully designed, the ceilings are high, and the linens and robes are by Frette. A peek-a-boo glass wall in the bathroom shower is a seductive touch (a blind can be lowered) and also makes everything feel more spacious. The exercise room on the 11th floor has floor-to-ceiling windows and an open-air terrace. Rooms on the north side are not as quiet, as they face a noisy strip of King Street restaurants and bars.

30 Mercer St., Toronto, ON M5V 1H3. www.germaintoronto.com. ℂ **866/345-9501** or 416/345-9500. Fax 416/345-9501. 122 units. From C$285 double. AE, DC, MC, V. Parking C$35. Subway: St. Andrew. Pets accepted (C$35 per pet). **Amenities:** Restaurant; bar; babysitting; concierge; health club; room service. *In room:* A/C, TV/DVD player, CD player, CD library, hair dryer, minibar, Wi-Fi (free).

Hôtel Le Germain Maple Leaf Square ★★ ☺   Last year, the small Le Germain chain opened a second location directly opposite the Air Canada Centre. The brand's flair is evident throughout, although the look is more post-industrial, with painted concrete walls and balconies. The bedrooms are inviting and bright, fitted with Frette and featuring waterfall-like showerheads and sumptuous beds. Giant close-up photos of hard-working athletes in training keep with the location. It's a perfect location for anyone with tickets to the ACC (some rooms even face a giant screen over the venue's entrance), but if you're not into the events and the Centre is open for business, you might prefer the original Germain Toronto.

75 Bremner Blvd., Toronto, ON M5J 0A1. http://germainmapleleafsquare.com. ℂ **888/940-7575.** 67 units. From C$324 double. AE, DC, MC, V. Parking C$35. Subway: Union Station. **Amenities:** Lounge/bar; babysitting; concierge; health club; room service. *In room:* A/C, TV (DVD player upon request), CD player, hair dryer, minibar, Wi-Fi (free).

Thompson Toronto ★★★   This swank downtown property is the first Canadian outpost of the New York–based boutique chain, and it lives up to all the hype and

expectations of the brand. The luxe rooms are chic yet comfortable; the service attentive, but not cloying; the location a welcome launching point for seeing the groovier
parts of the city, but also convenient to the theater district. The rooftop infinity swimming pool with its breathtaking views, along with the rooftop's cozy fireplace lounge,
offer a unique destination on the city's hotel scene. Ditto for the dining options,
which range from a diner (above-average fare; open 24/7) to an outpost of Scott
Conant's Italian upscale Scarpetta restaurant. Expect high-end fitness facilities,
including a yoga studio; a 40-seat screening room; SFERRA linens on your bed and
Carrera marble in the bathroom; and a serene, white-toned backdrop rich with
wooden touches and creative flare.

550 Wellington St. W., Toronto, ON M5V 2V4. www.thompsonhotels.com. © **888/550-8368** or
416/640-7778. 102 units. From C$245 double. AE, DC, MC, V. Valet parking C$35. Subway: St. Patrick,
then streetcar W to Bathurst St. **Amenities:** 2 restaurants; bar; lounge; babysitting; concierge; health
club; outdoor pool; room service. *In room:* A/C, TV/DVD player, CD player, hair dryer, minibar, Wi-Fi ($10
per day).

Moderate

Delta Chelsea ★★ ☺   Guest rooms here are bright and cheery, and a few have
kitchenettes. The pool, with an awesome four-story indoor waterslide, combined with
a children's center and babysitting, make this a particularly attractive option for families. Grown-up amenities include Deck 27, a lounge with a panoramic view of
Toronto. Business travelers should consider a room on the Signature Club floor,
which come with many in-room comforts like well-stocked desks and ergonomic
chairs. Weekend packages often combine tickets to the city's top attractions and
theaters.

33 Gerrard St. W. (just W of Yonge St.), Toronto, ON M5G 1Z4. www.deltahotels.com.© **800/243-5732**
or 416/595-1975. Fax 416/585-4362. 1,590 units. From C$179 double. Additional adult C$20. Children 17
& under stay free in parent's room. Multi-night packages available. AE, DC, DISC, MC, V. Parking C$29.
Subway: College. **Amenities:** 3 restaurants; 3 bars; babysitting; children's center; concierge; health club;
Jacuzzi; 2 pools (1 for adults only); sauna. *In room:* A/C, TV, hair dryer, Internet ($14 per day), MP3 dock-
ing station.

The Gladstone Hotel ★ 🏨   This lovely Victorian redbrick hotel, opened in 1889,
is the longest continually operating hotel in the city. Those first guests probably
wouldn't know what to make of the arty offerings of the Gladstone today. When artist
Christina Zeidler and her architecturally-inclined family (her father, Eb, designed the
Eaton Centre and Ontario Place) took over in 2005, they transformed the place while
preserving its heritage features, including the birdcage elevator. The hip public rooms
are now a hive of cultural activity, with offerings ranging from burlesque shows to
indie bands, and the Melody Bar hosts the city's most colorful weekend karaoke.
Rooms are featured on the website, comprising everything from lumberjack chic (a
four-poster bed anchored by tree trunks) to a teen-idol theme, where the walls are
plastered with retro posters, on offer. *Note:* If you're a light sleeper, this may not be
the place for you.

1214 Queen St. W. (at Gladstone Ave.), Toronto, ON M6J 1J6. www.gladstonehotel.com. © **416/531-
4635.** Fax 416/539-0953. 37 units. From C$195 double. AE, MC, V. Parking C$15. Subway: Osgoode, then
streetcar W to Gladstone Ave. **Amenities:** Restaurant; cafe; bar. *In room:* A/C, TV/DVD player, CD player,
hair dryer, Wi-Fi (free).

Hyatt Regency Toronto   Toronto's second Hyatt is located on King Street West
in a former Holiday Inn. Close to TIFF Bell Lightbox, theaters, the Financial District,

and the Convention Centre, it's a good bet for either leisure or business travel, with the usual fine standard of service associated with the Hyatt brand.

370 King St. W., Toronto, ON M5V 1J9. www.torontoregency.hyatt.com. ✆ **800/233-1234** or 416/343-1234. Fax 416/599-7934. 394 units. From C$179 double. Multi-night packages available. AE, DC, DISC, MC, V. Self-parking C$29. Subway: St Andrew. Pets accepted in some rooms. **Amenities:** 2 restaurants; bar; concierge; health club; room service. *In room:* A/C, TV, fax, hair dryer, Internet ($15 per day).

The Strathcona ★★ 🍃   If you want to be in the Financial District but don't want to pay a bundle, this is a good option. For years, the Strathcona has offered fair deals, and a recent renovation has made it more attractive. It sits in the shadow of the Fairmont Royal York, a short walk from most major downtown attractions. Although the Strathcona's rooms are on the small side, they're no less comfortable for their compact design. Lately, the hotel has taken some green initiatives, changing its lighting, reducing water usage, and becoming entirely smoke-free.

60 York St. (btw. Front St. W. & Wellington St. W.), Toronto, ON M5J 1S8. www.thestrathconahotel.com. ✆ **800/268-8304** or 416/363-3321. Fax 416/363-4679. 194 units. From C$155 double. AE, DC, MC, V. Subway: Union. Private parking nearby C$16–C$38. **Amenities:** Cafe; bar; babysitting; bike rental; children's center; concierge; access to nearby health club; room service. *In room:* A/C, TV, hair dryer, Wi-Fi ($10 per day).

Toronto Marriott Downtown Eaton Centre   It's a shopaholic's dream: a hotel in a mall—and not just any mall, but downtown's mega mall, the Eaton Centre. This hotel caters to the tourist crowd: The Marriott has desks set up to facilitate day-trip planning and other activities. Because of its location, this is a fine choice for determined sightseers. One caveat is that the area immediately surrounding the Eaton Centre is pickpocket heaven. On the upside, it's always busy in this neighborhood, so you won't want for company. Also, in summer, nearby Yonge-Dundas Square (p. 190) offers open-air concerts and films.

525 Bay St. (at Dundas St.), Toronto, ON M5G 2L2. www.marriotteatoncentre.com. ✆ **800/905-0667** or 416/597-9200. Fax 416/597-9211. 459 units. From C$179 double. AE, DC, DISC, MC, V. Parking C$30. Subway: Dundas. **Amenities:** 3 restaurants; bar; concierge; health club; Jacuzzi; indoor rooftop pool; room service; sauna. *In room:* A/C, TV, hair dryer, Wi-Fi ($16 per day).

Inexpensive

Baldwin Village Inn ★   If only there were more small, affordable, family-run hotels in Toronto like the Baldwin. This charming, friendly bed-and-breakfast—steps away from trendy Queen West, Kensington, and Chinatown—is located on the equally charming Baldwin Street. It's an historic, converted house with six rooms that are well cared for; bathrooms are shared, and there's a homey eat-in kitchen and a small garden in back. Reservations are a must. The owners, Roger and Tess, have opened a second location nearby, Sullivan by the Grange, for extended stays.

9 Baldwin St. (at McCall St.), Toronto, ON M5T 1L1. www.baldwininn.com. ✆ **416/591-5359.** 6 units. From C$95 single. Rates include continental breakfast. AE, MC, V. Subway: St. Patrick. **Amenities:** Lounge. *In room:* A/C.

Planet Traveller Youth Hostel ★ Canada's most eco-conscious hostel has a great locale on College Street, in the heart of Kensington and steps from Little Italy; sleek, clean rooms and dorms; and an attractive rooftop bar and indoor lounge. Two guys, one a hostel-owner and the other a green-tech venture capitalist, poured millions of dollars into making this a green enterprise fueled by a combination of solar-thermal hot water, geothermal heat transfer, pure solar power, and more. There are deals, too: You can get a private room for three or four at the same per-person rate, $30 a head, as it costs for a bed in a dorm.

357 College St., Toronto, ON M5T 1S5. theplanettraveler.com. ✆ **647/352-TRIP** (647/352-8747). 15 6-bed dorms, 11 private rooms. From C$30 dorm bed; from $80 private room. Rates include continental breakfast. MC, V. Subway: Osgoode, then the College streetcar W to Augusta. **Amenities:** Lounge; rooftop bar.

Hotel Victoria ★ 🎗 In a landmark downtown building near the Hockey Hall of Fame, the Victoria retains the glamorous touches of an earlier age, such as crown moldings and marble columns in the lobby. It's Toronto's second-oldest hotel (built in 1909), but the facilities are upgraded annually. Personal service and attention are a bonus not often found in budget accommodations. Standard rooms are on the small side, but are nicely put together; deluxe rooms are larger and have coffeemakers and mini-fridges. A recent major renovation has only sweetened the deal: New guest rooms offer LCD TVs and new furnishings.

56 Yonge St. (at Wellington St.), Toronto, ON M5E 1G5. www.hotelvictoria-toronto.com. ✆ **800/363-8228** or 416/363-1666. Fax 416/363-7327. 56 units. From C$160 double. Rates include continental breakfast. Additional adult C$15. AE, DC, MC, V. Parking in nearby garage C$14. Subway: King. **Amenities:** Restaurant; babysitting; access to nearby health club. *In room:* A/C, TV, hair dryer, Internet (free).

DOWNTOWN EAST

The east end is on the rise with an evolving strip of cutting-edge design and furniture stores, the attractive Distillery District, historic Corktown, and well-trod Little India and the Danforth.

Best for: Exploring off the beaten path.
Drawbacks: Things tend to be more spread out here, so be prepared to travel to eat, play, or sleep.

Very Expensive

The Ivy at Verity ★★ 🎗 This boutique hotel has just four rooms, each one luxuriously appointed with Hastens hand-crafted beds (the only ones in any hotel in the world, they claim), fine linens and furnishings, and a private terrace overlooking the charming courtyard of the adjoining French restaurant George. Bathrooms are equally opulent with soaking tubs, marble finishes, and lush toiletries. The hotel is part of the Verity Club—a private women's club with spa, fitness facilities, public rooms, and lounges—and all of the Club's services are available for hotel guests to use. The place is overwhelmingly feminine (and only women are allowed in the fitness facilities), but men are welcome. Room service is provided by the excellent restaurant.

111d Queen St. E. (near Jarvis St.), Toronto, ON M5C 1S2. www.theivyatverity.ca. ✆ **416/368-6006,** ext 300. 4 units. From C$330 double. Rates include continental breakfast. AE, DC, DISC, MC, V. Parking C$25. Subway: Queen. **Amenities:** Restaurant; bar; concierge; fitness club; pool; spa; Wi-Fi (free). *In room:* A/C, TV/DVD player; hair dryer.

Expensive

Cambridge Suites Hotel ★★ ◀ The emphasis at this all-suite hotel is comfortable home-away-from-home amenities, which makes it popular for extended stays. The smallest suite is a generous 51 sq. m (549 sq. ft.), and at the other end are deluxe duplexes. The desk areas are equipped with two two-line telephones and a fax, while the living areas offer fridge, microwave, and cookware, plus coffee, tea, and snacks. And if you hand over your shopping list, the staff will stock the fridge, too. Penthouse suites come with Jacuzzis and some with views.

15 Richmond St. E. (near Yonge St.), Toronto, ON M5C 1N2. www.cambridgesuitestoronto.com. ✆ **800/463-1990** or 416/368-1990. Fax 416/601-3751. 229 units. From C$240 suite. Rates include continental breakfast. AE, DC, DISC, MC, V. Parking C$25. Subway: Queen. **Amenities:** Restaurant; bar; babysitting; concierge; small health club; access to large health club nearby; Jacuzzi; room service; sauna; spa. *In room:* A/C, TV, fax, fridge, hair dryer, minibar, Wi-Fi ($12 per day).

Cosmopolitan Hotel ★★ This discrete, all-suite boutique property is tucked away on quiet Colborne Street, just off Yonge Street. No surprise then to discover it caters to a Zen sensibility of serenity in all aspects of its service, from decor to turn-down service (a gemstone is placed on the pillow, not a mint). Yoga mats, incense sticks, and a guided relaxation CD round out the room experience. If you're not blissed out by all this, head for Shizen Spa for more serious soothing.

8 Colborne St., Toronto, ON M5E 1E1. www.cosmotoronto.com. ✆ **416/350-2000.** Fax 416/350-2460. 80 suites. From C$229 suite. Rates include continental breakfast. AE, DC, DISC, MC, V. Valet parking C$33. Subway: King. **Amenities:** Wine bar; concierge; gym; room service; spa. *In room:* A/C, TV, DVD player, kitchen, Wi-Fi ($12 per day).

😊 family-friendly HOTELS

Delta Chelsea. This perennial family favorite has a Family Fun Zone, a multi-room play area with live bunnies and fish, a video arcade, and the only indoor water-slide in downtown Toronto. You can play together in the family pool here or drop off the tykes for babysitting. Kids will enjoy the in-room family movies, games, cookie jar (replenished daily), and nightly turn-down gift. Some of the Delta Chelsea's restaurants have half-price kids' menus, further reducing the strain on the family purse. See p. 57.

Four Seasons Hotel Toronto. A hop and a skip from the newly renovated Royal Ontario Museum, this hotel has its own attractions. Guests can borrow free bicycles and video games, and use the indoor pool. Upon arrival, room service brings the kids complimentary cookies and milk. The concierge and housekeeping staff can arrange babysitting services. See p. 64.

Hôtel Le Germain Maple Leaf Square. This boutique Canadian chain remains true its superior standard of thoughtful service, even for pint-sized guests, with special touches such as child-sized bathrobes and special linens with kid-friendly patterns. See p. 56.

Where to Stay in Downtown East

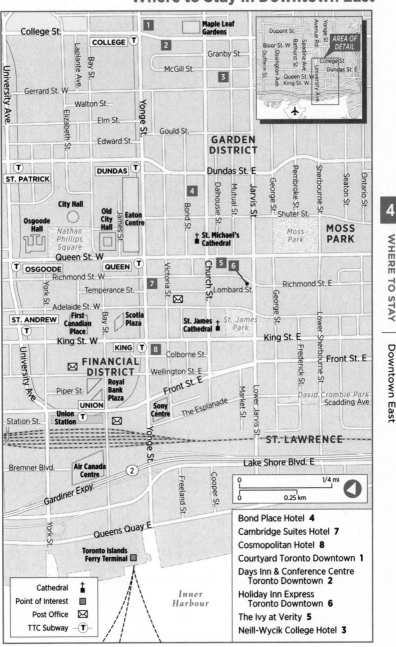

Bond Place Hotel 4

Cambridge Suites Hotel 7

Cosmopolitan Hotel 8

Courtyard Toronto Downtown 1

Days Inn & Conference Centre Toronto Downtown 2

Holiday Inn Express Toronto Downtown 6

The Ivy at Verity 5

Neill-Wycik College Hotel 3

summer-only STAYS

From September to early May, the dorms at the University of Toronto and at Ryerson Polytechnic University are full of students. But in summer, many of these rooms are rented out to budget-minded travelers. If you don't mind your in-room amenities on the Spartan side, you can save a lot of money this way—and get a great downtown or midtown location, too.

Massey College   Tucked away on a quiet street on the University of Toronto downtown campus sits the very attractive Massey College, designed by renowned architect Ron Thom. It's an exclusive graduate college, and the summer residence program offers a handful of tasteful, if spare, rooms—all set around a beautiful courtyard. Personal touches are a bonus:

The porter greets you upon arrival with your own key to the gate, and breakfast is included. You can use the public rooms, such as the library. Book a double suite, and you'll have a sitting area, private bathroom, and a wood-burning fireplace. Rooms are available from May through late August.

4 Devonshire Place (near Harbord & St George sts.), Toronto, ON M5S 2E1. **www.masseycollege. ca. ☏ 416/946-7843** or 416/978-1759. 12 units, 8 w/shared bathroom. C$55 single; C$85 double (2 twin beds). Rates include breakfast. MC, V. Subway: St George. **Amenities:** Cafe; breakfast room & restaurant (during limited periods).

Neill-Wycik College Hotel   During the school year, this is a Ryerson residence. Some students work here in the summer, when the Neill-Wycik morphs into

Courtyard Toronto Downtown ★ ☺   Most Courtyard-brand properties in the Marriott chain are usually out of the city center. This one near Yonge and College streets is an exception, convenient to get around on foot and on the subway line. The lobby, with its double-sided fireplace, has a surprisingly intimate feel, given the size of the 575-room hotel. Tour groups, which often book here, have a separate reception area. The guest rooms aren't big, but they are comfortable, with smart features such as windows that open and additional sinks outside the bathrooms. Ongoing refurbishments keep guest rooms looking fresh, rather than lived in. While Courtyards are generally regarded as business hotels, this one has family-friendly facilities, such as a children's wading pool.

475 Yonge St. (1 block N of College St.), Toronto, ON M4Y 1X7. www.courtyard.com/yyzcy. ☏ **800/847-5075** or 416/924-0611. Fax 416/924-8692. 575 units. From C$149 double. AE, DC, MC, V. Parking C$30. Subway: College. **Amenities:** 2 restaurants; bar; health club; room service. *In room:* A/C, TV, hair dryer, minibar, Wi-Fi (free).

Inexpensive

Bond Place Hotel ★   The location is right—a block from the Eaton Centre, around the corner from the Canon and Elgin theaters—and so is the price. Perhaps that's why this hotel tends to be popular with tour groups. The rooms are on the small side. Book as far in advance as you can; the hotel is usually packed, especially in summer. *Note:* This hotel is part-way through an extensive renovation, so while noise and disruption might be an issue, the plus-side is that refurbished rooms are a cut above the old ones. Most public rooms are completely redone.

65 Dundas St. E. (at Bond St.), Toronto, ON M5B 2G8. www.bondplace.ca. ☏ **800/268-9390** or 416/362-6061. Fax 416/360-6406. 287 units. From C$119 double. Additional adult C$15. Multi-night

a guesthouse. Rooms have beds, chairs, desks, and phones, but no air-conditioning or TVs (although there is a TV lounge). Groups of five bedrooms share two bathrooms and one kitchen with a refrigerator and stove. The hotel has two roof decks, on the 5th and 23rd floors. It's less than a 5-minute walk to the Eaton Centre.

96 Gerrard St. E. (btw. Church & Jarvis sts.), Toronto, ON M5B 1G7. **www.neill-wycik.com**. ℂ **800/268-4358** or 416/977-2320. Fax 416/977-2809. 281 units, all w/shared bathroom. C$45 single; C$80 double (2 twin beds); C$110 family (2 adults, plus children). MC, V. Limited on-site parking (C$10); private lots offsite. Subway: College. **Amenities:** Cafe; sauna.

Victoria University at the University of Toronto   This is a steal for this very expensive neighborhood (just a 2-min. walk from tony Yorkville). Victoria University offers simple rooms with plain furnishings (a bed, desk, and chair are standard), but the surroundings are splendid. Many of the rooms are in Burwash Hall, a 19th-century building that overlooks a peaceful, leafy quad. Guests are provided with linens, towels, and soap.

140 Charles St. W. (btw. Queen's Park & St. Thomas St.), Toronto, ON M5S 1K9. **www.vicu.utoronto.ca** ℂ **416/585-4524.** Fax 416/585-4530. 700 units, all w/shared bathroom. C$60 single; C$80 double (2 twin beds). Rates include breakfast. MC, V. Parking C$18/day or C$38/week. Subway: Museum. **Amenities:** Access to health club w/Olympic-size pool; tennis courts. *In room:* No phone.

packages available. AE, DC, DISC, MC, V. Off-site parking C$25. Subway: Dundas. **Amenities:** Restaurant; bar; concierge; room service. *In room:* A/C, TV, hair dryer, Wi-Fi ($13 per day).

Holiday Inn Express Toronto Downtown   The main selling point of this no-frills hotel is its location, close to the Financial District and the Eaton Centre. It often offers special promotions, so be sure to ask. Rooms tend to be small, with standard amenities.

111 Lombard St. (btw. Adelaide & Richmond sts.), Toronto, ON M5C 2T9. www.ichotelsgroup.com. ℂ **800/228-5151** or 416/367-5555. Fax 416/367-3470. 196 units. From C$139 double. Rates include continental breakfast. AE, DC, DISC, MC, V. Parking C$20. Subway: King or Queen. **Amenities:** Breakfast bar. *In room:* A/C, TV, hair dryer, Wi-Fi (free).

MIDTOWN

Most of the hotels in midtown are located in or near Yorkville, with Bloor Street the southern border of this area.

Best for: High-end shopping along Mink Mile and in Yorkville. It's also a pretty area to stroll around, and it's home to a handful of fine art galleries, the ROM, and a number of good restaurants and bars.

Drawbacks: It's expensive.

Very Expensive

Windsor Arms Hotel ★★   It's a tiny and very tony property with a condo tower on top. The Windsor Arms once held the only five-star status in town and has had its ups and downs. But for years, it's been known as a dignified and exclusive destination

WHERE TO STAY | Midtown

with just 28 rooms, almost all of which are suites. The rooms range from 46 to 139 sq. m (500–1,500 sq. ft.) and are outfitted with top-line linens and amenities. The clubby atmosphere combines with attentive service. A salt-water pool with a poolside fireplace, part of the excellent spa, is a bonus. The restaurants are equally high-end and the afternoon tea suitably elegant.

18 St Thomas. (at Yorkville Ave.), Toronto, ON M5S 2Z7. www.windsorarmshotel.com. © **416/971-9666.** 28 units. From C$250 double. AE, DC, DISC, MC, V. Parking C$35. Subway: Bay. **Amenities:** 2 restaurants; 2 bars/lounges; concierge; health club; Jacuzzi; indoor pool; room service. *In room:* A/C, TV/DVD player, CD player, hair dryer, minibar, Wi-Fi (free).

Four Seasons Hotel Toronto ★ ☺ Although its days are numbered in this location—the new Four Seasons opens mid-2012—the legend lives on. The Rolling Stones call this home in Toronto, and during the Toronto International Film Festival, you can't get in for love or money. The hotel, in the ritzy Yorkville district, has earned a reputation for offering fine service and complete comfort. Rooms tend to be on the small side (a standard is only about 30 sq. m/323 sq. ft.) and are by now a bit tired. Corner rooms have charming balconies offering great views of the street scene below. Take a window seat at the Avenue bar off the lobby for the serious sport of people-watching; you never know who might walk by.

21 Avenue Rd. (at Yorkville Ave.), Toronto, ON M5R 2G1. www.fourseasons.com/toronto. © **800/268-6282** or 416/964-0411. Fax 416/964-2301. 380 units. From C$305 double. Multi-night discounts & packages available. AE, DC, DISC, MC, V. Parking C$30. Subway: Bay. **Amenities:** 2 restaurants; 2 bars/lounges; babysitting; bike rental; concierge; health club; Jacuzzi; indoor/outdoor pool; room service. *In room:* A/C, TV/DVD player, CD player, hair dryer, minibar, Wi-Fi ($15 per day).

The Hazelton Hotel ★ This luxury boutique hotel has a lot going for it. At just 77 rooms, it's the right size for Yorkville, and it has the best outdoor patio for people-watching (the Four Seasons' is indoor). Perks include heated bathroom floors and laptop-sized safes. The decor is understated masculine glamour in both public spaces and guest rooms (designed by local design whiz Yabu Pushelberg). Rooms are spacious, and bathrooms are indulgent, with a TV on the wall above the sink. The hotel also boasts a Mark McEwan restaurant, ONE, and a VIP screening room that seats 25.

118 Yorkville Ave. (at Hazelton Ave.), Toronto, ON M5R 1C2. www.thehazeltonhotel.com. © **866/473-6301** or 416/964-6300. Fax 416/963-6399. 77 units. From C$480 double. AE, DC, DISC, MC, V. Parking C$35. Subway: Bay. **Amenities:** Restaurant; babysitting; concierge; health club; indoor lap pool; room service; spa. *In room:* A/C, TV/DVD player, CD player, hair dryer, minibar, MP3 docking station, Wi-Fi (free).

Park Hyatt Toronto ★★★ This venerable hotel commands a prime location opposite the Royal Ontario Museum at the corner of Bloor Street West and Avenue Road. It's glamorous and grown up, and boasts a great rooftop hotel bar (author Mordecai Richler famously called its 18th-floor Roof Lounge the only civilized place in Toronto). The Park Hyatt's two towers are linked by a lobby dotted with Eastern-inspired objets d'art. The guest rooms in the newer North Tower are generously proportioned: the smallest is 46 sq. m (495 sq. ft.). The older, but frequently refurbished, rooms in the South Tower offer unobstructed views of downtown Toronto. The ground-floor restaurant **Annona** is a treat, as is the Stillwater Spa, which is a popular destination for locals.

4 Avenue Rd. (at Bloor St. W.), Toronto, ON M5R 2E8. www.parktoronto.hyatt.com. © **800/233-1234** or 416/925-1234. Fax 416/924-6693. 346 units. From C$289 double. Multi-night packages available. AE,

Where to Stay in Midtown

Point of Interest ■
TTC Subway —Ⓣ

Bata Shoe Museum

Royal Ontario Museum ■

Gardiner Museum of Ceramic Art ■ 7

Four Seasons Hotel Toronto **5**
The Hazelton Hotel **4**
Holiday Inn Bloor Yorkville **1**
Howard Johnson Yorkville **3**
Massey College **9**
Park Hyatt Toronto **2**
The Sutton Place Hotel **8**
Victoria University
    at the University of Toronto **6**
Windsor Arms Hotel **7**

University of Toronto Art Centre — **Barnicke Gallery** ■

Provincial Legislature

DC, DISC, MC, V. Valet parking C$34. Subway: Museum or Bay. **Amenities:** Restaurant; 2 bars; concierge; health club; Jacuzzi; room service; sauna; spa. *In room:* A/C, TV, fax, hair dryer, Internet (free), minibar.

Expensive

The Sutton Place Hotel ★   The Sutton Place presents the perks of a small hotel, with detail-oriented, personalized service not often found in a 300-plus–room property. In addition to hosting a galaxy of stars, the hotel draws sophisticated business and leisure travelers in search of serious pampering. Guest rooms are spacious, and a few suites have full kitchens. Not that you'd want to cook while you're here—the ground-floor **Accents** restaurant serves continental fare, and across the street, Bistro 990 produces good classic bistro fare. One downside is that the Sutton Place stands alone in its neighborhood. It's about a 10- to 15-minute walk to attractions such as the Royal Ontario Museum (see p. 107) and the Yorkville shopping district.

955 Bay St. (at Wellesley St.), Toronto, ON M5S 2A2. www.toronto.suttonplace.com.© **866/378-8866** or 416/924-9221. Fax 416/924-1778. 311 units. From C$189 double. Additional adult C$29. Children 17 & under stay free in parent's room. AE, DC, MC, V. Parking C$25. Subway: Wellesley. **Amenities:** Restaurant; bar; babysitting; concierge; health club; indoor pool; room service; sauna. *In room:* A/C, TV, hair dryer, minibar, Wi-Fi ($16 per day).

> ### Bed & Breakfasts in Toronto
>
> A B&B can be an excellent alternative to standard hotel accommodations. **Toronto Bed & Breakfast Reservation Service** (✆ 877/922-6522; www.toronto bandb.com) has a short but wide-ranging list of accommodations in the city. The organization will make your reservation and send you a confirmation. The **Downtown Toronto Association of Bed and Breakfast Guest Houses** (✆ 416/410-3938; www.bnbinfo.com) has listings for most of metro Toronto, not just downtown. **Bed and Breakfast Canada** (✆ 800/239-1141 or 905/524-5855; www.bbcanada.com) has a very long list of independent B&B operators.
>
> For a memorable, out of the ordinary stay, consider staying at one of the eight B&Bs located on the Toronto Islands. The cottage-like communities of Ward's Island and Algonquin Island are just a 10-minute ferry ride, but a world, away from the bustle of downtown. Some accommodations are summer seasonal, others have 1-week minimum stays. What they all share is the rare treat of staying in a park setting with wonderful views back to the city. Remember if you're out downtown to catch the last ferry back to Ward's Island (around 11:30pm), or you'll have to hire a water taxi. For a complete list of island accommodations, see www. torontoisland.org.

Moderate

Holiday Inn Bloor Yorkville 🦪 Considering this hotel's tony location—steps from Yorkville and several museums, including the Royal Ontario Museum (see p. 107)—the price is hard to beat. The rooms are small but comfortable, and have well-lit worktables. All rooms have free wireless access, but there aren't many other amenities or services. This is a good home base for leisure travelers who prize location over other considerations. If you're not planning to hang out a lot in your hotel room, it's a small trade-off for the price.

280 Bloor St. W. (at St. George St.), Toronto, ON M5S 1V8. www.holidayinn.com ✆ **888/HOLIDAY** (888/465-4329) or 416/968-0010. Fax 416/968-7765. 209 units. From C$140 double. Multi-night & other packages available. AE, DC, DISC, MC, V. Parking C$22. Subway: St. George. **Amenities:** Restaurant; coffee shop; babysitting; health club; room service. *In room:* A/C, TV, hair dryer, Wi-Fi (free).

Howard Johnson Yorkville 🦪 This hotel is a bargain in a very expensive neighborhood. The Yorkville location is excellent, which compensates for small rooms (you're probably not going to want to spend much time there, as is the case with many value-priced hotels).

89 Avenue Rd. (btw. Yorkville & Webster aves.), Toronto, ON M5R 2G3. www.hojoyorkville.com. ✆ **800/446-4656** or 416/964-1220. Fax 416/964-8692. 69 units. From C$150 double. Rates include continental breakfast. AE, DC, MC, V. Parking C$22. Subway: Bay or Museum. **Amenities:** Concierge; Wi-Fi (free). *In room:* A/C, TV, hair dryer.

AT THE AIRPORT

Expensive

Sheraton Gateway Hotel in Toronto International Airport ★ They named this hotel right—it is both a gateway to the city and the closest sleep you'll get to the gateway to board a plane. Connected by skywalk to Terminal 3 (and a free SkyTrain to Terminal 1), this hotel offers comfortable, spacious rooms and, most importantly, soundproof windows. Club rooms have extra perks, such as ergonomic chairs, a fax/printer/copier, and access to a private lounge that serves complimentary breakfast and snacks. Some guest rooms have been tailored for visitors with disabilities.

Terminal 3, , Toronto, ON L5P 1C4. www.sheraton.com. ℂ **800/325-3535** or 905/672-7000. Fax 905/672-7100. 474 units. From C$209 double. AE, DC, DISC, MC, V. Parking C$28. **Amenities:** Restaurant; bar; babysitting; concierge; health club; Jacuzzi; indoor pool; room service; sauna. *In room:* A/C, TV, fridge, hair dryer, Internet (free).

Moderate

Hilton Toronto Airport ★   The one convenience of staying out by Pearson International Airport is that rooms tend to be larger, and this Hilton is no exception. The 152 mini-suites each have king-size beds in the bedrooms, sofa beds in the living room, color TVs in both rooms, and three phones. The double rooms feature personal TV screens, much like larger versions of what you get on an airplane but at the foot of your bed. Another lure is the chain's well-regarded business-oriented amenities.

5875 Airport Rd., Mississauga, ON L4V 1N1. www.hilton.com. ℂ **866/565-4555** or 905/677-9900. Fax 905/677-7782. 419 units. From C$169 double. Additional adult C$25. Children under 16 stay free in parent's room. Multi-night packages available. AE, DC, DISC, MC, V. Parking C$15. **Amenities:** Restaurant; bar; free airport transfers; children's center; concierge; nearby golf course; health club; indoor & outdoor seasonal pools; room service; sauna; spa. *In room:* A/C, TV, fax, hair dryer, Internet ($13 per day), minibar, MP3 docking station.

Toronto Marriott Airport Hotel   Leisure travelers can benefit from weekend discounts here when the business crowd is not around. Rooms are comfortable and spacious, with standard amenities and no surprises. They've been spruced up a bit lately with down comforters and fluffier pillows. It's not home, but it's not bad for a short stay.

901 Dixon Rd. (at Carlingview Dr.), Toronto, ON M9W 1J5. www.marriott.com. ℂ **800/905-2811** or 416/674-9400. Fax 416/674-8292. 424 units. From C$179 double. Additional adult C$20. Multi-night packages available. AE, DC, DISC, MC, V. Parking C$18. **Amenities:** 2 restaurants; cafe; bar; free airport transfers; babysitting; concierge; nearby golf course; health club; Jacuzzi; sky-lit indoor pool; room service; sauna. *In room:* A/C, TV, hair dryer, minibar, Wi-Fi ($16 per day).

WHERE TO EAT

Toronto is a good place to eat. The city's rich multicultural makeup ensures a kaleidoscopic banquet. In fact, it's hard to find a taste that Toronto can't satisfy. But the one thing you won't find is an entrenched culinary tradition; food culture is an ever-changing work-in-progress that offers a good deal of gusto and, on occasion, some appetizing originality.

best DINING BETS

o **Best Patio:** If it's people-watching you crave, check out the **Drake** on West Queen West: It's great for relaxing at the sidewalk bars and roof lounges, and savoring the famous BBQs. (See p. 76.) If you're looking for fine dining in a leafy locale, try **Trattoria Giancarlo** in Little Italy for its pretty patio, good Italian fare, and excellent wine cellar. See p. 75.

o **Best Pizza:** Neapolitan pizza—paper-thin crust, light on toppings, and big on flavors—is all the rage in Toronto. Arguably the yummiest is to be found at the bustling **Pizzeria Libretto,** where an imported oven from Naples cooks the tasty pies in less than 2 minutes. (See p. 78.) On the other side of town, **Queen Margherita** is Libretto's equal, some say rival.

o **Best Charcuterie:** Toronto has taken its sweet time to fully embrace this trend, but at last, the top spots offer good and sometimes excellent charcuterie made in-house. With more than 40 kinds of cured, dried, and otherwise prepared meat, bone, and organ dishes, the **Black Hoof** reigns supreme. See p. 76.

o **Best for a Romantic Rendezvous:** When the sun sets, **Gilead Café** turns into **Gilead Bistro,** a perfect spot for an evening with someone special. The intimate room is alight with candles, the service is thoughtful, and the menus sublime. Most evenings, star chef Jamie Kennedy is behind the stove. See p. 81.

o **Best Tapas:** Partners Chris McDonald and Doug Penfold at **Cava** do tapas best with inventive dishes and more than 20 wines offered by the glass for pairing. (See p. 92.) **Torito** is a low-key, laid-back alternative. See p. 81.

o **Best Museum Restaurant:** The renovation at the Royal Ontario Museum brought with it the inspired **C5,** which some say is the best thing about the Museum's new look. See p. 83.

o **Best Bakery Lunch:** Toronto loves its tarts, croissants, and dainty desserts: The number of fine bakery-cafes is proof. A favorite is the pioneering **Patachou,** which brought true French pastries to the city back in the day and arguably still makes the best croissant in town. (See

PRICE CATEGORIES

Very Expensive	$30 and up	Moderate	$10–$20
Expensive	$20–$30	Inexpensive	Under $10

p. 95.) **Woodlot** also serves (daytime only) fine coffee and excellent pastries; there's a daily selection of savory and sweet croissants and exquisite individual quiches. See p. 76.

o **Best Hotel Restaurant:** Dining at **TOCA by Tom Brodi** at the new **Ritz Carlton** is a treat. The Canadian-themed dishes are crafted with care, and the service is refreshingly un-institutional. (See p. 75.) **Lai Wah Heen,** in the Metropolitan Hotel, is a longstanding favorite for Peking duck, great dim sum, and an impressive menu of mostly Cantonese specialties. See p. 70.

o **Best for Families:** **Grano** is an Italian restaurant that knows how to treat the *ragazzini*. Simple pastas, delicious breads and sweets, good salads, and the lively, warm atmosphere combine to make it feel like you're visiting family. (See p. 92.) **Mangia e Bevi,** in the Distillery District, is equally welcoming, with good pastas, pizzas, and salads—and a tolerant approach to little ones and their restless ways.

o **Best Japanese:** There are plenty of good sushi spots and Japanese restaurants to choose from, but there's little doubt of the fun and fine food to be had at the chaotic **Guu Izakaya,** with its great selection of small-plate dishes served in a pub-like atmosphere. A second location on Bloor Street West, which opened in spring 2011 under the name **Guu Sakabar,** is helping to lessen the notoriously long lines for the many Guu fans. See p. 82.

DOWNTOWN WEST

This is where you will find Toronto's highest concentration of great restaurants. **Little Italy,** which runs along College Street, generally has better bars and cafes than restaurants; the streets of **Chinatown,** which radiate from Spadina Avenue, are lined with brightly lit, busy eateries; and lately, **West Queen West, Dundas West,** and **Ossington Avenue** are all proving to be enticing destinations for dining.

Very Expensive

Bymark ★★ AMERICAN/BISTRO   In the heart of the financial district sits the most corporate of the Mark McEwan empire of swanky restaurants. The menu ranges from fancy burgers and frites to steaks and snazzy seafood—all of it presented in a grown-up atmosphere for the suits. The extensive wine list, which was a draw for big expense accounts before the recession hit, now offers good value, especially with a fine selection of wines by the glass. *Note:* McEwan also runs One restaurant in the Hazelton Hotel (116 Yorkville Ave., © 647/955-4865) and a new venture, Fabricca, an Italian restaurant in suburban Don Mills (49 Karl Fraser Rd.; © 416/391-0707).

66 Wellington St. W. (at Bay St.). © **416/777-1144.** www.bymarkdowntown.com. Reservations recommended. Main courses C$32–C$47. AE, DC, MC, V. Mon–Fri 11:30am–2:30pm; Mon–Sat 5–11pm. Subway: King, then walk W to Bay St.

Canoe Restaurant & Bar ★★★ CANADIAN   On the 54th floor of the TD Tower, this chic, modern dining room is famous for its panoramic views. But the professional service; sophisticated, elegant Canadiana cuisine; and fine wine cellar are what have established it as one of the city's best restaurants. Executives dominate at lunchtime, when the feel is distinctly corporate; dinner, with the twinkling cityscape backdrop, is more romantic. Thanks to the passion of executive chef Anthony Walsh and his crew, seasonal menus offer a selection of top ingredients from local purveyors. Standouts include delicately handled Nunavut caribou and Québec foie gras. Tasting menus, at C$100 per person (add C$50 for paired wines), are impressive and generous. If you're on a budget, drop in at the bar for a glass of Niagara wine and a nibble.

54th floor, Toronto Dominion Tower, 66 Wellington St. W. ℂ **416/364-0054.** www.oliverbonacini.com. Reservations required. Main courses C$39–C$44. AE, DC, MC, V. Mon–Fri 11:45am–2:30pm & 5–10:30pm. Subway: King.

Chiado ★★★ SEAFOOD/MEDITERRANEAN   Local Portuguese families flock here for special occasions; the atmosphere is an old-world balance of sophistication and warmth. At its core, it's a great fish restaurant, thanks in part to the fresh seafood flown in most days of the week, with perfectly grilled sardines and pan-seared monk-fish. The wine list is equally impressive, especially for those who believe Portuguese wines are plonk but are willing to reconsider. Upstairs is a less formal dining option: a bar with a small, but fine, menu. *Note:* Owner Albino Silva has also opened the smaller, more casual **Salt Wine Bar** on Ossington Avenue (ℂ **416/533-7258**) and the elegant **Adega** restaurant on Elm Street (ℂ **416/977-4338**).

864 College St. ℂ **416/538-1910.** www.chiadorestaurant.com. Reservations recommended. Main courses C$25–C$45. AE, DC, MC, V. Mon–Fri 11am–4pm; Mon–Sat 5–10pm. Subway: College, then a streetcar to Ossington Ave.

Lai Wah Heen ★★★ CANTONESE   This is one hotel dining room where you'll find more locals than visitors. The interior is vintage Art Deco; spare pictograms dominate the walls of the two-level space. The extensive menu is mainly Cantonese, and regulars come for the excellent Peking duck, dim sum (especially the Sunday brunch tasting menu), and delicacies such as alligator loin dumplings. There's a mid-town location, too: Lai Toh Heen (629 Mount Pleasant Rd.; ℂ **416/489-8922**).

In the Metropolitan Hotel, 110 Chestnut St. ℂ **416/977-9899.** www.laiwahheen.com. Reservations recommended. Main courses C$22–C$48. AE, DC, MC, V. Daily 11:30am–3pm; Sun–Thurs 5:30–10:30pm, Fri & Sat 5:30–11pm. Subway: St. Patrick.

Expensive

Ame ★★★ JAPANESE   The Rubino brothers, Michael and Guy, are local legends for their highly stylized restaurants and serious dedication to the culinary arts.

📎 A Note on Smoking

A provincial law came into effect in 2006 that banned smoking at restaurants in Ontario: There is no smoking indoors, and patios that have any sort of covering are also smoke-free. This has made for a great deal of confusion because tableside umbrellas that are close-set apparently count as covering, according to the law. You can smoke on uncovered patios.

Where to Eat in Downtown

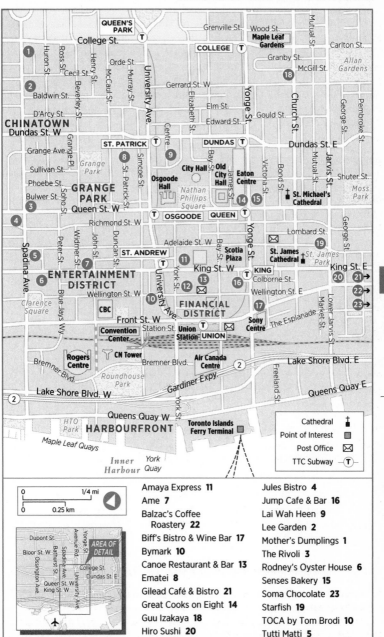

Amaya Express **11**

Ame **7**

Balzac's Coffee
    Roastery **22**

Biff's Bistro & Wine Bar **17**

Bymark **10**

Canoe Restaurant & Bar **13**

Ematei **8**

Gilead Café & Bistro **21**

Great Cooks on Eight **14**

Guu Izakaya **18**

Hiro Sushi **20**

Jules Bistro **4**

Jump Cafe & Bar **16**

Lai Wah Heen **9**

Lee Garden **2**

Mother's Dumplings **1**

The Rivoli **3**

Rodney's Oyster House **6**

Senses Bakery **15**

Soma Chocolate **23**

Starfish **19**

TOCA by Tom Brodi **10**

Tutti Matti **5**

This very modern lounge and restaurant, rich with wood and fine textiles, is their latest creation: a Japanese reinvention of their acclaimed Rain restaurant. The focus is on sushi and sashimi with a Robata grill, plus an elegant dinner menu. The vegetable tempura alone exemplifies the care chef Guy takes in the kitchen. There are dazzling cocktails, too. An ultra-hip destination, both for the fine fare and the idiosyncratic nature of the place, the choice of eating at the bar or in the dining room suits a range of budgets.

19 Mercer St. (at John St.). ✆ **416/599-7246.** http://amecuisine.com. Reservations recommended. Main courses C$15–C$25. AE, DC, MC, V. Mon–Wed 5:30–10pm; Thurs–Sat 5:30–11pm. Subway: St. Andrew, then W to John St. & S to Mercer St.

Brassaii ★★ BISTRO/INTERNATIONAL   This large, pretty space with a lovely courtyard is a Mediterranean restaurant and bar/lounge with good food, and extensive cocktail and wine lists. It's hip, but not trendy, in part thanks to the kitchen helmed by chef Bruce Woods, formerly of the very flashy Centro, and a new look launched last year. The menus are grown-up enough to feature ostrich, champagne risotto, and meatballs made of Kobe beef, and to satisfy late-night revelers looking for a sophisticated snack. The restaurant is named for the 1920s French photographer; his prints adorn the walls.

461 King St. W. ✆ 416/598-4730. www.brassaii.com. Reservations recommended. Main courses C$20–C$39. AE, MC, V. Mon–Fri 10am–2am; Sat & Sun 10am–3pm; Sat 5:30pm–2am. Subway: St. Andrew, then a streetcar W to Spadina Ave.

Buca ★★★ ITALIAN/PIZZA   Only the most popular restaurants can play a game of hide-and-seek and get away with it. And so it is with this hard-to-find Italian subterranean destination: down an alleyway with no signage, how silly. But it's worth the search for the exceptional fare. Chef Rob Gentile takes the accessible and comforting rustic foods of Italy and treats them with craft and care. Most everything is done in-house. The house-cured charcuterie and sausages are superior. Fresh pastas would make a *nonna* proud, especially the *agnolotti* stuffed with veal in a rich *ragu*. Pizzas are light and flavorful, and meats and whole fish are braised or grilled expertly. Vegetable sides, like all of the menu, are seasonal. (Menus change daily.) Even the desserts, such as a moist but not greasy olive oil cake, are irresistible. The team behind Brassaii owns the place; the service and decor are equally pro.

602 King St. W. ✆ **416/865-1600.** www.buca.ca. Reservations required. Main courses C$16–C$34. AE, MC, V. Mon–Fri 11am–3pm; Mon–Sat 5–11pm. Subway: St Andrew, then a streetcar W to Portland.

Foxley ★★ ASIAN/BISTRO   It was just 5 years ago that this unpretentious bistro opened on Ossington Avenue, leading a brigade of new eateries to what is now one the city's best strips for good food. Chef/owner Tom Thai, long known as a top sushi chef, creates beautiful small-plate dishes such as plump dumplings, steamed (often sustainable) fish dishes, smoked pork belly, and more. The flavor is fusion: pan-Asian with European and Mexican influences. Eat what you please since there's a fresh note to this cooking—light on salt and fat—and the reasonable prices are equally encouraging. The only drawback, really, is that they don't accept reservations. So arrive early, put your name and cellphone number on the list, and then trundle off for a drink along the strip while you wait.

207 Ossington Ave. ✆ **416/534-8520.** Reservations not accepted. Main courses C$7–C$24. Mon–Sat 5–11pm. Subway: Dundas St., then a streetcar W to Ossington Ave.; or Ossington Ave. (on Bloor line), then a bus S to Foxley St.

Where to Eat in the West End

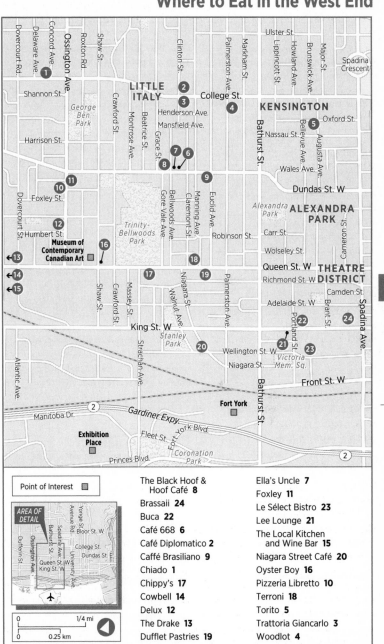

Point of Interest ■		
	The Black Hoof & Hoof Café **8**	Ella's Uncle **7**
	Brassaii **24**	Foxley **11**
	Buca **22**	Le Sélect Bistro **23**
	Café 668 **6**	Lee Lounge **21**
	Café Diplomatico **2**	The Local Kitchen and Wine Bar **15**
	Caffè Brasiliano **9**	Niagara Street Café **20**
	Chiado **1**	Oyster Boy **16**
	Chippy's **17**	Pizzeria Libretto **10**
	Cowbell **14**	Terroni **18**
	Delux **12**	Torito **5**
	The Drake **13**	Trattoria Giancarlo **3**
	Dufflet Pastries **19**	Woodlot **4**

LOCAL lovers UNITE!

Toronto is deep into a love affair with local foods. From top dining rooms to little cafes, from the new wave of pizzerias to the boom of burger joints, just about everywhere you look, cooks are tapping into local, farm-fresh sources, from great cheeses to pastured meats, organic fruits and vegetables, and plenty of local wine and craft beer to wash it all down. Whether the trend and its politics appeal, it's a good way to get a taste of the territory. There are too many to list in their entirety, but here are a few of the top locavore haunts.

Allen's. Burgers, brunch, and big salads: This 20-year neighborhood favorite inspired by, and named for, Joe Allen of New York is in fact a champion of local sources. The excellent meat, the heart of any great burger, is sourced from local farms and then ground on-site. The owners are so proud of their sources, they list the animal feed on the menu. The excellent wine list is local, too. See p. 90.

Cowbell. Chef Mark Cutrara is so dedicated to knowing his food, he took a year off to learn the art of butchery before opening this nose-to-tail star. He has the same commitment to his sources: local, small-scale, and often organic farms. If you're in town, check out the monthly "Farmers Dinners" that feature a member of the Cowbell family of suppliers.

Gilead Café and Bistro. You could say star Jamie Kennedy is Toronto's original locavore chef; he's been promoting these sources for decades, and to great effect. Kennedy is a maestro at the stove, and his suppliers reflect his high standards. After years of running a small restaurant empire, he's back in the kitchen at this modest and beautiful *boîte*. See p. 81.

Pangaea. Chef Martin Kouprie has a taste for locally sourced wild foods, so expect to find seasonal menus embellished with cattail hearts, wild mushrooms, wild berries, and what is arguably the last wild meat, caribou, on offer. See p. 86.

Ruby WatchCo. One prix-fixe dinner nightly with four courses and the main ingredients supplied by local purveyors. Celebrity chefs Lynn Crawford and Lora Kirk work closely with farmers, and the mutual respect is evidenced in the truly inspired results. See p. 82.

Jump Cafe & Bar ★★ AMERICAN   This sprawling space in Commerce Court can be tricky to find. Just follow the buzz: As the decibel level rises, you'll know you're on the right track. This is a spot to socialize, with table-hopping and schmoozing all around. The menus play it safe—salads, grilled meats, and house-made pastas—but guarantee a measure of panache. Even the onion rings are a notch above the norm. This is one of the city's chain of restaurants under Oliver & Bonacini (O&B) that includes Canoe, Auberge du Pommier, Biff Bistro, and a few O&B cafes around town.

1 Wellington St. W. ⓒ **416/363-3400.** www.oliverbonacini.com. Reservations required. Main courses C$17–C$36. AE, DC, MC, V. Mon–Fri 11:45am–midnight; Sat 5pm–midnight. Subway: King.

Lee Lounge ★★★ ASIAN   Celebrity chef Susur Lee returned to Toronto last year from his world-tour—New York, Singapore, and more—just long enough to open a much-awaited new restaurant, Lee Lounge. The restaurant/lounge replaces the groundbreaking, haute Susur, which closed years ago, and its most recent predecessor Madeleine. It adjoins the popular Lee restaurant through a wide door, and the sister restaurants serve small-plate Asian fare in a busy, often loud room, but the new Lounge is the true hot spot. Critics rave about the foie-gras-stuffed Peking duck,

Susur's signature Singapore slaw, salmon ceviche, and rich desserts, all of them reflecting the singular creative craft that has made the Iron Chef champion a star, even if he isn't here to run the kitchen.

601 King St. W. ✆ **416/603-2205.** www.susur.com/lee. Reservations required. Main courses C$7–C$38. AE, DC, MC, V. Mon–Sat 5:30pm–midnight. Subway: St Andrew, then W to Bathurst.

Le Sélect Bistro ★★ BISTRO Le Sélect is a Toronto tradition: a Parisian-style bistro that moved to Wellington Street West (a few blocks from its original home) a few years ago and has since remained as popular as ever. The patio is small but pretty in good weather, the esteemed wine cellar is a draw, and the favorites—such as steak-frites, savory tarts, duck confit, and rich desserts—are all nicely done. Try the artisan cheeses from Québec.

432 Wellington St. W. ✆ **416/596-6405.** www.leselect.com. Reservations recommended. Main courses C$20–C$30; 3-course prix-fixe menu C$35. AE, DC, MC, V. Sun–Thurs 11:30am–11:30pm; Fri & Sat 11:30am–midnight. Subway: Osgoode.

Niagara Street Café ★★ 🍴 BISTRO Owner Anton Potvin has flare, as does accomplished chef Nick Liu, and together they have created a lovely little bistro with an emphasis on local, organic, and artisanal ingredients. Don't worry, there's nothing righteous about the experience; it's pure pleasure, from the crispy snail and lettuce salad to the duck confit, the daily wild fish special, or the bison *bavette*. Desserts, made in-house, are worth saving room for; service with a smile adds another positive note. Brunch is a neighborhood draw.

169 Niagara St. (at King St.). ✆ **416/703-4222.** www.niagarastreetcafe.com. Reservations recommended. Main courses C$19–C$27. AE, DC, MC, V. Wed–Sun 6–10:30pm. Subway: St. Patrick, then King St. streetcar W to Niagara St.

TOCA by Tom Brodi ★★ CANADIAN/CONTINENTAL It's rare to find creative cuisine in a chain hotel (even one as upscale as Toronto's Ritz Carlton), but TOCA is an exception. Chef Brodi's passions define the elegant, accessible menus that highlight the best of Canadian foods. And it's evident he's having a good time at it. A fresh *burrata* from Ontario—a creamy fresh mozzarella—is brightened with pea shoots, basil, and a nibble of pressed watermelon. Soups are imaginative and soothing, such as consommé with stuffed pasta and duck confit. There are aged meats for serious carnivores and plenty of sustainable fish, such as a line-caught halibut and BC sablefish. The wine cellar impresses, the staff is friendly and attentive, and the room is splashy but comfortable in a modern, open way. The only negative is the piped-in hotel music that seems out of place.

1181 Wellington St. W. ✆ **416/585-2500.** http://tocarestaurant.com. Main courses C$16–C$43. AE, DC, MC, V. Daily 6:30–11am; Sun–Fri 11:30am–2:30pm; Mon–Sat 5:30–10:30pm. Subway: St. Patrick.

Trattoria Giancarlo ★★ ITALIAN In summer, the pretty patio in the heart of Little Italy is one of the strip's quietest. It's also where you'll find decent (modern) Italian fare, a cut above most of the food in this very touristy 'hood. Pastas are handled with particular skill, such as the bracingly fresh lemon and basil linguine, and salads and mains, including the popular thick veal chop, are also consistently good. There's a new addition: a dark and cool little wine bar adjoining the dining room, where peek-a-boo windows offer a chance to clandestinely watch the parade outside. There's one curious thing about this longstanding spot: The wine list is much more extensive than the chalkboard lists, so you have to do a little probing to find the best match.

41 Clinton St. (at College St.). ✆ **416/533-9619.** Main courses C$18–C$35. AE, DC, MC, V. Mon–Sat 6–11pm. Subway: College, then a streetcar W to Clinton St.

Woodlot Restaurant and Bakery ★★★ CANADIAN/ITALIAN A bit of farm in the city, a coy conceit that works to great effect. The warm, split-level, open room is as laid-bare as the cuisine: a handful of tables in a loft that look down on a communal, harvest table. The chefs toil away in an open kitchen with a wood-burning oven where just about everything—breads, pies, meats and fish—are cooked. Chef and co-owner David Haman's comforting, well-executed food is continental with an Italian influence, served in homestead portions, with a focus on local ingredients. Menus—one meat, one vegetarian—are small and feature savory pies, excellent soups (the French onion draws raves), fresh pastas with meaty *ragus,* and sides including mashed potatoes with marrow butter. Desserts, led by pastry chef Stephanie Bishop, and breads under Jeff Connell are not to be missed.

293 Palmerston Ave. ☎ **647/342-6307.** www.woodlotrestaurant.com. Main courses C$16–C$35. AE, C, MC, V. Tues–Sun 7:30am–3:30pm & 5pm–midnight. Subway: College, then a streetcar W to Palmerston Ave.

Moderate

The Black Hoof & Hoof Café ★★★ 🎁 BISTRO Nose-to-tail eating is taken to extremes, and to truly tasty heights, at this brilliant restaurant-bar and its sister brunch-and-bar bistro right across the street. Co-owner/chef Grant van Gameren's in-house charcuterie is the star, with the tongue sandwich drawing raves, but the pastas and soups are equally inspired. At the Café, brunch dish standouts include pancakes topped with rabbit confit and little bone-marrow doughnuts, all daring and beautiful. Be prepared to wait: The buzz around these two spots is deafening.

928 & 923 Dundas St. W. ☎ **416/551-8854** or 416/792-7511. Reservations not accepted. Main courses C$10–C$24. No credit cards. Restaurant Sun–Wed 6–11:30pm, Thurs–Sat 6pm–1am; cafe Thurs–Mon 10am–2pm & 6pm–2am. Subway: St. Patrick, then a streetcar W to Grace St.

Delux ★★ BISTRO Warmth and comfort come together in this small, simple bistro, both in lovely touches, such as cookies made-to-order (what could be more warming?), and in the satisfying Cuban-inspired French-bistro cuisine that is the creation of chef/owner Corinna Mozo. Lovely salads, garlicky roast chicken, a good Cubano sandwich, and frites are mainstays. The desserts are standouts, especially the coffee-flavored crème brûlée.

92 Ossington Ave. (at Humbert St.). ☎ **416/537-0134.** Reservations recommended. Main courses C$18–C$25. DC, MC, V. Tues–Thurs 6–10:30pm; Fri & Sat 6–11pm; Sun 10:30am–3pm & 6–10pm. Subway: Osgoode, then a streetcar W to Ossington Ave.

The Drake ★★ BISTRO A good spot that satisfies most appetites. You can come for a busy brunch, great smoked meats and ribs, burgers, a range of bars, a hopping night-time lounge, a sidewalk patio, or a full-on dining room that's good for big parties. The Drake is a destination for music, fun, and food, and the kitchens are overseen by excellent chef Anthony Rose. Groovy yet friendly, plus new BBQ menus and patios are currently in the works.

1150 Queen St. W. (at Beaconsfield Ave.). ℘ **416/531-5042.** www.thedrakehotel.ca. Main courses C$14–C$37. AE, DC, MC, V. Mon–Sat 11am–2:30pm; Sun 10:30am–2:30pm; daily 6–11pm. Subway: Osgoode, then a streetcar to Beaconsfield Ave.

Ematei ★★ JAPANESE/SUSHI   One of Toronto's most authentic sushi and *izakaya* spots, this place attracts regulars looking for fine fare who don't mind the drab decor. Don't miss the hot pots, grilled fish, tantalizing tempura, and hand-rolls. The best values are the three-course menus. Service is no-nonsense.

30 St Patrick St. ℘ **416/340-0472.** Main courses C$9–C$29. AE, DC, MC, V. Mon–Fri noon–2:30pm; daily 5pm–midnight. Subway: Osgoode.

Gallery Grill ★★ BISTRO/CONTINENTAL   This small, pretty restaurant sits perched above the University of Toronto's neo-Gothic Great Hall, so the setting is stunning, with daytime-only menus to match. Chef Suzanne Baby is a local, under-the-radar treasure whose elegant fare includes soups such as cardamom-scented carrot purée, fresh pastas, poached fish fillets, and fresh veggie dishes. It's all done with a continental flare, including the excellent eggs. The wines are selected with care, and the service is pleasant yet pro. Make time for a stroll around the campus after lunch.

7 Hart House Circle (at King's College Circle). ℘ **416/978-2445.** www.harthouse.utoronto.ca. Main courses C$14–C$18. AE, DC, MC, V. Sept–June Mon–Fri 11:30am–2:30pm; Sun 11am–2pm. Closed July, Aug & holiday weekends. Subway: Museum, then walk S to Harbord St. or take Bus 94.

Great Cooks on Eight ★★ LIGHT FARE   If you've shopped till you dropped at the Eaton Centre, take a break one big door south at this cafeteria-style cafe and restaurant on the eighth floor of the department store the Bay. It's a pleasant retreat for good lunchtime fare and a broad selection of teas and fine sweets, all at reasonable prices. If you're feeling inspired, consider signing up for one of the cooking classes that take place in the evening.

401 Bay St. (at Queen St.). ℘ **416/861-4333.** www.greatcooks.ca. Main courses C$7–C$17. AE, DC, MC, V. Mon–Fri 11:30am–3pm. Subway: Queen.

Lee Garden ★ CANTONESE   It's been around since 1978, back when the options for Cantonese cuisine were few in Toronto, and it has since satisfied crowds with consistently good, if predictable, menus that specialize in seafood, tofu, and veggie dishes. Meats are hearty, too. The signature dish is fork-tender grandfather's smoked chicken with honey and sesame seeds. Expect a crowd: This spot remains ever popular.

331 Spadina Ave. ℘ **416/593-9524.** Reservations not accepted. Main courses C$15–C$20. AE, MC, V. Daily 4pm–midnight. Subway: Spadina, then the LRT S to Baldwin St.

The Local Kitchen and Wine Bar ★★ ITALIAN   Parkdale's latest hot number is part authentic Italian trattoria, part contemporary Toronto. The crowded, convivial room is idiosyncratic, the service pro yet friendly, and the food absolutely fantastic. Chef Fabio Bondi arrives pre-dawn each morning to make stunning fresh pasta such as smoked gnocchi with creamy Taleggio cheese. Vegetables, fish, and meats are often on par with the noodles. The wine list is simple yet good, and each evening, there's an interesting wine highlighted, whether a rare Sicilian white or a new local vintage.

1710 Queen St. W. ℘ **416/534-6700.** Reservations not accepted. Main courses C$15–C$25. AE, DC, MC, V. Tues & Wed 5:30–10pm; Thurs–Sat 5:30–11pm. Subway: Osgoode, then a streetcar W to Triller Ave.

Oyster Boy SEAFOOD   Mollusk expert Adam Colquhoun runs a vibrant, fun, and very friendly bar and casual dining room where the fresh on-the-shell fare is superb and as fine as the cooked seafood, sourced mostly from Canadian suppliers. Fish and chips are excellent, pastas are generous, and the wine list features great pairings from Canada and abroad.

872 Queen St. W. (at Strachan Ave.). ℂ **416/534-3432.** Main courses C$11–C$17. AE, DC, MC, V. Mon-Wed 5-10pm; Thurs-Sun 5-11pm. Subway: Osgoode, then a streetcar W to Strachan Ave.

Pizzeria Libretto ★★ ITALIAN/PIZZA   This pizza parlor has been doing gang-buster business since opening its doors a few years ago. This was Toronto's first "authentic" Neapolitan-style pizzeria: The super-thin crusts cook in less than 2 minutes in a specially built and imported wood-burning oven that hovers around the 700-degree mark. Toppings are simple: in-house-made spicy sausage with tomato sauce, the classic Margherita, and nice veggie options. What's more, the pastas and salads are generous and delicious. The place is the brainchild of chef Rocco Agostino and partner Max Rimaldi, who are also behind the upscale, much-praised Italian wine bar **Enoteca Sociale** (1288 Dundas St. W.; ℂ **416/534-1200**).

221 Ossington Ave. ℂ **416/532-8000.** Reservations not accepted. Main courses C$11–C$25. AE, DC, MC, V. Mon-Sat noon-11pm; Sun 4-11pm. Subway: Dundas, then a streetcar W to Ossington Ave.

The Rivoli INTERNATIONAL   The Riv is better known as a club than a restaurant—the back room plays host to live music, stand-up comics, and poetry readings. The kitchen serves up jerk chicken, steamed curried mussels, salads, and a classic house burger. It's better than most bar food, for sure. Prices are fair, too.

332-334 Queen St. W. ℂ **416/597-0794.** www.rivoli.ca. Reservations accepted only for groups of 6 or more. Main courses C$11–C$20. AE, MC, V. Daily 11:30am-2am. Subway: Osgoode.

Rodney's Oyster House ★★ SEAFOOD   Rodney is Toronto's original "Oyster-man," one of only a handful left now. This spot is a favorite with nearby condo dwellers and office workers, but is also a draw as a destination. The maritime-inspired setting is unpretentious and includes whimsical touches such as fishing paraphernalia. The main draw is the super-fresh oysters, but chowders and pastas are very good, too. There's a new locale at 56 Temperance St. (ℂ **416/703-5111**).

469 King St. W. ℂ **416/363-8105.** www.rodneysoysterhouse.com. Reservations recommended (reservations cannot be made for the patio except for groups of 10 or more). Main courses C$10–C$29. AE, DC, MC, V. Mon-Sat 11am-1am. Subway: St. Andrew.

Terroni ★★ 🐟 ITALIAN/PIZZA   This was Toronto's first serious venture into true Southern Italian pizza. It's since grown to be something of a mini-empire and a tried-and-true place for fine, thin-crust pies; good pastas; traditional salads made with beans, greens, and sausage; and other traditional dishes and desserts made with *nonna's* kitchen in mind. It's a great value and always popular. There are other locations at 1 Balmoral Ave. (ℂ **416/925-4020**) and 106 Victoria St., Dundas Square (ℂ **416/955-0258**), as well as more serious dining rooms at Osteria Ciceri e Tria (106 Victoria St.; ℂ **416/504-1992**) and the new Bar Centrale in Midtown (1095 Yonge St.; ℂ **416/504-1992**).

720 Queen St. W. (at Claremont St.). ℂ **416/504-0320.** www.terroni.ca. Main courses C$10–C$23. AE, MC, V. Mon-Wed & Sun 9am-10pm; Thurs-Sat 9am-11pm. Subway: Osgoode, then a streetcar W to Claremont.

Tutti Matti ★★ ITALIAN   Chef/owner Alida Solomon, a native Torontonian, worked in Tuscan restaurant kitchens for years, and the results are worth a visit to her

WHERE TO EAT | Downtown West

A second CUP

Do you love coffee? Toronto has finally moved beyond a dependence on cookie-cutter chain coffee shops and is embracing a full-on barista movement. It seems every week there's a new spot opening up. Here's a very short list of some of the best, but ask around; there's likely a great cafe just around the corner, where the espresso is dynamite and the owner can talk beans all day. *Note:* most of these spots, Euro-style, open early and close before suppertime.

Balzac's Coffee Roastery. Building 60, 55 Mill St. ((*C* **416/207-1709**). The airy cafe invites lounging upstairs in the loft living room or downstairs near the roaster. Beans are fresh-roasted and then micro-roasted on the premises for super-freshness.

Dark Horse Espresso Bar. 682 Queen St. E. ((*C* **647/436-3460**); 215 Spadina Ave. ((*C* **416/979-1200**). Is it the caffeine? Everyone here buzzes—happily. Pleasant vibe, good pastries, lots of free newspapers and magazines, Wi-Fi for all . . . oh, and consistently excellent (fair-trade) joe. Who could ask for anything more?

Ella's Uncle. 916 Dundas St. W. ((*C* **416/703-8881**). There are two great things about this little, mostly take-out spot: Great brews from local roaster Classic Coffee (bonus: the roaster is eco-friendly), plus the yummy baked goods made in the dollhouse kitchen behind the bar. Really nice staff, too.

Ezra's Pound. 238 Dupont St. ((*C* **416/929-4400**); 913 Dundas St. W. ((*C* **647/346-8448**). You can sit down to warm croissants, a light lunch, or just plain great coffee—organic and fair-trade—where free Wi-Fi invites lingering in the pretty space. More tranquil than most coffee bars.

Sam James Coffee Bar. 297 Harbord St. ((*C* **647/341-2572**). Some claim this tiny spot, named for the owner/award-winning barista, serves the best brew in town. To be sure, the *crema* would make a mamma cry. The siphon coffee—you have to see it to understand—is a work of art. A Montreal roaster, Toi, Moi e Café, supplies the beans. Lovely pastries come from top chef J.P. Challet's catering company.

friendly restaurant. You'll find a combination of local ingredients, such as Ontario-made prosciutto and *salumi,* on the menu, along with traditional bean soups, house-made fresh pastas, good braised meats, and some satisfying desserts. The small open kitchen offers a bit of drama, and the atmosphere is convivial. Expect a somewhat noisy experience, but all in good fun *alla Italiana.* The wine list reveals Solomon's intimate knowledge of great Tuscan vintages. The lunchtime prix-fixe menu offers great value.

364 Adelaide St. W. (at Spadina Ave.). *C* **416/597-8839.** www.tuttimatti.com. Main courses C$14-C$34. AE, DC, MC, V. Mon–Fri noon–3pm; Mon–Sat 6–10:30pm. Subway: Osgoode, then any streetcar W to Spadina Ave. or Spadina streetcar to Adelaide St.

Inexpensive

Amaya Express ★ INDIAN This chain of Indian take-out and delivery spots are sprouting up all over town, and the bargains are hard to beat. They feature daily deals and coupons such as dinner specials for two people for C$40 or four for C$80 that include an appetizer, a choice of three items from the main menu, rice, and naan. Menus are wide-ranging, from rice pilafs to chicken madras, curries, and masalas, and a good selection of breads. There's a section of street foods that's worth a look:

Chicken pakoras and lamb kebabs are particularly noteworthy. And the food is good, sometimes truly delicious. There are full-service Amaya restaurants, too: The original Indian Room, at 1701 Bayview Ave. (© **416/322-3270**), is a cut above and suitable for a special occasion.

100 King St. W., First Canadian Place, Mezzanine Level; 200 Simcoe Place Food Court; 108 Ossington Ave.; 21 Davenport Rd.© **416/322-0020.** Main courses C$7–C$10. AE, DC, MC, V. First Canadian Place & Simcoe Place Mon–Fri 11:30am–5pm; Ossington & Davenport daily noon–10pm.

Café Diplomatico LIGHT FARE/ITALIAN/PIZZA   Talk about location! This is one of the best patios in Little Italy for kicking back and watching the parade go by. The scene varies from Italian grandmothers to community families and plenty of dressed-up visitors (especially on weekend nights). The food, however, is secondary: The pizzas are basic, sandwiches merely satisfying, and pastas are often poor. The Dip, as it's known, attracts long lines to secure a seat. Good fun. Eat elsewhere.

594 College St. (at Clinton St.).© **416/534-4637.** www.diplomatico.ca. Main courses C$5–$15. AE, DC, MC, V. Mon–Fri 8am–2am; Sat & Sun 8am–3am. Subway: Queen's Park, then a streetcar W to Clinton St.

Caffé Brasiliano 🍴 LIGHT FARE/PORTUGUESE   Need some fuel for the day? Look no further than this busy, very affordable spot where hordes of taxi drivers go for home-cooked meals. This traditional cafe moved across the street to expanded digs, which feature comfy booths, and serves buffet (read: steam-table) fare alongside rib-sticking specials including generous sandwiches, hot lasagna, and hearty soups. For dessert: The neighborhood specialty is a Portuguese custard tart with a touch of perfectly caramelized crust.

849 Dundas St. (at Euclid St.).© **416/603-6607.** Main courses C$5–C$10. No credit cards. Mon–Sat 6am–11pm. Subway: St Patrick, then a streetcar W to Claremont St.

Café 668 ★ ASIAN/VEGETARIAN   This vegetarian restaurant used to be a dingy spot at 668 Dundas St. W., but it has been reinvented as a sleek cafe/bistro offering the same Asian-fusion fare it won acclaim for, but in a much prettier room. Soups are a standout, as are the wide selection of noodles. Mock meats are, well, a poor stand-in. Salad rolls are fresh and worth a try. Overall, spicing can be through the roof, so take note from the friendly guide on the menu.

885 Dundas St. W. (at Claremont St.).© **416/703-0668.** www.cafe668.com. Main courses C$11–C$14. No credit cards. Tues–Fri 12:30–4pm & 6–9pm; Sat & Sun 1:30–9pm. Subway: St. Patrick, then a streetcar W to Claremont St.

Chippy's ★ SEAFOOD   Great, non-greasy fish and chips are hard to find, so little wonder this shoe-box spot on Queen West is a hit with its signature light batter (Guinness beer is a key ingredient) and chunky, home-cut fries. There's halibut, cod, and haddock for frying, and an assortment of garnishes, most of them not any improvement over a bit of ketchup or traditional malt vinegar. The location, across the street from the beautiful and sprawling Trinity Bellwoods Park, calls out for a good-weather picnic.

893 Queen St. W. (at Strachan Ave.).© **416/866-7474.** Main courses C$9–C$13. No credit cards. Sun–Wed 11:30am–8pm; Thurs–Sat 11:30am–9pm. Subway: Osgoode, then a streetcar W to Strachan Ave.

Jules Bistro ★★ FRENCH/BISTRO   A lunchtime hangout by day and a pretty cafe by night, this little French treasure serves up good quiches, lovely salads, crisp frites, sweet and savory crêpes, and buttery desserts. It's a simple, friendly spot with a suitably approachable wine list and price tag to match. A C$25 prix fixe menu is a steal. Regulars pack the place midday, and neighborhood locals linger over candlelit tables after dark.

147 Spadina Ave. (at Queen St. W.). © **416/348-8886.** Reservations recommended. Main courses C$13–C$20; prix-fixe menu C$25. AE, DC, MC, V. Mon–Fri 11:30am–9pm; Sat noon–5pm. Subway: Osgoode, then a streetcar W to Spadina Ave.

Mother's Dumplings ★ 🍴 CHINESE The website of this family-oriented, idiosyncratic spot proudly states: "No longer does our restaurant appear to be a hole in the wall." That's because this beloved dumpling spot moved to a new location, a welcome improvement from the plastic tables and chairs of yore. But new polish or not, this mom-and-pop spot remains one of the best places for Chinese dumplings in town. Even chefs drop by for the silken pockets made on-site, as well as fine noodles and more.

421 Spadina Ave (just N of College St.). © **416/217-2008.** www.mothersdumplings.com. Main courses C$3.50–C$8. DC, MC, V. Daily 11am–10pm. Subway: Spadina, then a streetcar S to College St.

Torito ★★ SPANISH/TAPAS Kensington Market—and Augusta Avenue, in particular—is filled with eateries, but this one is a little gem that serves small-plate, Spanish-rooted fare that is fun and fine, such as roasted quail with a pomegranate glaze, smoked trout with potato salad, and "tongue in cheek": braised tongue beside seared-and-braised cheek in a red-wine sauce. The wine list offers plenty of sherry and cava (sparkling Spanish wine), plus sangria for pairing.

276 Augusta Ave. © **647/436-5874.** www.toritotapasbar.com. Reservations not accepted. Tapas plates C$5–C$11. MC, V. Mon–Sat 5:30–11pm. Subway: Spadina, then a streetcar S to College St.

DOWNTOWN EAST
Expensive

Biff's Bistro & Wine Bar ★★ BISTRO The Oliver-Bonacini team that created a number of top-notch Toronto restaurants (Jump, Canoe, and Auberge du Pommier, among others) also invented this good-value, classic bistro. The setting is cozy but chic, and the menu features fine fare such as pan-fried halibut covered with thinly sliced potatoes, and traditional roast leg of lamb. The three-course dinner is a steal at C$33, with many choices for appetizers and mains. The good wine list focuses on Ontario. If you're heading to a Canadian Stage Company show or to the Sony Centre, you could not pick a better place to dine.

4 Front St. E. (at Yonge St.). © **416/860-0086.** www.oliverbonacini.com. Reservations strongly recommended. Main courses C$18–C$35. AE, DC, MC, V. Mon–Fri noon–2:30pm; Mon–Sat 5–10pm. Subway: Union or King.

Gilead Bistro & Café ★★★ 🍴🍷 CANADIAN/BISTRO After years of building a restaurant empire and then scaling back, star chef Jamie Kennedy is back behind the stove at this small, beautiful bistro. In other words, the food is sublime. Menus change daily and draw inspiration from local and seasonal ingredients. (Kennedy is a pioneering locavore.) Come for a light breakfast of fresh-baked pastries and organic yogurt; at lunch, try the chef's famous, thyme-scented frites alongside impossibly light battered whitefish. At dinner, the more sophisticated menu is a showcase for Kennedy's classical French training: *gallantine* of chicken, pork confit, succulent duck breast, delicately handled vegetables, soups that sing, and fine desserts. Wines are local, including some from Kennedy's own vineyard. Finding your way can be tricky: It's in a tiny alley in Corktown.

4 Gilead Place. © **647/288-0680.** www.jamiekennedy.ca. Reservations accepted for dinner & for parties of 6 or more at brunch. Main courses C$6–C$26. AE, DC, MC, V. Mon 8am–5:30pm; Tues–Sat 8am–11pm; Sun 10am–3pm. Subway: King, then a streetcar E to Trinity St. & walk 1 block E to Gilead Place.

Guu Izakaya ★★★ JAPANESE   It's loud, fun and chaotic—and the bright and delicious food keeps drawing crowds in spite of notoriously long lineups. A great selection of small-plate dishes is served in a pub-like atmosphere—an *izakaya* is a Japanese bar that serves food. Highlights include seared seafood, perfect pork belly, great noodles and sizzling hot pots. A second location on Bloor St West, Guu Sakabar, offers the same fine fare but in a quieter setting (559 Bloor St W.; © **647/343-1101**).

398 Church St. © **416/977-0999.** www.guu-izakaya.com/toronto. No reservations accepted. Small plates C$3.50–C$8. AE, DC, MC, V. Mon–Thurs5–11:30pm; Fri–Sat 4pm–midnight; Sun 4–11:30pm. Subway: College.

Hiro Sushi SUSHI   Take a seat at the bar, as many sushi aficionados do, and enjoy the spectacle of watching star chef Hiro Yoshida create beauty in front of your eyes. Pick from the master chef's selection of sushi and sashimi for a memorable experience. Soups are also inspired, and tempura is light as air.

171 King St. St. E. (at Jarvis St.). © **416/304-0550.** Main courses C$20–C$30. AE, DC, MC, V. Mon–Fri noon–2:30pm; Mon–Sat 6:30–10:30pm. Subway: King.

Ruby WatchCo. ★★★ BISTRO   Star chef Lynn Crawford, formerly of Four Seasons in Toronto and New York, teamed with Michelin-starred chef Lola Kirk to create a unique dining experience: There's one prix-fixe dinner offered nightly with four courses—no choices—and the main ingredients are supplied by local purveyors. At C$49 a head, the price might seem high, but given that the food is stellar and the atmosphere convivial, and the chefs work attentively on all details, the risky venture is proving a hit. Don't try to visit without a reservation.

730 Queen St. E. (at Broadview Ave.). © **416/465-0100.** www.rubywatchco.ca. Reservations required. Prix-fixe menu C$49. AE, MC, V. Tues–Sat 6–11pm. Subway: Broadview, then a streetcar S to Queen St. E.

Moderate

Edward Levesque's Kitchen ★★ BISTRO   An early arrival to the now-popular, once-empty Leslieville, this casual diner and bistro emphasizes local and organic products that up the quality overall. The burgers are good and are made fresh, as are the generous salads; breakfasts are excellent, including eggs poached in tomato sauce and fine frittatas. Bistro fare includes succulent leg of lamb, veggie risotto, and lovely desserts, including house-made pies.

1290 Queen St. E. © **416/465-3600.** www.edwardlevesque.ca. Reservations accepted for dinner. Main courses C$15–C$24. AE, MC, V. Sat & Sun 9am–3pm; Thurs & Fri 11:30am–2:30pm; Tues–Sat 5:30–10pm. Subway: Queen, then a streetcar E to Leslie St.

Tomi-Kro MEDITERRANEAN/ASIAN   Another Leslieville neighborhood haunt, this warm and friendly spot serves up fine Mediterranean-Asian fusion fare. John Coronius, a former partner in Lolita's Lust, named this (in Greek) "the little place." A bold sense of fun greets you at the door: lamps covered in hearts, blaring music, and nonsense declarations on the menu. The food, thankfully, is usually more serious. Pairings include octopus with sake.

1214 Queen St. E. (at Leslie St.). © **416/463-6677.** Main courses C$18–C$26. AE, DC, MC, V. Mon–Wed 6–10pm; Thurs–Sat 6–11pm. Subway: Queen, then a streetcar E to Leslie St.

Starfish SEAFOOD   Toronto has a thing for bivalves: There's a wealth of excellent oyster houses around town. Owner Patrick McMurray is a world-champion oyster-shucker, and he knows his goods. Stop by for some beautiful oysters or sample the excellent fish and chips, perfect prawns, or more substantial fare including poached and grilled fish and seafood. Beers and wines are well selected, and the ambience is cheerful.

100 Adelaide St. E. (at Church St.). ✆ **416/366-7827.** www.starfishoysterbed.com. Main courses C$18–C$35. AE, DC, MC, V. Mon–Fri noon–3pm; Mon–Sat 5–11pm. Subway: King.

Inexpensive

Mi Mi Restaurant VIETNAMESE   Authentic Vietnamese is the name of the game at this family-run spot, where locals go for fine barbecued meats, delicate seafood, well-done rice and noodle dishes, fine pho soups, and inspired rice rolls. The vibe is fun and relaxed; it may take a while to get a seat or for dishes to arrive, but it's worth the wait.

688 Gerrard St. E. (at Broadview Ave.). ✆ **416/778-5948.** Main courses C$5–C$17. No credit cards. Mon, Tues, Thurs & Fri 10am–10pm; Wed noon–10pm; Sat & Sun 10am–10:30pm. Subway: Broadview, then a streetcar S to Gerrard St.

MIDTOWN

Very Expensive

C5 ★★★ BISTRO/CANADIAN   The renovation of the Royal Ontario Museum remains controversial, but there's little argument that this beautiful restaurant, which is located on the top level and is headed by chef Ted Corrado, is worth a visit. The skylights and crisscrossing window segments provide a gorgeous view of the city. More importantly, the modern and chic dining room is host to fine dining with a distinct local flavor.

At the Royal Ontario Museum, 100 Queen's Park. ✆ **416/586-7928.** www.c5restaurant.ca. Reservations recommended for dinner. Main courses C$26–C$45. AE, DC, MC, V. Tues–Sat 11:30am–2:30pm; Thurs–Sat 5:30–10pm. Subway: Museum or Bay.

Mistura ★★★ ITALIAN   Owner-chef Massimo Capra, with his handlebar moustache and million-watt smile, is a fixture around town. With partner Paolo Paolini, he runs one of the city's best Italian restaurants. The risottos are, for starters, quite perfect, which is a testament to the kitchen's talent. There are handmade pastas, such as buckwheat noodles with pulled duck *ragu,* and entrees, including a C$56 Kobe beef steak, are top-notch. Sexy in decor, the place is great for romantic dinners, but it also caters to business clientele and family affairs. Service is pro, the wine list a lesson in fine Italian vintages (with a lot of New World wines, too). Upstairs is the more modest Sopra Supper Lounge, with equally fine fare and often live music.

265 Davenport Rd. ✆ **416/515-0009.** www.mistura.ca. Reservations recommended. Main courses C$22–C$56. AE, DC, MC, V. Mon–Wed 5:30–10pm; Thurs–Sat 5:30–11pm. Subway: Bay.

Expensive

earth ★★★ 🎁 BISTRO/INTERNATIONAL   Globe Bistro's (see p. 90) team has moved to Rosedale, and the news is good: Prices are trimmed, and the attractive dining room and lounge are hopping with locals who love chef Kevin McKenna's culinary talent and owner Ed Ho's gracious touch. Together, they share a serious commitment

Where to Eat in Midtown & Uptown

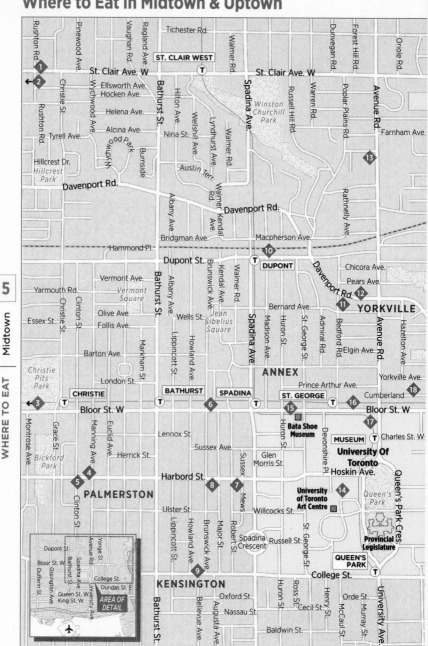

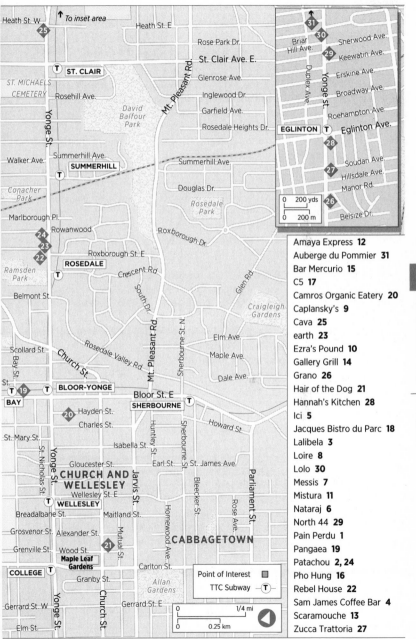

Amaya Express **12**
Auberge du Pommier **31**
Bar Mercurio **15**
C5 **17**
Camros Organic Eatery **20**
Caplansky's **9**
Cava **25**
earth **23**
Ezra's Pound **10**
Gallery Grill **14**
Grano **26**
Hair of the Dog **21**
Hannah's Kitchen **28**
Ici **5**
Jacques Bistro du Parc **18**
Lalibela **3**
Loire **8**
Lolo **30**
Messis **7**
Mistura **11**
Nataraj **6**
North 44 **29**
Pain Perdu **1**
Pangaea **19**
Patachou **2, 24**
Pho Hung **16**
Rebel House **22**
Sam James Coffee Bar **4**
Scaramouche **13**
Zucca Trattoria **27**

Point of Interest ■
TTC Subway —(T)—

5

WHERE TO EAT | Midtown

to local foods, so produce is local and seasonal. Meats are sourced from nearby farms and butchered on-site, and you can order your flesh by the ounce. Smart. The wood-burning oven is used to cook beautiful flatbreads and more, including a scrumptious suckling pig. A long list of wines by the glass, some local, and homey desserts round out the experience.

1055 Yonge St. (at Roxborough St. E.). © **416/551-9890.** www.globeearth.ca. Reservations required. Main courses C$17–C$25. AE, DC, MC, V. Mon–Fri 11:30am–11pm; Sat & Sun 11am–11pm. Subway: Rosedale.

Ici ★★ BISTRO/FRENCH When J. P. Challet, a popular and highly talented chef about town, landed at this neighborhood bistro with partner Jennifer Decorte, the news was welcome: This strip of Harbord Street needed just such a spot. A fight with the city to get a liquor license and other problems nearly ended the plans, but Ici won, and so did those who have come here frequently to dine. It's one of those places people treat as a home-away-from-home, where service is friendly (but professional), the room is warm and lively, and the food is delicious, a cut above bistro fare with just enough inventiveness and levity to pleasantly surprise. They call it Cuisine Nouveau Classique: Lobster thermidor is reinvented with a bit of spice and beef bourguignon topped with an onion tartlet. Desserts, mousses, and soufflés, are divine. Book ahead: There are only 24 seats, and they're in high demand.

538 Manning Ave. (at Harbord St.). © **416/536-0079.** www.jpco.ca. Reservations required. Main courses $14–$32. AE, MC, V. Wed–Sat 5:50–11pm. Subway: Museum, then the Harbord bus W to Manning.

Pangaea ★★★ INTERNATIONAL In a neighborhood with few good places to eat—it's all about work or shopping here—this truly delightful, high-end restaurant hops with chic regulars at lunch and dinner. Open for 15 years, the restaurant's chef/co-owner team of Martin Kouprie and Peter Geary deliver consistent elegance with fine food, attentive service, and a stellar cellar. The tone of the place is muted, even conservative, but behind the scenes, Kouprie's adventurous streak makes for an unusual selection of wild foods; think wild-caught fish (the restaurant is certified by Ocean Wise for its sustainable practices), wild mushrooms, wild berries—whatever is in season and inspires the chef.

1221 Bay St. © **416/920-2323.** www.pangaearestaurant.com. Reservations recommended. Main courses C$29–C$44. AE, DC, MC, V. Mon–Sat 11:30am–11:30pm. Subway: Bay.

Moderate

Bar Mercurio ★ ITALIAN There's something quintessentially Italian about this casual trattoria (it's not a bar) that stays open from breakfast through to late suppers. You can come for an espresso and brioche, return for excellent pizzas made in the wood-burning oven at lunch and—why not?—stroll back for dinner and sample the signature beef medallion with crab or some fine pastas and salads. Whatever time of day, linger on the noisy patio or inside (often equally boisterous); take your time. Across the street is the stylish (and more subdued) L'Espresso (© **416/585-2233**), good for brunch and a great deal for lunch.

270 Bloor St. W. (at St. George St.). © **416/960-38770.** Main courses C$14–C$32. AE, MC, V. Mon–Sat 7am–11pm. Subway: St. George.

Jacques Bistro du Parc ★ FRENCH It's a rarity: a Yorkville restaurant that has nothing trendy or pretentious about it. Husband-and-wife Jacques and Martine Sorin have been faithfully running this charming little brasserie for 35 years, and little has changed, or indeed, has needed to. The omelets are perfectly cooked and properly buttery, salads are fresh and generous (particularly the niçoise), and quiches are very good, too. On a bitter day, the French onion soup is as warm and welcoming as the place itself.

126A Cumberland St. ☎ **416/961-1893.** www.jacquesbistro.com. Reservations recommended at lunch & on weekends. Main courses C$16–C$32. AE, MC, V. Mon–Sat 11:30am–3pm & 5–10:30pm. Subway: Bay.

Loire ★★ FRENCH   For a while, this pretty bistro was too hot to handle: It was tough to get in, and sometimes service came with an attitude. But things have lightened up, and it's now a convivial spot for fine and sometimes inventive French fare. Chef Jean-Charles Dupoire and top sommelier Sylvain Brissonnet are clearly enjoying their hard-earned accolades. Both hail from the Loire region, so expect French classics and plenty of beautiful wines and perfect pairings. Dupoire is stretching a bit, adding fusion touches to standards, and to good ends. Lake Erie whitefish comes with a chili-cornmeal crust and a garlic comfit, lemon polenta, and salsa *verde*. Regulars opt for the burgers, lamb, or beef.

119 Harbord St. ☎ **416/850-8330.** www.loirerestaurant.ca. Reservations recommended. Main courses C$17–C$27. AE, MC, V. Tues–Fri noon–2:30pm; Tues–Sat 5:30–10pm. Subway: Spadina, then the LRT S to Harbord St.

Messis ★★ 🍴 BISTRO/INTERNATIONAL   Nearly 20 years old, this simple bistro is Eugene Shewchuk's vision realized: He wanted to create an accessible and pleasant spot with good food and fair prices, a place where cooks can happily eat. The menu changes frequently, keeping as its mainstays Italian pastas and Mediterranean meat dishes, and ranging into Asia, too. Thin-crust pizzas are kept simple, and mains tend to stick to a small selection of two meats, one fish. It's all very good. To boot, it was one of the first fine restaurants along the Harbord Street strip, which now has good options from one block to the next. The California-dominated wine list is as reasonably priced as the food.

97 Harbord St. ☎ **416/920-2186.** www.messisrestaurant.ca. Reservations accepted. Main courses C$13–C$25. AE, MC, V. Sun–Thurs 5:30–10pm; Fri & Sat 5:30–11pm. Subway: Spadina, then the LRT S to Harbord St.

Inexpensive

Caplansky's 🎒 ☺ DELICATESSEN   Montréal's smoked meat is rightfully famous. Now, Toronto has a fantastic version to call its own. Zane Caplansky's fatty, um, marbled pastrami-on-rye is the main attraction: The hand-cut slices of pink, salty goodness are also featured in hash browns, with eggs, in a burger, and numerous other worthy ways. Choose your fat content: lean, medium, or full-on. Students and profs, foodies and families all make pilgrimages. There are other deli delights at this spacious new spot with a great patio. Try the pickled tongue, the lox, or if you're feeling sanctimonious, the salad (protein provided by only chick peas). The kids' menu includes kosher hot dogs.

356 College St. W. ☎ **416/500-3852.** http://caplanskys.com. Main courses C$10–C$13. V. Sun–Tues 10am–10pm; Wed–Sat 10am–11pm. Subway: Osgoode, then the College streetcar W to Brunswick Ave.

Camros Organic Eatery 🎒 HEALTH FOOD/LIGHT FARE/VEGETARIAN   Yonge and Bloor streets are a major intersection, yet the food options nearby are mostly dreadful; in other words, mostly fast-food chains. But this terrific little find is a great alternative. Saffron and cinnamon scent the air: a signal to the fact this is Persian cuisine. The emphasis is on health-conscious eating; every dish is vegetarian and made from certified organic produce. Try the cabbage roll stuffed with nutty brown rice, bright peppermint, sweet tomatoes, and tarragon; or the *ghorme sabzi,* a satisfying savory stew of kidney beans and spinach. There's more to love about this place, including comprehensive ingredient lists to help people with food allergies and takeout containers that are 100% biodegradable.

25 Hayden St. © **416/960-0723.** www.camroseatery.com. Reservations not accepted. 2-item combo C$7.50. MC, V. Mon–Fri 11:30am–7:30pm. Subway: Yonge/Bloor.

Lalibela ☺ ETHIOPIAN   This is delicious Ethiopian cuisine with plenty of vegetarian options, rich with flavor and a friendly vibe, too. It's a winning combination; little wonder a second location has opened up (1405 Danforth Ave.; © **416/645-0486**). If you don't know your *yemiser wat* from your *asa gulashe,* have no fear: The staff will guide you to what you're looking for and prepare custom tasting platters. It's great for kids, too, with a special menu of small tasting portions or, for fussy eaters, mac-and-cheese and fries.

869 Bloor St. W. © **416/535-6615.** www.lalibelaethiopianrestaurant.com. Main courses C$5–C$12. V. Daily 10am–2am. Subway: Ossington, then walk 1 block E.

Nataraj ★ INDIAN   There's usually a bit of a wait for a table, especially at dinnertime—Nataraj's cuisine is popular with Annex residents and university students given its good value and better-than-fair Northern Indian menus. The decor is tired, but this isn't a place to linger anyway. Line up, sit down, order curries, tandoori chicken, rich veggie dishes such as the *chana* masala (chickpeas cooked with potatoes, tomatoes, onions, and spices) and the *saag paneer* (house-made cottage cheese cooked in onion and spinach), and be on your merry way. The tandoor-baked breads are good for scooping up the special relishes, such as the *kachumbor* (cucumber, tomato, and onion marinated in lime juice).

394 Bloor St. W. © **416/928-2925.** Reservations not accepted. Main courses C$9–C$13. AE, DC, MC, V. Mon–Fri noon–2:30pm; daily 5–10:30pm. Subway: Spadina.

Pho Hung VIETNAMESE   Students love the generous portions and mainstream tastes of this bright Vietnamese soup-and-noodle spot. Favorites include the lemongrass-scented broth, beef noodle soup, filling rice dishes, spring rolls, and the Vietnamese milkshakes. There is a second location in Chinatown, at 350 Spadina Ave. (© **416/593-4274**).

200 Bloor St. W. © **416/963-5080.** Main courses C$8–C$12. V. Mon–Sat 11am–10pm. Subway: St. George or Museum.

THE DANFORTH/THE EAST END

The general theme along the Danforth has long been Greek, although today there is more variety: good pubs, bars, restaurants, and lounges line the busy thoroughfare. You can still come for good and middling (but cheap) Greek, too.

Expensive

Aravind ★★ INDIAN   There's a thriving Little India strip in Toronto with lots of friendly and cheap eateries and a number of fair curry joints, but this is a unique haven of more sophisticated southern Indian cuisine—specifically, Keralan—executed by the talented Raj Kozhikott and his son, Aravind Kozhikott. Local and Canadian ingredients are proudly sourced, and the combination brings standards such as mulligatawny soup, masala *dosas,* and banana-leaf-wrapped fish to new heights. The

Where to Eat on the Danforth & The East End

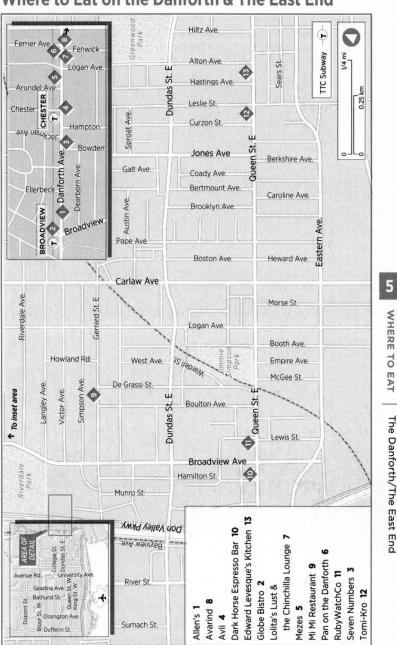

Allen's **1**
Avarind **8**
Avli **4**
Dark Horse Espresso Bar **10**
Edward Levesque's Kitchen **13**
Globe Bistro **2**
Lolita's Lust &
the Chinchilla Lounge **7**
Mezes **5**
Mi Mi Restaurant **9**
Pan on the Danforth **6**
RubyWatchCo **11**
Seven Numbers **3**
Tomi-Kro **12**

portions are generous, but not for sharing, and it's best to bring an appetite for starters, mains, and even desserts such as delicate fruit purees. The modern dining room is uninspired, the atmosphere one of a considered, family venture. Carnivores be forewarned: The menu is vegetarian- and fish-based.

596 Danforth Ave (near Pape Ave). ⓒ **647/346-2766.** Reservations recommended. Main courses C$14–C$21. AE, DC, MC, V. Sun 11am–2pm; Tues–Sun 5:30–10pm. Subway: Pape, then a short walk west.

Globe Bistro ★★ BISTRO   There's a chic dining room, a cool bar, a breezy patio, and some very fine cooking at this popular neighborhood bistro. Owner Ed Ho and chef Kevin McKenna have created a go-to destination with staying power, in part due to a great wine cellar and generous deals, such as half-price bottles on Sunday. The vibe is fun, the dishes sometimes stellar, such as the Muscovy duck breast and elk loin. You can also make a meal of the many tantalizing starters. There is a definite local-and-seasonal bent that is genuine.

24 Danforth Ave. ⓒ **416/466-2000.** www.globebistro.com. Reservations recommended. Main courses C$19–C$29. AE, DC, MC, V. Mon–Fri 11:30am–2pm, Sun 11am–2pm; daily 6–11pm. Subway: Broadview.

Lolita's Lust & the Chinchilla Lounge ★ AMERICAN/BISTRO   Relaxed, fun, and accessible, this restaurant and lounge offers a break from the Danforth's Greek theme with pretty good food. Lolita's Burger has a reputation as irresistible: bacon, white cheddar, and caramelized onions top a mile-high beef patty. Desserts are popular, too, with safe bets including bread pudding with caramel and chocolate sauce. The upstairs Chinchilla Lounge is often booked for private parties, but when it's not, it's a hopping spot for martinis.

513 Danforth Ave. ⓒ **416/465-1751.** www.lolitaslust.ca. Reservations recommended. Main courses C$15–C$29. AE, MC, V. Daily 5pm–2am. Subway: Chester.

Moderate

Allen's ★★ AMERICAN   This time-honored pub, burger joint, and casual dining room takes its name and inspiration from the institution in New York City. Take note of the excellent beef, lamb, and pork—the heart of any great burger—which is sourced from local farms and then butchered and ground on-site. Pastas, salads, and mains are all consistently good. Brunch, especially when the lovely patio is open, is a treat. Desserts are comfort food: pies and homey sweets. The selection of beers—on tap and in bottles—is another draw. The fine wine list is focused on local.

143 Danforth Ave. (at Broadview Ave.). ⓒ **416/463-3086.** www.allens.to. Main courses C$10–C$26. AE, DC, MC, V. Mon–Fri 11:30am–1am; Sat & Sun 11am–1am. Subway: Broadview.

Avli ★ GREEK   Always noisy, occasionally raucous, this taverna serves up some of the best Greek standards on the Danforth—non-greasy, thoughtfully prepared, and carefully seasoned. *Meze* starters are de rigueur: *kopanisti* (spicy feta with peppers) and hummus, for those who want cold food; grilled octopus and steamed mussels, for those who like it hot. The half chicken stuffed with cashews, dates, apples, and rice is exquisite, and the meat *moussaka* is the best around. Like the menu, the wine list is both extensive and very reasonably priced.

401 Danforth Ave. ⓒ **416/461-9577.** www.avlirestaurant.com. Reservations recommended. Main courses C$12–C$22. AE, DC, MC, V. Daily noon–midnight. Subway: Chester.

Pan on the Danforth ★ GREEK   Pan feels like a spot for a celebration: Staff are friendly; weekend nights, in particular, are busy and humming; and the vibe is all Mediterranean warmth. This long-established eatery serves Greek classics—dips and starters are especially conventional—but the quality is good and often a notch above competitors on the strip. Portions are generous, and fish and lamb dominate. The well-chosen wine list favors the New World. The crowd is fairly sophisticated, which may explain the cryptic message over the bar: YOU'VE DONE IT ALREADY. On weekend evenings, diners are treated to live music: traditional Greek bouzouki on Fridays and jazz piano on Saturdays (there's also a belly dancer who turns up for performances on other evenings, too).

516 Danforth Ave. © **416/466-8158.** www.panonthedanforth.com. Reservations recommended. Main courses C$16–C$25. AE, MC, V. Sun–Thurs noon–11pm; Fri & Sat noon–midnight. Subway: Chester or Pape.

Inexpensive

Mezes GREEK   This sophisticated space doles out exactly what it promises. *Mezes* are light snacks meant to keep you going until it's time for dinner. Still, it's worth spoiling your appetite to indulge here (especially given the often pedestrian offerings on the strip). Choices range from grilled calamari and octopus to spicy eggplant dip and leek pie. Save room for the honey-sweet baklava. Bonus: There's a heated patio, so you can dine alfresco, even when the weather is less than balmy.

456 Danforth Ave. © **416/778-5150.** www.mezes.ca. Reservations accepted till 7:30pm. Appetizers C$4–C$10. AE, MC, V. Mon–Thurs 11am–midnight; Fri & Sat 11am–1am; Sun noon–midnight. Subway: Chester.

Seven Numbers ☺ ITALIAN   This super-popular, Italian family trattoria began life on Eglinton Avenue West, and then took hold on the Danforth. So, whether east or west, everyone gets to enjoy the generous, well-prepared and mamma-inspired fare such as grilled veggies, fresh pastas, flavorful salads, and Italian standards like *bistecca*. Rosa Marinuzzi runs the business with her sons. The cheerful atmosphere is sincere, not a show: pure, simple fun.

307 Danforth Ave. (at Broadview Ave.). © **416/322-5183.** www.sevennumbers.com. Main courses C$7–C$17. AE, DC, MC, V. Tues–Sat 5–11pm; Sun 5–10pm. Subway: Broadview.

UPTOWN

This area is too large to be considered a neighborhood, stretching as it does from north of Davenport Road to Steeles Avenue. While it doesn't have the concentration of restaurants that the downtown area enjoys, a number of stellar options make the trip north worthwhile.

Very Expensive

Auberge du Pommier ★★★ 🍴 FRENCH   Don't have time to drop by your French country house this weekend? Then this cozy, fine-dining room that exudes Provençal-style charm is a ready alternative. Chef Jason Bartenger combines classical French technique with the best of Canadian ingredients. Service is equally refined, as is the extensive wine list. Creamy lobster and white-bean soup, and baked artichokes stuffed with French goat cheese, are lovely starters. Entrees, such as pan-seared scallops with braised oxtail in a cabernet *jus* keep up the pace. Crème brûlée isn't always on the dessert menu (which changes with the season, just like the regular menu), but be sure to order it when available.

4150 Yonge St. © **416/222-2220.** www.oliverbonacini.com. Reservations strongly recommended. Main courses C$36–C$44. AE, DC, DISC, MC, V. Mon–Fri 11:45am–2:30pm; Mon–Thurs 5–9pm, Fri & Sat 5:30–9:30pm. Subway: York Mills.

North 44 ★★★ INTERNATIONAL   The soft lighting and strategically situated mirrors wrap the dining room—and its occupants—in a lovely glow. Upscale regulars succumb to the seduction of a three-course meal. Celebrity chef Mark McEwan's menu, which changes with the seasons, borrows from Mediterranean, American, and Asian sources, with inspired results. On the list of main courses, you might find grilled veal tenderloin with orange peppercorns, toasted barley, and root veggies, or roasted Muscovy duck breast with orange-soy marinade and foie gras. There are always a few pasta and pizza choices. The wine list is loftily priced and built to suit the high-end fare. Service is seamless.

2537 Yonge St. ✆ **416/487-4897.** www.north44restaurant.com. Reservations required. Main courses C$31–C$53. AE, DC, MC, V. Mon–Sat 5–11pm. Subway: Eglinton.

Scaramouche ★★★ 🍴 INTERNATIONAL   Tucked into a tony midtown apartment building with beautiful views over the city, Scaramouche isn't easy to find. But it's worth the effort. Chef Keith Froggett and maitre d' Carl Corte have been quietly perfecting one of the city's finest restaurants for more than 25 years. Understated and elegant, the menus are laden with luxe ingredients like caviar, foie gras, truffles, and oysters; main dishes include venison loin wrapped in smoked bacon and a rich, red-wine glaze. Top pastry chef Joanne Yolles has returned after years at Pangaea (see p. 86), so the sweets are equally stunning. The wine list has a broad reach, and there's a nice selection of cognacs. The formal dining room, which is best for special occasions, is complemented by the adjoining casual pasta bar and grill.

1 Benvenuto Place (off Avenue Rd.). ✆ **416/961-8011.** www.scaramoucherestaurant.com. Reservations required. Main courses C$34–C$47. AE, DC, MC, V. Dining room Mon–Sat 5:30–10pm; pasta bar Mon–Fri 5:30–10:30pm, Sat 5:30–11pm. Subway: St. Clair, then a streetcar W to Avenue Rd. & walk 4 blocks S to Edmund Ave.

Expensive

Cava ★★★ SPANISH/TAPAS   Chef Chris McDonald is a local legend for his culinary prowess, which was honed at his formal (and former) Avalon restaurant. Now with partner and chef Doug Penfold, he is the driving force at Cava, where inventive, small-plate dishes—sometimes daring, but always delicious—offer Iberian-inspired menus with salt cod cakes, beef cheeks, and more. House-cured charcuterie is not to be missed: think smoky chorizo and dried salamis, plus Iberico ham hand-cut to order (a skill in itself). There are more than 20 well-selected wines offered by the glass for pairing. The vibe is delightfully low-key, although professionalism informs everything, from service to sweets. And speaking of desserts, Xococava (✆ **416/979-9916**), next door, is worth a visit on its own for rich, artisan chocolates, silken ice creams, and more, all made on-site.

1560 Yonge St. ✆ **416/979-9918.** www.cavarestaurant.ca. Reservations strongly recommended. Tapas plates C$3.50–C$18. AE, DC, MC, V. Daily 5–10pm. Subway: St. Clair.

Moderate

Grano ★★ ☺ ITALIAN   While Toronto has no shortage of Italian eateries, few spots have as much ambience as Grano. Thanks to owners Robert and Lucia Martella—he's in the front; she's in the kitchen below—this is an institution for celebrating the joys of Italian culture and Canada's inspired Italo riches. The busy trattoria sprawls over several dining areas, including a small and quiet courtyard at the back that is heavenly on sunny days. This high-energy spot attracts couples, friends, and families with bambini in tow. The cooking is hearty, with lovely pastas, breads baked on-site, tender *osso buco,* and ricotta gnocchi paired with shrimp in a white-wine sauce. A nice feature: You can order many dishes in appetizer-sized portions or more substantial portions for sharing. The desserts are a delight—you must try the white chocolate and raspberry tart at least once.

2035 Yonge St. ℰ **416/440-1986.** www.grano.ca. Reservations recommended. Main courses C$14–C$24. AE, DC, MC, V. Mon–Fri 9:30am–11pm; Sat 9am–11pm. Subway: Davisville or Eglinton.

Lolo ★ ✦ BISTRO   Lolo is airy and bright, with white walls and a relaxed ambience. More importantly, the menu—and the prices—are refreshingly down-to-earth. The mains are bistro classics, from the roasted Cornish hen (updated with a citrus-basil glaze) to the grilled rib-eye steak with green-peppercorn sauce and crispy frites. In addition to the a la carte menu, a prix-fixe option serves up three courses for a mere C$25. All of the desserts—including a fine lemon tart—are made on the premises.

2590 Yonge St. ℰ **416/483-2590.** Reservations recommended. Main courses C$15–C$25; prix-fixe menu C$25. AE, DC, MC, V. Daily noon–3pm & 5–10pm. Subway: Eglinton, then walk 6 blocks N to Albertus Ave.

Zucca Trattoria ★★★ ITALIAN   Inviting in spirit and truly Italian in the kitchen, this pretty trattoria has been winning quiet accolades from fans for more than a decade. It's chef Andrew Milne-Allan's baby, and most nights, the chef is at the stove. *Agnolotti* and other fresh pastas made by the maestro are consistently great. There are meaty ragouts, poppy-seed sauces, plenty of delicate vegetables, and entrees that feature local purveyors such as the fine Cumbrae Farms. (Milne-Allan can be seen shopping at farmers markets throughout the year.) The grilled whole fish, which changes according to what's fresh, also proves a standout. Desserts are restrained and lovely.

2150 Yonge St. (at Berwick Ave.). ℰ **416/488-5774.** Reservations recommended. Main courses C$16–C$36. AE, DC, MC, V. Daily 5:30–10pm. Subway: Eglinton or Davisville.

Inexpensive

Hannah's Kitchen LIGHT FARE   National magazines and newspapers have published several of its recipes, but this cubbyhole-like eatery remains defiantly low-key. Diners seat themselves at wooden banquettes or tiny tables. The menu includes many pasta dishes, both cold (pesto *radiatore* salad with chicken and pine nuts is the top pick) and hot (the penne *arrabiata* is the spiciest in town), with three or four daily specials. Occasional forays into the exotic include a few Indonesian rice dishes and the ever-popular pad Thai. Desserts are a must, so check out the selection behind the counter on your way in.

2221 Yonge St. ℰ **416/481-0185.** Reservations not accepted. Main courses C$7–C$14. MC, V. Mon–Fri 10am–10pm. Subway: Eglinton.

Pain Perdu ✦ FRENCH/LIGHT FARE   It's a sit-down bakery and lovely daytime spot for fine quiches, cheesy sandwiches like a fine croque monsieur, and a wealth of lovely pastries. The owner is from the Basque region, so also expect a wicked gateaux Basque, which is a buttery, custard tart infused with anise. The namesake dish is a kind of Gallic French toast baked with cream and topped with fruit.

736 St. Clair Ave. W. (at Christie St.). ℰ **416/656-7246.** Main courses C$5–C$7. DC, MC, V. Tues–Fri 7am–7pm; Sat 7am–5pm; Sun 8am–4pm. Subway: St. Clair, then a streetcar W to Christie St.

Rebel House LIGHT FARE   Friendly service combines with better-than-average pub grub and an impressive selection of microbrews (almost entirely Canadian) to make for a popular neighborhood spot. In summer, the gorgeous patio is a bonus. The food isn't exotic, but it's good: The spinach and apple salad is fresh, the Québécois *poutine* fine with beer drinking, and the steak frites decent. Most main courses are priced below C$15.

1068 Yonge St. ✆ **416/927-0704.** www.rebelhouse.ca. Reservations not accepted. Main courses C$8–C$23. AE, MC, V. Restaurant Mon–Sat 11:30am–11pm, Sun 11:30am–10pm; bar Mon–Sat 11:30am–1am, Sun 11:30am–11pm. Subway: Rosedale.

OUT OF TOWN

Toronto is a sprawling city, and as it has expanded, restaurants have cropped up in formerly out-of-the-way regions. If you have a car, you might want to head out of town for some great dining just an hour or two beyond the city limits.

Very Expensive

Eigensinn Farm & Haisai Restaurant ★★★ 🛍 CANADIAN/INTERNA-TIONAL   Michael Stadtländer, perhaps the most famous and celebrated chef working in Canada today, is an artist. He's always on the move, with new art installations, ongoing documentary series, and events that promote the Canadian culinary scene. Last year, in addition to the beloved Eigensinn Farm restaurant, run by he and his wife Nobuyo Stadtländer, the couple opened Haisai in the nearby town of Singhampton. So Stadtländer fans have a choice: Haisai on weekends or Eigensinn on weekday evenings. Briefly, Haisai is a small restaurant and bakery and Eigensinn is the family farmstead with an intimate dining room. The focus is über-local, and had been long before it was trendy, and the cooking is heaven. Dishes include braised meats, poached fish, produce from the farm rendered perfect, exquisite desserts, and more. At both restaurants, the simplicity and friendly-relaxed vibe are deceptive; techniques are masterful. *Note:* BYOB at the Farm.

Eigensinn: 449357 10th Concession, Singhampton. ✆ **519/922-3128.** Reservations required. Prix fixe menu from C$275. AE, DC, MC, V. Call for hours of operation; hours change w/the season.

Haisai: 794079 Country Rd., RR2, Singhampton. ✆ **705/445-2748.** www.haisairestaurantbakery.com. Reservations required for dinner. AE, DC, MC, V. Bakery items from C$4; Mains from C$45. Bakery: Wed–Sat 8:30am–6pm, Sun 9am–6pm; dinner: one seating Fri & Sat at 7pm.

Moderate

Ancaster Mill ★★ CONTINENTAL   The setting is lovely, so little wonder it's still a popular spot for weddings, banquets, and other events. Yet chef Jeff Crump has turned this old-time country spot into a go-to destination for Toronto diners who love hearty, honest fare that celebrates the best of the local season. Pigs are roasted whole, the lamb rack is quite perfect, vegetables are turned into gnocchi and rich sides, and the desserts are simply splendid.

548 Old Dundas Rd, Ancaster. ✆ **905/648-1828.** www.ancastermill.com. Reservations recommended. Main courses C$20–C$35. AE, MC, V. Tues–Sat 11:30am–10pm; Sun 9:30am–2:30pm & 5–9pm.

PRACTICAL INFORMATION

The Big Picture

Toronto delivers an enticing array of good places to eat, whatever pleases your palette. There's authentic Thai and Ethiopian, French bistros, an emerging Canadiana cuisine with a flare for wild foods, excellent Indian, Portuguese grills, Halal and Kosher, frenetic and fantastic Japanese, oodles of good Italian, and more. It's hard to find a

SWEET TREATS: TORONTO'S BEST dessert CAFES

I've got a serious sweet tooth, and to my mind, dessert should be its own food group. Here are some of the city's most delicious places to satisfy a sugar craving and do some people-watching at the same time.

Dufflet Pastries. 787 Queen St. W. (✆ **416/504-2870**). On menus around town, you'll sometimes see mention of "desserts by Dufflet." It's an institution: popular for everything from butter tarts to berry pies or three-tiered cakes heavy with icing and rich with flavor. The cafe also serves light fare.

Patachou. 1120 Yonge St., at Roxborough St. (✆ **416/927-1105**); 835 St. Clair Ave. W. (✆ **416/927-1105**). Toronto knew little about proper French pastries when this bakery opened almost 30 years ago, but this family-owned patisserie set the bar, and it has remained unchallenged since. Croissants are chewy inside, crisp and flaky on the outside; brioches are perfect; and a range of sweets—bright fruit tarts, deep chocolate sweets such as the éclair or rich opera cake—are outstanding. The chic yet friendly cafes also serve lovely continental breakfasts and fine lunches.

Senses Bakery. 2 Queen St. E. (✆ **416/364-7303**). The menu has some light, lunch-appropriate food, but the real draw is the divine collection of pastry confections and chocolates.

SOMA Chocolate. In the Distillery District, 55 Mill St. (✆ **416/815-7662**). Owners David Castellan and wife Cynthia Leung run the best chocolatier in town. Beans are carefully sourced from far-flung locales for fair-trade and organic certifications, with taste a factor above all. Then, in this micro-factory where the process is on view, the beans are roasted, turned into paste (which is where most chocolatiers begin their work), and spun into beautiful truffles, exquisite bars, irresistible (chocolate) cakes, cookies, and more. In summer, have a gelato. In winter, don't miss the house specialty, a *bicerin* (beech-er-een) made with melted chocolate, espresso, and warm milk. There's plenty to take away, too.

taste that Toronto can't satisfy, from greasy diners to organic vegan "bars," molecular gastronomy to good pub grub.

Many of the city's best restaurants offer second locales, such as mini empires from celebrity chefs Mark McEwan and Jamie Kennedy and the ever-expanding Oliver & Bonacini chain of a dozen destinations like Canoe, Auberge du Pommier, and the Bell Lightbox's Luma and Canteen. A love of the local, seasonal movement only gains in popularity each year, naturally inviting more wine lists that focus on Ontario VQA vintages from Niagara and Prince Edward County. And it's supplying some new discoveries, like the rustic Woodlot, the friendly neighborhood Ici, even Sicilian pizzerias like Libretto.

The new slate of luxury hotels has added some tantalizing tastes to a hotel-dining scene that in the recent past was exciting on the boutique front but pretty safe and institutional beyond. TOCA by Tom Brodi at the Ritz Carlton and Scarpetta at the Thompson Toronto are two favorites.

More good news: In comparison to other big cities, it all adds up to a fairly affordable feast. The bad news is that high taxes on food and alcohol—add a good 30%—put a dent in the budget, even if menu prices are generally fair. Oh, and Toronto has earned a reputation for a habit of snooty service: it's still true, but on the decline as the city's culinary scene matures.

Reservations

Whenever you can, book ahead if you're planning to dine at one of Toronto's top restaurants. That said, many of the hottest spots do not accept reservations for dinner. It's common for diners to arrive early, leave their name and cell-phone number at the door and skip out for a stroll or a drink until the table is ready. Many Toronto restaurants now accept reservations through **Open Table** (www.opentable.com)—check individual websites for details.

Dining Hours

Restaurant hours vary. Lunch is typically served from noon to 2pm; dinner begins around 6pm—the busiest window is 7pm to after 9pm, especially on weekends when two seatings are standard at the best restaurants. Reservations are recommended when accepted.

Tipping

The standard tip in Toronto calculates as 15%, although 20% is pretty common if it's been above average. Groups of six or more can anticipate an automatic added service charge of 15% to 20%—this serves as the tip and diners are not expected to leave an additional amount unless service was outstanding. Keep in mind that your bill will also include a 13% tax (HST, which stands for a "harmonized sales tax"). It all adds up to a good 30% hike to the menu prices. Also, wine and other alcoholic beverages tend to be pricey in part because the provincial government levies high taxes and also because restaurateurs often charge as high as a 30% markup. Some establishments let you bring your own and add a corkage fee.

RESTAURANTS BY CUISINE

The prices within each review refer to the cost in Canadian dollars of individual main courses, using the following categories: Very Expensive ($$$$), main courses at dinner average more than C$35; Expensive ($$$), C$25 to C$35; Moderate ($$), C$15 to C$25; and Inexpensive ($), C$15 and less. Restaurants are listed alphabetically at the end of the index in the back of this book.

AFRICAN
Lalibela (Midtown, $, p. 88)

AMERICAN
Allen's ★★ (The East End, $$, p. 90)
Bymark ★★ (Downtown West, $$$$, p. 69)
Jump Cafe & Bar ★★ (Downtown West, $$$, p. 74)
Lolita's Lust & the Chinchilla Lounge ★ (The East End, $$$, p. 90)

ASIAN
Café 668 ★ (Downtown West, $, p. 80)
Foxley ★★★ (Downtown West, $$$, p. 72)

Lee Lounge ★★★ (Downtown West, $$$, p. 74)
Tomi-Kro (Downtown East, $$, p. 82)

BISTRO
Biff's Bistro & Wine Bar ★★ (Downtown East, $$$, p. 81)
The Black Hoof & Hoof Café ★★★ (Downtown West, $$, p. 76)
Brassaii ★★ (Downtown West, $$$, p. 72)
Bymark ★★ (Downtown West, $$$$, p. 69)
C5 ★★★ (Midtown, $$$$, p. 83)

5

WHERE TO EAT | Restaurants by Cuisine

Delux ★★★ (Downtown West, $$, p. 76)

The Drake ★★ (Downtown West, $$, p. 76)

earth ★★★ (Midtown, $$$, p. 83)

Edward Levesque's Kitchen ★★ (Downtown East, $$, p. 82)

Foxley ★★ (Downtown West, $$$, p. 72)

Gallery Grill ★★ (Downtown West, $$, p. 77)

Gilead Bistro & Café ★★★ (Downtown East, $$$, p. 81)

Globe Bistro ★★ (The East End, $$$, p. 90)

Ici ★★ (Midtown, $$$, p. 86)

Jules Bistro (Downtown West, $, p. 80)

Le Sélect Bistro ★★ (Downtown West, $$$, p. 75)

Lolita's Lust & the Chinchilla Lounge ★ (The East End, $$$, p. 90)

Lolo ★ (Uptown, $$, p. 93)

Messis ★★ (Midtown, $$, p. 87)

Niagara Street Café ★★ (Downtown West, $$$, p. 75)

Ruby WatchCo. ★★★ (Downtown East, $$$, p. 82)

CANADIAN

C5 ★★★ (Midtown, $$$$, p. 83)

Canoe Restaurant & Bar ★★★ (Downtown West, $$$$, p. 70)

Eigensinn Farm ★★★ (Out of town, $$$$, p. 94)

Gilead Bistro & Café ★★★ (Downtown East, $$$, p. 81)

TOCA by Tom Brodi ★★ (Downtown West, $$$, p. 75)

Woodlot ★★★ (Downtown West, $$$, p. 76)

CHINESE

Lai Wah Heen ★★★ (Downtown West, $$$$, p. 70)

Lee Garden ★ (Downtown West, $$, p. 77)

Mother's Dumplings ★ (Downtown West, $, p. 81)

CONTINENTAL

Ancaster Mill ★★ (Out of town, $$, p. 94)

Gallery Grill ★★ (Downtown West, $$, p. 77)

TOCA by Tom Brodi ★★ (Downtown West, $$$, p. 75)

DELI

Caplansky's (Midtown, $, p. 87)

FRENCH

Auberge du Pommier ★★★ (Uptown, $$$$, p. 91)

Ici ★★★ (Midtown, $$$, p. 86)

Jacques Bistro du Parc ★ (Midtown, $$, p. 86)

Jules Bistro (Downtown West, $, p. 80)

Loire ★★ (Midtown, $$, p. 87)

Pain Perdu (Uptown, $, p. 93)

Patachou (Midtown, $$, p. 95)

GREEK

Avli ★ (The East End, $$, p. 90)

Mezes (The East End, $, p. 91)

Pan on the Danforth ★ (The East End, $$, p. 90)

HEALTH FOOD

Camros Organic Eatery (Midtown, $, p. 87)

INDIAN

Amaya Express ★ (Multiple locations, $, p. 79)

Aravind ★★ (The East End, $$$, p. 88)

Nataraj ★ (Midtown, $, p. 88)

INTERNATIONAL

Brassaii ★★ (Downtown West, $$$, p. 72)

earth ★★★ (Midtown, $$, p. 83)

Eigensinn Farm ★★★ (Out of town, $$$$, p. 94)

Messis ★★ (Midtown, $$, p. 87)

Pangaea ★★★ (Midtown, $$$, p. 86)

North 44 ★★★ (Uptown, $$$$, p. 92)

The Rivoli (Downtown West, $$, p. 78)

Scaramouche ★★★ (Uptown, $$$$, p. 92)

ITALIAN

Bar Mercurio ★ (Downtown West, $$, p. 86)

Buca ★★★ (Downtown West, $$$, p. 72)

Grano ★★ (Uptown, $$, p. 92)

The Local Kitchen and Wine Bar ★★ (Downtown West, $$, p. 77)

Mistura ★★★ (Midtown, $$$$, p. 83)

Pizzeria Libretto ★★ (Downtown West, $$, p. 78)

Seven Numbers (The East End, $, p. 91)

Terroni ★★ (Downtown West, $$, p. 78)

Trattoria Giancarlo ★★ (Downtown West, $$$, p. 75)

Tutti Matti ★★ (Downtown West, $$, p. 78)

Woodlot ★★★ (Downtown West, $$$, p. 76)

Zucca Trattoria ★★★ (Uptown, $$, p. 93)

JAPANESE/SUSHI

Ame ★★★ (Downtown West, $$, p. 70)

Ematei ★★ (Downtown West, $$, p. 77)

Hiro Sushi ★★ (Downtown East, $$$, p. 82)

LIGHT FARE

Amaya Express ★ (Multiple locations, $, p. 79)

Camros Organic Eatery (Midtown, $, p. 87)

Café Diplomatico (Downtown West, $, p. 80)

Caffé Brasiliano (Downtown West, $, p. 80)

Dufflet Pastries (Downtown West, $$, p. 95)

Great Cooks on Eight ★★ (Downtown West, $$, p. 77)

Hannah's Kitchen (Uptown, $, p. 93)

Pain Perdu ★ (Uptown, $$, p. 93)

Patachou (Midtown, $$, p. 95)

Rebel House (Uptown, $, p. 93)

Senses Bakery (Downtown East, $, p. 95)

SOMA Chocolate (The East End, $$, p. 95)

MEDITERRANEAN

Chiado ★★★ (Downtown West, $$$$, p. 70)

Tomi-Kro (Downtown East, $$, p. 82)

PIZZA

Buca ★★★ (Downtown West, $$$, p. 72)

Pizzeria Libretto ★★ (Downtown West, $$, p. 78)

Terroni ★★ (Downtown West, $$, p. 78)

PORTUGUESE

Caffé Brasiliano (Downtown West, $, p. 80)

SEAFOOD

Chiado ★★★ (Downtown West, $$$$, p. 70)

Chippy's ★ (Downtown West, $, p. 80)

Oyster Boy ★★ (Downtown West, $$, p. 78)

Rodney's Oyster House ★★ (Downtown West, $$, p. 78)

Starfish (Downtown East, $$, p. 83)

SPANISH

Cava ★★★ (Uptown, $$$, p. 92)

Torito Tapas Bar ★★★ (Downtown West, $, p. 81)

VEGETARIAN

Café 668 ★ (Downtown West, $, p. 80)

Camros Organic Eatery (Midtown, $, p. 87)

VIETNAMESE

Mi Mi Restaurant (Downtown East, $, p. 83)

Pho Hung (Midtown, $, p. 88)

WHERE TO EAT | Restaurants by Cuisine

WHAT TO SEE & DO

T oronto presents a wealth of attractions. If your pleasure is simply getting to know the city, you're off to the races: There are plenty of things to do, see, and taste in the downtown core that together offer an easy 101 introduction to Toronto. The major museums, art galleries, and sports venues are here; plus, given the residential nature of the heart of the city, these top attractions are located in neighborhoods also worth exploring.

There are day trips to consider, too: True wilderness, sublime beaches, a giant theme park and equally impressive zoo, and pretty regions of wine country that are also culinary destinations in their own right are all a drive, or train ride, away.

Keep in mind that new in 2012 are added lakeside attractions such as Sugar Beach; an eco-facelift for the shopping stretch of Mink Mile; a new sake brewery in, where else, the Distillery District; and more. For history buffs, the 200th anniversary of the War of 1812 is the inspiration behind a series of events at Old Fort York, as well as other significant sites, such as the battlefield at Fort Erie and the town of Queenston.

Some attractions can easily take up an entire day, such as the Ontario Science Centre, Harbourfront, the Toronto Islands, and Canada's Wonderland. For less ambitious outings, explore the many parks, the thriving arts scene, or the shopping opportunities. And pack a good pair of walking shoes because the best way to appreciate Toronto is on foot.

THE TOP ATTRACTIONS

Art Gallery of Ontario ★★★   If you go to only one major attraction while you're in Toronto, let it be the AGO. Fresh from a top-to-bottom renovation—and reinvention—by Toronto-born Frank Gehry, it is a wonder. Gehry's vision is throughout; the fabulous, circular floating staircase is especially impressive. There are skylights in some rooms, adjusted every day to best display the works (to spectacular effect with Lawren Harris's paintings of the arctic). Gorgeous Galleria Italia lets you view the scene on Dundas Street down below while you take a rest from the art. Most of all, there's a dramatic increase in the amount of viewing space. Gehry's work is inspired yet practical, a rarity in today's starchitect-driven renovations of public spaces.

There's a lot to see: The collection numbers 79,450 pieces and growing.

What to See & Do in Downtown

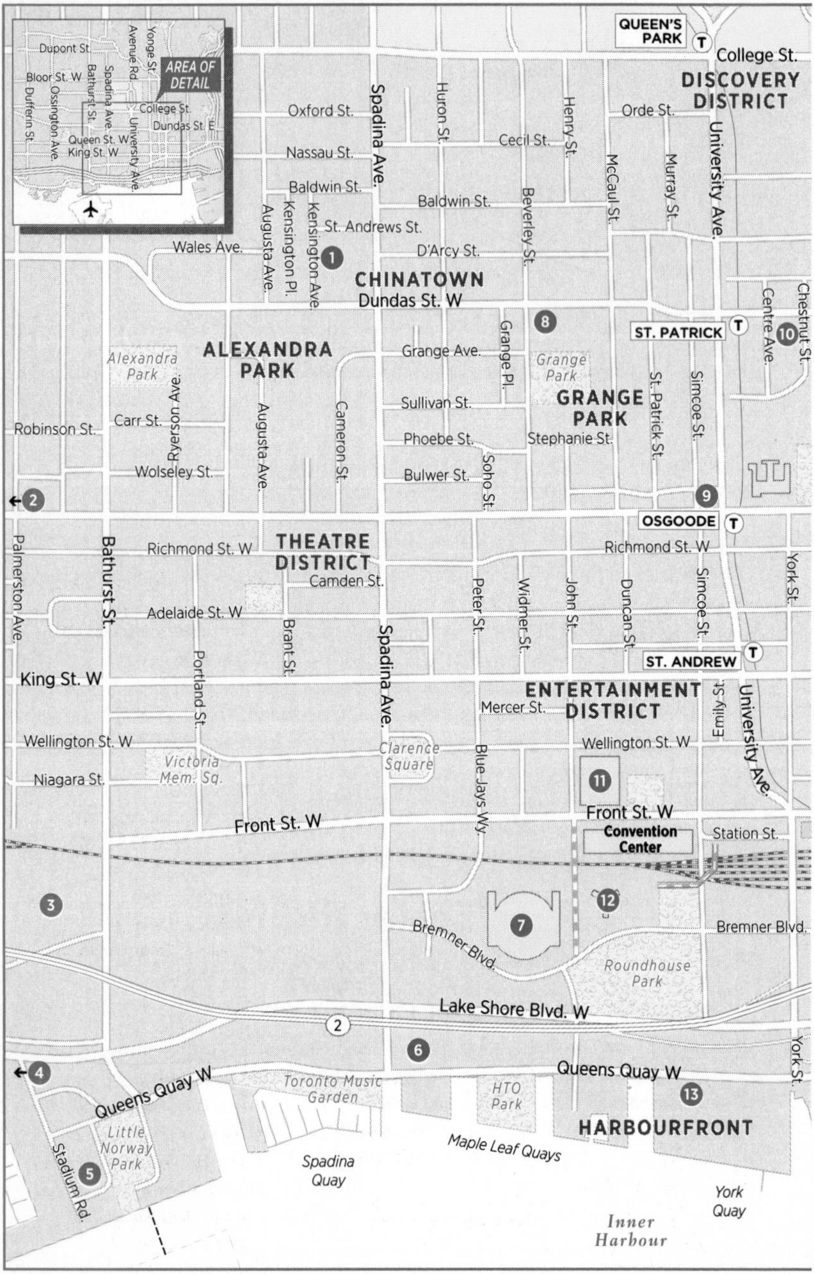
AREA OF DETAIL
Dupont St.
Bloor St. W
Dufferin St.
Ossington Ave.
Bathurst St.
Spadina Ave.
Avenue Rd.
Yonge St.
University Ave.
College St.
Dundas St. E
Queen St. W
King St. W
QUEEN'S PARK
College St.
DISCOVERY DISTRICT
Oxford St.
Nassau St.
Baldwin St.
Spadina Ave.
Huron St.
Henry St.
Cecil St.
Orde St.
McCaul St.
Murray St.
University Ave.
Beverley St.
Augusta Ave.
Kensington Pl.
Kensington Ave.
St. Andrews St.
Wales Ave.
D'Arcy St.
CHINATOWN
Dundas St. W
ST. PATRICK
Centre Ave.
Chestnut St.
ALEXANDRA PARK
Alexandra Park
Grange Ave.
Grange Pl.
Grange Park
GRANGE PARK
St. Patrick St.
Simcoe St.
Ryerson Ave.
Augusta Ave.
Cameron St.
Sullivan St.
Robinson St.
Carr St.
Phoebe St.
Stephanie St.
Wolseley St.
Soho St.
Bulwer St.
OSGOODE
Palmerston Ave.
Bathurst St.
Richmond St. W
THEATRE DISTRICT
Camden St.
Richmond St. W
York St.
Adelaide St. W
Brant St.
Peter St.
Widmer St.
John St.
Duncan St.
Simcoe St.
ST. ANDREW
King St. W
Portland St.
ENTERTAINMENT DISTRICT
Emily St.
University Ave.
Mercer St.
Wellington St. W
Clarence Square
Blue Jays Wy.
Wellington St. W
Victoria Mem. Sq.
Niagara St.
Front St. W
Front St. W
Convention Center
Station St.
Bremner Blvd.
Bremner Blvd.
Roundhouse Park
Lake Shore Blvd. W
Queens Quay W
Queens Quay W
Toronto Music Garden
HTO Park
York St.
HARBOURFRONT
Little Norway Park
Stadium Rd.
Maple Leaf Quays
Spadina Quay
York Quay
Inner Harbour

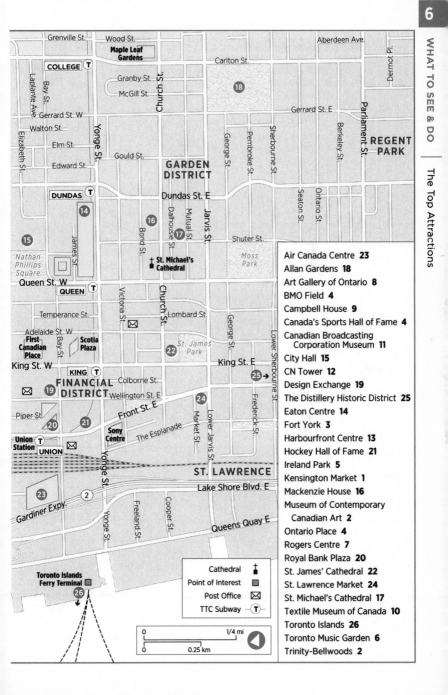

Grenville St.
Wood St.
Maple Leaf Gardens
Aberdeen Ave.
Dermot Pl.
COLLEGE Ⓣ
Granby St.
Carlton St.
⑱
McGill St.
Church St.
Bay St.
Laplante Ave.
Gerrard St. W
Gerrard St. E
Parliament St.
Berkeley St.
REGENT PARK
Walton St.
Elizabeth St.
Elm St.
George St.
Pembroke St.
Sherbourne St.
Yonge St.
Edward St.
Gould St.
GARDEN DISTRICT
Seaton St.
Ontario St.
DUNDAS Ⓣ
⑭
Dundas St. E
⑮
James St.
⑯
Bond St.
Dalhousie St.
⑰
Mutual St.
Jarvis St.
Shuter St.
Moss Park
Nathan Phillips Square
† St. Michael's Cathedral
Queen St. W
QUEEN Ⓣ
Temperance St.
Victoria St.
Lombard St.
Church St.
George St.
Adelaide St. W
First Canadian Place
Bay St.
Scotia Plaza
St. James Park
⑫
King St. E
Lower Sherbourne St.
King St. W
KING Ⓣ
FINANCIAL DISTRICT
Colborne St.
Wellington St. E
⑲
⑳
Front St. E
Market St.
Lower Jarvis St.
Frederick St.
㉔
㉕→
Piper St
㉑
Sony Centre
The Esplanade
Union Station Ⓣ
UNION Ⓣ
ST. LAWRENCE
Yonge St.
Lake Shore Blvd. E
㉓
②
Gardiner Expy.
Freeland St.
Cooper St.
Queens Quay E
Toronto Islands Ferry Terminal
㉖

Air Canada Centre **23**
Allan Gardens **18**
Art Gallery of Ontario **8**
BMO Field **4**
Campbell House **9**
Canada's Sports Hall of Fame **4**
Canadian Broadcasting Corporation Museum **11**
City Hall **15**
CN Tower **12**
Design Exchange **19**
The Distillery Historic District **25**
Eaton Centre **14**
Fort York **3**
Harbourfront Centre **13**
Hockey Hall of Fame **21**
Ireland Park **5**
Kensington Market **1**
Mackenzie House **16**
Museum of Contemporary Canadian Art **2**
Ontario Place **4**
Rogers Centre **7**
Royal Bank Plaza **20**
St. James' Cathedral **22**
St. Lawrence Market **24**
St. Michael's Cathedral **17**
Textile Museum of Canada **10**
Toronto Islands **26**
Toronto Music Garden **6**
Trinity-Bellwoods **2**

Cathedral †
Point of Interest ■
Post Office ⊠
TTC Subway Ⓣ

0   1/4 mi
0   0.25 km

A Tiny Gem of a Gallery

The Ontario College of Art and Design (OCAD), located steps away from the AGO, has its own gallery. Called the **OCAD Professional Gallery**, it was launched in 2007 to explore the connections between art and design. So far, the tiny 111-sq.-m (1,195-sq.-ft.) space has shown work by Canadian Karim Rashid (famous for his stylish housewares and table accessories) among others. Located at 100 McCaul St., the gallery is open from Wednesday to Friday 1 to 7pm, and on weekends from noon to 6pm. There is no admission fee. For more information, call 🕿 **416/977-6000** or visit www. ocad.ca.

Local media magnate the late Ken Thomson donated his beautiful and extensive collection of paintings, carved miniatures, medieval triptychs, and model ships to the AGO. The Thomson Collection is central to the gallery: Alone, it spans 20 rooms and includes an unparalleled collection of great Canadian art—think the Group of Seven, David Milne—and international drawings, such as Peter Paul Rubens' masterpiece *The Massacre of the Innocents*. (One note: Thomson believed that art should be allowed to speak for itself, in other words, unencumbered by the usual explanatory and identifying tags; instead, a palette identifies the artists.)

And there's far more to see. The AGO's European collection ranges from the 14th century to the French Impressionists. The Canadian compilation is strong and includes Inuit art, ranging from a breathtaking collection of carved miniatures dating back to 9000 B.C. to the contemporary vivid paintings of Norval Morrisseau. The AGO is also famous for its collection of Henry Moore sculptures, which number more than 800. (The artist gave them to Toronto as a tribute to local citizens' enthusiasm for his work: In the 1960s, public donations helped to bring his sculpture *The Archer* to decorate Nathan Phillips Square; an inspired move that cost then-mayor Philips his job.) In one room, 14 or so of his large works are displayed; there is also one on display outside the gallery, where everyone can appreciate it. There are also shows that apply mixed media to explore lesser known artists, combining private artifacts, documentary portraits and notes on the broader context of the artist featured. All in all, a top-notch experience.

317 Dundas St. W. (btw. McCaul & Beverley sts.). 🕿 **416/977-0414.** www.ago.net. C$20 adults, C$16 seniors, C$11 students (w/ID) & children 6–17, free for children 5 & under; free admission Wed 6–8:30pm. Tues & Thurs–Sun 10am–5:30pm; Wed 10am–8:30pm. Closed Jan 1 & Dec 25. Subway: St. Patrick.

CN Tower ★ ☺ The CN Tower may no longer be the world's tallest freestanding structure (thanks, Burj Dubai), but it's still an impressive attraction—even if it's something that most locals agree is better to visit than to live with.

However you approach Toronto—on an island-airport flight or on the highway—the first thing you see is this slender structure. Glass-walled elevators glide up the 553m (1,814-ft.) tower, first stopping at the 346m-high (1,135-ft.) Look Out level. (The truly fearless can ride up in the vertiginous glass-*floored* elevator, which the CN Tower opened in 2008.) Walk down one level to experience the Glass Floor, which is great for a dizzying face-plant: Through it, you can see all the way down to street level. Take comfort: The floor won't break. The glass can withstand the weight of 14 adult hippos.

Above the Look Out is the world's highest public observation gallery, the Sky Pod, 447m (1,467 ft.) above the ground. From here, on a clear day, the sweeping vista stretches across Lake Ontario to the south and across the cityscape to the north. Atop the tower sits a 102m (335-ft.) antenna mast: It took 31 weeks, with the aid of a giant Sikorsky helicopter, to complete the operation.

> ## Tough Enough
>
> To resist the elements, the CN Tower is built of sturdy stuff—contoured, reinforced concrete covered with thick, glass-reinforced plastic—and designed to keep ice accumulation to a minimum. The structure can withstand high winds, snow, ice, lightning, and earth tremors. What's more, this super-strength structure is hollow on the inside.

For a 35th anniversary celebration, the EdgeWalk opened in summer 2011. An elevated, narrow (1.5m/ 5-ft.) ledge 116 stories above ground, it circles around the perimeter of the tower's main pod and claims to be "the world's highest full circle hands-free walk." Thrill-seekers are locked into harnesses that are attached to a pulley system and then head off for a gravity-defying walk. Definitely not for vertigo sufferers. It also comes with a bracing fee of C$175.

Some perennial draws are the IMAX Theatre and the flight simulators. A series of interactive displays showcases the CN Tower, along with such forerunners as the Eiffel Tower and the Empire State Building.

301 Front St. W. ℭ **416/868-6937.** www.cntower.ca. Observation C$23 adults, C$21 seniors, C$15 children 4–12; Total Tower Experience (Look Out, Glass Floor, Sky Pod, IMAX & 2 rides) C$35 adults. Daily 9am–11pm (shorter hours in winter). Closed Dec 25. Subway: Union, then walk W on Front St.

The Distillery District ★★★   This was home to the Gooderham and Worts Distillery, founded in 1832 and once Canada's largest distilling company. In 2003, this 45-building complex (empty save the film crews that used it as a set) was reinvented as an historic district with galleries and cafes inhabiting the 19th century buildings. A miller named James Worts, who immigrated from Scotland in 1831, built the first building on the site: a windmill intended to power a grain mill (the millstone he brought with him is still on display). His brother-in-law, William Gooderham, soon joined him in the business. In 1834, Worts's wife died in childbirth, and in despair, Worts drowned himself in the mill's well. Gooderham took over the business and adopted Worts's son, who eventually joined the business.

The charming complex is an excellent example of 19th-century industrial design. Most of the buildings were made with Toronto's own red brick; you'll see it in everything from the buildings to the streets themselves. One exception is the mill building, which is stone.

The Distillery District has launched an ambitious program of events throughout the year, including a blues festival, a jazz festival, and an outdoor art exhibition; also, a farmers' market takes place on summer weekends. It's also home to the Soulpepper Theatre Company, the Sandra Ainsley gallery, and top chocolatier Soma, as well as a handful of pubs and patios. See chapter 10 for the performing-arts information.

55 Mill St. ℭ **416/367-1800.** www.thedistillerydistrict.com. Free admission. Subway: King, then a streetcar E to Parliament St.

Harbourfront Centre ★ ☺   This cultural center encompasses a 38-hectare (94-acre) strip of waterfront land, once-abandoned warehouses, charming piers, and an

What to See & Do in Midtown

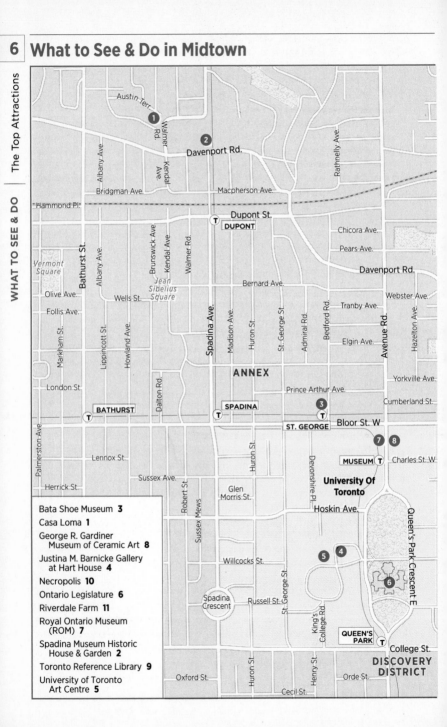

Bata Shoe Museum **3**

Casa Loma **1**

George R. Gardiner
    Museum of Ceramic Art **8**

Justina M. Barnicke Gallery
    at Hart House **4**

Necropolis **10**

Ontario Legislature **6**

Riverdale Farm **11**

Royal Ontario Museum
    (ROM) **7**

Spadina Museum Historic
    House & Garden **2**

Toronto Reference Library **9**

University of Toronto
    Art Centre **5**

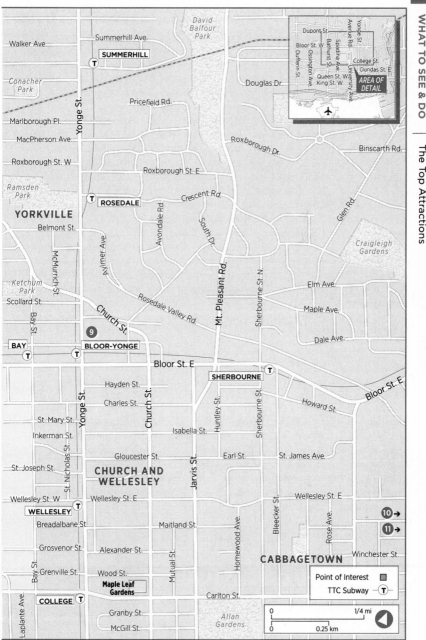

old smokestack. The center, which opened in 1974, is a stunning urban playground and one of the most popular destinations for locals and visitors alike—a great place to spend time strolling, picnicking, gallery-hopping, biking, shopping, and sailing.

Queen's Quay, at the foot of York Street, is the first stop on the LRT line from Union Station (you can also get there in 5 min. on foot, walking south from Front St. along a walkway under the Gardiner Expwy.). From here, boats depart for harbor tours and ferries leave for the Toronto Islands. In this renovated warehouse, you'll find the Premiere Dance Theatre and two floors of shops. York Quay also has a decent art gallery with rotating art installations. There's an information booth with a calendar of events, also available online (www.harbourfrontcentre.com).

Harbourfront has several venues devoted to the arts. The **Power Plant** is a contemporary art gallery with some excellent and often edgy shows; behind it is the **Du Maurier Theatre Centre.** At the **Craft Studio,** you can watch artisans blow glass, throw pots, and make silk-screen prints. You can buy their works at **Bounty Contemporary Canadian Craft Shop.** The **Artists' Gardens** features outdoor gardens created by local and visiting landscape architects, designers, and other artists.

More than 4,000 events take place annually at Harbourfront, the biggest of which are two literary gems: the **Harbourfront Reading Series** in June and the **International Festival of Authors** in October (see "Calendar of Events," in chapter 2). Other happenings include dance, theater, music, film, children's programs, multicultural festivals, and marine-themed events. Harbourfront is best in summer but a great destination year-round, especially with the pretty skating rink and other activities for wintertime fun. In midwinter, the winds blowing off Lake Ontario can be wicked, so dress appropriately.

235 Queens Quay W. © **416/973-4000.** www.harbourfrontcentre.com. Subway: Union, then LRT to Queen's Quay or York Quay.

Ontario Science Centre ★★★ ☺ Since this pioneering interactive science museum opened in 1969, generations of Toronto's kids, and their offspring, have proven loyal fans. It's not surprising: The hands-on approach to exploring the wide world of science is absolutely thrilling. With more than 800 exhibits, there is an abundance of things to touch, push, pull, or crank. Test your reflexes, or balance, or heart rate, or grip strength; watch frozen-solid liquid nitrogen shatter into thousands of icy shards; study slides of butterfly wings, bedbugs, fish scales, or feathers under a microscope; land a spaceship on the moon; see how many lights you can turn on or how high you can elevate a balloon using pedal power. The fun goes on and on.

In addition, the city's only planetarium, an Omnimax cinema, and a collection of small theaters showing assorted documentaries and slide shows are located here. A recent addition is the C$40-million Weston Family Innovation Centre, with new

---

A Real Deal

You can save a lot of money visiting Toronto's attractions by purchasing a **Toronto CityPass.** See the CN Tower, Casa Loma, the Ontario Science Centre, the Royal Ontario Museum, and the Toronto Zoo for C$59 adults, C$39 kids 4 to 12. Each booklet of tickets is valid for 9 days from the time the first one is used. For a list of ticket vendors or to purchase online, visit **www.citypass.com.**

exhibit halls and a focus on interactive learning and problem-solving. There are also some outdoor improvements, including a music-making water garden. The food is much less exciting: Spots for hungry visitors are Galileo's Bistro, a buffet-style restaurant, and Valley Marketplace, a cafeteria. The on-site gift shop, a Mastermind outlet, has a good collection of educational toys and games. This is one Toronto attraction that always seems to be busy (blame school groups), so arrive at 10am to see everything. Make no mistake: The OSC provides a full day's entertainment.

770 Don Mills Rd. (at Eglinton Ave. E.). © **416/696-3127,** or 416/696-1000 for Omnimax tickets. www.ontariosciencecentre.ca. OSC C$18 adults, C$14 seniors & children 13–17, C$11 children 4–12, free for children 3 & under; Omnimax C$12 adults, C$9 seniors & children 13–17, C$8 children 4–12, free for children 3 & under. Combination discounts available. Fall–spring daily 10am–5pm; summer daily 10am–7pm. Closed Dec 25. Subway: Yonge St. line to Eglinton Ave., then 34 Eglinton bus E to Don Mills Rd. By car: From downtown, take Don Valley Pkwy. to Don Mills Rd. exit & follow signs.

Royal Ontario Museum ★★ ☺   This is Canada's largest museum and the fifth largest on the continent, with 6 million objects in its collections. The massive and controversial renovation by starchitect Daniel Libeskind has had mixed reviews from visitors and locals: some love it, others decry the design. The new crystal wing, which houses six galleries, hangs out over Bloor Street, hiding the main entrance. (Finding your way in is just one of the inconveniences of the design.) From the interior of the crystal, there are peek-a-boo views to the street below, but it's best to focus on the content here, rather than the playful and often irritating renovation. Fortunately, there's plenty to see, with particular strengths in natural history and world cultures.

Don't miss the Chinese galleries, which feature an intact Ming tomb, as well as the Bishop White Gallery of Chinese Temple Art; wonderful galleries exploring the ancient world (Egypt, Greece, Cyprus, and Bronze Age Aegean are standouts); dazzling dinosaurs, including the largest mounted dinosaur in Canada at 27m (90 ft.) long; a newly improved Bat Cave (a very popular draw for kids); and galleries devoted to biodiversity in the animal kingdom. (In fact, the Museum's Centre for Biodiversity and Conservation Biology is a world leader in preservation.) Hands-on galleries invite children to play educational games such as the CIBC Discovery Gallery's "dinosaur dig" (a hit with would-be paleontologists), and a teepee, costumes, and castles add to the attractions for tots. The four totem poles are remarkable, too, as are the mummies.

You can easily spend a day here, especially if you eat at either the refined C5 (one of the city's top restaurants) or at the cafeteria-style Food Studio in the basement.

100 Queen's Park. © **416/586-8000.** www.rom.on.ca. C$24 adults, C$21 seniors & students (w/ID), C$16 children 4–14, free for children 3 & under; free admission Wed 4:30–5:30pm; half-price admission Fri 4:30–9:30pm. Sat–Thurs 10am–5:30pm; Fri 10am–9:30pm. Closed Dec 25. Subway: Museum.

The major museums are pricey in Toronto, especially when compared with the smart and progressive freebie programs in cities like London. The ROM is particularly expensive, with a C$24 admission for adults and additional charges for special exhibitions. The list below will help you save on admission fees. Just keep in mind that these free or discounted times do change, so check before you visit.

- **Art Gallery of Ontario:** Free admission every Wednesday from 6 to 8:30pm.
- **Bata Shoe Museum:** Pay-what-you-can admission every Thursday from 5 to 8pm (suggested donation is C$5).
- **Royal Ontario Museum:** Free admission every Wednesday from 4:30 to 5:30pm; half-price admission every Friday from 4:30 to 9:30pm (note that these policies do not apply to special exhibitions, which are always ticketed at the full price).
- **Textile Museum of Canada:** Pay-what-you-can admission every Wednesday from 5 to 8pm; also, the website often offers coupons for C$1 off regular-priced admissions.

The Toronto Islands ★★★ ☺ In only 7 minutes, an 800-passenger ferry takes you to 245 hectares (605 acres) of island parkland crisscrossed by shaded paths and quiet waterways—a glorious spot to walk, bike, picnic, feed the ducks, putter around in boats, picnic, or soak up the sun. Of the 14 islands, the 2 major ones are **Centre Island** and **Ward's Island.** The first is the most popular with tourists (see note below on Centreville); Ward's is more residential (about 600 people live on the islands). Originally, the land was a peninsula, but in the 1800s, storms shattered it into islands.

On Centre Island, families enjoy **Centreville** (✆ **416/203-0405;** www.centre island.ca), an old-fashioned amusement park that's been in business since 1966. You won't see the usual neon signs, shrill hawkers, and greasy hotdog stands. Instead, you'll find a turn-of-the-20th-century village complete with a Main Street; tiny shops; a firehouse; and the Far Enough Farm, where the kids can pet lambs, chicks, and other barnyard animals. The kids will also love trying out the antique cars, fire engines, old-fashioned train, authentic 1890s carousel, flume ride, and aerial cars. An all-day rides pass costs C$21 for 1.2m (4 ft.) tall and under, C$30 for those taller than 1.2m (4 ft.); a family pass for four is C$90. Centreville is open from 10:30am to 6pm daily from mid-May to Labour Day, and weekends in early May and September.

Centreville Amusement Park, 84 Advance Rd., Centre Island. ✆ **416/392-8193.** www.toronto.ca/parks/island/. Round-trip fare C$6.50 adults, C$4 seniors & students 15–19, C$3 children 3–14, free for children 2 & under. Ferries leave from docks at the bottom of Bay St. Subway: Union Station, then the LRT to Queen's Quay.

Toronto Zoo ★★ ☺ At 284 hectares (702 acres) of parkland, it's one of the largest zoos in the world, with some 5,000 animals representing more than 500 species, plus an extensive botanical collection. Pavilions—including Africa, Indomalaya, Australasia, and the Americas—and outdoor paddocks house the plants and animals.

One popular zoo attraction is at the **African Savanna** project. It re-creates a market bazaar and safari through Kesho (Swahili for "tomorrow") National Park, past such special features as a bush camp, a white rhino, and several watering holes. It also includes the **Gorilla Rainforest,** one of the most popular sights at the zoo and the largest indoor gorilla exhibit in North America. Another hit is Splash Island, a kids-only water park that includes a replica of a Canadian Coast Guard ship.

In 2011, the zoo was at the center of media attention when it decided to relocate the very popular elephants to a warmer locale; the flip side is that they have brought in 12 African penguins, an endangered species, and built them a 557-sq.-m (6,000-sq.-ft.) splash pad and pool, complete with underwater windows for viewing.

Ten kilometers (6¼ miles) of walkways offer access to all areas of the zoo. Be prepared to walk long distances, but during the warmer months, the Zoomobile takes visitors around the major walkways to view the animals in the outdoor paddocks. The zoo has restaurants, a gift shop, first aid, and a family center. Visitors can rent strollers and wagons, and borrow wheelchairs. The African pavilion has an elevator for strollers and wheelchairs. There are several parking areas and plenty of picnic tables.

361A Old Finch Ave. (N of Hwy. 401 & Sheppard Ave.), Scarborough. ℭ **416/392-5900.** www.toronto zoo.com. C$23 adults, C$17 seniors, C$13 children 4–12, free for children 3 & under. Summer daily 9am–7:30pm; spring & fall daily 9am–6pm; winter daily 9:30am–4:30pm. Last admission 1 hr. before closing. Closed Dec 25. Subway: Bloor-Danforth line to Kennedy, then bus no. 86A N. By car: From downtown, take Don Valley Pkwy. to Hwy. 401 E, exit on Meadowvale Rd. & follow signs.

MORE MUSEUMS

Bata Shoe Museum ★★ Imelda Marcos: Eat your heart out. This modern museum houses the shoe-magnate Bata family's 10,000-item collection. The attractive building, designed by Raymond Moriyama, suggests a whimsical shoebox. The main gallery, "All About Shoes," traces the history of footwear, beginning with a plaster cast of some of the earliest known human footprints that date to 4 million B.C. You'll come across such specialty shoes as spiked clogs used to crush chestnuts in 17th-century France, Elton John's 12-inch-plus platforms, and Canadian Prime Minister Pierre Trudeau's well-worn sandals. One display focuses on Canadian footwear fashioned by the Inuit, while another highlights 19th-century ladies' footwear. The second-story galleries house changing exhibits, which have taken on some serious topics, such as a history of foot binding in China.

327 Bloor St. W. (at St. George St.). ℭ **416/979-7799.** www.batashoemuseum.ca. C$14 adults, C$12 seniors, C$8 students (w/ID), C$5 children 5–17, free for children 4 & under. Tues, Wed, Fri & Sat 10am–5pm; Thurs 10am–8pm; Sun noon–5pm. Subway: St. George.

Black Creek Pioneer Village ★ ☺ In this quaint reconstruction of a Victorian-era village, costumed interpreters cheerily answer questions about life in the 19th century. The original pioneers on this land were Daniel and Elizabeth Strong, a newlywed couple in 1816 who cleared 40 hectares (99 acres) of wilderness for farming and built a log house in their spare time. Eventually, a village developed around this site, and many of the existing buildings date from the 1860s. Every day is different here, so on any given day, you might find "villagers" spinning, sewing, rail splitting, sheep shearing, or threshing. You can count on sampling the villagers' homey cooking, wandering through the cozily furnished homesteads, visiting the working mill, shopping at the general store, and rumbling past the farm animals in a horse-drawn wagon. The beautifully landscaped village has more than 30 restored buildings to explore.

1000 Murray Ross Pkwy. (at Steeles Ave. & Jane St.), Downsview. ℭ **416/736-1733.** www.blackcreek. ca. C$15 adults, C$14 seniors & students, C$11 children 5–15, free for children 4 & under. May & June

Mon–Fri 9:30am–4pm; Sat, Sun & holidays 11am–5pm. July to Labour Day Mon–Fri 10am–5pm; Sat, Sun & holidays 11am–5pm. Sept–Dec Mon–Fri 9:30am–4pm; Sat, Sun & holidays 11am–4:30pm. Closed Jan–Apr, Dec 25 & 26. Subway: Finch, then bus no. 60 W to Murray Ross Pkwy.

Canadian Broadcasting Corporation Museum ★ ☺ The CBC has been Canada's national broadcaster since 1936—and from that date forward, its history intersects with the country's own. But this is anything but a time capsule. The museum has interactive exhibits that are fun for kids and shows film clips (including great documentary clips) that engage all ages. Temporary exhibits explore subjects such as radio sound effects or honor much-loved programs (such as Canadian childhood favorites *The Friendly Giant* and *Mr. Dressup*). The building is also a site for concerts and other performances, many of them free.

250 Front St. W. ✆ **416/205-5574.** www.cbc.ca/museum. Free admission. Mon–Fri 9am–5pm. Subway: Union.

Design Exchange Located in the old Stock Exchange Building, the Design Exchange—or DX, as it prefers to be known—has become an important Canadian design museum. It features work from a range of disciplines, from architecture to fashion, landscape design to interactive media design. The Resource Centre has a library-like collection of design books, magazines, and other materials that can be viewed by appointment (Mon, Wed, and Fri afternoons).

234 Bay St. ✆ **416/363-6121.** www.dx.org. Free admission; special exhibits C$10 adults. Mon–Fri 10am–5pm; Sat & Sun noon–5pm. Subway: King.

George R. Gardiner Museum of Ceramic Art ★★ It's a rarity: a museum dedicated to the ceramic arts. Plus, since its renovation that expanded it from 1,765 sq. m (19,000 sq. ft.) to 2,694 sq. m (29,000 sq. ft.), it is a beautiful and tranquil space to explore. There's plenty to see here, from pre-Columbian relics, including Olmec and Maya figures, to objects from Ecuador, Colombia, and Peru. It's clearly a collection curated with passion. Among the highlights are objects from the Swan Service—a 2,200-piece set that took 4 years (1737–41) to make—and a collection of commedia dell'arte figures. There are free guided tours on Tuesday, Thursday, and Sunday at noon. Popular chef Jamie Kennedy runs a pretty cafe here, so you can stay for lunch (keep the cafe in mind, too, if you're visiting the ROM across the street).

111 Queen's Park. ✆ **416/586-8080.** www.gardinermuseum.on.ca. C$12 adults, C$8 seniors, C$6 students (w/ID), free for children 12 & under. Mon–Thurs 10am–6pm; Fri 10am–9pm; Sat & Sun 10am–5pm. Closed Jan 1 & Dec 25. Subway: Museum.

💬 Signs & Whispers

Have you ever wandered around a neighborhood that intrigued you, wishing that you could get some inside information on the place? Now, thanks to [murmur], you can—at least, in a few Toronto districts, including Kensington Market, the Art & Design District on West Queen West, the Annex around Bloor Street West, and Fort York. Look for signs that have a green ear logo and a phone number underneath; when you dial that number, you'll hear an interesting tidbit that will deepen your appreciation for what you're seeing. The project was developed as part of the city of Toronto's Culture Capital program, and its creators hope to eventually expand it throughout the city. Visit **www.murmurtoronto.ca** for details.

WHERE TO eat WHEN YOU'RE GOING TO . . .

It's a growing trend that has thankfully come to Toronto: Decent food at museums, galleries, and other attractions. To make your planning easier, here are some of Toronto's top attractions where you can find inspiration for the belly, as well as the mind, all under one roof:

○ **The Art Gallery of Ontario:** The newly renovated AGO has two fine options: **FRANK** restaurant (expensive, top-notch cuisine) and the **AGO Café** (cheap and cheerful salads and sandwiches). Both are run by the same kitchen, which is headed by local star chef Anne Yarymowich. The emphasis is on local, and the wine list offers a good sampling of Ontario's top wines.

○ **CN Tower:** The CN Tower's restaurant, **360,** is a little pricey and touristy; but if you enjoy a panoramic view—and a rotating one, at that—with your foie gras and filet mignon, this might be your ticket. The prix-fixe menus offer good value. The wine cellar is built to impress.

○ **Four Seasons Centre for the Performing Arts:** Toronto has a perfect culinary match for its sleek, modern opera house: the neighboring **Nota Bene.** Run by the pair who steered what was Toronto's top dining room, Splendido, this is a more casual affair with delicious fare. Book ahead.

○ **The Air Canada Centre:** This complex prides itself on a range of tempting goods, from de rigueur hot dogs and beer to three fine-dining rooms, a wine cellar of more than 600 labels, and one of the country's top sommeliers. The vast kitchen feeds the teams, too. For a casual bite, there are dozens of concessions on-site, including customized hot dogs at Burkie's Dog House and Chef Jamie Kennedy's famous French fries. The Air Canada Club (☎ **416/815-5983**) is the most luxurious of the three restaurants. See p. 120.

○ **Ontario Science Centre:** While people who work at the OSC love to point out that it's in the geographic center of Toronto, it's Nowheresville as far as food is concerned (though the museum does have its own restaurant). But if you head north to the new Don Mills Centre, you'll find **McEwan Foods,** a tony gourmet store run by celebrity chef Mark McEwan, with chairs and tables for lunch and snacks.

○ **Royal Ontario Museum:** The ROM has two dining spots: The elegant (and expensive) **C5** (see p. 83) gets consistent raves from local critics, while the cafeteria-style **Food Studio** serves up middling lunches and suppers to keep you fueled for a long day at the museum.

Justina M. Barnicke Gallery at Hart House ★ 👜 Hart House is the cultural heart of the University of Toronto community, and the Justina M. Barnicke Gallery is one of its treasures. A tiny treasure, it nonetheless houses a fine collection of Group of Seven paintings and other Canadian artworks, both historical and contemporary. The Barnicke is a two-room gallery that features an ever-changing series of monthly exhibits. Occasionally, historical works are on show, but the focus is on works by

If you have access to a car and happen to be a fan of Canadian landscape painters (such as the Group of Seven, David Milne, and Emily Carr), drive the 40km (25 miles) north to Kleinburg for this very beautiful gallery. The McMichael sits on 40 hectares (99 acres) of conserved land, a bucolic setting that would have inspired many of the artists featured in its collection. It was founded by Robert and Signe McMichael in 1965, when they donated their property, home, and collection to the province of Ontario. Today, the collection includes more than 6,000 works. If you intend to visit, call ahead; the McMichael does shut down some galleries while preparing new shows, and its hours (normally daily 10am–4pm) are sometimes shortened. It's located at 10365 Islington Ave., Kleinburg (✆ 888/213-1121 or 905/893-1121; www.mcmichael.com). Admission is C$15 adults, C$12 seniors and students with ID, free for children 5 and under; parking is C$5.

contemporary artists working with various media. Works from the collection are scattered throughout the hallways and rooms of Hart House (it's a public building, so feel free to wander and explore; just remember that the small plaques naming the work and its artist are hidden on the lower-right side of each frame or canvas).

At Hart House, 7 Hart House Circle. ✆ **416/978-8398.** www.jmbgallery.ca. Free admission. Mon–Sat noon–5pm (shorter hours in summer; call ahead). Subway: St. George or Museum.

Museum of Contemporary Canadian Art ★ MOCCA has relocated to the very hot Art & Design District on Queen Street West. The ever-growing collection includes works by Stephen Andrews, Geneviève Cadieux, Ivan Eyre, Betty Goodwin, Micah Lexier, Arnaud Maggs, and Roland Poulin, among many others. MOCCA's mandate has been widening in recent years, and that has made it a must-visit. Some of the temporary exhibits, such as the 2010 exhibit on the Andy Warhol's transsexual star Candy Darling, have proven show-stoppers. In 2011, the popular exhibit "This Is Paradise" featured visual art, fashion, performance, music, and theater that combined to offer a look into the lives and inspirations of the (at least locally) infamous Cameron Public House of the Queen Street West art scene of 1980s Toronto. There is an air of irreverence and playfulness that makes this museum a delight to experience.

952 Queen St. W. ✆ **416/395-7430.** www.mocca.ca. Free admission; donation requested. Tues–Sun 11am–6pm. Closed all statutory holidays. Subway: Osgoode, then a streetcar W to Shaw St.

Textile Museum of Canada ★ This museum is internationally recognized for its collection of historic and ethnographic textiles and related artifacts; although, due to its specialized nature, it's really suited to those with an interest in the wide world of fabrics. There are fine Oriental rugs and tapestries from all over the world, a gallery that presents the work of contemporary artists, and the museum, which is so small only a fraction of the collection is on display at any given time. The space is vibrant and interesting.

55 Centre Ave. ✆ **416/599-5321.** www.textilemuseum.ca. C$15 adults, C$10 seniors, C$6 students & children 5–14, free for children 4 & under. Thurs–Tues 11am–5pm; Wed 11am–8pm. Closed Jan 1 & Dec 25. Subway: St. Patrick.

University of Toronto Art Centre ★ 🎁 This is a real find—and one that very few people outside the Toronto university community know about. You enter the center from the University College quad, an Oxford-style cloistered garden that in itself is a work of art. Inside, you'll find a gallery housing the Malcove Collection, which consists mainly of Byzantine art dating from the 14th to the 18th centuries. There are early stone reliefs and an assortment of icons. One of the Malcove's gems was painted by a German master in 1538: Lucas Cranach the Elder's *Adam and Eve*. The rest of the Art Centre is devoted to temporary exhibitions, which offer University College's collection of Canadian art and other special exhibits.

15 King's College Circle. ✆ **416/978-1838.** www.utac.utoronto.ca. Free admission. Tues–Fri noon–5pm; Sat noon–4pm. Closed all statutory holidays. Subway: St. George or Museum.

Exploring the Neighborhoods

Toronto is a patchwork of neighborhoods, and the best way to discover its soul and flavor is to meander along its streets. On foot, you can best appreciate the sights, sounds, and tastes that lend each area its particular character. Below are some of the most interesting neighborhoods.

DOWNTOWN WEST

Art & Design District ★★★   Also known as West Queen West. Queen Street west of Bathurst Street used to be a no-man's land—not because it was dangerous, but because little of importance was believed to be that far from the downtown core. How times have changed: This is one of the liveliest 'hoods in the city (one magazine dubbed it the coolest in the country). It's home to the **Museum of Contemporary Canadian Art**, or MOCCA (p. 112); chic hotels the **Drake Hotel** (p. 54) and the **Gladstone Hotel** (p. 57); and a bounty of good cafes, small clubs, and restaurants.

West Queen West is all funky fun. It's got great shops, including **Type Books** (p. 170) for great reads and local scribes, and excellent art galleries, such as the **Stephen Bulger** (p. 166). The clothing boutiques are exceptional: glamorous **Cabaret** (p. 175) for vintage, **Girl Friday** (p. 174) for original designs, and **Delphic** (p. 172) for menswear. It also has some fine-but-affordable dining, such as **Oyster Boy** (p. 78). Take the subway to Osgoode and the streetcar over to Bathurst, and start walking west from there.

Chinatown ★★   Stretching along Dundas Street west from Bay Street to Spadina Avenue, and north and south along Spadina Avenue, Chinatown is home to some of Toronto's 350,000 Chinese-Canadian residents. Packed with crammed shops and loud restaurants, it has bilingual street signs and red-painted poles topped by dragons along Spadina.

As you stroll through Chinatown, stop in at some of the shops and teahouses. A couple of popular stores include **Tap Phong** (p. 165) and **B&J Trading** (p. 178). A walk through Chinatown at night is especially exciting—the sidewalks fill with people, and neon lights shimmer everywhere. You'll pass gleaming noodle houses, windows hung with rows of glossy-brown cooked ducks, record stores selling the Top 10 in Chinese, and trading companies filled with Asian produce.

To get to Chinatown, take the subway to St. Patrick station and walk west. For more details, see "Walking Tour 1: Chinatown & Kensington Market," in chapter 7.

Little Italy ★★   Along College Street, between Euclid and Shaw, Little Italy competes with West Queen West as one of the hottest spot in the city (although Dundas West and Ossington are contenders). The area hums at night as people crowd the coffee bars, pool lounges, nightclubs, and trattorie. Notable restaurants in the area include longstanding favorite **Trattoria Giancarlo,** with its nice patio and its cool little adjoining wine bar, plus the new and very hot **L.A.B.** and **Sottovoce,** which also has a good terrace for people-watching. There's lots more, from burgers to pizzas and a nice little street-side fish eatery. A great boutique in the area is **Sim & Jones,** which features chic, smart casual clothing for women. To get here, ride any College Street streetcar west to Euclid Avenue.

Queen Street West ★ This street was once considered the heart of Toronto's avant-garde scene. That would be a stretch today. Sure, it's home to several clubs—such as the **Rivoli** (p. 195) and the Horseshoe—where major Canadian artists and singers have launched their careers (see chapter 9), but it's also where you'll find mainstream shops such as Club Monaco, Gap, and Le Chateau. Edgy? Not anymore. (See "Art & Design District," above, if you want a walk on the—somewhat—wilder side.)

Queen Street West officially starts at Yonge Street, but it doesn't really pick up, style-wise, till you cross University Avenue. This is prime shopping territory, with one-of-a-kind clothing boutiques such as **Fresh Collective** (p. 171) and **Peach Berserk** (p. 174). You'll also find a number of antiquarian bookstores, antiques and/or junk shops, nostalgic record emporiums, kitchen supply stores, and discount fabric houses. To start exploring, take the subway to Osgoode and walk west along Queen Street West.

DOWNTOWN EAST

The Beaches This is one of the neighborhoods that makes Toronto a unique city. Here, near the terminus of the Queen Street East streetcar line, you can stroll or cycle along the lakefront boardwalk. Because of its natural assets, it has become a popular residential neighborhood for young boomers and their families, and Queen Street has plenty of browse-able stores, such as **Book City** (p. 167). Just beyond Waverley Road, you can turn down through Kew Gardens to the boardwalk and walk all the way past the Olympic Pool to Ashbridge's Bay Park. To get to the Beaches, take the Queen Street East streetcar to Woodbine Avenue.

Leslieville ★ Queen Street East between Broadview and Leslie Street has become the place to shop for well-priced antique and vintage furniture. Stop in at **Zig Zag** (p. 162), **G.U.F.F.** (p. 162), and **Uppity!**. Vintage clothing is another Leslieville specialty: Stop in at **Gadabout** (p. 175) or **Thrill**

of the Find (p. 175). This is also a great spot for lounges (such as **Barrio,** p. 199) and bistros (such as **Edward Levesque's Kitchen,** p. 82).

MIDTOWN

Mirvish Village One of the city's most illustrious characters is the late Honest Ed Mirvish, who started his career in the 1950s with a no-frills department store at the corner of Markham and Bloor streets (It's still there, 1 block west of Bathurst St.). Even from blocks away, neon signs race and advertisements touting bargains hit you from every direction. Among his other accomplishments, Mirvish saved the Royal Alexandra Theatre on King Street from demolition; established a row of adjacent restaurants for theater patrons; and developed this block-long area with art galleries, restaurants, and bookstores. The late, great Mirvish was also responsible for saving and renovating London's Old Vic.

Stop by and browse, and don't forget to stop for a tour of the singular **Honest Ed's** (see "The Best Bargains," on p. 168). To start your visit, take the subway to Bathurst.

Bloor-Yorkville ★ It's tonier here than ever after the recent completion of a C$20-million "transformation project" that widened boulevards and added greenery. This area stretches north of Bloor Street West, between Avenue Road and Bay Street. Since its founding in 1853 as a village outside the city proper, Yorkville has experienced many transformations, and it's going through another right now. In the 1960s, it was Toronto's answer to Haight-Ashbury. In the 1980s, it became the hunting ground of the chic, who spent liberally at **Hermès, Chanel,** and **Cartier.** Today, the area is still a shopper's paradise from high-end **Holt Renfrew** (p. 171) to bargain-basement **Winners** (p. 169). If you want to be really decadent, visit the **Stillwater Spa** (p. 130) at the Park Hyatt hotel or the **Holt Renfrew Spa** (p. 130). The Aquatic Reiki treatment at the Stillwater—which takes place in a water-filled room—is a memorable experience.

If you're an architecture buff, take a look at architect Raymond Moriyama's redbrick building on Bloor Street at the end of

Yorkville Avenue that houses the **Toronto Reference Library.** Step inside, and you'll find one of Toronto's most serene spots. To reach Yorkville, take the subway to Bay.

THE EAST END

Danforth/Greektown This eclectic area along Danforth Street east of the Don River is lined with quaint, often two-story buildings that together form a critical mass of mostly Greek restaurants, plus an assortment of shops, pubs, and clubs. Visitors can browse the traditional Greek stores, including **Akropol**, a Greek bakery at no. 458

(✆ **416/465-1232**) that displays stunning multi-tiered wedding cakes in the window. The neighborhood is becoming more ethnically diverse, and its new character is reflected by stores such as **Blue Moon** (no. 375; ✆ **416/778-6991**), which sells beautiful crafts from the developing world (the store supports only producers that provide healthy working conditions and fair pay), and **El Pipil** (no. 267; ✆ **416/465-9625**), which has colorful clothing, knapsacks, and jewelry. To get to the Danforth, ride the subway to Broadview and walk east.

ARCHITECTURAL HIGHLIGHTS

Toronto is a beautiful city in spite of itself—or, rather, in spite of some of the city planners and developers who, supposedly in the name of progress, have torn down valuable elements of the city's architectural legacy. Toronto grew by leaps and bounds in the Victorian and Edwardian eras, which is why there are so many stunning buildings from those times (take a walk around the **University of Toronto campus** for a quick introduction to the different styles, or the **Ontario Legislature** and the **Old City Hall**). However, much of the 20th century wasn't as kind: Clumsy planners plunked the Gardiner Expressway near the waterfront—making what should have been prime parkland into a wasteland—and roughly 28,000 buildings were demolished between 1955 and 1975. A few of the buildings that went up during that era were stunners, such as Ludwig Mies van der Rohe's black-glass **Toronto-Dominion Centre** and Viljo Revell's **New City Hall.** And although Toronto has its share of forgettable buildings, enough Gothic-inspired ones survived to allow the city to make a convincing stand-in for New York on-screen. The good news here and now: Toronto is in the throes of an impressive architectural Renaissance, from Gehry's AGO to Libeskind's ROM (love it or hate it), Alsop's quirky OCAD building to Jack Diamond's Four Seasons Hotel stunner, and much, much more. If you're interested in exploring Toronto's architectural history, the Toronto Society of Architects runs walking tours from June to September, and the Design Exchange offers year-round programs on the topic.

Casa Loma ★★★ ☺ A kitschy glitch in the city's skyline to locals, this castle on a hill offers an inspiring view of the sweep of the city. But while you can admire the view for free, it's worth visiting the interior of the castle, too. The elegant rooms and period furniture are appropriately grand. If you're up for it, climb the towers (one Norman, one Scottish, both great).

Sir Henry Pellatt, who built it between 1911 and 1914, had a lifelong fascination with castles. He studied medieval palaces and gathered materials and furnishings from around the world, bringing marble, glass, and paneling from Europe; teak from Asia; and oak and walnut from North America. He imported Scottish stonemasons to build the massive walls that surround the 2.5-hectare (6¼-acre) site.

Wander through the majestic Great Hall, with its 18m-high (59-ft.) hammer-beam ceiling; the Oak Room, where three artisans took 3 years to fashion the paneling; and the Conservatory, with its elegant bronze doors, stained-glass dome, and pink-and-

Walk This Way

Several doors on the first story of Casa Loma open to a grand terrace that overlooks the gardens; most visitors step out, look at the gorgeous fountain and flowers below, and then proceed with the castle tour, which is truly a mistake. From the terrace, it's almost impossible to see the entrances to several winding paths that lead around the extensive grounds and command amazing views. Follow the grand staircase down and enjoy a leisurely ramble.

green marble. The castle encompasses battlements and a tower; Peacock Alley, designed after Windsor Castle; and a 1,800-bottle wine cellar. A 244m (801-ft.) tunnel runs to the stables, where Spanish tile and mahogany surrounded the horses.

The tour is self-guided; pick up an audiocassette, available in eight languages, upon arrival (it's included in the price of admission). From May to October, the gardens are open, too. There's also a Druxy's deli (part of a local chain) on-site, which is good to know, as there aren't many dining options nearby.

The City of Toronto declared in 2011 that it will once again manage the estate, which has lagged for decades in the hands of the Kiwanis Club. Now a debate is underway: What should it become next? A museum of the city or a luxe hotel or simply an improved version of what it is now?

1 Austin Terrace. ✆ **416/923-1171.** www.casaloma.org. C$20 adults, C$14 seniors & children 14-17, C$11 children 4-13, free for children 3 & under. Daily 9:30am–5pm (last entry at 4pm). Closed Dec 25. Subway: Dupont, then walk 2 blocks N.

City Hall ★   An architectural spectacle, City Hall houses the mayor's office and the city's administrative offices. Daringly designed in the late 1950s by Finnish architect Viljo Revell, it consists of a low podium topped by the flying-saucer-shaped Council Chamber, enfolded between two curved towers. Its interior is as dramatic as its exterior. A free brochure detailing a self-guided tour of City Hall is available from its information desk; the tour can also be printed from the website below in French, Chinese, German, Italian, Japanese, Korean, Portuguese, and Spanish.

In front stretches **Nathan Phillips Square** (named after the mayor who initiated the project). In summer, you can sit and contemplate the flower gardens, fountains, and reflecting pool (which doubles as a skating rink in winter), as well as listen to concerts. A recently reopened outdoor ramp allows for meandering above the square and through a new system of elevated gardens. Here, you'll find Henry Moore's *The Archer* (formally, *Three-Way Piece No. 2*), purchased through a public subscription fund, and the Peace Garden, which commemorates Toronto's sesquicentennial in 1984. In contrast, to the east stands the **Old City Hall,** a green-copper-roofed Victorian Romanesque-style building.

100 Queen St. W. ✆ **416/338-0338.** www.toronto.ca/city_hall_tour/nps.htm. Free admission. Self-guided tours Mon–Fri 8:30am-4:30pm. Subway: Queen, then walk W to Bay St.

Eaton Centre ★   Does a mall really deserve a star? Perhaps this one does. Buttressed at both ends by 30-story skyscrapers, this urban shopping center stretches from Dundas Street south along Yonge Street to Queen Street (557,418 sq. m/6 million sq. ft.). An upscale **Sears** department store anchors the north section, while the south end is the Bay and its buzz-making collection of high-end fashions in the Room. More than 285 stores and restaurants, and two garages, fill the rest. Twenty million people shop here annually.

While it's easy to get carried away in the shops of Eaton Centre, don't overlook Trinity Square, on the west side of the building near the Sears department store. The complex surrounds two of Toronto's oldest landmarks: **Church of the Holy Trinity**, dating to 1847, and **Scadding House** (𝒞 **416/598-4521**), home of Trinity's rector. Concerned citizens demanded that the developers not block sunlight from reaching the buildings. They got their way—the sun continues to shine on the church's twin towers.

If you can, drop by on a Monday: Holy Trinity hosts an eclectic concert series called **"Music Mondays"** that features everything from modern jazz to Hindustani classical music (see the church's website at www.holytrinity toronto.org for the schedule, or call 𝒞 **416/598-4521**, ext. 222). Concerts take place at 12:15pm, and there is a requested C$5 donation.

Inside, the structure opens into the impressive **Galleria,** a 264m-long (866-ft.) glass-domed arcade dotted with benches, orchids, palm trees, and fountains; it's further adorned by Michael Snow's 60 soaring Canada geese, titled *Step Flight*. The birds are made from black-and-white photos mounted on cast fiberglass frames. But let's face it: You're probably here to shop (see chapter 8 for guidance).

Dundas & Yonge sts. 𝒞 **416/598-8700.** www.torontoeatoncentre.com. Mon–Fri 10am–9pm; Sat 9:30am–7pm; Sun noon–6pm. Subway: Dundas or Queen.

Ontario Legislature ★ At the northern end of University Avenue, with University of Toronto buildings to the east and west, lies Queen's Park, a lovely green place in the heart of the city. Embedded in its center is the rose-tinted sandstone-and-granite Ontario Legislature, which has stood here since 1893. The *New Yorker* comic writer Bruce McCall labeled it an example of "Early Penitentiary" style, but many find it stately and attractive. Be sure to call ahead before you visit to make sure that the building will be open to the public that day. Try to take the Friday afternoon "Art & Architecture" tour that runs between 2 and 3:30pm (it's free, but advance reservations are required to participate). If you're interested in observing the Ontario Legislature in session, consult its schedule on the website.

111 Wellesley St. W. (at University Ave.). 𝒞 **416/325-7500.** www.ontla.on.ca. Free admission. Early Sept to late May Mon–Fri 8:30-am-5pm; late May to early Sept daily 8:30-am-5pm. Call for tour information & reservations. Subway: Queen's Park.

Royal Bank Plaza Shimmering in the sun, Royal Bank Plaza looks like a pillar of gold, and with good reason. During its construction, 70,874g (2,500 oz.) of gold went into the building's 14,000 windows as a coloring agent. More important, the structure is a masterpiece of architectural design. Two triangular towers of bronze mirror glass flank a 40m-high (131-ft.) glass-walled banking hall. The external walls of the towers are built in a serrated configuration so that they reflect a phenomenal mosaic of color.

In the banking hall, hundreds of aluminum cylinders hang from the ceiling, the work of Venezuelan sculptor Jesús Raphael Soto. Two levels below, a waterfall-and-pine-tree setting is naturally illuminated from the hall above.

Front & Bay sts. Free admission. Subway: Union.

St. James' Cathedral ★★★ This early English Gothic–style Anglican cathedral owes its existence at least in part to a group of American Loyalists. They joined with a group of British immigrants to found a congregation in 1797, and they were given a plot of land, which today is bounded by Church, King, Jarvis, and Adelaide streets. They started building Toronto's first church on this site in 1803. The original frame building was enlarged in 1818 and replaced in 1831—and that burned down in 1839. The first cathedral replaced it, only to be destroyed in the great fire of 1849. The present building was begun in 1850 and completed in 1874. It boasts the tallest steeple in Canada. Inside, there's a Tiffany window in memory of William Jarvis, one of Toronto's founding fathers.

In addition to being a great work of architecture, St. James' is a good place to stop and rest for a bit. Unless there's a service going on, it doesn't draw much of a crowd, so it feels like a private oasis in the middle of downtown. St. James' also hosts free concerts every Tuesday at 1pm from September to June. The adjoining park is pretty, too, especially in summer months.

65 Church St. ℂ **416/364-7865.** www.stjamescathedral.on.ca. Free admission. Sun–Fri 7:30am–5:30pm; Sat 9am–3pm. Subway: King.

St. Michael's Cathedral ★★★ The principal seat of the Catholic archdiocese of Toronto, St. Michael's is another 19th-century neo-Gothic structure. Built between 1845 and 1848, it originally had a plain interior design with clear-glass windows and white walls. That changed in 1850, when Armand de Charbonnel became the second Bishop of Toronto. Charbonnel was a Frenchman who lived in Montréal, and at first, he was so opposed to his new post that he traveled to Rome to beg Pope Pius IX to change his mind. The pope had other ideas and used Charbonnel's visit to consecrate him in the Sistine Chapel. However, when the new bishop finally arrived in Toronto in September 1850, he threw himself into beautifying St. Michael's. He sold lands that he owned in France and donated the proceeds to the cathedral. He bought dazzling stained-glass windows from France, built interior chapels, and commissioned paintings; he also imported the Stations of the Cross from France (that's why they're in French).

St. Michael's is particularly venerated for its musical tradition. It has its own boys' choir—which has won awards internationally—and of the four Masses they sing weekly, three are on Sunday.

65 Bond St. ℂ **416/364-0234.** www.stmichaelscathedral.com. Free admission. Mon–Sat 6am–6pm; Sun 6am–10pm. Subway: Queen or Dundas.

Looking Sharp

No building in Toronto is more distinctive than the **Sharp Centre for Design.** While it doesn't dominate Toronto's skyline the way that the CN Tower does, it's a work of stark originality. Designed by renowned architect Will Alsop, it opened in 2004 to near-universal shock—and acclaim—including a Worldwide Architecture Award from the Royal Institute of British Architects. The upper portion of the structure is referred to as the "table top," and its white-and-black checkerboard body stands 26m (85 ft.) above the street on 12 spindly, colorful legs. It's most dramatic at night, when it's lit by 16 large metal lights with blue bulbs. Sadly, it's open only to students of the Ontario College of Art and Design, not the public. Located on McCaul Street, just south of Dundas Street West, you'll see it in the "Chinatown & Kensington Market" tour, on p. 134.

The Big O

The University of Toronto has some of the most eclectic architecture in the city. Unfortunately, one of the most talked-about buildings is one that you can't get inside: the **Graduate House**, located at the campus's western edge at 60 Harbord St. (at Spadina Ave.). Designed by architect Thom Mayne, this award-winning building looks not unlike a concrete bunker, and the giant UNIVERSITY OF TORONTO sign only has the last letter visible at most viewing angles, earning the structure the nickname "The Big O." There are many more new and interesting buildings on campus, such as the Leslie Dan Faculty of Pharmacy, with a design much sexier than its name would suggest. Naturally, since the architect is none other than Norman Foster.

Toronto Reference Library   Step inside—a pool and a waterfall gently screen out the street noise, and the space opens dramatically to the sky. Light and air flood every corner. This 1977 six-story structure is another masterwork by Toronto architect Raymond Moriyama, who also designed the Bata Shoe Museum (see p. 109). Recent reconstruction has only improved the space: The addition of the Bram & Bluma Appel Salon on the second floor provides a space for free literary and cultural programming organized by the library.

789 Yonge St. ✆ **416/395-5577.** Free admission. Year-round Mon–Thurs 10am–8pm, Fri & Sat 10am–5pm; Thanksgiving–Apr also Sun 1:30–5pm. Subway: Yonge/Bloor.

HISTORIC BUILDINGS

Campbell House ★   This lovely old house has a small art gallery filled with rotating exhibitions. An 1822 mansion, it belonged to Sir William Campbell, a Loyalist and sixth chief justice of Upper Canada. The man's home has been beautifully restored (complete with a lovely collection of period furniture), even if it *was* moved several blocks from its original location in 1972. Guided tours take about half an hour and provide insight into Toronto's early history.

160 Queen St. W. (at University Ave.). ✆ **416/597-0227.** www.campbellhousemuseum.ca. C$6 adults, C$4 seniors & students (w/ID), C$3 children 5–12. Year-round Mon–Fri 9:30am–4:30pm; May–Oct also Sat & Sun noon–4:30pm. Closed Dec 25. Subway: Osgoode.

Colborne Lodge   This charming, English-style Regency cottage with a three-sided veranda was built from 1836 to 1837 to take advantage of the view of Lake Ontario and the Humber River. Today, it's set amid downtown's soaring office towers, but in the 1830s, it was considered way out in the country and a bother to travel to during the harsh winters. In 1873, the owner, a Toronto surveyor and architect named John Howard, donated the house and surrounding land to the city in return for an annual salary. That created the impressive and expansive High Park (see "Parks, Gardens & Cemeteries," below), a great recreational area. Don't miss the lovely offerings of the on-site, historic food program.

High Park. ✆ **416/392-6916.** C$6 adults, C$4 seniors & students (w/ID), C$3 children ages 5–12. Tues–Sun noon–5pm; call ahead as hours vary. Subway: High Park.

Fort York ★ ☺   For those interested in history—especially military history—this is a treat. This historic base was established by Lt. Gov. John Graves Simcoe in 1793 to defend "little muddy York," as Toronto was then known. Americans sacked it in April 1813, but the British rebuilt that same summer. Fort York was used by the military until 1880 and was pressed back into service during both world wars.

You can tour the soldiers' and officers' quarters; clamber over the ramparts; and in summer, view demonstrations of drills, music, and cooking. If you can, try to visit on Victoria Day, Canada Day, or Simcoe Day (see "Holidays," p. 23), when there are plenty of special events. These include the ever-popular Kids' Drill, in which kids get to take part in a military exercise. For 2012, watch out for special exhibits that commemorate the War of 1812.

100 Garrison Rd. (off Fleet St., btw. Bathurst St. & Strachan Ave.).© **416/392-6907.** www.fortyork.ca. C$8 adults, C$4 seniors & children 13–18, C$3 children 6–12, free for children 5 & under. Mid-May to early Sept daily 10am–5pm; early Sept to mid-May Mon–Fri 10am–4pm, Sat & Sun 10am–5pm. Subway: Bathurst, then streetcar no. 911 S.

Mackenzie House   This Greek Revival brick row house dates from the mid–19th century. It was once the home of William Lyon Mackenzie, a fiery orator and newspaper editor who had a most unusual career. He became Toronto's first mayor in 1836 . . . and then, in 1837, he led the Upper Canada rebellion against British rule. Mackenzie fled to the United States with a bounty on his head but returned to Toronto after influential friends arranged a pardon. Some of those same friends bought this house for him, and Mackenzie lived here from 1859 until his death in 1861. It's furnished in 1850s style, and in the back is a print shop modeled after Mackenzie's own. Mackenzie was born in Scotland, and celebrations for Hogmanay and Robbie Burns Day are always special here.

82 Bond St.© **416/392-6915.** C$6 adults, C$4 seniors & students, C$3 children 5–12, free for children 4 & under; higher admission rates on holidays. May–Aug Tues–Sun noon–5pm; Sept–Dec Tues–Sun noon–4pm; Jan–Apr Sat & Sun noon–5pm. Subway: Dundas.

Spadina Museum Historic House & Garden ★   This circa-1866 mansion with spectacular seasonal gardens reopened in 2010 after an extensive, expensive renovation. The result is worth a visit: Now a museum run by the City of Toronto, it's a year-round destination to get a sense of domestic life in Toronto in the 1920s and '30s. The garden is also themed: It's a Victorian-Edwardian masterpiece. The Austin family occupied the house from 1866 to 1980, and successive generations modified and added to the house and its decor.

285 Spadina Ave. © **416/392-6910.** www. toronto.ca/spadinamuseum. Free admission. Gardens Mon–Fri 9am–4pm. Subway: Dupont.

Park Yourself Here

Spadina House is the next-door neighbor of Casa Loma (p. 115). Between the two is a small but lovely park that is almost hidden by the trees that shade it. Many visitors don't notice it, but locals love it. Grab a bench here if you want to take a breather.

FOR SPORTS FANS

Air Canada Centre ★   This sports and entertainment complex is home to the Maple Leafs (hockey) and the Raptors (basketball). Longtime fans were crushed when the Leafs moved here in 1999 from Maple Leaf Gardens—the arena that had housed the team since 1931—but the Air Canada Centre has quickly become a fan favorite; the center was designed with comfort in mind (the seats are wide and upholstered). Seating is on a steeper-than-usual grade so that even the "nosebleed" sections have decent sightlines. When the teams are off the field (or ice), it serves as a concert venue.

40 Bay St. (at Lakeshore Blvd.).℃ **416/815-5500.** www.theaircanadacentre.com. Subway: Union, then the LRT to Queen's Quay.

BMO Field ★   With a capacity of 20,000, it's home to Canada's national soccer team, as well as the popular Toronto FC. This is Canada's first soccer-specific stadium and, despite some initial hiccups with the quality of the playing surface, it's won many plaudits for the intimate atmosphere and infectious attitude of the noisy fans, who sing cheers and chants throughout the matches.

BMO Field, 170 Princes Blvd., Exhibition Place.℃ **416/360-GOAL** (416/360-4625). www.torontofc.ca/ bmo-field. Tickets $C26–$C120. Subway: Bathurst, then streetcar no. 511 S to end of line.

Canada's Sports Hall of Fame   In the center of Exhibition Place, this three-floor space celebrates the country's greatest male and female athletes in all major sports. Complementing the displays are touch-screen computers that tell you everything you could want to know about particular sports personalities and Canada's athletic heritage.

115 Princes Blvd., Exhibition Place.℃ **416/260-6789.** Free admission. Mon–Fri 10am–4:30pm. Subway: Bathurst, then streetcar no. 511 S to end of line.

Hockey Hall of Fame ★★ ☺   Ice hockey fans will be thrilled by the artifacts collected here. They include the original Stanley Cup, a replica of the Montréal Canadiens' locker room, Terry Sawchuck's goalie gear, Newsy Lalonde's skates, and the stick Max Bentley used. You'll also see photographs of the personalities and great moments in hockey history. Most fun are the shooting and goalkeeping interactive displays, where you can take a whack at targets with a puck or don goalie gear and face down flying video pucks or sponge pucks.

In Brookfield Place, 30 Yonge St. (at Front St.).℃ **416/360-7765.** www.hhof.com. C$15 adults, C$12 seniors, C$10 children 4-18, free for children 3 & under. Mon–Fri 10am–5pm; Sat 9:30am–6pm; Sun 10:30am–5pm. Closed Jan 1 & Dec 25. Subway: Union.

Rogers Centre ★   This is home to the Toronto Blue Jays baseball team and the Toronto Argonauts football team. In 1989, the opening of this stadium, then known as SkyDome, was a gala event. The stadium represents an engineering feat, featuring the world's first fully retractable roof and a gigantic video scoreboard. It is so large that a 31-story building would fit inside the complex when the roof is closed.

1 Blue Jays Way.℃ **416/341-2770.** www.rogerscentre.com. Subway: Union, then follow the signs & walkway.

MARKETS

Toronto's markets, a part of its heritage, are thriving today. In summer and fall, there are dozens of farmers markets operating throughout the city's residential neighborhoods and beyond, even at New City Hall. Antique markets run year-round, and open-air markets such as Kensington are part of the city's fabric. Make like a local and dive into the fray. In addition to the markets listed below, check out the smaller farmers markets at the **Distillery District** (p. 103) and at **Riverdale Farm** (p. 128), plus the wealth of choices that have sprouted at Dufferin Grove, the Green Barns at Wychwood, the Evergreen Brickworks, and beyond.

Kensington Market ★★　This colorful, lively area should not be missed. You'll hear Caribbean, Portuguese, Italian, and many other languages and dialects as merchants spread out their wares. Think: squid and crabs in pails; live chickens and pigeons; local breads; cheese from around the world; apples, pears, peppers, ginger, and spices; West Indies mangoes; and salted fish from Portuguese dories. There's also lace, fabrics, and other colorful remnants. Kensington Avenue itself is a treasure trove of vintage clothing stores. You'll see a lot of junk here, but amazing finds can be had at shops such as **Courage My Love** (see p. 175). Most of the shops display their wares outdoors in decent weather, adding to the color and charm of the area. *Note:* There's no market on Sunday.

> ### Coffee Break
>
> One Kensington Market spot that's worth a stop is **Ideal Coffee** (84 Nassau St.; ✆ 416/362-7700). This groovy little cafe serves organic and fair-trade beans, and roasts its own. A great cup of joe to keep you on the go.

Bounded by Dundas St., Spadina Ave., Baldwin St. & Augusta Ave. No phone. Most stores Mon–Sat noon–6pm. Subway: St. Patrick, then Dundas St. streetcar W to Kensington St.

St. Lawrence Market　This handsome food market is, in fact, two tiers. The primary market runs throughout the week in a vast building constructed around the facade of the second City Hall, built in 1850. Vendors sell meat, fish, fruit, vegetables, and dairy products, as well as other foodstuffs. The second one operates Saturday only, across the road, and is busy with local farmers and their wares. The best time to visit is early Saturday morning, shortly after the farmers arrive. Don't miss the gallery and city archives on the second floor of the South Market: Historic shows about the city are mounted here, and it's free, too.

92 Front St. E. ✆ **416/392-7219.** Tues–Thurs 8am–6pm; Fri 8am–7pm; Sat 5am–5pm. Subway: Union.

PARKS, GARDENS & CEMETERIES

Downtown

Allan Gardens ★ ☺　What a difference a few years can make. Allan Gardens used to be down at the heels and seedy, but since the University of Toronto relocated its Botany Greenhouses here in 2004, this park has been infused with new life. This was actually Toronto's first civic park, created on the 4 hectares (10 acres) donated to the city by Mayor George William Allan. Originally called the Horticultural Gardens, the city renamed the park after Allan died in 1901. The stunning glass-domed Palm House conservatory dates back to 1910 and contains six greenhouses. It has been joined by U of T's restored and renovated greenhouses, now called the Allan Gardens Children's Conservatory.

Btw. Jarvis, Sherbourne, Dundas & Gerrard sts. ✆ **416/392-1111.** Free admission. Daily dawn–dusk. Subway: Dundas.

Ireland Park ★★ 🎁　In 1847, Toronto was a city of 20,000—until 38,000 Irish immigrants arrived that summer. On June 21, 2007, this memorial to the Irish Famine was opened at Éireann Quay by Mary McAleese, president of Ireland. The park was inspired by Rowan Gillespie's "Departure" series of famine figures, which stand on Dublin's Liffey quayside, depicting Irish emigrants looking out to sea. There are seven figures in Dublin and five in Toronto's new park: They reach out to one another across the sea. The figures in Ireland Park were also created by Gillespie, and they are called the "Arrival" series. There is also a memorial in the park to the more than 1,100 who died just after their arrival; as their names are discovered, they are inscribed in a limestone wall. Although it's tucked away, it's a worthwhile trek to find it and pause to think on this key time in history.

At Bathurst St. & Queens Quay W. (across from Bathurst Quay). © **416/601-6906.** www.irelandpark foundation.com. Free admission. Daily dawn–dusk. Subway: Union, then the LRT to Spadina Ave. & walk W to Bathurst St.

Toronto Music Garden ★★★   Toronto is a city of gardens, but this one along Toronto's waterfront is a favorite of many locals. Cellist Yo-Yo Ma and landscape designer Julie Moir Messervy created the Toronto Music Garden to invoke Bach's "First Suite for Unaccompanied Cello." The prelude is represented by the undulating curves of a river-scape; the allemande by a forest grove that's filled with wandering trails; the courante by a swirling path through wildflowers; the *menuett* by a pavilion of formally arranged flowerbeds; and finally the gigue, with giant grass steps that lead you back to the real world. It's tough to translate the experience into words, but the music garden is a don't-miss spot if you visit Toronto in warm weather.

475 Queens Quay W. © **416/338-0338.** Free admission. Daily dawn–dusk. Subway: Union, then the LRT to Spadina.

Trinity Bellwoods Park ★ 👪   This gorgeous neighborhood park was originally part of a military reserve when Toronto was still a small town called York and the British troops were garrisoned at Fort York (p. 119). Eventually, parcels were sold to retiring officers, but in 1851, Bishop John Strachan bought up some of the land in order to found a college. Strachan was furious at the University of Toronto's decision to become a secular school, and he founded the Anglican Trinity College in 1852 (of course, Trinity is now part of the University, though it has kept its Anglican traditions). The buildings were torn down, but the impressive stone-and-wrought-iron gates that face Queen Street West still remain, and there are Victorian lampposts illuminating the main paths at night. Given the colorful neighborhood it's located in (the Art & Design District), it's no surprise that Trinity Bellwoods has hosted some interesting events, including an anarchist book fair and weekly, ongoing drumming circles. It's a family park, good for picnics and people-watching. Be on the lookout for the legendary albino squirrels who reside here—there's a coffee shop across the street named in honor of the rodents.

Btw. Dundas St. W., Crawford St., Queen St. W. & Gore Vale Ave. © **416/392-1111.** Free admission. Daily dawn–dusk. Subway: Osgoode, then a streetcar W to Bellwoods Ave.

Music Alfresco

The **Toronto Music Garden** hosts some of the city's best summer concerts. From late June to mid-September, you can count on listening to live music here every Thursday at 7pm and on Sunday at 4pm. Sometimes, you'll hear classical music—especially by the baroque composers—but the programs are rather eclectic. Recent offerings have included Spanish flamenco music and traditional Chinese melodies. All performances are free.

Midtown

High Park ★ ☺   This 161-hectare (398-acre) park in the far west of Midtown was architect John G. Howard's gift to the city. He lived in Colborne Lodge, which still stands in the park (p. 119). There's a large lake here called Grenadier Pond (great for ice skating in winter); a small zoo; a swimming pool; tennis courts; sports fields; bowling greens; and vast expanses of green for baseball, jogging, picnicking, cycling, and more. The Dream in High Park, an annual Shakespearean offering in the open air, is staged each summer and draws crowds who often picnic on-site.

1873 Bloor St. W. (S to the Gardiner Expwy.). No phone. www.toronto.ca/parks. Free admission. Daily dawn–dusk. Subway: High Park.

Necropolis ★   If you have a fascination with historic cemeteries, definitely make a stop here. Located in Midtown East, this is one of the city's oldest cemeteries, dating to 1850. Some of the remains were originally buried in Potters Field, where Yorkville stands today.

Before strolling through the cemetery, pick up a History Tour brochure at the office. You'll find the graves of William Lyon Mackenzie, leader of the 1837 rebellion, as well as those of his followers Samuel Lount and Peter Matthews, who were hanged for their parts in the rebellion. (Mackenzie himself went on to become a member of Parliament. Go figure.) Other notables buried in the 7.2-hectare (18-acre) cemetery include George Brown, one of the fathers of Confederation; Anderson Ruffin Abbot, the first Canadian-born black surgeon; Joseph Tyrrell, who unearthed dinosaurs in Alberta; and world-champion oarsman Ned Hanlan. Henry Langley, who designed the Necropolis' porte-cochere and the Gothic Revival chapel—as well as the spires of St. James' and St. Michael's cathedrals (p. 117 and 118)—is also buried here.

200 Winchester St. (at Sumach St.). © **416/923-7911.** www.mountpleasantgroupofcemeteries.ca. Free admission. Daily 8am–dusk. Subway: Castle Frank, then bus no. 65 S on Parliament St. to Wellesley St. & walk 3 blocks E to Sumach St.

Uptown & Further Afield

Edwards Gardens   This quiet, formal 14-hectare (35-acre) garden is part of a series of parks that stretch over 240 hectares (593 acres) along the Don Valley. It's not easily reached by public transit, so be prepared to make a special and long trip. Gracious bridges arch over a creek, rock gardens abound, and roses and other seasonal flowers add color and scent. (The bridges are a favorite spot for wedding photos, and in seasonal weather, the line of brides and grooms can seem never-ending.) The garden is famous for its rhododendrons. The Civic Garden Centre operates a gift shop and offers free walking tours on Tuesday and Thursday at 11am and 2pm. The Centre also boasts a fine horticultural library.

777 Lawrence Ave. E. (at Leslie St.). © **416/392-8188.** www.toronto.ca/parks. Free admission. Daily dawn–dusk. Subway: Eglinton, then bus no. 51 (Leslie) or 54 (Lawrence).

Evergreen Brick Works ★★★ ☺   Be prepared: You have to hike it here on foot over a lush path, take a shuttle from Broadview subway station, or drive and pay for parking. Once the home of the city's founding brick factory, it has been reinvented by the dynamic Canadian Evergreen foundation (national in scope: its business is to "green" cities) to include a farmers market that runs year-round on Saturday mornings, a cafe and restaurant featuring local goods under the Café Belong moniker, marshlands, a beautiful park, and thoughtful exhibits that take advantage of the unique setting of the age-old kilns where Toronto's signature red bricks were once formed. A taste of past and present, the Brick Works is proving to be one of the city's most attractive locales for brilliant events. There are programs for families, parties for grown-ups, and much more.

550 Bayview Ave. (C) **416/596-1495.** http://ebw.evergreen.ca Free admission. Subway: Broadview Station, then free shuttle bus to the site (see website for schedule). By car: From downtown, take River St. just N of Gerrard St. to Bayview Ave., then follow Bayview Ave. to the site.

Scarborough Bluffs ★★ On the eastern edge of Toronto is a natural wonder that's well worth a half-day visit. The Scarborough Bluffs are unique in North America, and their layers of sand and clay offer a remarkable geological record of the great Ice Age. Rising up to 105m (345 ft.) above Lake Ontario, they stretch out over 14km (8¾ miles). The first 45m (148 ft.) contains fossil plants and animals that were deposited by the advancing Wisconsin Glacier 70,000 years ago. The bluffs were given their name in 1793 by Lady Elizabeth Simcoe, wife of the first Lieutenant Governor of Upper Canada (Ontario); as she sailed to York, as Toronto was then known, she was reminded of the cliffs of Yorkshire.

S of Kingston Rd. No phone. www.toronto.ca/parks. Free admission. Daily dawn–dusk. Subway: Victoria Park, then no. 12 Kingston Rd. bus to Brimley Rd. & about a 15-min. walk S along Brimley Rd. By car: From downtown, take Don Valley Pkwy. to Hwy. 401 E, exit on Brimley Rd. & drive S.

ESPECIALLY FOR KIDS

The city puts on a fabulous array of special events for children at **Harbourfront.** In February, there's **ALOUD: A Celebration for Young Readers.** Come April, **Spring Fever** welcomes the season with egg decorating, puppet shows, and more; on Saturday mornings in April, the 5-to-12 set enjoys **cushion concerts.** For information, call (C) **416/973-4000** or visit **www.harbourfrontcentre.com**.

For more than 30 years, the **Lorraine Kimsa Theatre for Young People** (165 Front St. E., at Sherbourne St.; (C) **416/862-2222** for box office or 416/363-5131 for administration) has been entertaining youngsters. Its season runs from August to May.

The 11th annual **Sprockets Toronto International Film Festival for Children** screens more than 100 entries from 29 countries. Like the Toronto International Film Festival in September, the screenings, to be held in April, take place around the city. Call (C) **416/968-FILM** (416/968-3456) for details or visit **www. sprockets.ca**.

Help! We've Got Kids is an all-in-one print and online directory for attractions, events, shops, and services appropriate for kids younger than 13 in the greater Toronto area. It doesn't provide a lot of detail about most of the entries, but the listings make a great starting point. Visit **www.helpwevegotkids.com**.

Look for the "Kids" icon in the sections above for the following Toronto-area attractions that have major appeal for kids of all ages. The best venues (at least, from a kid's point of view) are these:

o **Black Creek Pioneer Village:** For crafts, costumes, and an entertaining take on history. See p. 109.
o **Harbourfront:** Kaleidoscope is an ongoing program of creative crafts, active games, and special events on weekends and holidays. There are also a pond, winter ice skating, and a crafts studio. See p. 103.

o **Ontario Science Centre:** Kids race to be the first at this paradise of hands-on games, experiments, and push-button demonstrations—800 of them. See p. 106.

o **Toronto Zoo:** One of the best in the world, modeled after San Diego's—the animals in this 284-hectare (702-acre) park really do live in a natural environment. See p. 108.

For more specialized interests:

o **Evergreen Brick Works:** For hands-on learning experiences in cooking, ecology, markets, and treats. See p. 124.

o **Casa Loma:** The stables, secret passageway, and fantasy rooms capture children's imaginations. See p. 115.

o **CN Tower:** Especially the simulator games and the glass floor. See p. 102.

o **Fort York:** For its reenactments of battle drills, musket and cannon firing, and musical marches with fife and drum. See p. 119.

o **High Park:** Wide-open spaces, plus the chance to hang out with llamas. See p. 124.

o **Hockey Hall of Fame:** Who wouldn't want the chance to tend goal against Mark Messier and Wayne Gretzky (with a sponge puck), and to practice with the fun and challenging video pucks? See p. 121.

o **Royal Ontario Museum:** The top hits are the Ancient Egypt Gallery, the Hands-On Biodiversity Gallery, and the Maiasaur Project. See p. 107.

o **Toronto Islands–Centreville:** Riding a ferry to this turn-of-the-20th-century amusement park is part of the fun. See p. 108.

Ontario Place ☺ For all its Space Age looks, this is really just a fun amusement park, more thrilling than Centreville on Centre Island (p. 108), but small in comparison with Paramount Canada's Wonderland (see below). From a distance, you'll see five steel-and-glass pods suspended on columns 32m (105 ft.) above the lake, three artificial islands, and a huge geodesic dome. The five pods contain a multimedia theater, a children's theater, a high-technology exhibit, and displays that tell the story of Ontario in vivid kaleidoscopic detail. The dome houses Cinesphere, where specially made IMAX movies are shown year-round.

Ontario Place has many attractions targeted at kids, starting with the **H2O Generation Station,** a gigantic "soft play" structure with twisting slides, towers, and walkways. The **Atom Blaster**—which claims to be Canada's largest foam-ball free-for-all—is fun for the whole family. Younger children will enjoy the **MicroKids** play area with its ball pit, climbing platforms, and other tot-appropriate draws.

A Storybook Sanctuary

The **Osborne Collection of Early Children's Books** is a treasure trove for bibliophiles of all ages. Located at the Lillian H. Smith Branch of the Toronto Public Library (239 College St.; ✆ 416/393-7753), the collection includes a 14th-century manuscript of Aesop's fables, Victorian and Edwardian adventure and fantasy tales, 16th-century schoolbooks, storybooks once owned by British royalty, an array of "penny dreadfuls" (cheap thrillers from the days when a paperback book cost a penny), and Florence Nightingale's childhood library. Special exhibits at the Osborne often feature whimsical subjects. You can visit the library weekdays between 10am and 6pm or Saturdays from 9am to 5pm.

Retro Thrills

With the fanfare given to the new rides Paramount Canada's Wonderland introduces each summer, many park-goers overlook the older attractions. The Wild Beast is one of the original roller coasters, and it's still one of the best. The first few times you hurtle along the track, you'll be convinced that the whole rickety structure is about to fall down at any moment. Guess what—it was designed to feel that way! Other tried-and-true favorites include the Minebuster and the Dragon Fire. A bonus: shorter queues!

At night, the **Molson Amphitheatre** accommodates concert-goers in the reserved seating area under the canopy and on the surrounding grass. For concert information, call ✆ **416/260-5600;** for tickets, call **Ticketmaster** (✆ **416/870-8000**).

955 Lakeshore Blvd. W. ✆ **416/314-9811,** or 416/314-9900 for recorded info. www.ontarioplace.com. Grounds only C$18 adults, C$12 seniors & children 4–5, free for children 3 & under, separate fees for rides & events (pricing varies by month); Play All Day pass C$34 adults, C$18 seniors & children 4–5, free for children 3 & under. Park open mid-May to Labour Day daily 10am–dusk; evening events end & dining spots close later. Closed (except Cinesphere) early Sept to early May. Subway: Bathurst, then Bathurst St. streetcar S.

Paramount Canada's Wonderland ★ ☺ An hour north of Toronto lies what some say is Canada's answer to Disney World. The 120-hectare (297-acre) park features more than 200 attractions, including 65 rides, a water park, a play area for tiny tots (KidZville), and live shows. Because the park relies on a local audience for most of its business, there are new attractions each year. Some of the most popular have been the Behemoth, Canada's biggest, fastest, and tallest rollercoaster; the Fly, a roller coaster designed to make every seat feel as though it's in the front car (the faint of heart can't hide at the back of this one!); Sledge Hammer, a "menacing mechanical giant" that stands 24m (79 ft.) tall and hurls riders through accelerated jumps and free-falls; Cliffhanger, a "super swing" that executes 360-degree turns and makes riders feel immune to gravity; and the Xtreme Skyflyer, a hang-gliding and skydiving hybrid that plunges riders 46m (151 ft.) in a free-fall. The roller coasters range from the looping, inverted Top Gun to the track-free suspended Vortex.

The Splash Works water park offers a huge wave pool and water rides spread over 8.1 hectares (20 acres), from speed slides and tube rides to special scaled-down slides and a kids' play area. You'll also find Hanna-Barbera characters, including Scooby-Doo, strolling around the park (and ready to get their picture taken with the kids). Additional attractions include Wonder Mountain and its high divers (they take the 20m/66-ft. plunge down Victoria Falls to the mountain's base), restaurants, and shops.

9580 Jane St., Vaughan. ✆ **905/832-7000** or 905/832-8131. www.canadaswonderland.com. Pay-One-Price Passport (includes unlimited rides & shows, but not special attractions or Kingswood Music Theater) C$45 adults, free for children 2 & under; check website for specials. June 1 to June 25 Mon–Fri 10am–8pm, Fri & Sat 10am–10pm; June 26 to Labour Day daily 10am–10pm; late May & early Sept to early Oct Sat & Sun 10am–8pm. Closed mid-Oct to mid-May. Subway: Yorkdale or York Mills, then GO Express Bus to Wonderland. By car: From downtown, take Yonge St. N to Hwy. 401 & go W to Hwy. 400. Go N on Hwy. 400 to Rutherford Rd. exit & follow signs. From the N, exit at Major Mackenzie Dr.

Riverdale Farm ★★   Situated on the edge of the Don Valley Ravine, this working farm located on 3 hectares (7½ acres) right in the city is a favorite with small tots. They enjoy watching the cows, pigs, turkeys, and ducks—and can get close enough to pet many animals, such as the rabbits. Because this really is a working farm, you'll see all of the chores of daily life, such as horse grooming, cow and goat milking, egg collecting, and animal feeding. Adults should note that the farm shop has some seasonal produce and baked goods, and that there's a farmers' market on-site Tuesdays from May to October.

201 Winchester St. (at Sumach St.). ✆ **416/392-6794.** Free admission. Daily 9am–5pm. Subway: Castle Frank, then bus no. 65 S on Parliament St. to Wellesley St. & walk 3 blocks E to Sumach St.

ORGANIZED TOURS

For summer weekends, it's always a good idea to make tour reservations in advance. At slower times, you can usually call the same day or simply show up.

Bus Tours

Try the **Hop-On Hop-Off City Tour** offered by **Gray Line** (184 Front St. E.; ✆ **416/594-3310;** www.grayline.ca). The good thing is that it goes to such major sights as the Eaton Centre, City Hall, Casa Loma, Yorkville, Chinatown, Harbourfront, the Rogers Centre, and the CN Tower, and a ticket allows you to get on and off the bus over a 2-day period. These narrated tours, which operate daily starting at 10am, cost C$35 adults, C$31 seniors, and C$18 children 4 to 11; free for children 3 and under.

OUTDOOR ACTIVITIES

Toronto residents love the great outdoors, whatever the time of year. In summer, you'll see people cycling, boating, and hiking; in winter, they are skating and, out of town for the most part, skiing and snowboarding.

For additional information on facilities in the parks, golf courses, tennis courts, swimming pools, beaches, and picnic areas, contact **Toronto Parks and Recreation** (✆ **416/392-8186;** www.toronto.ca/parks). Also, see "Parks, Gardens & Cemeteries," earlier in this chapter.

Beaches

The Beaches is the neighborhood along Queen Street East from Coxwell Avenue to Victoria Park. It has a charming boardwalk that connects the beaches, starting at **Ashbridge's Bay Park,** which has a sizable marina. **Woodbine Beach** connects to **Kew Gardens Park** and is a favorite with sunbathers and volleyball players. Woodbine also boasts the **Donald D. Summerville Olympic Pool.** Snack bars and trinket sellers line the length of the boardwalk.

Many locals prefer the beaches on the **Toronto Islands.** The ones on **Centre Island,** always the busiest, are favorites with families because of such nearby attractions as **Centreville.** The beaches on **Ward's Island** are much more secluded. They're connected by the loveliest boardwalk in the city, with masses of fragrant flowers and raspberry bushes along its edges. **Hanlan's Point,** also in the Islands, is Toronto's only nude beach.

Canoeing & Kayaking

The **Harbourfront Canoe and Kayak School** (283A Queens Quay W.; ℂ 800/960-8886 or 416/203-2277; www.paddletoronto.com) rents canoes and kayaks; call ahead if you are interested in taking private instruction.

You can also rent canoes, rowboats, and pedal boats on the **Toronto Islands** just south of Centreville.

Cross-Country Skiing

Just about every park in Toronto becomes potential cross-country skiing territory as soon as snow falls. Best bets are Sunnybrook Park and Ross Lord Park, both in North York. For more information, contact **Toronto Parks and Recreation** (ℂ 416/392-8186; www.toronto.ca/parks). Serious skiers interested in day trips to excellent out-of-town sites, such as Horseshoe Valley, can contact **Trakkers Cross Country Ski Club** (ℂ 416/763-0173; www.trakkers.ca), which also rents equipment.

Cycling

With biking trails through most of the city's parks and more than 29km (18 miles) of street bike routes, it's not surprising that Toronto has been called one of the best cycling cities in North America. Favorite pathways include the **Martin Goodman Trail** (from the Beaches to the Humber River along the waterfront); the **Lower Don Valley** bike trail (from the east end of the city north to Riverdale Park); **High Park** (with winding trails over 160 hectares/395 acres); and the **Toronto Islands,** where bikers ride without fear of cars. For advice, call the **Ontario Cycling Association** (ℂ 416/426-7416), contact **Toronto Parks and Recreation** (ℂ 416/392-8186; www.toronto.ca/parks), or visit www.toronto.ca/livegreen/greenlife_onthego_cycling.htm. Bike lanes are marked on College/Carlton streets, the Bloor Street Viaduct leading to the Danforth, Beverly/St. George streets, Jarvis Street, and Davenport Road.

For a list of bike rental shops, contact the **Toronto Bicycling Network** (ℂ 416/766-1985; www.tbn.ca). One sure bet is **Wheel Excitement** (249 Queens Quay W., Unit 110; ℂ 416/260-9000; www.wheelexcitement.ca). If you're interested in cycling with a group or want information about daily excursions and weekend trips, contact the Toronto Bicycling Network.

Be forewarned: Like many other North American cities, the tensions between cyclists and car drivers are mounting, so be on your guard and take it easy.

Walk/Jog/Cycle in Peace

One of the best places to walk, jog, or cycle in the city is the path that connects downtown with the Don Valley Ravine and winds up at the **Evergreen Brick Works**. There's plenty of topography and the promise of a beautiful and tranquil spot to rest at the end of the journey. On Saturdays in summer, you can also refuel at the farmers market, where good prepared foods, often made with local and seasonal ingredients, make the trek back a breeze.

Fitness Centers

The **Metro Central YMCA** (20 Grosvenor St.; ℂ 416/975-9622; www.ymca toronto.org) has excellent facilities, including a 25m (82-ft.) swimming pool, all kinds of cardiovascular machines, Nautilus equipment, an indoor track, squash

spas IN THE CITY

In the past decade or so, Toronto has established a reputation for superior spas, some in hotels and others stand-alone facilities. Here's a short list of the best, and most unique to the city.

Elmwood Spa. 18 Elm St. (✆ **416/977-6751;** www.elmwoodspa.com). Just a stone's throw from the busy corner of Dundas and Yonge streets, and a convenient respite for shoppers who have exhausted themselves at the nearby Eaton Centre, this is a favorite day spa to while away many serene hours of pampering, dining, and quiet play. They really have it all: massages and facials, a range of water therapies that center around a pretty pool, steam rooms, a whirlpool, and a poolside lounge where spa cuisine and herbal teas are served. The service is top-notch and the brand so highly respected they have their own line of beauty products. Facials are a highlight.

Holt Renfrew Spa. Holt Renfrew, 50 Bloor St. W. (✆ **416/960-2909;** www.holt renfrew.com). Located in one of Toronto's most luxurious stores is, appropriately enough, one of the city's most luxurious

spas. Decorated in modern-chic blond wood and glass, the spa provides a good range of cosmetic services, from manicures to massage. If you've flown to Toronto, try their Jet Lag Facial, which rehydrates the skin and includes lymphatic leg therapy.

Stillwater Spa. Park Hyatt Toronto, 4 Avenue Rd. (✆ **416/924-5471;** www.still waterspa.com). Water is the theme at this spa in the Park Hyatt, and it undulates in streams under transparent floor panels and courses down walls in mini-waterfalls. Before you even get to the treatment rooms, you'll be dazzled by the changing areas, which include a whirlpool and sauna, and also private cabana-like nooks for reclining (personal TV screens come with a headset). There's something for everyone at this lovely spot, from manicures to hair "rituals," Swedish and Reiki massage to anti-stress treatments. For a taste of Canadiana, try a Canadian grain facial (with grain from Alberta) or the BC seaweed wrap. The hotel dining room, combined with the health menu at the Spa, offer culinary delights, too.

and racquetball courts, and aerobics classes. The **University of Toronto Athletic Centre** (55 Harbord St., at Spadina Ave.; ✆ 416/978-3436; www.ac-fpeh.com) offers similar facilities. Guest passes to both centers are C$25 per day.

For yoga aficionados, there's no better place to stretch than **Yoga Plus** (40 Eglinton Ave. E., 8th Floor; ✆ 416/322-9936; www.yogaplustoronto.com). A single class costs C$20; there's also a pay-what-you-can "Karma" class available. For a listing of all of Toronto's yoga studios, visit **www.yogatoronto.ca**, which covers the city and the Greater Toronto Area.

Golf

Toronto is obsessed with golf: There are more than 75 public courses within an hour's drive of downtown. Here's information on some of the best.

○ **Don Valley.** 4200 Yonge St., south of Highway 401 (✆ 416/392-2465). Designed by Howard Watson, this is a scenic par-71 course with some challenging elevated tees. The par-3 13th hole is nicknamed the Hallelujah Corner (it takes a miracle to make par). It's considered a good place to start your kids. Greens fees are C$30 to C$63.

o **Humber Valley.** 40 Beattie Ave., at Albion Road (✆ **416/392-2488**). The relatively flat par-70 course is easy to walk, with lots of shade from towering trees. The three final holes require major concentration (the 16th and 17th are par-5s). Greens fees are C$44 to C$52.

o **Glen Abbey Golf Club.** 1333 Dorval Dr., Oakville (✆ **905/844-1800;** www. glenabbey.ca). The championship course is one of the most famous in Canada. Designed by Jack Nicklaus, the par-73 layout traditionally plays host to the Canadian Open. Greens fees are C$135 to C$265.

Travelers who are really into golf might want to consider a side trip to the **Muskoka Lakes** (see chapter 10). This area, just 90 minutes north, has some of the best golfing in the country at courses such as **Taboo** and the **Deerhurst Highlands.**

Ice Skating & In-Line Skating

Nathan Phillips Square, in front of City Hall, becomes a free ice rink in winter, as does an area at Harbourfront Centre. Rentals are available on-site. More than 25 parks contain artificial rinks (also free), including Grenadier Pond in High Park—a romantic spot, with a bonfire and vendors selling roasted chestnuts. They're open from November to March.

Skate till You Drop?

Let's say you'd like to go skating, while your traveling companion wants to hit the shops. If you head to **Hazelton Lanes,** you can both get what you want. A central courtyard doubles as a skating rink. Better yet, the shopping center's **Customer Service Centre** (✆ **416/968-8600**) offers complimentary skate rentals. It's hard to beat a deal like that.

In summer, in-line skaters pack Toronto's streets (and sidewalks). Go with the flow and rent some blades from **Wheel Excitement** (see "Cycling," above).

Jogging

Downtown routes might include **Harbourfront** and along the lakefront, or through **Queen's Park** and the University. The **Martin Goodman Trail** runs 20km (12 miles) along the waterfront from the Beaches in the east to the Humber River in the west. It's ideal for jogging, walking, or cycling. It links to the **Tommy Thompson Trail,** which travels the parks from the lakefront along the Humber River. Near the Ontario Science Centre in the Central Don Valley, **Ernest Thompson Seton Park** is also good for jogging. Parking is available at the Thorncliffe Drive and Wilket Creek entrances.

These areas are generally quite safe, but you should take the same precautions you would in any large city.

Rock Climbing

Toronto has several climbing gyms, including **Joe Rockhead's** (29 Fraser Ave.; ✆ **416/538-7670;** www.joerockheads.com) and the **Toronto Climbing Academy** (100 Broadview Ave.; ✆ **416/406-5900;** www.climbingacademy.com). You can pick up the finer points of knot tying and belaying. Both gyms also rent equipment.

Snowboarding & Skiing

The snowboard craze shows no sign of abating, at least from January to March (or anytime there's enough snow on the ground). One popular site is the **Earl Bales**

Park (4169 Bathurst St., just south of Sheppard Ave.), which offers rentals. The park also has an alpine ski center, which offers both equipment rentals and coaching. Call (✆ **416/395-7931**) for more information.

Swimming

The municipal parks, including High and Rosedale parks, offer a dozen or so outdoor pools (open June–Sept). Several community recreation centers have indoor pools. For **pool information,** call ✆ **416/338-7665.**

Visitors may buy a day pass to use the pools at the **YMCA** (20 Grosvenor St.; ✆ **416/975-9622**) and the **University of Toronto Athletic Centre** (55 Harbord St., at Spadina Ave.; ✆ **416/978-4680**).

Tennis

There are 200 municipal parks across Toronto with tennis facilities. The most convenient are the courts in High, Rosedale, and Jonathan Ashbridge parks. They are open from April to October only. Call **Toronto Parks** (✆ **416/392-1111**) for information. The Toronto Parks website also has a brochure you can download; visit www.toronto.ca/parks.

SPECTATOR SPORTS

AUTO RACING The **Grand Prix of Toronto** (formerly the Molson Indy; ✆ **416/588-7223;** www.grandprixtoronto.com) takes place in July at the Exhibition Place Street circuit. Check the website for 2011 updates.

BASEBALL **Rogers Centre** (1 Blue Jays Way, on Front St., beside the CN Tower) is the home of the **Toronto Blue Jays.** For tickets, contact the Toronto Blue Jays at ✆ **888/OK-GO-JAY** (888/654-6529) or 416/341-1234, or http://toronto.bluejays.mlb.com.

BASKETBALL Toronto's basketball team, the **Raptors,** has its home ground in the **Air Canada Centre** (40 Bay St., at Lakeshore Blvd.). The NBA schedule runs from October to April. The arena seats 19,500 for basketball. For information, contact the **Raptors Basketball Club** (40 Bay St.; ✆ **416/815-5600;** www.nba.com/raptors). For tickets, call **Ticketmaster** (✆ **416/870-8000**).

FOOTBALL Remember Kramer on *Seinfeld?* He would watch only Canadian football. If you're not familiar with it, here's your chance to catch a game. **Rogers Centre** (1 Blue Jays Way) is home to the **Argonauts** of the Canadian Football

---

Stephen Colbert vs. the Raptors

Toronto's basketball team has been on Stephen Colbert's bad side since the very first episode of Comedy Central's *The Colbert Report* on October 17, 2005. At that time, Colbert put the Raptors "On Notice" for losing a game to Maccabi Tel Aviv, the Euroleague champions. Things got worse in early 2007: Because the Raptors' mascot came in ahead of the Saginaw Spirits' Steagle Colbeagle the Eagle (named after Colbert) in an online poll, Colbert demoted the Raptors to his "Dead to Me" board. Oh, the indignity of being on the same list as bowtie pasta, screw-cap wines, and men with beards!

League. They play between June and November. For information, contact the club at ✆ 416/341-2700 or visit www.argonauts.on.ca. For tickets, call **Ticketmaster** (✆ 416/870-8000).

GOLF TOURNAMENTS Canada's national golf tournament, the **Bell Canadian Open,** usually takes place at the **Glen Abbey Golf Club** (✆ 905/844-1800) in Oakville, about 40 minutes from the city. Most years, it runs over the Labour Day weekend.

HOCKEY Hockey isn't Canada's national sport, believe it or not (that's lacrosse), but it's undoubtedly the most popular. The **Air Canada Centre** (40 Bay St., at Lakeshore Blvd.) is the home of the **Toronto Maple Leafs** (http://mapleleafs.nhl. com). The team hasn't won a Stanley Cup since 1967, but droves of fans stick with the franchise nonetheless. Though the arena seats 18,700 for hockey, tickets are not easy to come by because many are sold by subscription. The rest are available through **Ticketmaster** (✆ 416/870-8000).

HORSE RACING Thoroughbred racing takes place at **Woodbine Racetrack** (Rexdale Blvd. and Hwy. 427, Etobicoke; ✆ 416/675-6110 or 416/675-7223). It's famous for the Queen's Plate (usually contested on the third Sun in June); the Canadian International, a classic turf race (Sept or Oct); and the North America Cup (mid-June). Woodbine also hosts harness racing in spring and fall.

SOCCER Toronto's new soccer club, the **Toronto FC** (http://toronto.fc.mlsnet. com), is beloved by Torontonians. It's the first non-U.S. team in Major League Soccer. They play at BMO Field at Exhibition Place; it was built for the FC, and it holds 20,195 spectators. For tickets, call **Ticketmaster** (✆ 416/870-8000).

TENNIS TOURNAMENTS Canada's international tennis championship, the **Rogers Cup,** takes place in Toronto *and* Montréal every August (the men's and women's championships alternate cities each year). In 2012, the men play in Toronto, the women in Montréal. For more information, call ✆ 877/283-6647 or check www.lovemeansnothing.ca.

CITY STROLLS

Toronto is a great city for walking. The patchwork of dynamic ethnic neighborhoods, the impressive architecture, and the many parks all combine to encourage visitors to lace up and hit the streets. To boot, there are small cafes and eateries for refueling along the way or for taking a lazy break. But because the city is such a sprawling place, you'll need to pick your route carefully . . . unless you're happy to wander.

The walking tours in this chapter aren't designed to provide an overview, but rather to guide you through the most colorful and exciting neighborhoods in the city, which feature worthwhile sights on almost every corner.

WALKING TOUR 1: CHINATOWN & KENSINGTON MARKET

START:	**St. Patrick subway station.**
FINISH:	**Queen's Park subway station.**
TIME:	**At least 2 hours. Depending on how long you want to linger at the Art Gallery of Ontario and at various stops, perhaps as long as 8 hours.**
BEST TIMES:	**Tuesday through Saturday during the day.**
WORST TIMES:	**Monday, when the Art Gallery is closed.**

This walk takes you through the oldest of Toronto's existing Chinatowns (the city's original Chinatown was on York St., between King and Queen sts., but skyscrapers replaced it long ago). Although at least four Chinatowns exist today, and most Chinese live in the suburbs, the intersection of Dundas Street and Spadina (pronounced spa-*dye*-na) Avenue is still a major shopping and dining area for the Asian communities.

Kensington has changed dramatically over the years. Originally a Jewish community, it then became home to Portuguese and other European immigrants, and then changed again as the bordering Chinatown expanded at the same time shopkeepers from the Caribbean, the Middle East, and elsewhere arrived. There are several Asian herbalists and grocers, as well as West Indian and Middle Eastern shops. Kensington Avenue has the greatest concentration of vintage clothing stores in the city as well as some good grub and excellent cafes for refueling.

Walking Tour: Chinatown & Kensington Market

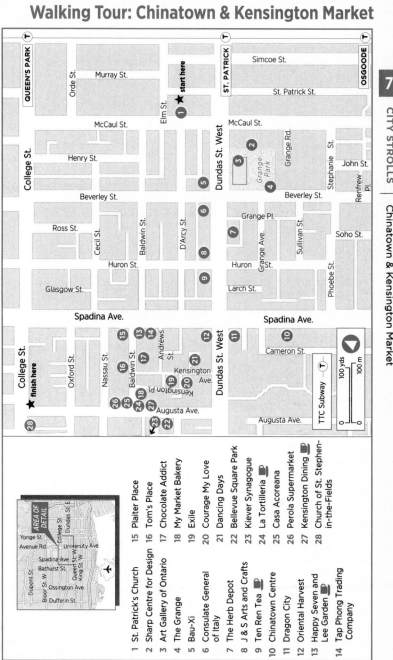

1 St. Patrick's Church
2 Sharp Centre for Design
3 Art Gallery of Ontario
4 The Grange
5 Bau-Xi
6 Consulate General of Italy
7 The Herb Depot
8 J & S Arts and Crafts
9 Ten Ren Tea 🍵
10 Chinatown Centre
11 Dragon City
12 Oriental Harvest
13 Happy Seven and Lee Garden 🍵
14 Tap Phong Trading Company

15 Plaiter Place
16 Tom's Place
17 Chocolate Addict
18 My Market Bakery
19 Exile
20 Courage My Love
21 Dancing Days
22 Bellevue Square Park
23 Kiever Synagogue
24 La Tortilleria 🍵
25 Casa Acoreana
26 Perola Supermarket
27 Kensington Dining 🍵
28 Church of St. Stephen-in-the-Fields

From the St. Patrick subway station, exit on the NW corner of Dundas St. and University Ave., and walk W on Dundas St. Turn right onto McCaul St. At no. 131, you'll see:

1 St. Patrick's Church

Built in 1861 for Toronto's Irish Catholic community, this church became the base of German-speaking Catholics from 1929 to the late 1960s. Inside, you'll find some of the most beautiful stained glass in Toronto. The church is also a popular site for concerts.

Go back toward Dundas St. and walk W; looking S on McCaul St., you'll see:

2 Sharp Centre for Design

This is one of the city's more controversial contributions to the recent surge in new and bold architecture. Will Alsop's building, which is part of the Ontario College of Art & Design, looks like a checkerboard box on stilts. The Sharp Centre won a Worldwide Award from the Royal Institute of British Architects in 2004; they described it as "courageous, bold, and just a little insane." Admire the insanity from the outside; visitors are not allowed beyond the lobby, although there is a shop worth a look.

Continue W along Dundas St. On your left is the:

3 Art Gallery of Ontario

Newly renovated—by local boy Frank Gehry, who grew up around the corner—and now blessed with the brilliant Thomson Collection, the AGO is arguably Toronto's best gallery. Visit for the stellar collection of paintings by Canadian legends and European masters, the best collection of Henry Moore sculpture in the world, the photography gallery, and much more. A recent gift from local collector and philanthropist Dr. Ydessa Hendeles added 32 Canadian and international contemporary artworks—the most significant single gift of contemporary art in the AGO's 110-year history.

Walk behind the AGO, following Beverley St. S. Behind the AGO, you'll find:

4 The Grange

This historic mansion was the original home of the Art Gallery of Ontario. Built in 1817, the Georgian mansion is still part of the AGO. Although there are tours of the kitchens, most of the building now houses the AGO's members club. The surrounding Grange Park is charming, if a bit rough in spots.

Retrace your steps to Dundas St. W. and cross so that you're on the N side of the street. On this block, you'll find:

5 Bau-Xi

This gallery, at 340 Dundas St. W., represents contemporary Canadian artists. It's been in business since 1965 and offers a worthwhile perspective on the national current art scene.

Walk W along Dundas St.; at the NW corner of Beverley and Dundas sts. is the:

6 Consulate General of Italy

It doesn't look like a government building: The rambling late-19th-century mansion, with its sandy-colored brick, quasi-Gothic windows and wrought-iron decoration, is a beauty. Too bad you can't go in.

You're now walking into the heart of Chinatown, with its grocery stores, bakeries, trinkets, and emporiums selling herbs and handcrafts.

What follows are some of my favorite stops along the stretch of Dundas St. between Beverley St. and Spadina Ave. On the S side, or the left side as you go W, is:

7 The Herb Depot

At nos. 407–409, this market carries every herb under the sun. Many are a mystery, but the terrific English-speaking herbalists and acupuncturists on duty are happy to help. Several markets in Chinatown carry similar wares, but this one is the best bet for those who don't speak Chinese.

On the N side of the street is:

8 J & S Arts and Crafts

This shop, at no. 430, is a good place to pick up souvenirs, including kimonos and happi coats, kung-fu suits, cushion covers, and all-cotton Chinatown T-shirts. **Kim Moon,** no. 438, is an Asian bakery that features abalone cookies, deep-fried lotus crisps, and dim sum pork buns (my husband is a huge fan).

9 Ten Ren Tea 🍵

Ten Ren Tea sells all kinds of tea—black, oolong, green—stored in large canisters at the back of the store. Charming ceramic teapots and cups are on sale here, along with gnarled root ginseng. You can break here for tea—but even if you don't want to sit down, the staff will probably urge you to sample an unfamiliar variety in a tiny cup. 454 Dundas St. ✆ 416/598-7872.

Cross Dundas St. so that you are on the S side of the street again. Turn left at Spadina Ave. and walk S to the first stoplight. Cross Spadina Ave. at this light and directly ahead of you is:

10 Chinatown Centre

This huge complex at 222 Spadina Ave. is now the go-to Chinatown mall. It has an impressive array of businesses under one roof: **Clean Slate Beauty** is here, as is **Fortune Jade** (which stocks costume jewelry, as well as real pieces), and **Kid's House,** which has great deals on clothing for children. There's also a food court and a Super 8 motel.

Walk N on Spadina Ave.; at the SW corner of Spadina and Dundas is:

11 Dragon City

This mall at 280 Spadina Ave. is smaller—and far quieter—than Chinatown Centre. Still, it's notable for a few things. The pet store **Downtown Pet Centre** is in the basement; they have emperor sharks, fancy *orandas,* and piranhas to watch in the aquariums, as well as a great collection of gear for your dog/cat/bird/fish at home. Dragon City also has Hui's Pharmacy, a Canada Post outlet inside Sun Wa bookstore, and free Wi-Fi throughout the building.

Cross Dundas St. and walk N on Spadina Ave.; at no. 310 is:

12 Oriental Harvest

Look at all the different provisions—chili and fish sauces, fresh meat and fish (including live tilapia in tanks), preserved plums, chrysanthemum tea and other infusions, moon cakes, and large sacks of rice. There's also a great selection of Kasugai Japanese-made gummy candies (my favorite flavor is lychee) and sweet rice snacks to keep you going.

13 Happy Seven and Lee Garden 🍵

For fine, reasonably priced food, a Chinatown favorite is Happy Seven (358 Spadina Ave.; ✆ 416/971-9820). If you don't mind lining up, head for the ever-popular Lee Garden (331 Spadina Ave.; ✆ 416/593-9524; p. 77).

Continuing N, cross St. Andrews St. to reach:

14 Tap Phong Trading Company

This shop, at 360 Spadina Ave., stocks terrific wicker baskets of all shapes and sizes, as well as woks and ceramic cookware, attractive mortars and pestles, and other household items.

Cross Baldwin St., and you'll come to:

15 Plaiter Place

At 384 Spadina Ave., Plaiter Place has a huge selection of wicker baskets, bird-cages, woven blinds, bamboo steamers, hats, and other souvenirs. **Fortune Housewares,** no. 388, carries kitchen and household items—including brand names—for prices at least 20% lower than most other spots in the city.

Now double back to Baldwin Street. You're heading into the heart of the **Kensington Market** area, which is particularly rich with cultural diversity. Once, it was primarily a Jewish market; later, it became a Portuguese neighbor-hood. Today, it is largely Asian and Caribbean, but its past lives on in many ways.

Head back to Baldwin St. and walk W; you'll find:

16 Tom's Place

This traditional haberdasher—located at 190 Baldwin St.—is a place where you can still haggle for a deal on good, Made-In-Italy men's shirts. The store also sells women's clothing, but it's mostly the men's suits and clothing that draw crowds.

Across the street is:

17 Chocolate Addict

Located at 185 Baldwin St., this tiny temple to chocolate has some tasty, unusual offerings (mmm, wasabi truffles . . .).

Across the street and down a few shops, look for:

18 My Market Bakery

At 172 Baldwin St. is one of the market's finest bakeries, with plenty of fresh goods baked on-site, plus a selection from some other small bakeries around town. Good for breads, pastries, and cookies, too.

Further down the street, at no. 64, is Tutti Frutti, a well-stocked health-ori-ented grocery store (great for those with food allergies or celiac disease).

As you stroll S along Kensington Ave. and pass St. Andrews St., you will find a series of secondhand- and vintage-clothing stores:

19 Exile

At 62 Kensington Ave., on the west side of the street, this store has good jeans, leather jackets, and assorted accessories.

20 Courage My Love

The best spot for cheap but chic vintage clothing is at no. 14. It stocks retro gowns and wedding dresses, suits, and accessories, as well as new jewelry and beads for do-it-yourself projects. The C$5 rack out front (in nice weather) has some great deals; if you take some of these exquisite but damaged dresses and coats to a tailor, you can end up with beautiful, original pieces for a song.

21 Dancing Days

At no. 17 (on the east side of the street), you'll find party-ready glad rags that will make you look like an extra in *Grease*.

When you reach Dundas St., turn right and walk 1 block to Augusta Ave. Turn right on Augusta Ave. As you walk N and cross Wales Ave., you'll find:

22 Bellevue Square Park

On maps, this park is often referred to as Denison Square. Either way, it's a lovely spot. While you're checking out the statue of Canadian actor Al Waxman, you may smell whiffs of marijuana in the air. Kensington Market is home to a few head shops, and smoking cannabis in public—while illegal—is not uncommon in and around the park.

Stroll through the park; at the corner of Bellevue Ave. and Denison Sq., you'll find:

23 Kiever Synagogue

This building, at 28 Denison Sq., was completed in 1927. Architect Benjamin Swartz designed it with Byzantine style in mind. The most striking features are the twin domes atop the building (sadly, the building isn't open to the public). The Kiever Synagogue was the first specifically Jewish building designated an historic site by the province of Ontario.

Turn back toward Augusta Ave., and you'll see:

24 La Tortilleria 🍴

This tiny spot—just a few stools inside and, weather permitting, tables out front—serves good corn tortillas made daily. Tacos and bottled drinks from Mexico round out the tiny menu. 198 Augusta Ave.; ✆ 647/723-8760.

Walk N on Augusta Ave. to:

25 Casa Acoreana

An old-fashioned store at no. 235, it stocks a full range of fresh coffees, as well as great pecans and filberts.

Just up the street is:

26 Perola Supermarket

This store, at 247 Augusta Ave., is great for cassava and strings of peppers—ancho, *arbol, pasilla*—that are hung up to dry. Check out the bins of other exotic fruits and herbs, too.

27 Kensington Market 🍴

The Aspetta Caffe (207 Augusta Ave.; ✆ 416/916-8275) is a perfect perch if you want to people-watch while sipping a *caffe* and having a tasty panini or pasta. If you're in the neighborhood at dinnertime, try the charming Torito (276 Augusta Ave.; ✆ 647/436-5874) for tapas.

Continue N along Augusta Ave. to College St. Turn W on College St., and you'll find:

28 Church of St. Stephen-in-the-Fields

This small but historically significant church has had to fight hard to ward off the condo developers circling Kensington Market. Ironically, the Anglican Diocesan Council wanted to sell its own church, and the local community—many of whom have no religious connection to the church—came together to save it. The building is a lovely example of Gothic Revival architecture, built in 1858, and contains some splendid stained-glass windows.

On College St., hop on an eastbound streetcar, which will deliver you to the Queen's Park subway station. The southbound train will take you downtown.

WALKING TOUR 2: **WYCHWOOD**

START:	**Dupont subway station.**
FINISH:	**Pain Perdu or Patachou on St. Clair West.**
TIME:	**2 to 4 hours.**
BEST TIME:	**Weekdays during business hours or Saturday mornings.**
WORST TIMES:	**Sundays, when many buildings are closed or reserved for weddings.**

This eclectic tour takes in the city archives; a castle; a stately home; a toll keeper's house; and two artist enclaves, one in a sylvan glade, the other in a former public-transit parking lot. The castle is a tale in itself: Toronto's kitschy chateau, Casa Loma, is a museum and events destination, complete with Elizabethan-style chimneys, Rhineland turrets, secret passageways, and an underground tunnel. Built about 100 years ago, it was a dream-come-true for a wealthy financier who, in the long term, had greater architectural ambitions than cash. The neighborhoods involved include busy Davenport; the magical park-like setting of Wychwood Park, with its stately homes; the pretty Hillcrest area, another residential gem; and finally, the new and very progressive development of an old "barn" for streetcars that was saved from ugly development by a brilliant partnership between Artscape, the city's primo art cooperative, and the Stop Food Community Centre, a leading activist organization that works to feed, with dignity, Toronto's poor. Any day of the week, stop by what's known as the Green Barns, and you might find there's a screening of a topical documentary on food politics, an exhibit of resident artists' work, children from the nursery school playing outside, or a bustling farmers market that runs year-round.

From the Dupont subway station, walk N on Spadina Rd. under the train bridge and to:

1 City of Toronto Archives

This often-overlooked repository at 255 Spadina Rd. is the closest thing Toronto has to a museum of the city. Ongoing exhibits, largely photography-based, reflect events and themes in the city's past. The collection has more than 1 million images, dating from 1856.

Walk 100m (328 ft.) N to the top of Spadina Rd., at Davenport Rd., and look up at the zigzagging flight of stairs you are about to climb:

Walking Tour: Wychwood

1 City of Toronto Archives
2 The Baldwin steps
3 Spadina Museum
4 Casa Loma
5 Sir Henry's Cafe
6 Tollkeeper's Park
7 Wychwood Park
8 Artscape Wychwood Barns
9a Pain Perdu
9b Patachou

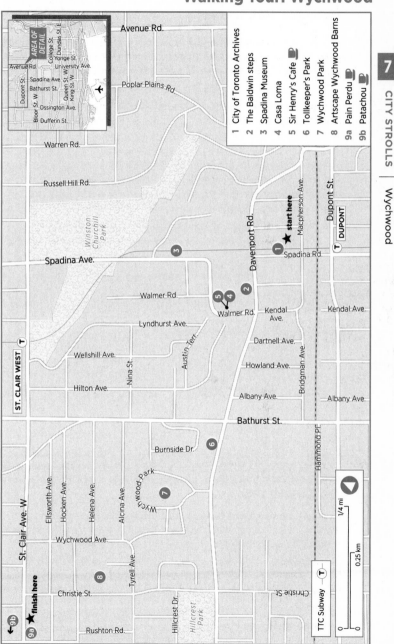

2 The Baldwin Steps

This part of Spadina Road ends at the base of a zigzagging flight of stairs that ascends the pre–Ice Age shoreline of the ancient Lake Iroquois. A public right-of-way that dates from the 1800s, The Baldwin Steps are a rare example in the city of a thigh-burning incline. The panoramic views of downtown and Lake Ontario are worth the effort. The steps are named after Robert Baldwin, a former premier of Ontario who owned land in this well-to-do neighborhood.

Continue on the path for 50m (164 ft.), with Toronto's turreted wonder, Casa Loma, on your left. Instead of visiting, though, turn right into the lush garden setting of this more subdued stately mansion:

3 Spadina Museum: Historic House & Gardens

The historic home of financier James Austin was occupied by the family for more than 100 years, from 1866 until 1980, when it became a city-run museum. In 2010, the interior was completely renovated and updated from a 19th-century setting to one focused on the inter-war years, with an emphasis on decorations from the 1920s. The grounds are as sumptuous as the interiors.

It's just a hop, skip, and a jump across the street to a more exuberant neighbor:

4 Casa Loma

Sir Henry Pellatt, who built this faux chateau between 1911 and 1914, studied medieval palaces and then gathered materials and furnishings from around the world, bringing marble, glass, and paneling from Europe; teak from Asia; and oak and walnut from North America. He then imported Scottish stonemasons to build the massive walls that surround the 2.5-hectare (6¼-acre) site. The architect was a local talent E. J. Lennox.

Wander through the majestic Great Hall, with its 18m-high (59-ft.) hammer-beam ceiling; the Oak Room, where three artisans took 3 years to fashion the paneling; and the Conservatory, with its elegant bronze doors, stained-glass dome, and pink-and-green marble. The castle encompasses battlements and a tower, and a 244m (801-ft.) tunnel runs to the stables, where Spanish tile and mahogany surrounded the horses.

5 Sir Henry's Café 🍽

Situated on the lower level in what was originally designed as Sir Henry's private exercise room, Sir Henry's Café is just a cafeteria-style coffee shop and feels pretty down-market from the surroundings. But if you're in need of some quick fuel, this is the only stop around. (✆ 416/913-3247).

From Casa Loma, walk down Walmer Rd., then turn right along Davenport Rd. to Bathurst St. The NW corner of the intersection is home to one of the oldest structures in the city, a toll keeper's cottage:

6 Tollkeeper's Park

This little home, built in 1835, is where hapless toll keepers tried to extract pennies from passing horse-drawn traffic along Davenport Road until tolls were abolished in 1890. It's also a rare example of vertical (rather than horizontal) wood planking. The simple living conditions in the two-bedroom home attest to the terms of the office: Any uncollected tariffs were deducted from their pay. A small interpretive center, where costumed docents regale visitors with stories of life in Muddy York, is connected to the house.

Continue W on the N side of Davenport Rd. until you reach the sign for Wychwood Park Private Grounds:

7 Wychwood Park

Don't let the "private" sign deter you: Step through the stone gate to enter another world tucked into the heart of the city. The fortunate residents of this secret enclave like to keep the wooded setting to themselves; another sign just inside the gate—"Danger Deep Water Quicksand"—is merely a ruse to deter visitors. Immediately ahead is a pond (often featuring the resident swan) and a fork in the road. The route to the left is a little shorter, but both are pleasant, taking you past many English-style Arts-and-Crafts homes designed by Toronto architect Eden Smith. Marmaduke Matthews envisioned an artist colony when he built the first home here in 1874, naming it after Wychwood Forest in Oxfordshire, England. This early example of a planned community retains its natural landscaping and bucolic setting.

Exit Wychwood Park at the N end and walk N on Wychwood Ave. 2 blocks until you get to:

8 Artscape Wychwood Barns

It's hard to imagine, as you come out at the top of these winding, tree-lined roads, that a TTC streetcar repair barn operated here until the 1990s. Now, it's one of the city's most successful transformations of industry into arts space. Artscape Wychwood Barns opened in 2009; attractions include studios for the 2 dozen artists-in-residence, ongoing exhibits of new work, and archival images of the old Barns. The Stop Food Community Centre, a leading activist organization that fights poverty and pushes political agendas on the food front, runs the food side of the space with a bake oven, greenhouse, community kitchen, and classroom on-site. There are lots of events to check out, from movies to fab dinners/fundraisers. (www.thestop.org). A bustling Saturday farmers market is complete with picnic-like prepared foods, such as butternut squash empanadas and some of the best fish tacos anywhere. If the weather cooperates, sit outside with a bite to eat and watch the parade of dogs, kids, farmers, and shoppers. Kick back: You've earned it.

Walk 2 blocks N to St. Clair Ave. W., where there are plenty of great cafes and restaurants:

9 Pain Perdu or Patachou

Try Pain Perdu (736 Saint Clair Ave. W.; ℂ 416/656-7246) for great quiches and *croques monsieur*, or Patachou (833 St Clair Ave W.; ℂ 416/782-0122) for buttery croissants and lovely pastries.

WALKING TOUR 3: ST. LAWRENCE & DOWNTOWN EAST

START:	**Union Station.**
FINISH:	**King subway station.**
TIME:	**2 to 3 hours.**
BEST TIME:	**Saturday, when the St. Lawrence Market is in full swing.**
WORST TIME:	**Sunday, when it's closed.**

At one time, this area was at the center of city life. Today, it's a little off center, yet it has some historic and modern architectural treasures and a wealth of history in and around the St. Lawrence Market.

1 Union Station

Check out the interior of this classical revival beauty, which opened in 1927 as a temple to and for the railroad. The shimmering ceiling, faced with vitrified Guastavino tile, soars 27m (89 ft.) above the 79m-long (259-ft.) hall.

Across the street, at York and Front sts., stands the:

2 Fairmont Royal York

The venerable railroad hotel is a longtime gathering place for Torontonians. It's the home of the famous Imperial Room cabaret and nightclub, which used to be one of Eartha Kitt's favorite venues. The hotel was once the tallest building in Toronto and the largest hotel in the British Commonwealth. Check out the lobby, with its coffered ceiling and opulent furnishings. One floor up on the mezzanine is a new **gallery** of black-and-white photographs that cover the hotel's long and illustrious history.

3 The Royal York ☕

Okay, you're just getting started, but it would be a missed opportunity to not stop in for a bite at one of the many good dining options at the Royal York (p. 54). The roof garden, where the hotel grows its own mint for mojitos, is also home to several honeybee hives. Expect an eco-conscious menu.

As you leave the hotel, turn left and walk E on Front St. At the corner of Bay and Front sts., look up at the stunning:

4 Royal Bank Plaza

The two triangular gold-sheathed towers rise 41 floors and 26 floors, respectively. A 40m-high (131-ft.) atrium joins them, and 68kg (150 lb.) of gold enhances the mirrored glass. Webb Zerafa Menkes Housden designed the project, which was built between 1973 and 1977.

Cross Bay Street and continue east on Front Street. On the south side of the street is the impressive sweep of **One Front Street,** the main post office building (okay, not an exciting-sounding sight, but an attractive one).

On the N side of the street is:

5 Brookfield Place

Go inside to view the soaring galleria. Skidmore, Owings, and Merrill, with Bregman + Hamann, designed it in 1993. The twin office towers connect through a

Walking Tour: St. Lawrence & Downtown East

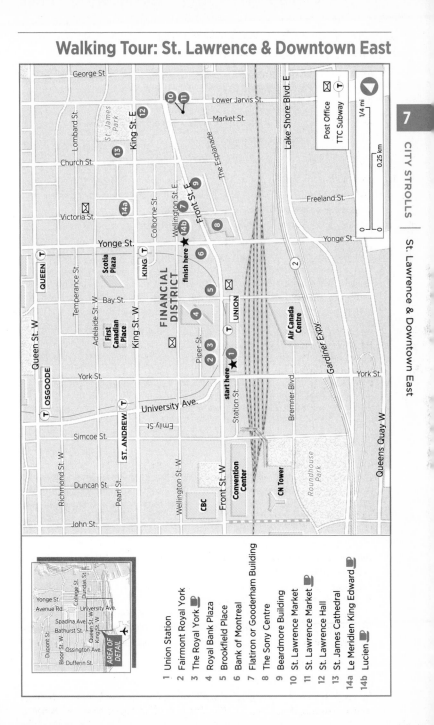

Map labels:

George St.
Lower Jarvis St.
Lombard St.
St. James Park
Market St.
King St. E
Church St.
St. James Park
The Esplanade
Lake Shore Blvd. E
Victoria St.
Colborne St.
Freeland St.
Yonge St.
Wellington St. E
Front St.
Yonge St.
Temperance St.
Scotia Plaza
QUEEN
KING
finish here
FINANCIAL DISTRICT
Adelaide St. W
First Canadian Place
Bay St.
Air Canada Centre
Queen St. W
King St. W
Piper St.
UNION
York St.
OSGOODE
Gardiner Expy.
York St.
University Ave.
Emily St.
ST. ANDREW
start here
Station St.
Bremner Blvd.
Simcoe St.
Queens Quay W
Richmond St. W
Wellington St. W
Convention Center
Roundhouse Park
Duncan St.
Pearl St.
CBC
Front St. W
CN Tower
John St.

Post Office
TTC Subway
1/4 mi
0.25 km

Legend:

1 Union Station
2 Fairmont Royal York
3 The Royal York
4 Royal Bank Plaza
5 Brookfield Place
6 Bank of Montreal
7 Flatiron or Gooderham Building
8 The Sony Centre
9 Beardmore Building
10 St. Lawrence Market
11 St. Lawrence Market
12 St. Lawrence Hall
13 St. James Cathedral
14a Le Meridien King Edward
14b Lucien

Inset map:

Yonge St.
Avenue Rd.
University Ave.
College St.
Dundas St.
Spadina Ave.
Bathurst St.
Queen St. W
King St. W
Dupont St.
Bloor St. W
Ossington Ave.
Dufferin St.
AREA OF DETAIL

huge glass-covered galleria five stories high, spanning the block between Bay and Yonge streets. Designed by artist-architect Santiago Calatrava of Bregman + Hamann, it links the old Midland Bank building to the twin towers.

On Front St., turn left and continue to the NW corner of Yonge and Front sts., stopping to notice the:

6 Hockey Hall of Fame

The ornate old building may be a surprise—built in 1885, it used to be a Bank of Montreal. Inside, the banking hall rises to a beamed coffered ceiling with domed skylights of stained glass. If you're a hockey fanatic, this is your shrine (p. 121).

From here, you can look ahead along Front St. and see the weird mural by Derek M. Besant that adorns the famous and highly photogenic:

7 Flatiron or Gooderham Building

This building was the headquarters of George Gooderham, who expanded his distilling business into railroads, insurance, and philanthropy; the original factories are now the Distillery District. At one time, his liquor business was the biggest in the British Empire. The very attractive five-story building occupies a triangular site, with the windows at the western edge beautifully curved and topped with a semicircular tower. The design is by David Roberts.

At the SW corner of Yonge and Front sts., you can stop in at:

8 The Sony Centre

The Sony Centre for the Performing Arts sits across Scott Street from the **St. Lawrence Centre.** In 1974, when the Sony was called the O'Keefe Centre, Mikhail Baryshnikov defected from the Soviet Union after performing here. The ballet has moved buildings, but this remains a busy theater with musicals and such.

Continue E along Front St. to the:

9 Beardmore Building

At 35–39 Front St. E., this and the many other cast-iron buildings lining the street were the heart of the late-19th-century warehouse district, close to the lakefront and railheads. At no. 45 is **Nicholas Hoare,** one of the coziest bookstores in the city.

Continue E along Front St., crossing Church St. and then Market St., to the:

10 St. Lawrence Market

The old market building on the right holds this great market hall, which was constructed around the city's second city hall (1844–45). The pedimented facade that you see as you stand in the center of the hall was originally the center block of the city hall. Today, the market is packed with vendors selling fresh eggs, Mennonite sausage, seafood, meats, cheeses, and baked goods. Upstairs is a small gallery of city archival photographs. On Saturday, in the north building across the street, a farmers' market starts at 5am.

11 St. Lawrence Market 🍴

Don't forget the famous peameal (Canadian) bacon sandwiches at the Carousel Bakery. There's also Chris the Cheesemonger and Alex Farms for great cheeses, and St Urbain for fresh bagels right out of the wood-burning oven, Montreal-style. Get some smoked salmon from Mike's and make your own sandwich. Other nearby choices include Chefs House, the restaurant at George Brown Chef School.

Exit the market where you came in. Cross Wellington St. and cut through Market Lane Park and the shops at Market Sq., past the N market building. Turn right onto King St. to:

12 St. Lawrence Hall

This was the focal point of the community in the mid–19th century. This hall, once the site of grand city occasions, political rallies, balls, and entertainment, was where Frederick Douglass delivered an antislavery lecture; Jenny Lind and Adelina Patti sang in 1851 and 1860, respectively; Gen. Tom Thumb appeared in 1862; and George Brown campaigned for Confederation. William Thomas designed the elegant Palladian-style building, which boasts a domed cupola.

Cross King Street and enter the 19th-century garden. It has a cast-iron drinking fountain for people, horses, and dogs, and flowerbeds filled with seasonal blooms.

If you like, rest on a bench while you admire the handsome proportions of St. Lawrence Hall and listen to the chimes of:

13 St. James' Cathedral

Adjacent to the garden on the north side of King Street, this is a beautiful Gothic church that is open to the public. The graceful building and its surrounding park make a serene setting to rest and gather one's thoughts, although the park can be a gathering place for some of the city's rougher citizens.

From here, you can view one of the early retail buildings, built when King Street was the main commercial street. **Nos. 129–35** was originally an Army and Navy Store; cast-iron, plate-glass, and arched windows allowed the shopper to see what was available in the store. Also note nos. 111 and 125. The **Toronto Sculpture Garden** (115 King St.; ✆ **416/485-9658**) is a quiet corner for contemplation.

14 King Street East 🍴

From St. James,' the venerable Le Meridien King Edward (37 King St. E.; ✆ 416/863-9700) is only a block away. You can stop for afternoon tea in the lobby lounge, or light fare or lunch in the Café Victoria (✆ 416/364-6363). For a memorable, fine-dining experience try the singular Lucien (36 Wellington St. E.; ✆ 416/504-9900), a favorite among locals.

From St. James' Cathedral, go S on Church St. for 1 block and turn right into Colborne St. From Colborne St., turn left down Leader Lane to Wellington St., where you can enjoy a fine view of the mural on the Flatiron Building and the rhythmic flow of mansard rooflines along the S side of Front St. Turn right and proceed to Yonge St.; then turn right and walk to King St. to catch the subway to your next destination.

WALKING TOUR 4: CABBAGETOWN

START:	**Allan Gardens.**
FINISH:	**Sumach and Gerrard streets (for streetcar to College Station).**
TIME:	**2 to 3 hours.**
BEST TIME:	**Tuesdays from May through October, when the Farmers' Market is open in Riverdale Park West.**
WORST TIME:	**There is no worst time; all of the other attractions on this tour can be seen on weekdays and weekends.**

Cabbagetown, one of the city's oldest neighborhoods, has gone from rags to riches more times than most can count. Built up in the 1840s by Irish immigrants fleeing the Great Famine, the name of the district comes from the cabbage plants they grew in their front yards. It has been both a wealthy enclave and a slum, but today, the residential streets have been gentrified, and the surrounding commercial streets are on an upswing.

1 Allan Gardens

This was Toronto's first civic park. For many years, it ran to the seedy side, but since the University of Toronto took over the care of the greenhouses in 2004, it has become a charming place to visit again (but not at night). The Children's Conservatory is well worth a look, but the crown jewel of the garden is the Edwardian Palm House.

At the corner of Carlton and Sherbourne sts., you'll see:

2 St. Luke's United Church

Known as Sherbourne Street Methodist when the first sermon was preached here in 1887, this is one of Toronto's most beautiful examples of religious architecture. From the outside, the imposing stonework and turrets make it look like a castle. Inside, the sanctuary has been completely refurbished in the past few years. The glorious stained-glass windows are the pièce de résistance (the church once had a wealthy congregation, and you'll see that the windows were all "dedicated" by businessmen trying to outdo one another).

On the N side of Carlton St. is:

3 St. Peter's Anglican Church

This parish was originally based in a cemetery chapel. In 1866, John Strachan, the Aberdeen-born Bishop of Toronto, opened this church. It's a pretty example of High Victorian Gothic, and later additions are in keeping with its original style.

Walk E along Carlton St. to:

4 Daniel et Daniel

This food shop at 248 Carlton St. (© **416/968-9275**) is a good place for simple but tasty fare, like meat pies and generous sandwiches. There are freshly baked pastries, pâtés, tarts, cakes, and other treats made in-house.

Walking Tour: Cabbagetown

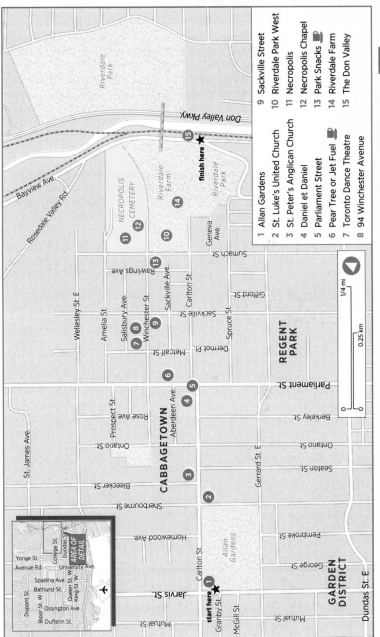

1 Allan Gardens
2 St. Luke's United Church
3 St. Peter's Anglican Church
4 Daniel et Daniel
5 Parliament Street
6 Pear Tree or Jet Fuel 🍽
7 Toronto Dance Theatre
8 94 Winchester Avenue
9 Sackville Street
10 Riverdale Park West
11 Necropolis
12 Necropolis Chapel 🍽
13 Park Snacks 🍽
14 Riverdale Farm
15 The Don Valley

You're now at the intersection with:

5 Parliament Street

Parliament Street got its name because the first Upper Canada government buildings in "muddy little York" (as Toronto was then known) were built at its southern end in 1793. Today, it's the main commercial artery of Cabbagetown. This isn't exactly trendy (at press time, Starbucks had yet to set up an outpost on this stretch), but you can make some great finds. At no. 480 is a branch of **Planet Aid,** the secondhand-clothing store that raises money for projects in the developing world. **Sharon's,** at no. 503, is a small but glamorous boutique with clothing and accessories. **Green's Antiques,** at no. 529, is a true gem, with plenty of great chairs, ottomans, and sofas, many of which have been newly upholstered by the talented staff.

6 Peartree or Jet Fuel ☕

One reliable place to grab a bite is the Peartree (507 Parliament St.; ℂ 416/962-8190), which serves hearty salads such as the goat cheese and spinach. Another great spot is Jet Fuel (519 Parliament St.; ℂ 416/968-9982), a coffee shop that has become a local landmark (bike couriers love this place). Everything here is made with espresso, so be prepared for a good jolt.

Turn right at Winchester St. (at the corner, you'll pass the Laurentian Room), and walk E. At the NE corner of the intersection of Winchester and Metcalfe sts., you'll see:

7 Toronto Dance Theatre

The former St. Enoch's Presbyterian Church was built in 1891 in a Romanesque Revival style. Oddly, the redbrick exterior makes the building (almost) blend in with the rest of the neighborhood (quite a feat, given its size).

Continue E to:

8 94 Winchester St.

This was once the home of magician Doug Henning. You can't go inside (it's someone else's home now), but a plaque at the front commemorates his life (1947–2000) and immortalizes him as "magician, teacher, politician." The first two are easy to get, but the last requires some explanation. In 1994, Henning stood for election to Parliament as a member of the Natural Law Party, an organization memorable mainly for its belief in levitation.

Continue walking E on Winchester St. and turn S onto:

9 Sackville Street

This quiet street had some of the loveliest homes in Cabbagetown. While the architecture is an eclectic mix, you'll mostly see variations on Victorian and Queen Anne styles. Walk down to Sackville Place (the street will be only on your left side). Across from it is Pine Terrace, a series of Victorian redbrick town houses built in 1886.

Walk N back to Winchester Ave. and follow it E to Sumach St., where you'll find:

10 Riverdale Park West

This is a lovely park that's a favorite with neighboring families. While you stop to enjoy the scenery, you can learn more about Cabbagetown's history. Look for the large maps and plaques in the park's northwestern corner, and you can learn all about many of the fascinating people who once called the neighborhood theirs. (Hint: Doug Henning fit in very well.) Depending on when you visit, you may find a farmers' market operating in the park, too.

Across from the park, on the N side of Winchester Ave., is the:

11 Necropolis

Walk under the Gothic-inspired porte-cochere to enter Toronto's city of the dead. This is the prettiest cemetery you could hope to find, and if you stop at the office (on the right side as you step under the archway), you can pick up a free map that will guide you to the final resting places of some of Toronto's famous inhabitants. Check out the imposing stone Celtic cross that marks the grave of William Lyon Mackenzie, the leader of the Upper Canada rebellion who later became the mayor of Toronto (see the entry for **Mackenzie House,** p. 120, for more details).

When you finish here, exit through the porte-cochere; on your right is the:

12 Necropolis Chapel

This small chapel is a lovely example of High Victorian Gothic style. Architect Henry Langley built it in 1872 (he's the same person who designed the towers at St. James' Cathedral, p. 117, and St. Michael's Cathedral, p. 118). The chapel and the adjoining porte-cochere are widely considered to be two of the finest pieces of Gothic Revival architecture in Canada. (Langley is buried in the Necropolis, and his grave is on the map mentioned above in stop 11.)

13 Park Snacks or Riverdale Farm 🍴

You won't find many places to grab a snack within the residential heart of Cabbagetown. The exception is Park Snacks (no phone), a take-out-only spot at the southwest corner of Winchester and Sumach sts. In summer, you can buy drinks, ice cream, or sandwiches here. Riverdale Park West provides many benches that are well shaded by trees. Year-round, you can buy snacks at Riverdale Farm (see stop 14, below).

On the eastern edge of the park, you'll see the entrance to:

14 Riverdale Farm

It's a rarity: a working farm in the heart of downtown. The grounds are clean and the animals very well cared for. It's a charming place to visit, particularly if you have children in tow, but even if you don't, you can appreciate the chicks, bunnies, cows, horses, rare-breed pigs, goats, and other animals. Watch out for baby animals, too.

When you leave the farm, turn to the left and follow its perimeter; this will give you a good view of:

15 The Don Valley

There's been a big movement to "Bring Back the Don" in Toronto, and the valley has been revitalized by it. The Don River is no longer a mighty force, but at least its valley is green. Across the valley, you can see the controversial renovation of the notorious Don Jail, which is becoming a health center. Also, consider leaving the area and wind your way north up the Bayview Extension to the revitalized Evergreen Brick Works (about a 15 minute hike), a unique heritage site that was once the city's brick factories. Today, it's an environmental project that offers a view into the past alongside beautiful parklands, a cafe, and on Saturday mornings, a bustling farmers market.

Walk S along Spruce St. to Gerrard St.; from here, you can catch any westbound streetcar, which will take you to College Station.

WALKING TOUR 5: **THE FINANCIAL DISTRICT**

START:	**The CN Tower, near the corner of John and Front streets.**
FINISH:	**A Queen Street West watering hole.**
TIME:	**2 to 4 hours.**
BEST TIME:	**Weekdays during business hours.**
WORST TIMES:	**Weekends, when the stock market is closed and the Financial District is dead.**

7

The Financial District

CITY STROLLS

Toronto's answer to Wall Street is a mix of old-fashioned—and very grand—bank buildings and modern towers that stretch to the sky.

Start by going up the:

1 CN Tower

Although it has become a symbol of the city, the CN Tower drew a great deal of criticism when it was built in 1975. It has since been recognized as an important symbol of a city trying to forge a new identity. Robert Fulford writes in *Accidental City* (Houghton Mifflin): "In the 1970s [Toronto] was struggling to shake off the dowdy self-image that was part of its heritage as a colonial city. . . . Torontonians were starting to consider, with shy pleasure, the novel idea that their city might be attractive, even enviable. . . . At that happy moment, the tower reinforced local exuberance and asserted the city's claim to even more attention." However you view it, the most enjoyable thing is the view *from* it. If you dare, lie down on the glass floor for a unique vertiginous experience.

Proof positive that the CN Tower is an attention-grabber is the dynamic area that has sprouted at its base, including dozens of condo towers, a new St Germain Hotel at Maple Leaf Square, and the charming Roundhouse and Steam Whistle Brewery.

Once you're back down at the base, exit at the corner of John and Front streets. From here, look to the right along Front Street to see the glistening golden Royal Bank towers (part of the Royal Bank Centre). The CBC Centre stretches along the north side of Front Street for a whole long block. Inside, you can peek at the lobby radio studios and take a nostalgic radio-TV trip in the free museum.

Walk N on John St. (with the CN Tower behind you) to King St. Turn right and walk 1 block to:

2 The Princess of Wales Theatre

Princess Diana opened it in 1993. Constructed for a production of *Miss Saigon,* the theater was the brainchild of impresario Ed Mirvish and his son, David. Try to pop inside for a peek at the 929 sq. m (10,000 sq. ft.) of murals created by Frank Stella. There's one on the exterior back of the building that's worth walking around to see.

Exit the theater and continue along King Street past a cluster of restaurants owned by Ed Mirvish. (Drop in to one to check out the larger-than-life decor Ed has purchased at antique closeouts.) You'll also pass a wall of newspaper clippings about this gutsy Torontonian. Booster and benefactor of the city, he started out in bleak circumstances as owner of a bankrupt store during the Depression.

Walking Tour: The Financial District

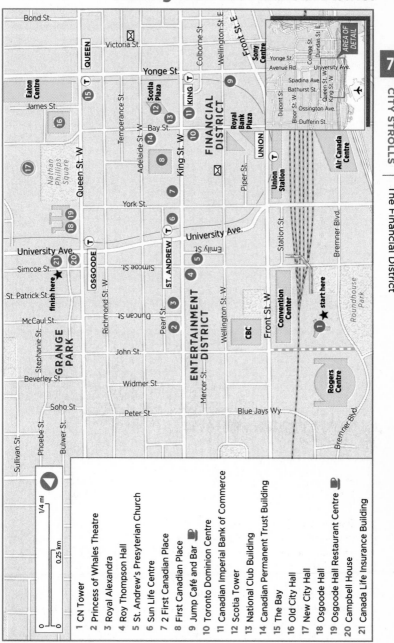

1 CN Tower
2 Princess of Whales Theatre
3 Royal Alexandra
4 Roy Thompson Hall
5 St. Andrew's Presyterian Church
6 Sun Life Centre
7 2 First Canadian Place
8 First Canadian Place
9 Jump Café and Bar
10 Toronto Dominion Centre
11 Canadian Imperial Bank of Commerce
12 Scotia Tower
13 National Club Building
14 Canadian Permanent Trust Building
15 The Bay
16 Old City Hall
17 New City Hall
18 Osgoode Hall
19 Osgoode Hall Restaurant Centre
20 Campbell House
21 Canada Life Insurance Building

He paid off the debt and launched **Honest Ed's** (see chapter 8), a discount store at Bloor and Bathurst streets that brought him fame and fortune. He saved the Royal Alex (see next stop) from demolition, and he and his son have become theater impresarios in Toronto and in London, where Ed outbid Andrew Lloyd Webber in 1982 for the Old Vic.

Cross Duncan St. Next you'll come to:

3 The Royal Alexandra

John M. Lyle built this beloved theater in 1906 and 1907 at a cost of C$750,000. In 1963, it was scheduled for demolition, but Ed Mirvish bought it for C$200,000 and refurbished it. Named after Queen Alexandra, wife of Edward VII, the magnificent Beaux Arts structure is Edwardian down to the last detail. It abounds with gilt and velvet, and green marble lines the entrance foyer.

Across the street from these two theaters stands the new **Metro Hall** (55 John St.), designed by Brisbin Brook Beynon. This building is pretty much a white elephant these days—it was constructed when Toronto had six separate municipal governments and a Metro Council for joint projects and concerns. On occasion, there are art installations on the first floor.

Also on the S side of the street, at the corner of King and Simcoe sts., is:

4 Roy Thomson Hall

The hall bears the name of newspaper magnate Lord Thomson of Fleet (a Canadian press baron who wound up taking a seat in the British House of Lords). Built between 1972 and 1982, and designed by Arthur Erickson, the building's exterior looks very Space Age. Inside, the mirrored effects are dramatic.

(A recent renovation fixed the once-poor acoustics, and the hall now justifiably hosts many of the city's top concerts.)

Continue walking east on King Street. You'll pass through the heart of the Financial District, surrounded by many towers owned and operated by banks and brokerage, trust, and insurance companies.

On the NE corner of King and Simcoe sts. rises the first of the towers that make up the Sun Life Centre; on the SE corner stands:

5 St. Andrew's Presbyterian Church

The church (1874–75) is a quietly inviting retreat from the city's pace and noise. It was designed by the city's premier architect of the time, W. G. Storm, in an inspired picturesque Scottish Romanesque style. Sun Life paid C$4.3 million for the church's air rights. The doors are often locked, but if they're open, duck inside to check out the gorgeous stained-glass window of a highlander in full regalia.

Continue along King St. to University Ave. Opposite, on the NE corner, is the:

6 Sun Life Centre's second tower

A Sorel Etrog sculpture marks this tower. Farther along the block, you'll find another sculpture, *Parent I,* by British sculptor Barbara Hepworth. It's in a courtyard setting, complete with a splashing fountain, at the northwest corner of York and King streets.

On the NE corner stands:

7 2 First Canadian Place

The north corner of the structure is the **Toronto Exchange Tower,** at the corner of Adelaide and York streets. The Sculptor's Society Gallery, which always has an interesting free show, is in 2 First Canadian Place.

Continue along King St. past:

8 First Canadian Place

It sits on the north side, and the **Standard Life** and **Royal Trust buildings** (part of the Toronto Dominion Centre) are on the south. At the end of this block, you'll reach Bay Street. The Standard Life building is the work of New York architect Edward Durell Stone with Bregman + Hamann; the marble facing contrasts with the TD Centre, which is black. Again, there are views of the magnificent towers of the Royal Bank Centre from here.

The intersection of Bay and King streets was once considered the geographical center of Toronto's financial power. During the mining booms in the 1920s and 1950s, Bay Street was lined with offices that were filled with commission salesmen peddling penny stocks.

If it's near lunchtime and your stomach is rumbling, this isn't a bad place to take a break:

9 Jump Cafe and Bar ☕

Your best bet for a leisurely lunch in this neighborhood is a block south and a block east of Bay and King sts., at Jump Cafe and Bar (p. 74). Or, for a more lofty experience, try the iconic Canoe (p. 70) atop the TD Tower (see below): It's one of the country's best restaurants featuring some of Canada's finest ingredients, and on a clear day, the views are stunning.

Our next stop, at King and Bay sts., is the:

10 Toronto Dominion Centre

Built between 1963 and 1969, the center was designed by Mies van der Rohe in his sleek trademark style. The black steel and dark-bronze-tinted glass tower rises from a gray granite base. Step inside and walk through the Royal Trust and Toronto Dominion Towers. Exit the TD Centre on Wellington Street and walk right; you'll come to a small staircase that leads to the courtyard behind the Toronto Dominion Bank Tower. Here, you'll find a patch of grass that holds half a dozen lazing bronze cows. Artist Joe Fafard's *Pasture* reminds the bankers and stockbrokers that Toronto's wealth derived from other stock, too.

Walk through the Centre to the King St. exit. Exit onto King St. and turn right to continue E. Cross Bay St. On the S side of King St., you'll come to the entrance to Commerce Court. Architecture buffs will want to go into the:

11 Canadian Imperial Bank of Commerce

Visit this building (built 1929–31) if only to see the massive banking hall—44m long (144 ft.), 26m wide (85 ft.), and 20m high (66 ft.)—with its coffered ceiling, gilt moldings, and sculpted friezes. Squirrels, roosters, bees, bears, and figures representing Industry, Commerce, and Mercury decorate the main entrance. For years, this 34-story building dominated the Toronto skyline. New Yorkers York and Sawyer, with Darling and Pearson, designed it. Note the carved heads on the top of the building depicting courage, observation, foresight, and enterprise. In the early 1970s, I. M. Pei was asked to design a new complex while preserving the old building. He set the new mercury-laminated stainless-steel bank tower back from King Street, creating Commerce Court.

Opposite, on the N side of King St., note the:

12 Scotia Tower

It's a red-granite building, designed by Webb Zerafa Menkes Housden between 1985 and 1988.

Walk back to Bay St. and turn right. You're now going N. At no. 303, on the E side, is the:

13 National Club Building

In 1874, the nationalist Canada First Movement, which had started in Ottawa in 1868, became centered in Toronto. It established a weekly, *The Nation,* entered politics (as the Canadian National Association), and founded the National Club, which moved here in 1907. Today, it's a prestigious private club.

Across the street on the W side, at the corner of Bay and Adelaide sts., stands the:

14 Canada Permanent Trust Building

Enter this structure, at 7 King St. E., to view the beautifully worked Art Deco brass and bronze—particularly the elevator doors, which are chased and engraved with foliage and flowers.

Cross Adelaide St. As you walk up Bay St., the magnificent Old City Hall is clearly in view. First, on the E side of Bay St., between Richmond and Queen sts., look at—or stop in to:

15 The Bay

The Hudson's Bay Company started out as a fur-trading business when the first French-speaking settlers came to Canada. Today, the Bay, long known for a mid-range selections of clothing and housewares, is reinventing itself as a competitor in high-end women's fashion and runway frocks. The place to see the new look is the Room at the Queen St location. Elsewhere, you'll still find wool blankets, simple housewares, and casual gear. (See chapter 8, "Shopping," for listings.)

Across Queen St. looms:

16 Old City Hall

This solid building, designed by Edward James Lennox, was built out of Credit River Valley sandstone. The Romanesque Revival style shows the obvious influence of H. H. Richardson. Begun in 1885, it opened in 1899, and for years, its clock tower was a skyline landmark. Today, the building houses the provincial criminal courts. Go in to see the impressive staircase, columns with decorative capitals, and mosaic floor. The stained-glass window (1898) by Robert McCausland depicts the union of Commerce and Industry watched over by Britannia. Note the carved heads on the exterior entrance pillars—supposedly portraits of political figures and citizens of the period, including the architect.

Exit along Queen St. and turn right. Pause at the intersection of Queen and Bay sts. Bay St., Toronto's equivalent of Wall St., curves at this intersection, offering a good view N and S. Cross Bay St., and you'll find yourself in Nathan Phillips Sq., with New City Hall looming above:

17 New City Hall

The city's fourth, it was built between 1958 and 1965 in modern sculptural style. It's the symbol of Toronto's postwar dynamism, although not everyone felt that way when it was built. According to Pierre Berton, Frank Lloyd Wright said of it, "You've got a headmarker for a grave and future generations will look at it and say: 'This marks the spot where Toronto fell.'" The truth is quite the opposite—this breathtaking building was the first architectural marker of an evolving metropolis. Finnish architect Viljo Revell won a design competition that drew entries by 510 architects from 42 countries, including I. M. Pei. The building has a great square in front with a fountain and pool; people flock here in summer to relax, and in winter to skate. The square's namesake, Nathan Phillips, was Toronto's first Jewish mayor.

City Hall also has some art worth viewing. Look just inside the entrance for *Metropolis,* which local artist David Partridge fashioned from more than 100,000 common nails. You'll need to stand well back to enjoy the effect. Henry Moore's sculpture *The Archer* stands in front of the building—thanks to Mayor Phil Givens, who raised the money to buy it through public subscription after city authorities refused. The gesture encouraged Moore to bestow a major collection of his works on the Art Gallery of Ontario (see chapter 6). Two curved concrete towers, which house the bureaucracy, flank the Council Chamber. From the air, the whole complex supposedly looks like an eye peering up at the heavens. Recently, the pretty, elevated walkways were opened to the public after decades; they're a good way to get a close look at the buildings and to the street scenes below.

From City Hall, walk W along Queen St. On your right, behind an ornate wrought-iron fence that once kept out the cows, you'll see:

18 Osgoode Hall

Since the 1830s, this has been the headquarters of the Law Society of Upper Canada, a professional association. Named after the first chief justice of Upper Canada, the building was constructed in stages. It started with the East Wing (built 1831–32), then the West Wing (built 1844–45), and the center block (built 1856–60). The last, designed by W. G. Storm with a Palladian portico, is the most impressive. Inside is the **Great Library**—34m long (112 ft.), 12m wide (39 ft.), and 12m high (39 ft.)—with stucco decoration and a domed ceiling. The Ontario Supreme Court is across Queen Street.

19 Osgoode Hall Restaurant 🍽

It's open only for lunch and during the academic year, but this unusual—and very good—restaurant is part of the Law School. The setting is the library, the menus are classic continental, and the clientele often show up in wigs and robes. You need to pass through a security check to get in, but it's worth it. 130 Queen St W., ((C) 416/947-3361).

Walk W 1 block to University Ave. On the NW corner, you can visit:

20 Campbell House

This elegant Georgian residence was home to Sir William Campbell, a Scot who moved to York in 1811 and rose to become chief justice of Upper Canada. A handsome piece of Georgian architecture, it was moved to this location from a few miles farther east.

Stretching NW behind Campbell House, on the NW side of University Ave., is the:

21 Canada Life Assurance Building

Atop the tower a neon sign provides weather reports—white flashes for snow, red flashes for rain, green beacon for clement weather, red beacon for cloudy weather. If the flashes move upward, the temperature is headed that way, and vice versa.

At University Ave. and Queen St., you can end the tour by boarding the subway at Osgoode station to your next destination, or continue walking W along Queen St. to explore its many shops and cafes.

SHOPPING

From shopaholics to casual browsers, Toronto offers plenty to interest anyone who likes to shop. As usual in this town, the wide range of choices is most easily broken down by neighborhood. The quaint, sometimes junky shops of Yonge Street deal in touristy trinkets, antiques, and local book chains like Book City, while Kensington Market is all vintage racks, most of them loaded down with clothing. Top labels like Gucci and Chanel line Mink Mile along Bloor Street West, which borders tony Yorkville where boutiques, such as MO851, a Canadian-owned leather store selling beautiful bags and cool jackets, reign. Downtown West leads to locally designed and generally hip finds like Fresh Baked Goods (knitwear, not pastries), Lilliput Hats on College St, and on Queen Street West, Preloved. An emerging design area along King Street East, in the heart of the historic Corktown neighborhood, promises dazzling showrooms featuring the latest in top brands. The city is also dense with ethnic pockets, from Little India in the east to Koreatown in the West, Little Italy(s) north and south, at least three Chinatowns to explore, and many more to suit your tastes.

That said, the economic crisis has had a visible impact in Toronto these past few years, and there are many empty storefronts downtown. The closures tumbled institutions such as veteran Pages Bookstore on Queen Street West and many mom-and-pop shops. Nonetheless, business is robust enough to nurture small enterprises like Type—with two stores—and sustain great indie stores such as Soundscapes on College Street, where you can buy CDs and hot tickets to live shows. The business of shopping is also enough of a draw to justify a major rejuvenation of the Mink Mile along Bloor Street West: It took 2½ years and cost millions, but the designer strip is now a pretty boulevard speckled with granite slabs, now worthy of the haute brands that line the street.

The Eaton Centre is Toronto's most famous shopping arcade, with more than 200 chain stores. Think: Banana Republic, Pottery Barn, Abercrombie & Fitch, and the Gap, plus two department stores, the Bay and Sears, at either end of the block-long mall. The Bay has been generating news in fashion circles with its reinvention from conservative to cutting-edge. Celebrity fashion editors and designers have come to visit and endorse the collections of frocks and more. But the case remains: The Eaton Centre is convenient yet generally boring. Be adventurous and check out local neighborhood shops to score deals on unique clothing, housewares, and antiques (see "Great Shopping Areas," below).

THE SHOPPING SCENE

While there are enough buys offered by the numerous international retailers in Toronto to pack a U-Haul with, don't forget the local talent. If your passion is fashion, there are great Canadian labels such as Anne Hung, Mercy, Lida Baday, Lydia K, Ross Mayer, and Comrags, for starters.

Toronto also has a bustling arts-and-crafts community, with many galleries, custom jewelers, and artisans. Some of the best are design-related, such as the eclectic collection at Swipe and Canadiana-with-cheek at MADE. If you're an art-lover, note that artwork brought into the United States is duty-free.

Stores usually open around 10am from Monday to Saturday. Closing hours change depending on the day. From Monday to Wednesday, most stores close at 6pm; on Thursday and Friday, hours can run to 8 or 9pm; on Saturday, closing is usually at 6pm. Most stores are open on Sunday, though the hours may be restricted—11am or noon to 5pm is standard.

All Toronto retailers charge shoppers for plastic bags; the charge for a plastic bag is C5¢. While the move was intended to boost Toronto's eco-friendliness, the fact that the bag tax doesn't go into any environmental fund (in fact, the "tax" money is kept by the shops) has caused a hullabaloo among some shoppers.

Almost every establishment accepts MasterCard and Visa, and a growing number take American Express.

Great Shopping Areas

DOWNTOWN

Chinatown The city's original Chinatown (there are three and counting) is in the heart of the city, steps away from Kensington Market and other shopping destinations. It is well worth a visit: You can peruse bins of touristy junk such as cheapo plastic toys and jewelry, or search out fine rosewood furniture, exquisite ceramics, homeopathic herbs, and a bounty of exotic foodstuffs. But don't try driving here: This is traffic purgatory and best navigated on foot.

The Eaton Centre Okay, you're short on time, but you still want to fit in all your shopping. If you don't mind chain stores, head to this city-center mall with 200 shops, including an Apple Store, Browns, Danier, Birks, Nine West, La Vie en Rose, Femme de Carriere, Williams Sonoma, Banana Republic, Mendocino, Laura Secord, H&M, and Indigo.

Queen Street West Queen Street West, between University Avenue and Bathurst Street, once *the* hip destination, is still a stomping ground for fashionistas in need of a fix. There's a mix of stores like the Gap and neighboring Canadian-based Le Chateau for budget fashions, M.A.C. Cosmetics, Kiehl's (originally of New York), and some fine local designer fare like Boomer (for men), and Comrags (for women). The groovy design store Urban Mode, which has moved just west of Bathurst, is good for cool oddities.

The Underground City Subterranean Toronto is a hive of shopping activity for the multitudes working in the Financial District. While you won't find many shops down here that don't have an aboveground location, the Underground City is a popular retreat for winter's coldest days and for summer heat waves, and it's convenient for those who have little time to explore beyond the neighborhood.

West Queen West Playing down its grittier roots, this hot neighborhood has earned the cutting-edge reputation once held by Queen Street West. The city has dubbed it the "Art & Design District." Starting at Bathurst Avenue and running west to Ossington Avenue and beyond, this is where you'll find a concentration of fashion talent, art galleries, and some of the best

Midtown Shopping: Bloor/Yorkville

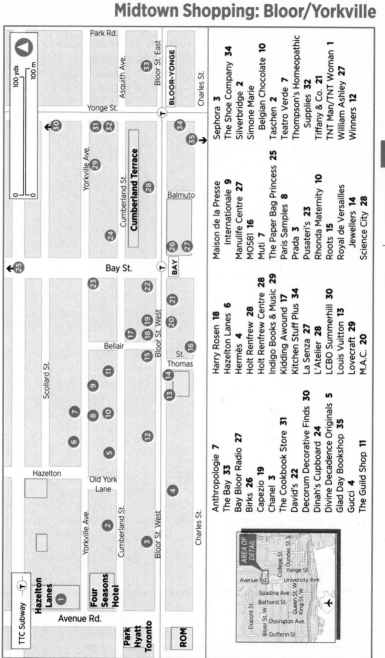

Anthropologie **7**
The Bay **33**
Bay Bloor Radio **27**
Birks **26**
Capezio **19**
Chanel **3**
The Cookbook Store **31**
David's **22**
Decorum Decorative Finds **30**
Dinah's Cupboard **24**
Divine Decadence Originals **5**
Glad Day Bookshop **35**
Gucci **4**
The Guild Shop **11**

Harry Rosen **18**
Hazelton Lanes **6**
Hermès **4**
Holt Renfrew **28**
Holt Renfrew Centre **28**
Indigo Books & Music **29**
Kidding Awound **17**
Kitchen Stuff Plus **34**
La Senza **27**
L'Atelier **28**
LCBO Summerhill **30**
Louis Vuitton **13**
Lovecraft **29**
M.A.C. **20**

Maison de la Presse
  Internationale **9**
Manulife Centre **27**
MO851 **16**
Muti **7**
The Paper Bag Princess **25**
Paris Samples **8**
Prada **3**
Pusateri's **23**
Rhonda Maternity **10**
Roots **15**
Royal de Versailles
  Jewellers **14**
Science City **28**

Sephora **3**
The Shoe Company **34**
Silverbridge **2**
Simone Marie
  Belgian Chocolate **10**
Taschen **2**
Teatro Verde **7**
Thompson's Homeopathic
  Supplies **32**
Tiffany & Co. **21**
TNT Man/TNT Woman **1**
William Ashley **27**
Winners **12**

new restaurants. While you're at it, walk north to the next major street, Dundas Street West, which is on the avant-garde of all fronts, from fashion to food.

MIDTOWN

The Mink Mile, Bloor Street West This strip of pricey real estate, known as Mink Mile, is bordered by Yonge Street to the east and Avenue Road to the west. It's where most of the top international names in fashion set up shop. If you're in the mood to see what Karl Lagerfeld is designing or to pick up a glittering bauble from Cartier or Tiffany, this is your hunting ground. The strip has undergone a long, drawn-out facelift and is all the prettier for it.

Yorkville One of Toronto's best known—and most expensive—shopping neighborhoods, it's where you'll find art galleries of note like The Guild Shop, designer boutiques, major outlets such as Toronto's only downtown Anthropologie and a Whole Foods location, and boutiques such as the Papery for curated stationery.

SHOPPING A TO Z
Antiques, Furniture & Housewares
ANTIQUES

Decorum Decorative Finds If you're going on an ocean voyage, can you resist a vintage Louis Vuitton trunk? The wares here range from tables and chaise lounges to oil paintings and old books. Wares are expensive, but also top of the line. 1210 Yonge St. ✆ **416/966-6829.** Subway: Summerhill.

G.U.F.F. 🛋 The name stands for "good used furniture finds," and this Leslieville store delivers on the promise. Much of the stock consists of wood pieces, often with a natural finish (not just tables and chairs, but cabinets and bed frames, too). There are also framed prints and mirrors. 1142 Queen St. E. ✆ **416/913-8025.** Subway: Queen, then a streetcar E to Bertmount Ave.

L'Atelier This is all about glamour. Napoleon III side tables share space with chrome bar stools and rococo Italian lamps. Many of the price tags hit four digits, but there are lovely accoutrements for moderate budgets, too. 1224 Yonge St. ✆ **416/966-0200.** Subway: Summerhill.

Zig Zag 🛋 This shop stocks a mélange of styles, but the specialty is early modernist pieces. The names to watch out for are Eames, Saarinen, Arne Jacobsen, and Warren Platner. 985 Queen St. E. ✆ **416/778-6495.** Subway: Queen, then any streetcar E to Carlaw Ave.

🎁 **Antiques Roadshow**

Seven times each year, more than 70 antiques dealers from Ontario and Québec descend on Centerpoint Mall for the **Heritage Antique Market.** The goods up for grabs include 19th- and 20th-century porcelains, jewelry, silver, furniture, and paintings. If you're in town when the market is on, you're in luck. Be sure to call ahead or check the website (www.heritageantiqueshows.com) for the schedule. The market takes place on statutory holidays. Centerpoint Mall is located at 6464 Yonge St. (at Steeles Ave.) and is accessible by subway (it's the Steeles stop on the Yonge Line). Call ✆ **416/483-6471** for more details.

FURNITURE

The Art Shoppe This veteran furniture store, more than 75 years old, deals in top-notch furniture that is laid out like set designs on a soundstage. A wide range of styles is on display, from gilt baroque to streamlined Art Deco. 2131 Yonge St. ℂ **416/487-3211.** www.theartshoppe.com. Subway: Eglinton.

Kiosk ★ A dynamic furniture and design spot known among the pros as a leading source for innovative, creative, and top-quality goods. Look for the latest from B&B Italia, Ligne Roset, and Poltrona Frau. The company's collection is steered by the owner's superlative eye for fine design. The collection of chairs alone is worth a visit. 288 King St. E. ℂ **416/539-9665.** www.kioskdesign.ca. Subway: King, then streetcar to Sherbourne St.

MADE ★ Smart and more than a little sassy, this small showroom of furniture and accessories is a retail gallery featuring works by artists, industrial designers, and other craftspeople. The pitch? Contemporary Canadiana with cheek, and an eco-bent, to boot. A sampling includes bookends that celebrate the iconic work of Group of Seven artist Lauren Harris, modular shelves, felt stools, and funky lamps. Even if you're not a shopper, it's fun to browse and admire the clever, often handmade, goods. 867 Dundas St. W. ℂ **416/607-6384.** www.madedesign.ca. Subway: Dundas, then streetcar W to Manning Ave.

HOUSEWARES, GLASS & DESIGN

Bergo Designs The selection here is a mix of international high-end standards like Alessi and Georg Jensen, and local finds like the Brothers Dressler, twin woodworkers who make beautiful pieces in their Toronto studio. There's also some architecturally inspired jewelry and watches by Frank Gehry. Prices veer to the high side, in keeping with the quality of goods. In the Distillery District, 55 Mill St. ℂ **416/861-1821.** www.bergo.ca. Subway: King, then a streetcar E to Parliament St.

Kitchen Stuff Plus This housewares shop sells brand-name goods from the likes of Umbra (see below) at discount prices. There is also a good selection of picture frames, wine racks, area rugs, candles, painted ceramics, and kitchen accessories. There are 11 locations around town. 703 Yonge St. ℂ **416/944-2718.** www.kitchenstuffplus.com. Subway: Yonge/Bloor.

Muti Murano glass designs and cheery ceramics from Italy dominate this store. Look a little closer, and you'll find a few French tapestries and tablecloths, too. 88 Yorkville Ave. ℂ **416/969-0253.** Subway: Bay.

Downtown Shopping: Queen Street West & West Queen West

Apple Store **44**
B&J Trading **21**
Bau-Xi Gallery **25**
The Bay **45**
Boomer **39**
Brian Bailey **5**
Browns **44**
Cabaret **14**
Canadian Tire **41**
Chapters **30**
Comrags **13**
Courage My Love **24**
Danier **44**
David Mason **29**
Decibel **38**
Delphic **10**
Eaton Centre **44**
Exile **23**
Fashion Crimes **34**
Femme de Carriere **44**

Fresh Baked Goods **19**
Fresh Collective **11**
Getoutside **31**
Girl Friday **9**
Grreat Stuff **6**
HMV **43**
I Miss You **4**
Indigo **44**

John Fluevog **36**
Kol Kid **12**
Lululemon Athletica **33**
Lush **35**
MADE **2**
Marilyn's **26**
Moores **47**
The Music Store **40**

Nicholas Hoare **48**
Nikolau Restaurant Equipment **17**
Olga Korper Gallery **1**
The Paper Place **7**
Peach Berserk **27**
Preloved **8**

Provenance Regional Cuisine **3**
Rotate This **15**
Sears **44**
Silver Snail **32**
Stephen Bulger Gallery **4**
Susan Hobbs Gallery **16**
Swipe Books **28**

Post Office ✉
TTC Subway —Ⓣ—

Nella Cucina   Feel like playing chef? This sleek, two-story destination for pros and home cooks alike has all you need, from Roos butcher blocks and cutting boards to top-of-the-line knives, grills, and assorted accessories. Open racks are lined with plastic condiment dispensers, 12-quart measuring cups, Le Creuset Dutch Ovens, and more. You also might want to sign up for one of the popular, one-off cooking classes led by popular local chefs. 876 Bathurst St. (just N of Bloor St. W.). ℂ **416/922-9055.** Subway: Bathurst.

Nikolaou Restaurant Equipment ★ 🎁   The name might lead you to believe that this is the place to go if you're on the hunt for a Hobart mixer or chef's whites, but in fact, this tiny, absolutely crammed store is a great place for home cooks to buy myriad quality kitchenware, from professional copper pans to Global knives and more. It's always busy, and the owners are sometimes grumpy dealing with amateur questions, so be prepared to take some time for exploring on your own. The effort usually pays off. 629 Queen St. W. (at Bathurst St.). ℂ **416/504-6411.** Subway: Osgoode, then a streetcar or walk W to Bathurst St.

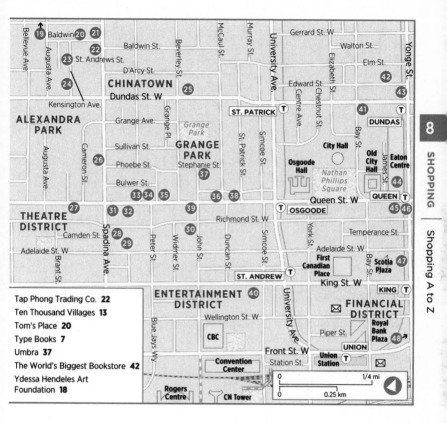

Tap Phong Trading Co. **22**
Ten Thousand Villages **13**
Tom's Place **20**
Type Books **7**
Umbra **37**
The World's Biggest Bookstore **42**
Ydessa Hendeles Art
Foundation **18**

Tap Phong Trading Co. 🏠 If you have only a few minutes in Chinatown, spend them here. You'll find beautiful hand-painted ceramics, earthenware, decorative items, kitchen utensils, and small appliances. Best of all, just about everything is inexpensive and of reliable quality. 360 Spadina Ave. *©* **416/977-6364.** Subway: Spadina, then the LRT to Baldwin St.

Umbra The screaming pink exterior is the award-winning work of a Toronto design firm, which is fitting for this "concept store" of a bold, global company. The two floors, brightly lit and sleek, carry the air of an art gallery, and each item features the designer's name, from a whimsical candelabra to a sleek desk, a round table to a neat tape dispenser. Designers are selected from around the world, and teams partner with design schools, such as the nearby Ontario College of Art and Design. Truly cool stuff. 165 John St. (just N of Queen St.). *©* **416/299-0088.** Subway: Osgoode, then a streetcar or walk W to John St.

William Ashley China All the top brands are here—Wedgwood, All-Clad, Baccarat, Lenox—and, as the weekly ads promise, all at amazing discount prices! This place, a popular spot for wedding registries, deals in huge volume. A Mink Mile staple, right across from Holt Renfrew, it's all service and smiles. Very traditional. Manulife Centre, 55 Bloor St. W. ✆ **416/964-2900.** Subway: Bloor at Yonge or Bay on the Bloor line & a short walk.

Art

Bau-Xi Gallery   After viewing the masterworks at the Art Gallery of Ontario, you can head across the street and buy your own. Founded in 1965 in Vancouver, Bau-Xi features contemporary works by artists from across the country. 340 Dundas St. W. ✆ **416/977-0600.** www.bau-xi.com. Subway: St. Patrick.

Corkin Gallery   Most items here are historical or contemporary fine-art photographs from around the world. They include works by André Kertész, Nan Goldin, Irving Penn, and Brett Weston, plus a small collection of modernist painting and sculpture. In the Distillery District, 55 Mill St. ✆ **416/979-1980.** www.corkingallery.com. Subway: King, then a streetcar E to Parliament St.

Eskimo Art Gallery ★★   This award-winning gallery has the largest collection of Inuit stone sculptures in Toronto. The focus is on contemporary, and especially emerging, artists. At any given time, it shows more than 500 pieces, including prints. 12 Queens Quay W. (opposite Westin Harbour Castle). ✆ **416/366-3000.** www.eskimoart.com. Subway: Union, then the LRT to Queen's Quay.

The Guild Shop ★ 🎒   This retail location of the Ontario Crafts Council is a longtime favorite among art-lovers (it's 80 years old this year). The store represents Canadian artists and is a good place to discover beautiful, unique, handmade objects—from pottery to painting, ceramics to sculptures—plus textiles. 118 Cumberland St., Yorkville. ✆ **416/921-1721.** www.craft.on.ca/store. Subway: Bay station at Cumberland exit, then cross the road.

Olga Korper Gallery   Established in 1973, this gallery houses contemporary Canadian and international works. Artists represented include Averbuch, John Brown, Sankawa, and the estate of Louis Comtois. 17 Morrow Ave. (off Dundas St. W.). ✆ **416/538-8220.** Subway: Dundas West.

Sandra Ainsley Gallery ★★   Specializing in glass sculpture, this renowned gallery represents Canadian, American, and international artists, including Dale Chihuly, Jon Kuhn, Peter Powning, Tom Scoon, Susan Edgerley, and David Bennett. The one-of-a-kind pieces have big price tags, but you can also find some affordable items, such as paperweights, vases, and jewelry. In the Distillery District, 55 Mill St. ✆ **416/214-9490.** www.sandraainsleygallery.com. Subway: King, then a streetcar E to Parliament St.

Stephen Bulger Gallery ★★ 🎒   If you're interested in fine-art photography, especially in the documentary tradition, this is the place to go in Toronto. The Gallery displays Canadian and international photography, both by established artists and up-and-comers, from Ruth Orkin to Pete Doherty. It is one of the driving forces behind CONTACT, Toronto's Annual Celebration of Photography, which has helped launch many careers. Artists represented include Robert Burley, Ruth Kaplan, Vincenzo Pietropaolo, and Alex Webb. This is also a place locals go for some of the city's best photography exhibits. 1026 Queen St. W. ✆ **416/504-0575.** www.bulgergallery.com. Subway: Osgoode, then a streetcar W to Ossington Ave.

Susan Hobbs Gallery 🎒   This small gallery in an unprepossessing warehouse far from the Yorkville crowd has been a major player in Canadian contemporary art since 1993. Hobbs represents some of Toronto's best artists, including Ian Carr-Harris,

Shirley Wiitasalo, Robin Collyer, and Sandra Meigs. 137 Tecumseth St. (at Queen St.). ✆ **416/504-3699.** www.susanhobbs.com. Subway: Osgoode, then any streetcar W to Tecumseth St.

Ydessa Hendeles Art Foundation ★ This is one of the most interesting contemporary art collections in the city. Hendeles features installations by international artists. Works on display include paintings, photography, and multimedia projects. Hours are limited, so call ahead to see if they're open when you're in town. 778 King St. W. ✆ **416/603-2227.** Subway: St. Andrew, then any streetcar W to Bathurst St.

Audiovisual & Electronic Goods

Apple Store ★★★ Mac geeks, take note: Toronto has *four* Apple stores. One is at the Yorkdale shopping center, one is at Fairview Mall, and one is at Sherway Gardens, all remote from the downtown core, but the Eaton Centre location provides easy access. Eaton Centre. ✆ **647/258-0801.** Subway: Dundas or Queen.

Bay Bloor Radio This 1,208-sq.-m (13,003-sq.-ft.) store carries the latest and greatest audio equipment, from portable units to in-home theater systems. Manulife Centre, 55 Bloor St. W. ✆ **416/967-1122.** www.baybloorradio.com. Subway: Bay.

Canadian Tire Don't be fooled by the name—this megastore carries far more than auto parts. It's a big department store, as well as a retailer of gardening goods in summer, baubles in festive season, and yes, tires year-round. There's another branch just north of Bloor Street, at 839 Yonge St. (✆ **416/925-9592**). 65 Dundas St. W. ✆ **416/979-9056.** www.canadiantire.ca. Subway: Dundas.

Henry's ★ This bi-level shop deals in analog and digital photography. The first floor has electronic equipment, darkroom supplies, and a photo-processing lab. Upstairs, a wide selection of secondhand cameras and gear is available. It's a favorite among pros for leading-edge equipment and archival-quality papers. 119 Church St. ✆ **416/868-0872.** Subway: Queen.

Books, Magazines & Newspapers
BOOKS

Book City ★ 🎁 For a small chain, Book City offers big discounts—many titles are discounted by 10% to 30%. The selection of international magazines is particularly good. Book City also has several branches around the city, including 716 Queen St. W. (✆ **416/964-1167**), 1950 Queen St. E. (✆ **416/698-1444**), and 348 Danforth Ave. (✆ **416/469-9997**). 501 Bloor St. W. ✆ **416/961-4496.** www.bookcity.ca. Subway: Bathurst.

Chapters ★★ While Indigo (see below) now owns and operates the Chapters bookstores, they retain their own charm. Browse-worthy and well stocked, these are comfortable stores where, pre-purchase, you can pick up a few titles, slide into a big chair, and sip a Starbucks latte. (Locals also recognize the scene as the one ridiculed by Toronto musician Ron Sexsmith's song "Jazz in the Bookstore.") The stores are open late, usually until 10 or 11pm on weeknights and midnight on weekends. 142 John St. ✆ **416/595-7349.** www.chapters.indigo.ca. Subway: Osgoode.

The Cookbook Store ★ 🍴 In a world where neighborhood bookstores are too often on life support, this gem, 20-plus years and kicking, stands out for its fine selection of cookbooks, food memoirs, and the best in food writing. If you're lucky enough to be in town for one of their many book launches, book the date—top chefs are often featured. (Julia Child, for one, was here.) 850 Yonge St. ✆ **416/920-2665.** www.cook-book. com. Subway: Yonge/Bloor.

THE BEST bargains

Like any big city, Toronto offers some great bargains. You just have to be prepared to hunt and appreciate it's luck of the draw if you find that vintage Hermès bag or brand-new Prada booty. Many Toronto retailers, including luxurious Holt Renfrew, have their own outlet shops. Here's my little black book of favorite foraging grounds. Happy hunting!

Dixie Outlet Mall ★   Ten minutes from Pearson International Airport, the Dixie Outlet Mall has more than 120 outlet shops, including Jay Set (which carries Peter Nygård fashions), La Vie en Rose lingerie, and chocolatier Laura Secord. It's a good bet you'll find something for yourself or a gift to take home. There's also a large Winners store (see below). 1250 S. Service Rd., Mississauga. © **905/278-7492.** Gardiner Expwy./Queen Elizabeth Way (QEW) W to Dixie Rd. exit; turn left & follow Dixie Rd. S to S. Service Rd.

Grreat Stuff   The place is packed with men's clothes; if you're not troubled by claustrophobia, dig in for some amazing deals. Business casual is this shop's

mainstay, though you can find *grreat* prices on Italian silk ties and brand-name suits. 870 Queen St. W. © **416/533-7680.** www. grreatstuff.com. Subway: Osgoode, then a streetcar W to Shaw St.

Honest Ed's World Famous Shopping Centre ★   Ed's is a Toronto institution; it's been in business for more than 60 years. The store is framed with flashing red and yellow lights both outdoors *and* indoors. "Don't just stand there, buy something!" blurts out one brazen sign. This idiosyncratic store has a deal on everything from housewares to carpets, clothing to toys. Crazy-making as shopping here can be, the bargains are unbeatable. In case you need to refuel after weaving through the maze of aisles, there's a **Lettieri** (p. 203) tucked into the corner at Bloor and Bathurst streets. 581 Bloor St. W. © **416/537-1574.** Subway: Bathurst.

Marilyn's 🎁   Here's a rare thing: knockdown prices paired with attentive service. The specialty is Canadian fashions for women, from sportswear to glamorous gowns. You can also attend in-store seminars on fashion-forward topics like

David Mason   This well-established store has moved into a new location. It stocks many travel books and a number of first editions of Canadian, American, and British works. The collections of 19th- and 20th-century literature are vast. 366 Adelaide St. W. © **416/598-1015.** www.davidmasonbooks.com. Subway: St. Andrew.

Glad Day Bookshop ★   This was the first gay-oriented bookstore in Canada, and it remains one of the best. The shelves hold a sizable collection of gay and lesbian fiction, biography, and history books, and the offerings have expanded to include magazines, CDs, videos, calendars, posters, and cards. 598A Yonge St., 2nd floor. © **416/961-4161.** Subway: Wellesley.

Indigo Books Music & More ★★ ☺   A Canadian-owned chain, Indigo offers an excellent selection of books and magazines, and a small selection of music. Like Chapters, Indigo comes complete with coffee shops and comfy seating. A favorite with night owls, they're open until 11pm or midnight every day. You'll also find branches at the Eaton Centre (© **416/591-3622**) and at 2300 Yonge St., at Eglinton Avenue (© **416/544-0049**). Manulife Centre, 55 Bloor St. W. © **416/925-3536.** www.chapters. indigo.ca. Subway: Yonge/Bloor or Bay.

traveling with just one suitcase. 200 Spadina Ave. ☎ **416/504-6777.** Subway: Spadina, then the LRT to Queen St. W.

Paris Samples This store snaps up designers' samples and marks them down 20% to 75%. The clothes range from wool pants to velvet dresses to micro-miniskirts. *Be forewarned:* The sizes are all under 14, and many clothes come only in the smallest sizes. 101 Yorkville Ave. ☎ **416/926-0656.** Subway: Bay.

The Shoe Company This small chain, with outlets around town, stocks good men's and women's shoes, from Unisa, Nine West, and others, many marked down. The emphasis is on trendy styles that might not be stylish for long, but won't hurt your pocketbook either. First Canadian Place, 711 Yonge St. ☎ **416/923-8388.** Subway: Yonge/Bloor.

Tom's Place ★★ After more than 40 years in business, Tom's Place looks sharper than ever. While the shop devotes an entire floor to women's wear, the best buys are in the men's department: You'll find brand-name merchandise by the likes of Armani and Valentino. Tom's Place

stocks sizes from 36 short to 50 tall. 190 Baldwin St. ☎ **416/596-0297.** Subway: Spadina, then the LRT to Baldwin St.

Winners This northern outpost of the U.S.-owned T.J. Maxx chain offers great deals on clothes for men and women (think Jones New York, Tommy Hilfiger, and even Stella McCartney as part of the Runway Selection). Some locations carry children's togs, too. There's also an ever-changing selection of housewares, cookware, linens, toiletries, and toys. The 3,716-sq.-m (40,000-sq.-ft.) outlet at College Park is always crowded, but its large, airy space is filled with deals (☎ **416/598-8800;** subway: College). The original, smaller location, in the Fashion District, is another good bet (57 Spadina Ave.; ☎ **416/585-2052;** subway: Spadina, then the LRT to King St. W.) as is the Scotia Plaza store in Toronto's Underground City; 40 King St. W.; ☎ **416/360-8162**). The shop on tony Bloor Street West outraged some of the strip's high-priced neighbors, but deal-obsessed shoppers love it. 110 Bloor St. W. ☎ **416/920-0193.** www.winners. ca. Subway: Bay.

Mabel's Fables ★ ☺ Children's bookstores can be as magical as the content they carry. This charming shop is stocked with classic and new titles, as well as a small but well-chosen selection of games, puzzles, and toys. They make a point of avoiding the major brands. On weekends, author visits and other special events take place. 662 Mount Pleasant. ☎ **416/322-0438.** www.mabelsfables.com. Subway: Eglinton, then bus no. 34 to Mount Pleasant & walk 2 blocks S.

Nicholas Hoare ★ This shop has the cozy feel of an English library, with hardwood floors, plush couches, and a fireplace. There's an extensive selection of Canadian and international fiction, as well as heavyweight art books and a small but good selection of children's titles. 45 Front St. E. ☎ **416/777-2665.** Subway: Union.

Silver Snail ★ ☺ Long before graphic novels entered the mainstream, this store opened the door to adults and kids alike in search of comic-book finds. There are collectables, books, posters, and other memorabilia, along with adult-oriented comics such as the *Sandman* series. 367 Queen St. W. ☎ **416/593-0889.** www.silversnail.com. Subway: Osgoode.

Sleuth of Baker Street ★★ If you love a good mystery, make a pilgrimage to Toronto's only crime-focused bookshop. Check the website before you visit so that you can take advantage of one of the shop's many author readings. Closed Mondays. 1600 Bayview Ave. (at Manor Rd. E.). ✆ 416/483-3111. www.sleuthofbakerstreet.ca. Subway: Eglinton, then bus no. 34 E to Mount Pleasant & walk 3 blocks S.

Swipe Books on Advertising and Design ★ 📚 Now located at the arts-collective studio building of 401 Richmond St. W., Swipe is legend among locals for its very thorough selection of books related to design, architecture, and advertising. Even if you're not looking for a particular title, it's a great place to browse beautiful books and explore the latest in international styles in buildings, public spaces, and private homes. You can also learn a thing or two about marketing machinations. This is the official bookstore of the RGD (Registered Graphic Designers of Ontario) and the ADCC (Advertising and Design Club of Canada). Great gizmos, too. 401 Richmond St. W. ✆ 416/363-1332. www.swipe.com. Subway: Queen or King, then streetcar W to Richmond St.

Type Books ★ 📚 This small, smart bookstore is run by a couple of English literature grads. Hip but not too cool, the selection includes serious fiction, fine books on food and art, a healthy collection of poetry, traditional and contemporary children's literature, and a lot of indie stuff that you'd have a hard time finding elsewhere. They make a point of featuring local talent. The mix has proven so popular that there's now a second location on Spadina north of St. Clair Avenue (427 Spadina Rd.). 883 Queen St. W. ✆ 416/366-8973. Subway: Osgoode, then a streetcar W to Trinity-Bellwoods.

University of Toronto Bookstore ★ 📚 This is one of the best-stocked independent booksellers in town, with textbooks galore, fiction, non-fiction, medical tomes, and impressive collections of Classics and Can Lit. As of year-end—that's May for college students—there's an annual blow-out sale. In the Koffler Centre, 214 College St. ✆ 416/978-7900. www.uoftbookstore.com. Subway: Queen's Park.

The World's Biggest Bookstore ★ Whether or not it is indeed the world's biggest, the 27km (17 miles) of bookshelves do contain a broad selection, as you'd expect, and a lot of remaindered stuff, too. The magazine racks alone seem endless. There's a lot to peruse, but the overly bright, bare-bones space doesn't make for a pleasant browse. 20 Edward St. ✆ 416/977-7009. Subway: Dundas.

MAGAZINES & NEWSPAPERS

Maison de la Presse Internationale This store fills up fast on weekends, drawing expats and locals alike to get that latest edition of *British Vogue, Paris Match,* or any number of international magazines and newspapers, all as current as you'll find. The second floor is devoted to paperback novels *en français*. 99 Yorkville Ave. ✆ 416/928-2328. Subway: Bay.

Department Stores

The Bay The Hudson's Bay Company started out as a fur-trading business when the first French-speaking settlers came to Canada. Today, the Bay, long known for its midrange selections of clothing and housewares, is reinventing itself as a competitor in high-end women's fashion and runway frocks. The new campaign has brought Sarah Jessica Parker and Anna dello Russo, among other celebrities, for champagne launches and elegant soirees. The place to see the new look is the Room at the Queen Street location. Elsewhere, you'll still find wool blankets, simple housewares, and casual gear. 176 Yonge St. (at Queen St.). ✆ 416/861-9111. www.thebay.com. Subway: Queen. 2nd location at 2 Bloor St. E. (at Yonge St.). ✆ 416/972-3333. Subway: Yonge/Bloor.

Fresh Perspective

Let's say you're pressed for time, and you want to hit a single store that will let you shop for truly distinctive clothing and giftware. Get yourself to **Fresh Collective**, a designer-run collective at 692 Queen St. W. ((C) 416/594-1313; www.freshcollective.com). You will find hip designs by local, up-and-coming labels—and you'll be able to talk to the people who made them because they staff the store themselves. The focus is primarily on designs for women (sorry, guys), but the eclectic offerings at any given time will also include baby togs and jewelry.

Holt Renfrew   This is Toronto's luxury department-store destination. Designers such as Donna Karan, Christian Lacroix, and Yves St. Laurent figure in the bright and stylish four levels of merchandise. While you're here, take time to visit the excellent Holt Renfrew Spa (p. 130) or the snazzy Holt Renfrew Café, which serves fine soups, sandwiches, and salads. The basement connects with an underground mall and features a casual cafe good for a quick bite. Holt Renfrew Centre, 50 Bloor St. W. (C) **416/922-2333.** www.holtrenfrew.com. Subway: Yonge/Bloor.

Sears   If you visited Toronto before 2000, you'll remember the gorgeous Eaton's department store, which anchored the Eaton Centre complex. Sears Canada, a run-of-the-mill chain, bought the Eaton's name and opened this department store in its place. It's more upscale than your average Sears. Eaton Centre. (C) **416/343-2111.** www.sears. ca. Subway: Dundas.

Fashion

Toronto has all of the requisite big-name European boutiques along Bloor Street West, between Yonge Street and Avenue Road. You'll find **Louis Vuitton** at no. 111; **Gucci** and **Hermès** at no. 130; and **Prada** and **Chanel** at the Colonnade shopping arcade at no. 131. But the listings below focus on shops particular to Toronto (with just a few exceptions). Also see "Hunting for Vintage" (p. 175) and "Shoes" (below).

CLOTHING FOR CHILDREN

Fashion Crimes ★   Toronto designer Pam Chorley's store looks like a princess's dressing room, complete with Venetian glass and ornate chandeliers. There are clothes for women here, too, but her Misdemeanors line makes gossamer gowns and ruby slippers for little girls who dream they're really princesses. 322½ Queen St. W. (C) **416/351-8758.** Subway: Osgoode.

Kol Kid   West Queen West isn't just for grown-ups, you know. This charming boutique carries Canadian- and European-made clothing for kids, plus toys and furnishings. 674 Queen St. W. (C) **416/681-0368.** Subway: Osgoode, then a streetcar W to Palmerston Ave.

Lovechild   A favorite with tiny tots who are already developing fashion savvy, Lovechild offers a selection of groovy clothes in a rainbow of colors. 2523 Yonge St. (C) **416/486-4746.** www.lovechild.ca. Subway: Eglinton.

CLOTHING FOR MEN & WOMEN

Danier   This Canadian chain carries suede and leather coats for men and women, as well as ladies' pants, skirts, and handbags. Most of the prices are very reasonable, and regular sales events knock the prices down 20% to 50%. Eaton Centre. (C) **416/598-1159.** www.danier.com. Subway: Queen.

lululemon athletica ★   The athletically inclined—especially yoga devotees—will delight in this shop. In addition to the Canadian house label's nicely designed workout wear, you'll find Ayurvedic skin care products by Christy Turlington, yoga mats, and other accessories. 342 Queen St. W. ✆ **416/703-1399.** www.lululemon.com. Subway: Osgoode, then a streetcar W to Spadina Ave.

MO851 ★   This Canadian-owned store based in Montreal has stores in New York, Paris, Taipei, and more. The boutique line specializes in beautiful bags, jackets and coats—all made with very fine leather—as well as belts and other accessories. The styles are classic and enduring. Even the raincoats are attractive enough to brighten a damp day. 23 St. Thomas St. ✆ **416/920-4001.** www.mo851.com. Subway: Bay subway, then a short walk W along Bloor St. & S on St. Thomas.

Roots   This is one Canadian retailer that seems to be universally loved. The clothes are casual, from hooded sweats to fleece jackets, and there's a small but good selection of leather footwear. Don't overlook the tykes' department, which has the same stuff in pint-sized versions. Other locations include the Eaton Centre (✆ **416/593-9640**). 95A Bloor St. W. ✆ **416/323-9512.** www.roots.ca. Subway: Bay.

Tilley Endurables ✦   The Tilley hat may not be Canada's greatest style moment, but it remains an institution. The company offers a full range of men's and women's clothing, as well as belts, socks, and other travel gear. Clothes are made to last and designed to be practical: extra pockets for hikers, waterproof vests for hunters, etc. Tilley has also branched out into travel underwear. (The claim is that although "sexy they may not be," a mere two pairs will get you around the world.) The store at Queen's Quay (207 Queens Quay W.; ✆ **416/203-0463**) is the most convenient, but the flagship store on Don Mills is unbeatable for choice. 900 Don Mills Rd. ✆ **800/363-8737** or 416/441-6141. www.tilley.com. Subway: Eglinton, then bus no. 34 E to Don Mills & walk 2 lights N to Barber Greene Rd.

TNT Man/TNT Woman 📖   The acronym stands for "The New Trend," and this small chain offers just that, with fashions from Betsey Johnson and Plein Sud for women, and Diesel and Iceberg jeans for men. There are also locations uptown at 368 and 388 Eglinton Ave. 87 Avenue Rd. ✆ **416/975-1960** (men's shop) or 416/975-1810 (women's shop). Subway: Bay.

CLOTHING FOR MEN

Boomer ★   Ever wonder where Barenaked Ladies or Moist get the glad rags they wear in their videos? Look no further than Boomer, a hip boutique that stocks staples such as Hugo Boss and Cinque, as well as the latest from Swedish trendsetter J. Lindeberg and more. 309 Queen St. W. ✆ **416/598-0013.** Subway: Osgoode.

Decibel   This trendy shop is a terrific spot to pick up the latest and greatest in casual wear. Labels range from well-known brands such as Kenneth Cole to up-and-comers such as Psycho Cowboy or Pusch (from Denmark and Calgary, respectively). 200 Queen St. W. ✆ **416/506-9648.** Subway: Osgoode.

Delphic   Expect to find fashion favorites such as Evisu Jeans, which are imported from Japan and other super-trendy fare. 706 Queen St. W. ✆ **416/603-3334.** Subway: Osgoode, then a streetcar W to Manning Ave.

Harry Rosen ★   Designed like a mini–department store, Harry Rosen carries the crème de la crème of menswear designers, including Hugo Boss, Brioni, and Versace. There is also a selection of work-worthy footwear and a famous "Great Wall of Shirts." Now the flagship store also claims Canada's only Tod's Place, the luxe international brand of shoes and leather accessories. 82 Bloor St. W. © **416/972-0556.** www.harryrosen. com. Subway: Bay.

Korry's This neighborhood spot stocks the latest from lines such as Canali, Canadian designer Copley, Pal Zileri, and Hugo Boss, as well as its own house brand of suits, Roberto, made with Italian wool. A great selection of samples, plus excellent ties at good prices, makes it a bargain-hunter's treasure trove, as well. 569 Danforth Ave. © **416/463-1115.** Subway: Pape station.

Moores 🎗 This spacious shop specializes in formal wear, but more casual clothes are in stock, as well. Most of the suits, sport coats, and dress pants are Canadian-made, and such international designers as Oscar de la Renta are represented, too. Sizes run from extra-short to extra-tall and oversize. The prices tend to be reasonable, and bargains abound. 100 Yonge St. © **416/363-5442.** www.mooresclothing.com. Subway: King.

CLOTHING FOR WOMEN

Anthropologie ★ This American-based women's clothing store chain has grown to hundreds of locations in less than 20 years, including one in downtown Toronto. Two floors of pretty florals, sexy dresses, skinny pants, whimsical jewelry, bags, dishes, and more all add up to a pleasant, if middle-of-the-road, shopping experience. It's hard to leave empty-handed. A second location is at the Shops at Don Mills, which is a hike from downtown. 80 Yorkville Ave. © **416/964-9700.** Subway: Bay, then walk 2 blocks N to Yorkville Ave.

Brian Bailey ★ Known for glamorous gowns, cocktail dresses, and smart suits, this Canadian designer is popular with clients who like their fashion statements to be classic and feminine. 878 Queen St. W. © **416/516-7188.** Subway: Osgoode, then a streetcar W to Shaw St.

Comrags ★ 👖 Designers Judy Cornish and Joyce Gunhouse create retro-inspired clothing that looks great on a range of body types. It's a label beloved for dresses, especially. Suits are snazzy, too. 654 Queen St. W. © **416/360-7249.** www.comrags.com. Subway: Osgoode, then a streetcar W to Palmerston Ave.

Ewanika 👖 The designs here are smart, modern, and generally good for work and play. Trish Ewanika designs tailored suits, dresses, and more that work for women who like a polished but understated look. 1083 Bathurst St. © **416/927-9699.** Subway: Bathurst, then walk or take the bus N to Dupont St.

Fashion Crimes ★ These glamorous dresses, designed by shop owner Pam Chorley, are a tribute to playful femininity and whimsical imagination. Many of the fabrics

---

🎁 Psst . . . Want a Free Yoga Class?

If you're in Toronto on a Wednesday or Sunday morning and feel an overwhelming urge to exercise, here's a secret you need to know: lululemon athletica offers **free hour-long classes** (Wednesday yoga is at 8am; Sunday is "Pilates-yoga fusion" at 9:30am). There's absolutely no charge or obligation to buy anything (though you may be tempted by the stylish workout gear that lines the walls). The classes take place at the store at 342 Queen St. W. (© **416/703-1399**). You should call the day before to make sure that the class is scheduled, but you can't make an advance reservation—participation is limited to the first 25 people to show up.

8

SHOPPING

Shopping A to Z

173

are made for Chorley in Paris, and you won't find them anywhere else. In addition to the elegant gowns, there are plenty of original accessories, including opera-length gloves, feathery boas, and glittering handbags. (Little girls have their own Misdemeanors line; see p. 171.) 322½ Queen St. W. ✆ **416/351-8758.** Subway: Osgoode.

Femme de Carriere ★   For a dose of Québécois savoir-faire, look no further than this elegant emporium. While the name translates as "career woman," the offerings range from shapely suits to evening-appropriate dresses and chic separates. Branches in shopping centers around town include First Canadian Place, Holt Renfrew Centre, and Fairview Mall. Eaton Centre. ✆ **416/595-0951.** Subway: Dundas or Queen.

Fresh Baked Goods ★ 🎁   This isn't a bakery. Owner Laura Jean, "the knitting queen," features a line of flirty knitwear made of cotton, mohair, wool, or lace. The staff is friendly; if you like a sweater but not its buttons, they'll sew on different ones from the store's sizeable collection, free of charge. They also do custom orders. 274 Augusta Ave. ✆ **416/966-0123.** www.freshbakedgoods.com. Subway: Spadina, then the LRT to Baldwin St. & walk 2 blocks W to Augusta Ave.

Girl Friday ★★ 🎁   Local designer Rebecca Nixon creates feminine dresses, suits, and separates for her shop under the name Girl Friday. The store also carries pieces from hip labels Nougat and Dish, but many come for Nixon's elegant yet affordable pieces. 740 Queen St. W. ✆ **416/364-2511.** www.girlfridayclothing.com. Subway: Osgoode, then a streetcar W to Claremont St.

Lilliput Hats ★ 🎁   If you're a hat fan, then Lilliput's is a must-visit for stunning designs made by the owner, Karyn Gingras. Her creations have been worn by Celine Dion and Whoopi Goldberg, among others. 462 College St. ✆ **416/536-5933.** www.lilliputhats.com. Subway: Queen's Park, then a streetcar W to Bathurst St.

Maxi Boutique   Variety is the name of the game at this long-established boutique in the heart of Greektown. Labels include homegrown talent such as Lida Baday, as well as international brands such as Naf Naf, Miss Sixty, and Betsey Johnson. 575 Danforth Ave. ✆ **416/461-6686.** Subway: Pape.

Peach Berserk ★ 🎁   Toronto designer Kingi Carpenter creates dramatically printed silk separates, dresses, and coats. Don't look for demure florals—prints range from bold martini glasses to the ironic "Do I Look Fat in This?" logo. Refreshing fashion with a sense of humor. 507 Queen St. W. ✆ **416/504-1711.** www.peachberserk.com. Subway: Osgoode, then a streetcar W to Spadina Ave.

Preloved ★★   The original Toronto boutique was destroyed by a fire in 2008. Since then, Preloved has reopened in a storefront across from Trinity-Bellwoods Park. The store's pieces really *are* one of a kind: The shop's owners breathe new life into vintage clothing and cast-off jeans and T-shirts by changing the shapes and adding details such as vintage lace. The roster of celeb fans includes Alanis Morissette. 881 Queen St. W. ✆ **416/504-8704.** Subway: Osgoode, then a streetcar W to Trinity-Bellwoods Park.

Rhonda Maternity   Red-hot mamas-to-be should check out this glamorous boutique. The stylish suits, sweater sets, and sportswear are this store's exclusive designs. 110 Cumberland St. ✆ **416/921-3116.** www.rhondamaternity.com. Subway: Bay.

Trove ★ 🎁   Trove started out primarily as a jewelry store, but expanded both in size and goods to now include groovy shoes, fun hats, and other accessories, plus a good selection of handbags. 793 Bathurst St. (at Bloor St. W.). ✆ **416/516-1258.** www.trove.ca. Subway: Bathurst.

HUNTING FOR vintage

In-the-know shoppers will tell you that Toronto has had a truly great vintage-shopping scene since the '70s. From couture and designer finds to simple smocks, collectibles to impulse buys, if you're prepared to rummage, you can find it at the treasure troves below.

Cabaret ★★ This shop features glamorous eveningwear of bygone eras—all in prime condition. Cabaret employs a seamstress to make repairs, and all clothing is dry-cleaned before it hits the sales floor. Be prepared to pay, though; this isn't one of the cheaper sources for vintage. 672 Queen St. W. ⓒ **416/504-7126.** Subway: Osgoode, then a streetcar W to Palmerston Ave.

Courage My Love ★ 🐟 With its mix of vintage clothing and new silver jewelry (the owner buys most of it in Mexico), Courage is a Kensington Market favorite. Dresses run from '50s velvet numbers to '80s jersey, with a few bias-cut 1930s gowns appearing once in a blue moon. There are also cashmere sweaters and handbags worthy of a night at the Stork Club and racks of worn shirts, jeans, shoes, and accessories. 14 Kensington Ave. ⓒ **416/979-1992.** Subway: Spadina, then the LRT to Dundas St. W.

Divine Decadence Originals ★ The price tags at this glamorous shop are sky high, but the dresses are so magnificent and well-maintained that the store feels like a couture museum. Take a look at the Lanvins and Balenciagas of years gone by. If that perfect dress is not quite a perfect fit, owner Carmelita Blondet can adjust to your size. 128 Cumberland St., 2nd floor ⓒ **416/324-9759.** Subway: Bay.

Exile Secondhand jeans, leather jackets, and classic T-shirts line the racks in this Kensington Market stalwart. Bargains turn up in odd places, such as the Anne Klein scarf at the bottom of a last-chance bin. 62 Kensington Ave. ⓒ **416/595-7199.** Subway: Spadina, then the LRT to Baldwin St.

Gadabout 👔 This jampacked Leslieville shop stocks outfits according to era, from Edwardian through the '70s. The quality is good, and pieces are dry-cleaned before they make it onto the racks. But everything is packed in so tight that shopping here can feel exhausting after a while. There are also menswear and a jumble of accessories and memorabilia. It's a good destination for the intrepid shopper who likes the hunt as much as the find. 1300 Queen St. E. ⓒ **416/463-1254.** www.gadabout.ca. Subway: Queen, then a streetcar E to Alton Ave.

I Miss You ★★ 👔 This gorgeous shop on Ossington bills itself as "modern vintage fashion," which means more emphasis on pieces from the '60s and '70s. The quality is excellent, and the clothes have been repaired (or lovingly preserved). Prices are reasonable, and discoveries include treasures such as vintage Hermès handbags. 63 Ossington Ave. ⓒ **416/916-7021.** Subway: Osgoode, then a streetcar W to Ossington Ave.

The Paper Bag Princess ★ L.A. has had a Paper Bag Princess boutique for several years, but only recently did its owner, Toronto native Elizabeth Mason, decide to open a location in her hometown. This store is a treasure trove, and its boudoir-like setting makes it a sexy place to shop. The mint-condition Chanel and Pucci outfits cost a bundle, but what else would you expect? Mason is also a designer in her own right, and her dresses grace the likes of Maria Bello and Ayelet Zurer. 287 Davenport Rd. ⓒ **416/925-2603.** www.thepaperbagprincess.com. Subway: Bay.

Thrill of the Find 👔 An easy store to navigate, this airy space has well-organized women's clothing on a few racks, with designer names such as Chanel featured in a separate couture section. 1172 Queen St. E. ⓒ **416/461-9313.** Subway: Queen, then a streetcar E to Jones Ave.

LINGERIE

La Senza 🖋 This Montréal-based chain carries moderately priced but eye-catching bra-and-panty sets, nighties, plush unisex robes, and patterned boxers. An assortment of slippers, candles, bath mousse, and picture frames rounds out the offerings. Holt Renfrew Centre, 50 Bloor St. W.✆ **416/972-1079.** www.lasenza.com. Subway: Yonge/Bloor.

Linea Intima ★ 🛍 While there's no shortage of fabulous undergarments at this boutique, the real reason to visit is owner Liliana Mann's encyclopedic knowledge of what suits the female form. This extends to prosthetics and bras that are designed for women who have had mastectomies. 1925 Avenue Rd.✆ **416/780-1726.** www.lineaintima.com. Subway: York Mills, then a bus W along Wilson Ave. to Avenue Rd. & walk 6 blocks S to Brooke Ave.

Secrets From Your Sister ★ 🛍 Thanks to Oprah, we know that the vast majority of women in North America are wearing the wrong bra size. That won't be true of you if you visit this store, which carries a terrific selection of bras to suit figures as dissimilar as Audrey Hepburn and Jayne Mansfield, and everything in between. 560 Bloor St. W.✆ **416/538-1234.** www.secretsfromyoursister.com. Subway: Bathurst.

SHOES (MEN'S, WOMEN'S & CHILDREN'S)

Browns ★ To treat your feet to fabulous footwear by Cesare Paciotti or Stuart Weitzman, beat a path to this shoe shop for both men and women. While you're here, check out Browns' own house label, which is well designed and less pricey. There's also athletic footwear from Puma and Adidas, and a good selection of handbags. Browns has several branches around town. Eaton Centre.✆ **416/979-9270.** www.browns shoes.com. Subway: Queen.

Capezio Whether you're looking for the perfect pair of ballet slippers or an up-to-the-minute design from Steve Madden or Guess, you'll find it here. All the shoes and other leather goods are for women. 70 Bloor St. W.✆ **416/920-1006.** Subway: Bay.

David's For serious shoppers only. This high-end store stocks elegant footwear for men and women—from Bruno Magli, Bally, and Sonia Rykiel, as well as the store's own collection—but prices are accordingly steep. 66 Bloor St. W.✆ **416/920-1000.** Subway: Bay.

Getoutside The store doesn't look like much, with its utilitarian shelving and lighting, but it stocks an amazing variety of sneakers from manufacturers around the world. Moccasins made by Laurentian Shoes, a Québec-based company, are also on show. 437 Queen St. W.✆ **416/593-5598.** www.getoutsideshoes.com. Subway: Osgoode.

John Fluevog ★★★ Famous for his Goth footwear, this Vancouver designer also creates shoes and boots in a kaleidoscope of colors. These shoes aren't for shrinking violets, but their funky chic will get your attention without having to stomp your feet. 242 Queen St. W.✆ **416/581-1420.** www.fluevog.com. Subway: Osgoode.

Mephisto These shoes are made for walking—particularly because they're made from all-natural materials. Devotees of this shop, now in its third decade, swear that it's impossible to wear out Mephisto footwear. 1177 Yonge St. ✆ **416/968-7026.** Subway: Summerhill.

Food & Wine

FOOD

The Big Carrot Who says health food can't be fun? This large-scale emporium stocks everything from organic produce to vitamins to all-natural beauty potions. Stop in at the cafe for a vegetarian snack or light meal. 348 Danforth Ave.✆ **416/466-2129.** www.thebigcarrot.ca. Subway: Chester.

The Bonnie Stern School   Crammed to the rafters with cooking accoutrements (such as stovetop grills) and exotic books, this store also features the raw ingredients you need to produce fine cuisine. It carries top-notch olive oil, balsamic vinegar, Asian sauces, and candied flower petals. If you take a course or seminar, you get a 10% discount on purchases. 6 Erskine Ave. ✆ **416/484-4810.** www.bonniestern.com. Subway: Eglinton.

The Cheese Boutique ★ 🎁   Cheese reigns supreme here, and any serious lover of fine *fromage* will want to visit the city's most notable aging cave. But the selection of top-end goods goes well beyond dairy: meats, charcuterie, spices, oils, teas, sweets, breads, even fresh produce, are all in stock. It's a little out of the way, so best to make it an excursion, perhaps en route for picnic fixings to nearby High Park. 45 Ripley Ave. ✆ **416/762-7292.** Subway: Jane, then a bus S on the Kingsway to Ripley Rd.

Dinah's Cupboard ★ 🎁   A charming neighborhood shop stocked with fine teas, coffees, spices, pastas, exotic rices, and plenty of biscuits, this is also a favorite stop for quick lunch fare. The salads, soups, and sandwiches are delicious. Plenty of dishes are ready for take-away, from rich and creamy mac-and-cheese to more sophisticated stuffed chicken and roasted vegetables. There are a few tables, too, for dining in. 50 Cumberland St. (at Bay St.). ✆ **416/921-8112.** Subway: Bay, then a short walk north to Cumberland St.

House of Tea   Visitors to this shop can drink in the heady scent of more than 150 loose teas. And the selection of cups, mugs, and tea caddies runs from chic to comical. 1017 Yonge St. ✆ **416/922-1226.** Subway: Rosedale.

Provenance Regional Cuisine ★ 🎁   Chef Alex Johnson runs this friendly, high-quality neighborhood grocery and gourmet-to-go shop. The emphasis is on local and sustainable, with options such as wild-rice-and-fish pies, brilliant chowders, unctuous lasagna made with béchamel and sweet potato, well-selected pickings of fruits and vegetables in season, plus fine cheeses and charcuterie. Look for the Forbes Wild Foods label for gifts to take home: exotic fare like spruce-tip jelly and wild-mushroom mustards. 800 Dundas St W. ✆ **416/504-9889.** www.provenancecuisine.ca. Subway: Dundas, then streetcar W to Palmerston.

Pusateri's ★   The Pusateri's store up at Lawrence Avenue and Avenue Road is a Toronto institution—and this younger Yorkville sibling is becoming one. The store stocks high-end sweets, meats, produce, and groceries. Travelers will appreciate the gourmet prepared meals that can be eaten on the go. 57 Yorkville Ave. ✆ **416/785-9100.** www.pusateris.com. Subway: Bay.

Simone Marie Belgian Chocolate   All of the rich truffles, colorful almond *dragées*, and fruit jellies in this shop are flown in from Belgium. 126A Cumberland St. ✆ **416/968-7777.** Subway: Bay.

SOMA Chocolatemaker ★★ 🎁   It's rare to find chocolatiers who make their creations from bean to bar. Co-owners Cynthia Leung and David Castellan source cocoa beans from around the world and make their chocolate on-site. The open-lab design of the place allows you to watch the process, and it's also an inviting place to hang out and savor one of the house specialties, like the warm coffee-and-chocolate drink *bicerin* (bee-cha-reen) or a cool, rich gelato. Don't forget to buy some to take home, especially the remarkable blends. A second location at John and King streets offers a menu of well-crafted lunch fare, in addition to sweets. In the Distillery District, 55 Mill St. ✆ **416/815-7662.** www.somachocolate.com. Subway: King, then a streetcar E to Parliament St.

Sugar Mountain Confectionery Remember Pez, candy necklaces, and lollipop rings? Sugar Mountain carries the tooth-aching sweets of youth, several of which have been elevated to cult status. Teens are drawn to this store, but the biggest customers are nostalgic boomers. 2291 Yonge St. ℂ **416/486-9321.** Subway: Eglinton.

Xococava ★ 🎁 If you've got an adventurous palette, this place offers exquisite chocolates and fine ice creams with plenty of exotica on the side. Sure, you can get pure chocolate—and it's heavenly—but you might be tempted by bacon and caramel ice cream or black mushroom truffles. The coffee is brilliant, too. 1560 Yonge St. ℂ **416/979-9918.** Subway: St. Clair, then a short walk N to Delisle Court.

WINE

In Ontario, Liquor Control Board of Ontario (LCBO) outlets include small boutiques, big stores, and some (wine and beer only) locations at grocery or convenience stores. It's a government monopoly that rattles many a citizen who would prefer more choices. At least there's plenty on offer. Look for tastes you won't find easily elsewhere, such as locally produced wines (Niagara and Prince Edward County are producing exceptional vintages), as well as the popular ice wine, an intensely sweet dessert wine that has won awards the world over. There are LCBO outlets all over the city, and prices are the same at all of them. The nicest shop is the **LCBO Summerhill** (10 Scrivener Sq.; ℂ **416/922-0403;** subway: Summerhill). Built into a former train station, this outpost hosts cooking classes, wine and spirits tastings, and party-planning seminars. Other locations are at the Manulife Centre (55 Bloor St. W.; ℂ **416/925-5266**), 20 Bloor St. E. (ℂ **416/368-0521**), the Eaton Centre (ℂ **416/979-9978**), and Union Station (ℂ **416/925-9644**). See **www.lcbo.com** for information about products and special in-store events.

Gifts & Unique Items

B&J Trading 🎁 This Chinatown store stocks a wide assortment of goods, but its claim to fame is the gift wrap department. The store has unusual wrapping papers, bows, and bags—but best of all are the beautiful presentation boxes that could almost be gifts themselves. 378 Spadina Ave. ℂ **416/586-9655.** Subway: Spadina, then a streetcar S to Nassau St.

The Paper Place ★ 🎁 In addition to being popular with artists, this shop has all the boxes, papers, and handmade cards you could ever need to create exquisite giftwrappings. Better yet, it stocks instruction books! 887 Queen St. W. ℂ **416/703-0089.** www.thepaperplace.ca. Subway: Osgoode, then any streetcar W to Ossington Ave.

Teatro Verde ★★ Life is drama, so why should the items you fill your home with be dull? That seems to be the question at Teatro Verde, where even table coasters are things of beauty. In 2009, the owners moved to a renovated Georgian mansion on Yorkville Avenue, so there are even more statuettes, table linens, art books, and other delights on show now. 100 Yorkville Ave. ℂ **416/966-2227.** www.teatroverde.com. Subway: Bay.

Ten Thousand Villages ★★ Everything at these stores arrived via fair-trade programs, so the artisans who make the items benefit directly from the sale of their work. In addition to hand-crafted housewares, there are jewelry, toys, Palestinian olive oil, shea-butter skin-care products, and really good Brazil nuts. There are also branches at 474 Bloor St. W. (ℂ **416/533-8476**) and 362 Danforth Ave. (ℂ **416/462-9779**). 709 Queen St. W. ℂ **416/703-2263.** www.tenthousandvillages.com. Subway: Osgoode, then a streetcar W to Bathurst St.

Health & Beauty

Lush   This clever U.K.-based emporium stocks a selection of fizzy bath bombs, skin lotions and potions, and an ever-changing variety of soaps stacked in jagged, jewel-colored slabs. All products are sold by weight. 312 Queen St. W. ☎ **416/599-5874.** www.lush.com. Subway: Osgoode.

M.A.C. ★   M.A.C. was founded in Toronto and is now owned by Estée Lauder. This flagship store is perpetually packed, especially on weekends, but if you call ahead, you can schedule an appointment for a makeup lesson. In addition to cosmetics, the store carries skin- and hair-care supplies. 89 Bloor St. W. ☎ **416/929-7555.** www.maccosmetics.com. Subway: Bay.

Noah's ✔   This is a mecca for health nuts. Noah's boasts aisle after aisle of vitamins and dietary supplements, organic foods and "natural" candies, skin-care and bath products, and books and periodicals. The staff is well informed and helpful. A smaller but more centrally located outlet is at 667 Yonge St. (at Bloor St.; ☎ **416/969-0220**). 322 Bloor St. W. ☎ **416/968-7930.** Subway: Spadina.

Sephora   This French chain of cosmetic and beauty shops is a one-stop destination for any makeover, with hair products, make-up, skincare, fragrance, and more. There are many locations around town. The one on the Mink Mile is particularly attractive. 131 Bloor St. W. ☎ **416/531-1100.** Subway: Bay Station or Queen's Park, then a short walk.

Thompson's Homeopathic Supplies 🎁   This is just like an old-fashioned apothecary, with endless rows of potions behind a wooden counter. It has a homeopathic remedy for everything, from the common cold to dermatitis to conjunctivitis. The staff is friendly and knowledgeable. 844 Yonge St. ☎ **416/922-2300.** Subway: Yonge/Bloor.

Jewelry

Birks ★   This Canadian institution, founded in 1879, is synonymous with good quality. Among the silver, crystal, and china is an extensive selection of fine jewelry, including exquisite pearls and knockout diamond engagement rings (the diamonds themselves were mined in northern Canada). A children's section is filled with such keepsakes as Royal Doulton Bunnykins china and whimsical picture frames by Nova Scotia's Seagull Pewter. Don't miss the showcase of antique estate jewelry. A smaller branch is at the Eaton Centre (☎ **416/979-9311**). Manulife Centre, 55 Bloor St. W. ☎ **416/922-2266.** www.birks.com. Subway: Bay.

Royal de Versailles Jewellers   This shop carries an eye-catching assortment of pearls, gold, and platinum. The designs range from classic to funkier, playful styles. There are also watches by the likes of Piaget, Cartier, Rolex, and Tag Heuer, as well as a Bulgari boutique. 101 Bloor St. W. ☎ **416/967-7201.** Subway: Bay.

Silverbridge   Most of the necklaces, bracelets, rings, and earrings here are silver, but a few are in 18-karat gold and platinum. Designer Costin Lazar has a modern sensibility, and he will also take on custom work. Watches by Georg Jensen and Ole Mathiesen are also available. 162 Cumberland St. ☎ **416/923-2591.** www.silverbridge.com. Subway: Bay.

Tiffany & Co.   Diamonds are still a girl's best friend at this Art Deco–style shop. Precious gems and designs by Elsa Peretti and Paloma Picasso are on the first level; the second floor holds silver jewelry, stationery, and housewares. 85 Bloor St. W. ☎ **416/921-3900.** www.tiffany.com. Subway: Bay.

Leather Goods

Taschen! Exclusive designer handbags, luggage, wallets, and other accessories are mainstays here. Many are European imports, and quality is high. 162 Cumberland St. ✆ **416/961-3185.** Subway: Bay.

Malls & Shopping Centers

Atrium on Bay This two-level complex has more than 60 shops selling clothing, jewelry, furniture, and more. Bay & Dundas sts. ✆ **416/980-2801.** Subway: Dundas.

Bayview Village ★ 👜 Elegantly designed and moderately sized, Bayview Village is home to several independent boutiques, as well as some chain stores (such as Chapters bookstore). It's also a place to come for fine food: an Oliver & Bonacini restaurant is here. 2901 Bayview Ave. (at Sheppard Ave.). ✆ **416/226-0404.** Subway: Bayview.

College Park This shopping center, originally a beautiful Art Deco building and Eaton's department stores, underwent a long renovation. It now houses a giant Winners store (see "The Best Bargains," on p. 168) and not much else. A little sad, actually. 444 Yonge St. ✆ **416/597-1221.** Subway: College.

Eaton Centre ★ A downtown mall is a bit of an oddity, but this is one popular destination. More than 200 shops and restaurants spread over four levels in the Eaton Centre, which takes up 2 entire city blocks. 220 Yonge St. ✆ **416/598-2322.** www.toronto eatoncentre.com. Subway: Dundas or Queen.

Fairview Mall This massive shopping complex, with its 260 stores, has been around for years, but until the Sheppard subway line opened, it wasn't easily accessible by public transit. Now that the subway brings you right to the door, you can easily shop at Toronto's first H&M store, as well as the Bay, Sears, Birks, Femme de Carriere, La Senza, Harry Rosen, and Danier. 1800 Sheppard Ave E. ✆ **416/491-0151.** www. fairviewmall.com. Subway: Don Mills.

First Canadian Place ★ A piece of the labyrinth of the underground city, this complex houses 120 shops and restaurants, and stages free noontime events each week, with performances as diverse as Opera Atelier's *Handel* recital and the dancing monks of the Tibetan Drikung Monastery. Ongoing art exhibitions are also featured. King & Bay sts. ✆ **416/862-8138.** Subway: King.

Hazelton Lanes ★ Hazelton is a two-level complex with about 90 shops, including the Whole Foods Market, high-end fashions for kids, and bauble-rich boutiques.

📎 An Outlet for People Who Hate Outlets

Vaughan Mills is a massive shopping complex 32km (20 miles) north of Toronto (close to Canada's Wonderland; p. 127). This clean, modern mall is home to **Holt Renfrew Last Call** (the only Holt Renfrew discount center in the province), the world's largest **Tommy Hilfiger** store, and Canada's largest Toys"R"Us/Babies"R"Us. Most of the stores in Vaughan Mills aren't outlets, but there are just enough to make sure you get an easy deal (plus, there's a massive **Winners** store—do you really need more?). The only catch is that you do need to drive to get here (take Hwy. 401 to Hwy. 400, then drive north and exit at Bass Pro Mills Dr., which leads directly to the mall). For more information, call ✆ **905/879-2110** or visit www.vaughanmills.com.

The charming courtyard at the center transforms into an ice-skating rink in winter. It has had its ups and downs over the years, so be prepared for some shuttered stores along the way. 55 Avenue Rd. © **416/968-8602.** www.hazeltonlanes.com. Subway: Bay.

Holt Renfrew Centre   Anchored by the chic Holt Renfrew department store, this small underground concourse is more down to earth, price-wise. It connects with the Manulife Centre and the Hudson's Bay Centre. 50 Bloor St. W. © **416/923-2255.** Subway: Yonge/Bloor.

Manulife Centre ★   More than 50 posh shops—including William Ashley, Indigo Books Music & More, and an LCBO outlet (Liquor Control Board of Ontario)—occupy this complex. The Manulife connects to the Holt Renfrew Centre underground. 55 Bloor St. W. © **416/923-9525.** Subway: Bay.

Royal Bank Plaza   Part of Toronto's underground city, the Royal Bank Plaza connects to Union Station and the Royal York Hotel. Its 60-plus outlets include a variety of shops, two full-service restaurants, and a food court. The building above is worth a look, too. See p. 117. Bay & Front sts. © **416/974-5570.** Subway: Union.

Shops at Don Mills   Toronto's latest mall is a truly suburban affair: outdoor, yet made for cars, not pedestrians. But there are some unique shops, such as McEwan (a food emporium created by top chef Mark McEwan), and Canada's first Anthropologie store (there is a second location in Yorkville). Worth a stop if you're already out at the Ontario Science Centre. 1090 Don Mills Rd. (at Lawrence Ave. E.). © **416/447-6087.** www.shopsatdonmills.ca. Subway: Pape, then Don Mills bus no. 25; alternatively, go to Eglinton, then take the Lawrence 54 bus; either way, the bus ride will take roughly 20 min.

Markets

Kensington Market ★★   This neighborhood has changed dramatically over the years. Originally a Jewish community, it became home to Portuguese and other European immigrants, and then changed again as the bordering Chinatown expanded at the same time shopkeepers from the Caribbean, the Middle East, and elsewhere arrived. There are several Asian herbalists and grocers, as well as West Indian and Middle Eastern shops. Kensington Avenue has the greatest concentration of vintage clothing stores in the city, as well as some good grub and excellent cafes for refueling. It's home to exceptional empanadas, a cutting-edge butcher, fish shops, and grocers selling produce at deep discounts. For a full description, see "Walking Tour 1: Chinatown & Kensington Market," in chapter 7. Along Baldwin, Kensington & Augusta aves. No phone. Subway: Spadina, then the LRT to Baldwin St. or Dundas St. W.

St. Lawrence Market ★   This market is a local favorite for fresh produce, and it even draws people who live a good distance away. The peameal-bacon sandwiches are famous. Check out the gallery on the second floor, a quiet retreat from the busy market, where exhibits about the city are mounted, with free admission. Hours are Tuesday through Thursday from 8am to 6pm, Friday from 8am to 7pm, and Saturday from 8am to 5pm. On Saturday, there is also the farmers market from 5am, when the farmers arrive, to 1pm. See p. 122 for a complete description. 92 Front St. E. © **416/392-7219.** www.stlawrencemarket.com. Subway: Union.

Music

HMV   This is the flagship Toronto store of the British chain. (You'll find smaller outlets throughout the city.) The selection of pop, rock, jazz, and classical music is large. Best of all, you can listen to a CD before you buy it. 333 Yonge St. © **416/586-9668.** Subway: Dundas.

The Music Store   On the Toronto Symphony Orchestra's home turf, this attractive shop includes several TSO CDs in its collection of classical and choral music. Roy Thomson Hall, 60 Simcoe St. © **416/593-4822.** Subway: St. Andrew.

Rotate This ★ 🎁   Low-key but well stocked, this is an excellent bet if you're interested in the local indie scene. In addition to CDs (new and used), there's plenty of vinyl, with countertop turntables you can use as listening stations. 801 Queen St. W. © **416/504-8447.** Subway: Osgoode, then a streetcar W to Claremont Rd.

Soundscapes ★ 🎁   This neighborhood shop carries an excellent selection of new and local talent, indie bands, essential standards, eclectic finds, and more. You can also buy tickets for hot shows around town. The staff is helpful and knowledgeable. Definitely worth a look. 572 College St. © **416/537-1620.** Subway: College, then a streetcar W to Manning Ave.

Wild East ★ 🎁   This is a great source for new and secondhand CDs and DVDs. Wild East is a strong supporter of both local talent and international indie acts, so you'll find music here that you won't get anywhere else. 360 Danforth Ave. © **416/469-8371.** Subway: Chester.

Sex Toys

Lovecraft ★   Believe it or not, Lovecraft is downright wholesome. Sure, there are the requisite bad-girl (and -boy) lingerie and toys, but much of the shop stocks joke gifts, T-shirts with suggestive slogans, and an impressive collection of erotic literature (no porn mags). The staff is friendly and the atmosphere playful. Safe sex is promoted, too. 27 Yorkville Ave. © **877/923-7331** or 416/923-7331. www.lovecraftsexshop.com. Subway: Bay.

Toys

Kidding Awound ☺ 🎁   Wind-up gadgets are the specialty here—hundreds of 'em. There are also some antique toys (which you won't let the kids near) and gag gifts. 91 Cumberland St. © **416/926-8996.** Subway: Bay.

Mastermind Toys ★ ☺   This Canadian-owned chain stocks toys for all ages, sizes, and quirks. The stores are well laid out, and staff is helpful. With dozens of major brands and some of the top lines—like Playmobil, Plan Toys, and Lamaze—it's one of the best options in Toronto, especially if you want to avoid the big-box stores. There are many locations, although they tend to be on the city's outskirts. There's also a location in the Ontario Science Centre. 2134 Queen St. © **416/699-3797.** www.mastermind toys.com. Subway: Queen, then a streetcar E to Glen Manor.

Science City ★ ☺   Kids and adults alike will love this tiny store filled with games, puzzles, models, kits, and books—all related to science. Whether your interest is astronomy, biology, chemistry, archaeology, or physics, you'll find something here. Holt Renfrew Centre, 50 Bloor St. W. © **416/968-2627.** www.sciencecity.ca. Subway: Yonge/Bloor.

TORONTO AFTER DARK

There's no lack of things to do in Toronto after the sun goes down. The city is a genuine mecca for top-notch theater, with some acclaimed productions actually premiering in Toronto before heading to Broadway or London's West End. Notable local performing arts organizations include the Canadian Stage Company, the Canadian Opera Company, the National Ballet of Canada, Soulpepper (which has earned a reputation as one of North America's most creative theater companies), the Tafelmusik Baroque Orchestra and Chamber Choir, and the Toronto Symphony Orchestra.

Toronto's many dance and music venues also host the crème de la crème of Canadian and international performers. Some of the best entertainment is in Toronto's comedy clubs, which have served as training grounds for stars such as Jim Carrey, Mike Myers, Dan Aykroyd, and John Candy.

There's plenty going on at the Sony Centre for the Performing Arts—formerly known as the Hummingbird Centre, Four Seasons Centre for the Performing Arts, Roy Thomson Hall, Massey Hall, the new and impressive Koerner Hall, and at other theaters around town.

The hottest news on the nightlife front is Ossington Avenue. This used to be a quiet stretch, but it's now the place to go for the coolest watering holes. The action has spilled onto the adjacent Dundas Street West strip, too. Some spots to look for: the Communist's Daughter, Dakota Tavern, Watusi, Reposado, and Sweaty Betty's.

MAKING PLANS For listings of local performances and events, check out *Where Toronto* (www.where.ca/toronto) and *Toronto Life* (www.torontolife.com), as well as the *Toronto Star* (www.thestar.com). For up-to-the-minute lists of hot-ticket events, check out the free weeklies (and their informative websites) *Now* (www.nowtoronto.com) and *The Grid* (www.thegridto.com), available around town in newspaper boxes and at bars, cafes, and bookstores. The city website www.toronto.com also boasts lengthy lists of performances. Events of particular interest to the gay and lesbian community are listed in *Xtra!* (www.xtra.ca), another free weekly available in newspaper boxes and many bookstores. The Torontoist blog (www.torontoist.com) is also a great source for upcoming performances, while www.tobars.com/ covers the bar and club scene thoroughly.

GETTING TICKETS For almost any theater, music, or dance event, you can buy tickets from Ticketmaster (© **416/870-8000;** www.ticketmaster.ca). To avoid the service charge on each ticket (not just each order)

Downtown After Dark

PERFORMING ARTS
Air Canada Centre **40**
Buddies in Bad Times Theatre **21**
Canadian Opera Company **19**
Canadian Stage Company **33**
Canon Theatre **28**
The Carlu **20**
Dancemakers **39**
Distillery District **39**
The Elgin and Winter Garden
Theatre Centre **28**
Factory Theatre **3**
Fleet Dance Theatre **41**

Four Seasons Centre for the
Performing Arts **19**
Glenn Gould Studio **11**
Lorraine Kimsa Theatre for
Young People **38**
Massey Hall **26**
Molson Amphitheatre **5**
National Ballet of Canada **19**
Native Earth
Performing Arts Theatre **39**
Princess of Wales Theatre **13**
Rogers Centre **10**
Roy Thomson Hall **15**

Royal Alexandra Theatre **14**
Sony Centre for the Performing Arts **32**
St. James Cathedral **35**
The St. Lawrence
Centre for the Arts **33**
St. Michael's Cathedral **29**
Soulpepper **39**
Theatre Passe Muraille **2**
TIFF Bell Lightbox **12**
Toronto Dance Theatre **41**
Toronto Mendelssohn Choir **15**
Toronto Symphony Orchestra **15**
Yonge-Dundas Square **25**

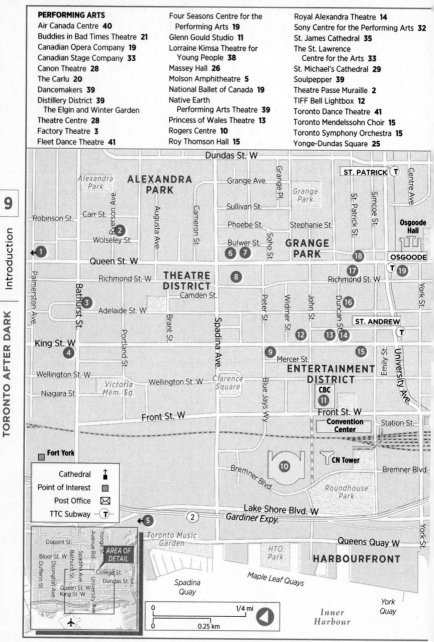

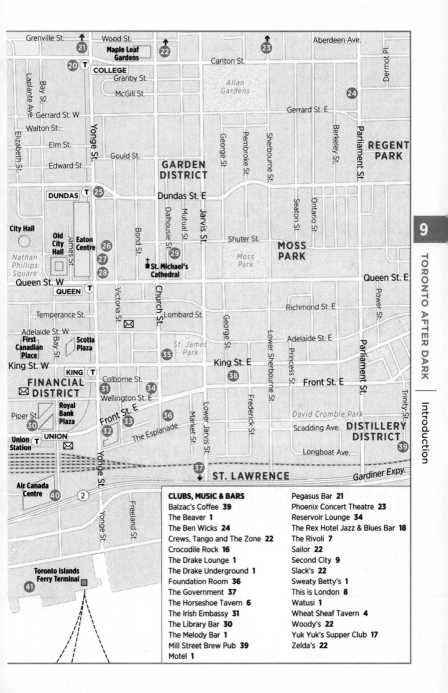

CLUBS, MUSIC & BARS

Balzac's Coffee **39**	Pegasus Bar **21**
The Beaver **1**	Phoenix Concert Theatre **23**
The Ben Wicks **24**	Reservoir Lounge **34**
Crews, Tango and The Zone **22**	The Rex Hotel Jazz & Blues Bar **18**
Crocodile Rock **16**	The Rivoli **7**
The Drake Lounge **1**	Sailor **22**
The Drake Underground **1**	Second City **9**
Foundation Room **36**	Slack's **22**
The Government **37**	Sweaty Betty's **1**
The Horseshoe Tavern **6**	This is London **8**
The Irish Embassy **31**	Watusi **1**
The Library Bar **30**	Wheat Sheaf Tavern **4**
The Melody Bar **1**	Woody's **22**
Mill Street Brew Pub **39**	Yuk Yuk's Supper Club **17**
Motel **1**	Zelda's **22**

discount TICKETS

Want to take in a show, but don't want to spend a bundle? Drop by the T.O.Tix booth ★ (☎ **416/536-6468,** ext. 40), which sells half-price day-of-performance tickets. The booth is in Yonge-Dundas Square, just across the street from the Eaton Centre. T.O.Tix accepts cash, debit cards, Visa, and MasterCard, and all sales are final. The booth is open Tuesday to Saturday from noon to 6:30pm; it's closed Sunday and Monday (tickets for performances on those days are sold on Sat). You can also buy tickets via the website www.totix.ca, but be warned that not all tickets are available online. Also available on the website are hipTIX, where students between the ages of 15 and 29 can score C$5 tickets for certain shows.

sold over the phone, head to a ticket center. They're scattered throughout the city; call the information line for the lengthy list of locations.

THE PERFORMING ARTS

Toronto's arts scene offers something for every taste year-round. The city's arts institutions are widely renowned, and top-notch international performers regularly pass through town.

Theater

Big-budget musicals—think *Cats* and *Mamma Mia!*—continue to dominate Toronto's larger theaters, but a number of excellent boutique companies also exist. Many of the smaller troupes have no permanent performance space, so they move from venue to venue. A few festivals offer great times to drop in and capture the flavor of Toronto's theater life: Luminato in early June (www.luminato.com), the Summer Works Theatre Festival in early August, which is Canada's largest juried theater festival (www.summerworks.ca), and the Fringe Festival (☎ **416/966-1062;** www.fringetoronto.com), usually held for 12 days starting in early July and featuring more than 100 casts from Canada and beyond.

LANDMARK THEATERS & PERFORMANCE VENUES

Canon Theatre ★   This beautiful venue has had a tumultuous history. It got its start as the Pantages Theatre in 1920, and its opulent design (by the famous theater architect Thomas Lamb) was widely admired. However, the theater's fortunes sank in 1929—not because of the stock-market crash, but because its owner was embroiled in a legal battle. Eventually, the gorgeous space was carved into six cinemas. It was rescued and dramatically renovated by the Livent production company, which also brought back its original name, and the new 2,250-seat Pantages Theatre was home for many years to Andrew Lloyd Webber's lavish *The Phantom of the Opera.* But after Livent collapsed, the theater went dark for a long time. Fortunately, its current owners—who have renamed it the Canon—have turned over the theater's management and programming to Mirvish Productions, Toronto's leading theater promoters and owners of the Royal Alex and the Princess of Wales Theatre (both listed below). In recent years, it has hosted such shows as *Spamalot* and *The Harder They Come.* 244 Victoria St. ☎ **416/872-1212.** www.mirvish.com. Subway: Dundas or Queen.

After Dark from Chinatown to Bloor Street

Brunswick House **11**	Lettieri **8**
Cafe Diplomatico **5**	Linux Cafe **2**
Comedy Bar **1**	Madison Avenue Pub **13**
The Communist's Daughter **6**	Mod Club Theatre **3**
Dakota Tavern **6**	The Pilot **16**
El Convento Rico **3**	The Roof **15**
El Mocambo **19**	Sneaky Dee's **17**
Future Bakery **10**	St. Patrick's Church **20**
The Garrison **6**	Supermarket **18**
Henhouse **6**	Sutra Tiki Bar **4**
Koerner Hall **14**	Tafelmusik Baroque Orchestra **12**
Lee's Palace **9**	Tarragon Theatre **7**
	Trinity-St. Paul's United Church **12**

The Elgin and Winter Garden Theatre Centre ★★ These landmark theaters first opened their doors in 1913, and the Centre is now a designated National Historic Site, owned and operated by the Ontario Heritage Trust. Both the Elgin and the Winter Garden have been restored to their Edwardian gilded glory, and the theaters vie with the Royal Alexandra and the Princess of Wales Theatre (see below for both) for major shows and attention. The Centre has been deemed the last operating double-decker theater. The downstairs Elgin is larger, seating 1,500 and featuring a lavish domed ceiling and gilded decoration on the boxes and proscenium. Frescoes adorn the striking interior of the 1,000-seat Winter Garden. Suspended from the ceiling and lit with lanterns are more than 5,000 branches of beech leaves, which have been preserved, painted, and fireproofed. Both theaters offer everything from

Broadway musicals and dramas to concerts and opera performances, with the Toronto International Film Festival utilizing the Elgin as a cinema. 189 Yonge St. © **416/872-5555** for tickets or 416/314-2901 for administration. Subway: Queen.

Four Seasons Centre for the Performing Arts ★★★   Toronto's opera house, which opened in 2006, is a stunner. Designed by architect Jack Diamond of the renowned Toronto firm Diamond and Schmitt, it has a simple exterior, resembling a house of glass. Inside, in the tradition of truly grand opera houses, there are three stages: main, rear, and side. But the masterstroke in the Four Seasons Centre's design is its perfect acoustics. No small feat given that the structure is set on not one but two major thoroughfares, and a subway line rumbles beneath it. This is home to both the Canadian Opera Company (p. 192) and the National Ballet of Canada (p. 193). 145 Queen St. W. © **416/363-8231** for tickets or 416/363-6671 for administration. www.fourseasons centre.ca. Subway: Osgoode.

Princess of Wales Theatre ★   This spectacular 2,000-seat, state-of-the-art facility was built for the Toronto run of *Miss Saigon,* with a stage large enough to accommodate the landing of the helicopter in that production. Later, it was home to *The Lion King, Hairspray,* and the ill-fated stage adaptation of the epic *The Lord of the Rings.* More recently, it has featured *The Sound of Music.* Frank Stella, who painted 929 sq. m (10,000 sq. ft.) of colorful murals, decorated the exterior and interior walls. People in wheelchairs have access to all levels of the theater (not the norm in Toronto). 300 King St. W. © **416/872-1212.** www.mirvish.com. Subway: St. Andrew.

Royal Alexandra Theatre ★★   The 1,495-seat Royal Alex is a magnificent spectacle, never mind the show! Constructed in 1907, it owes its current health to discount-store czar and impresario Ed Mirvish, who refurbished it (as well as the surrounding area) in the 1960s. Inside, it's a riot of plush reds, gold brocade, and baroque ornamentation. Recent productions here have included *Dirty Dancing,* a musical based on the movie, and *Rock of Ages.* Avoid the vertigo-inducing second balcony and the seats "under the circle," which don't have the greatest sight lines. Be forewarned that legroom is very limited here. 260 King St. W. © **416/872-1212.** www.mirvish. com. Subway: St. Andrew.

Roy Thomson Hall ★★★   This important concert hall is home to the Toronto Symphony Orchestra (p. 192), which performs here from September to June, and to the Toronto Mendelssohn Choir (p. 192). Since it opened in 1982, it has also hosted an array of international musical artists, including Yo-Yo Ma, Jessye Norman, and Kiri Te Kanawa. The hall was designed to give the audience a feeling of unusual intimacy with the performers—none of the 2,812 seats is more than 33m (108 ft.) from the stage. This is one of the few venues where you can feel happy in the "nosebleed" seats. With Roy Thomson's perfect acoustics, who cares about sightlines? 60 Simcoe St. © **416/872-4255** for tickets or 416/593-4822 for administration. www. roythomson.com. Subway: St. Andrew.

The St. Lawrence Centre for the Arts ★★   For 3 decades, the St. Lawrence Centre has presented top-notch theater, music, and dance performances. The facade of the building is unattractive, but the theaters inside

Farther Afield

Don't forget that two major theater festivals—the Shaw Festival (www. shawfest.com) in Niagara-on-the-Lake and the renowned Stratford Festival (www.stratfordfestival.ca) in Stratford— are only an hour or two away. See chapter 10 for details.

9

The Performing Arts

TORONTO AFTER DARK

are comfortable (and there's more legroom than, say, the Royal Alex). The Bluma Appel Theatre is home to the Canadian Stage Company (p. 190), and the smaller Jane Mallet Theatre features the Toronto Operetta Theatre Company, among others. This is a popular spot for lectures, too. 27 Front St. E. (✆ **416/366-7723.** www.stlc.com. Subway: Union.

MAJOR CONCERT HALLS & AUDITORIUMS

The Carlu★   Located on the seventh floor of College Park, this was considered one of the grandest concert halls in Canada when it opened in 1931. Like so many other venues in Toronto, the Carlu was shuttered in the 1970s. Now, the 1,200-seat concert hall is back in favor, and its architecture is believed to be one of the best surviving examples of Art Moderne in the world (it was created by Jacques Carlu, the architect also responsible for New York's Rainbow Room). The concerts here tend to be charity benefits, with hefty price tags for tickets. College Park, 444 Yonge St., 7th floor. (✆ **416/597-1931.** www.thecarlu.com. Subway: College.

Distillery District ★★★   This was once the home of the Gooderham and Worts Distillery, Canada's largest distilling company in the 19th century. The 45-building complex is an outstanding example of industrial design from the Victorian age (p. 103). In 2003, it was reinvented as the Distillery District, which includes galleries, restaurants, and shops. The district also houses several performing-arts venues, including the Case Goods Theatre and the state-of-the-art Young Centre for the Performing Arts. The Dancemakers (p. 192), Soulpepper (p. 191), and Native Earth (p. 191) troupes now perform here. 55 Mill St. (✆ **416/367-1800.** www.thedistillerydistrict.com. Subway: King, then a streetcar E to Parliament St.

Fleck Dance Theatre   Part of the sprawling Harbourfront Centre (p. 189) by the waterfront, this 446-seat theater (formerly the Premiere Dance Theatre) is specifically designed for dance performances and is where you can catch some of Toronto's leading contemporary dance companies. Queen's Quay Terminal, 207 Queens Quay W. (✆ **416/973-4000.** www.harbourfrontcentre.com. Subway: Union, then the LRT to York Quay.

Glenn Gould Studio ★   Located on the main floor of the Canadian Broadcasting Centre, this 341-seat radio concert hall offers chamber music, jazz, roots music, and spoken-word performances. Its name celebrates the great, eccentric Toronto pianist whose life was cut short by a stroke in 1982. 250 Front St. W. (✆ **416/205-5555.** www.cbc.ca/glenngould/. Subway: Union.

Koerner Hall ★★   Opened in 2009, this is a jewel on Toronto's performing arts scene. Designed by the renowned KPMB Architects group, the concert hall seats 1,135 patrons. The centerpiece of the Royal Conservatory of Music's TELUS Centre for Performance and Learning, it has received rave reviews for its acoustics and has attracted such international stars as Steve Reich, Frederica von Stade, Ravi Shankar, and Baaba Maal in genres ranging from jazz to blues to world music to classical. 273 Bloor St. W. (✆ **416/408-2825.** www.rcmusic.ca. Subway: St. George or Museum.

Massey Hall ★★   This landmark 1892 building is one of Canada's premier music venues. Its 2,753 seats are not the most comfortable in town, but the flawless acoustics will make you stop squirming. It has hosted now-legendary concerts from the likes of Charlie Parker and Neil Young, and its programming runs the gamut from classical to pop to rock to jazz. Recent visitors have included Norah Jones, Diana Krall, Jimmy Cliff, and Pat Metheny. Each year, Gordon Lightfoot plays a string of concerts here. This is also a popular stop for lectures. 178 Victoria St. (✆ **416/872-4255** for tickets or 416/593-4822 for administration. www.masseyhall.com. Subway: King.

Sony Centre for the Performing Arts ★   If you visited Toronto before 1997, you might remember this as the O'Keefe Centre; if you visited before 2007, it was the Hummingbird Centre. Now known as The Sony Centre for the Performing Arts, it reopened in October 2010 after a C$30-million renovation and restoration, in time to celebrate the building's 50th anniversary. Artists who have appeared in this storied venue range from Richard Burton and Liz Taylor to Bob Dylan, the Clash, and Radiohead. Star architect Daniel Libeskind, the man responsible for the Royal Ontario Museum's controversial crystal galleries (p. 107), has designed a residential tower that will loom over the theater. 1 Front St. E. ✆ **416/872-2262.** www.sonycentre.ca. Subway: Union.

Toronto Centre for the Arts   Built in 1993, this gigantic complex is home to the Toronto Philharmonia, an acclaimed classical orchestra. It also hosts international performers and shows such as a long and successful run of *Jersey Boys*. The Toronto Centre is a half-hour subway ride from downtown and located in a neighborhood with generally lame food options. Best advice: Have a really early pre-theater dinner before making the trek (see the "Uptown" section in the dining chapter for ideas). 5040 Yonge St. ✆ **416/733-9388.** www.tocentre.com. Subway: North York Centre.

Yonge-Dundas Square ★   Toronto's open-air entertainment venue is across the street from the Eaton Centre. Summer is its liveliest season: Events include a Tuesday-night film series, a "Serenades in the Square" series featuring local musicians every Wednesday at lunchtime, and weekly Indie Friday concerts in the evenings. When not in use for events, this is a public square where you can stroll or sit by the fountains. This is also the home of the T.O.Tix discount-tickets booth (p. 186). Yonge & Dundas sts., SE corner. ✆ **416/979-9960.** www.ydsquare.ca. Subway: Dundas.

THEATER COMPANIES & SMALLER THEATERS

Buddies in Bad Times Theatre ★   Proudly provocative, this not-for-profit company has been dedicated to gay, lesbian, and queer theatrical expression since its founding in 1979. Their edgy work is not for everyone (the list of upcoming productions identifies shows that are "not for the faint of heart," and they mean it), but Buddies produces shows that you simply won't see anywhere else. The theater has also staged Canadian adaptations of some well-known works, such as Ibsen's *Hedda Gabler*. Controversial playwright Sky Gilbert helped build the theater's cutting-edge reputation. 12 Alexander St. ✆ **416/975-8555.** www.artsexy.ca. Tickets C$20–C$30; pay-what-you-can admission to some performances. Subway: Wellesley.

Canadian Stage ★★★   Formerly known as CanStage, this company performs an eclectic variety of Canadian (from the likes of Michel Tremblay and Robert Lepage) and international plays. Their productions are often ground-breaking. They perform at the Bluma Appel Theatre, which seats 875, and the Berkeley Theatre, a more avant-garde, intimate (240-seat) space. Bluma Appel Theatre (St. Lawrence Centre): 27 Front St. E.; Berkeley Theatre: 26 Berkeley St. ✆ **416/368-3110.** www.canadianstage.com. Tickets C$30–C$75; Mon pay-what-you-can admission. Senior & student discounts may be available 30 min. before performance. Subway for St. Lawrence Centre: Union; for Berkeley Theatre: King, then any streetcar E to Berkeley St.

Factory Theatre ★   Since it opened in 1970, the Factory Theatre has focused on presenting Canadian plays, from political dramas to over-the-top comedies. The theater likes to call itself "the home of the Canadian playwright." Performances showcase up-and-coming scribes, as well as such established playwrights as the internationally-acclaimed George F. Walker, who has had 23 shows produced here. The options veer

MORE THAN church MUSIC

Everyone knows that a church is where you go to listen to choir music—but in Toronto, several churches double as performance spaces for classical or opera ensembles. **Trinity-St. Paul's United Church** (427 Bloor St. W.; ℂ **416/964-6337;** www.trinitystpauls.ca) is home to Toronto's acclaimed Tafelmusik Baroque Orchestra & Chamber Choir (p. 192). **St. James' Cathedral,** at 65 Church St. (ℂ **416/364-7865;** www.stjames cathedral.on.ca), hosts everything from solo performances of classical cellists to youth choirs from abroad, as well as its own high-quality 18-voice Cathedral Choir and organ recitals. **St. Patrick's Church** (141 McCaul St.; ℂ **416/483-0559**) is where the Tallis Choir of Toronto (ℂ **416/286-9798;** www.tallis choir.com) often performs (its repertoire is mostly Renaissance and Tudor music). And if you happen to love real church music, stop in at **St. Michael's Cathedral** (65 Bond St.; ℂ **416/364-0234;** www. stmichaelscathedral.com). Its internationally-acclaimed Boys Choir regularly sings at three weekend masses.

from experimental to traditional. 125 Bathurst St. ℂ **416/504-9971.** www.factorytheatre.ca. Tickets C$15–C$37. Subway: St. Andrew, then any streetcar W to Bathurst St. & walk S to Adelaide St.

Lorraine Kimsa Theatre for Young People ★★ ☺   Toronto's such a theater town that even tiny tots (and the rest of the family) get their own performance center. For more than 30 years, the always-enjoyable Lorraine Kimsa Theatre (formerly known as the Young People's Theatre) has mounted whimsical productions such as *Jacob Two-Two Meets the Hooded Fang* (by the late, great Mordecai Richler) and children's classics like *You're a Good Man, Charlie Brown.* This theater company is particularly committed to diversity in its programming and in its artists. 165 Front St. E. ℂ **416/862-2222** for tickets or 416/363-5131 for administration. www.lktyp.ca. Tickets C$15–C$30. Subway: Union, then a streetcar E to Jarvis St.

Native Earth Performing Arts Theatre ★   A small company dedicated to performing works that express and dramatize the native Canadian experience and to encouraging the use of theater as a form of communication within the Native community. Playwright Tomson Highway, author of *Dry Lips Oughta Move to Kapuskasing,* was one of the company's founders. The company also performs at other theaters around town. Performing at the Case Goods Theatre in the Distillery District, 55 Mill St. ℂ **416/367-1800.** www.nativeearth.ca. Tickets C$15–C$30. Subway: King, then a streetcar E to Parliament St.

Soulpepper ★★★   Founded in 1997, this artist-created classical repertory company presents theatrical masterpieces of the 20th century, under the able artistic direction of Albert Schultz Theatre. Education and youth outreach are key parts of their mandate. The highly respected—and award-winning—group recently staged *Glengarry Glen Ross* and the Canadian classic *Billy Bishop Goes To War.* Performing at the Young Centre in the Distillery District, 55 Mill St. ℂ **416/866-8666.** www.soulpepper.ca. Tickets C$40–C$75; C$20–C$22 for ages 21–30 through www.stageplay.ca. Subway: King, then a streetcar E to Parliament St.

Tarragon Theatre ★   Opened in 1971, Tarragon produces original works by such famous Canadian literary figures as Michel Tremblay, Michael Ondaatje, and Judith Thompson, alongside works from the likes of David Hare and David Mamet, as well as the occasional classic. There are two small theaters on-site—or three, if you count

9

TORONTO AFTER DARK

The Performing Arts

191

the 60-seat rehearsal hall, which is occasionally used for performances. 30 Bridgman Ave. (near Dupont & Bathurst sts.). © **416/531-1827 for tickets** or 416/536-5018 for administration. www.tarragontheatre.com. Tickets C$21–C$39. Subway: Bathurst.

Theatre Passe Muraille ★ This theater started in the late 1960s, when a pool of actors began experimenting and improvising original Canadian material. It continues to produce innovative, provocative theater by such contemporary Canadian playwrights as John Mighton, Daniel David Moses, and Wajdi Mouawad. There are two stages—the Mainspace seats 220; the more intimate (if rather uncomfortable) Backspace seats 70. 16 Ryerson Ave. © **416/504-7529.** www.passemuraille.on.ca. Tickets C$15–C$35. Subway: Osgoode, then any streetcar W to Bathurst St.

Classical Music & Opera

Canadian Opera Company ★★★ Canada's largest opera company, the fifth largest in North America, was founded in 1950. Performances take place at the Four Seasons Centre for the Performing Arts (p. 188), a venue built with opera aficionados in mind. To give you an idea of how popular the Canadian Opera Company is, its performances have been at 99% capacity for the past 4 years. More than three-quarters of the tickets are held by subscribers, making this a tough "get" for visitors—so plan ahead. The COC is now headed by new music director Johannes Debus. A new series of standing-room tickets sold for about $15 the day of the performance regularly sells out. 145 Queen St. W.© **416/363-8231** for tickets or 416/363-6671 for administration. www.coc.ca. Tickets C$62–C$292. Subway: Osgoode.

Tafelmusik Baroque Orchestra & Chamber Choir ★★ This internationally acclaimed ensemble plays baroque compositions by the likes of Handel, Bach, and Mozart on authentic period instruments. Their annual *Messiah* concerts always sell out. Visiting musicians frequently join the 19 permanent performers. It gives a series of concerts at Trinity-St. Paul's United Church (47 Bloor St. W.) and stages other performances in Massey Hall (p. 189) and the Toronto Centre for the Arts (p. 190). 427 Bloor St. W. © **416/964-6337.** www.tafelmusik.org. Tickets C$32–C$82. Subway for Trinity-St. Paul's: Yonge/Bloor; for Massey Hall: King; for Toronto Centre for the Arts: North York Centre.

Toronto Mendelssohn Choir ★ This world-renowned group first performed in Massey Hall in 1895. Today, it calls Roy Thomson Hall home. Its repertoire ranges from Verdi's *Requiem,* Bach's *St. Matthew Passion,* and Handel's *Messiah* to the soundtrack of *Schindler's List.* TMC has recorded for Naxos and EMI. 60 Simcoe St. © **416/598-0422.** www.tmchoir.org. Tickets C$30–C$100. Subway: St. Andrew.

Toronto Symphony Orchestra ★★★ The TSO has been revitalized under the direction of Peter Oundjian and the improved acoustics of their home venue. They perform anything from classics to jazzy Broadway tunes to new Canadian works at Roy Thomson Hall from September to June. 60 Simcoe St.© **416/593-4828.** www.tso.on.ca. Tickets C$33–C$99. Subway: St. Andrew.

Dance

Dancemakers Now under the artistic direction of choreographer Michael Trent, Dancemakers has, over the past 4 decades, gained international recognition for its provocative mix of stylized physical movement and theater. It is based in the Distillery District, in a state-of-the-art 98-seat performance venue. Case Goods Theatre in the Distillery District, 55 Mill St.© **416/367-1800.** www.dancemakers.org. Tickets C$20–C$25.

It was big news back in 2006 when Toronto's opera house—the Four Seasons Centre for the Performing Arts—opened its doors. The irony was that Toronto, a city that had never had an opera house, was already a North American magnet for opera lovers. **The Canadian Opera Company** (see above) is just one reason to visit. Others include **Opera Atelier** (℃ 416/703-3767; www.operaatelier.com), a renowned company that produces baroque operas (Monteverdi, Mozart, and Gluck are perennially popular). The **Toronto Opera Repertoire** (℃ 416/698-9572; www.toronto-opera.com) is dedicated to making classic opera accessible to all, using supertitles in English and keeping ticket prices democratically low. **Tapestry New Opera Works** (℃ 416/537-6066; www.tapestrynewopera.com) is dedicated to the production of original works of Canadian opera and musical theater. For a provocative and fantastical take on chamber opera, check out the **Queen of Puddings Music Theatre** (℃ 416/203-4149; www.queenofpuddingsmusictheatre.com). The company has performed in London's Convent Garden. Further evidence of Toronto's passionate love of opera has been the enthusiastic response to the Metropolitan Opera's *Live in HD* series, in which opera is screened in movie theaters around the globe. Go to www.metopera.org/hdlive for ticket info.

National Ballet of Canada ★★★ Perhaps the most beloved and famous of Toronto's cultural icons is the National Ballet of Canada. English ballerina Celia Franca launched the company in Toronto in 1951 and served as director, principal dancer, choreographer, and teacher. Over the years, the company has achieved great renown. The legendary Canadian ballerina Karen Kain became its artistic director in 2005. The company shares the Four Seasons Centre for the Performing Arts (p. 188) with the Canadian Opera Company. Its repertoire includes the classics (you can always count on *The Nutcracker* every December) and works by luminaries such as George Balanchine, as well as from some Canadian choreographers. 145 Queen St. W. ℃ **866/345-9595** or 416/345-9595 for tickets, or 416/345-9686 for administration. www.national.ballet.ca. Tickets from C$45–C$200. Subway: Osgoode.

Toronto Dance Theatre The city's leading contemporary-dance company was founded in 1968, bringing an inventive spirit and original Canadian dance to the stage. Christopher House has been the company's director since 1994. House's choreography is widely acclaimed and has earned him multiple awards. TDT tours internationally and often performs at Fleck Dance Theatre, Queen's Quay Terminal, 207 Queens Quay W. Office: 80 Winchester St. ℃ **416/973-4000** for tickets or 416/967-1365 for administration. www.tdt.org. Tickets C$30–C$45.

Cinema

Cinematheque Ontario and Bell Lightbox ★★ 🎭 A division of the Toronto International Film Festival, Cinematheque Ontario has been showing the best in world cinema for the past 20 years. The programs include directors' retrospectives, plus new films from France, Germany, Japan, Bulgaria, and other countries that you won't find in the first-run theaters around town. Now in its new home, Bell Lightbox programming has expanded to a year-round calendar and includes exhibitions,

GREAT music ON A BUDGET

As the cost of concert tickets spirals ever upward, it can be frustrating to budget for an evening out. But there are some places you can count on scoring a deal. One best bet is **University of Toronto's Faculty of Music** (© 416/978-3744; www.music.utoronto.ca), which offers a full range of instrumental and choral concerts and recitals. They are held at various locations around the St. George Campus, including Walter Hall, and many performances are free of charge. It's also worth checking out who's performing at the **Royal Conservatory of Music** (273 Bloor St. W.; © 416/408-2825; www.rcmusic.ca). There are concerts by well-known jazz vocalists or international ensembles, as well as free recitals given by faculty members and students, plus the COC presents free lunchtime concerts in the Richard Bradshaw Amphitheatre (© 416/363-8231; www.fourseasons centre.ca).

seminars, and more. Screenings at the new Bell TIFF Lightbox, 350 King St. W. © **416/968-FILM** (416/968-3456). www.cinemathequeontario.ca. Tickets C$12 adults, C$8 seniors & students. Subway: King, then streetcar W to John St.

Pop & Rock Music Venues

Toronto is known for possessing one of the most active live-music scenes in North America. Tickets are available through Ticketmaster (© **416/870-8000**; www.ticket master.ca). In addition to the previously mentioned Roy Thomson Hall and Massey Hall, these are the major pop and rock music venues. Ticket prices vary widely depending on both the venue and the act.

Air Canada Centre Better known as a sports venue (it's home to the Maple Leafs and the Raptors), the Air Canada Centre also hosts popular musical acts. Neil Young has performed here, as have Tom Petty, Michael Buble, and Mariah Carey. 40 Bay St. (at Lakeshore Blvd). © **416/815-5500**. www.theaircanadacentre.com. Subway: Union, then the LRT to Queen's Quay.

Molson Amphitheatre ★ This is a favorite summer spot because you can listen to music by the shore of Lake Ontario. The amphitheatre seats 9,000, the cheaper lawn section another 7,000. It regularly draws some of the biggest names in rock, pop, and country. Ontario Place, 909 Lakeshore Blvd. W. © **416/260-5600**. www.livenation.com/venue/molson-canadian-amphitheatre-tickets. Subway: Bathurst, then the Bathurst streetcar S to Exhibition Place (last stop).

Rogers Centre The biggest venue in the city, it is not used regularly for music but occasionally draws superstar like U2 and AC/DC. This venue is about as intimate as a parking lot. If you're seated in the 400 or 500 levels, you'll be watching the show on the JumboTron unless you bring your binoculars. Steer clear of the seats next to the JumboTron, or you won't see anything at all. 1 Blue Jays Way. © **416/341-3663**. www.rogers centre.com. Subway: Union.

The Club & Music Scene

A few hints before you head out for the evening. The drinking age in Ontario is currently 19, and most establishments enforce the law. Expect long queues on Friday and Saturday after 10pm at downtown clubs. Bars and pubs are open daily from 11am to 2am. During such special events as the Toronto International Film Festival, the North By Northeast Music Festival (NXNE), and Pride, a number of downtown bars are allowed to stay open until 4am. If you're out at closing time, you'll find the subway shut down, but late-night buses run along Yonge and Bloor streets. Major routes on streets such as College, Queen, and King operate all night. To find out what's on, see "Making Plans," earlier in this chapter.

Comedy Clubs

Toronto must be one heck of a funny place. How else to explain why a disproportionate number of comedians, including Jim Carrey and Mike Myers, hail from here. The annual Just for Laughs festival delivers laughs every July, and the city's comedy clubs are thriving.

Comedy Bar   This new kid on the comedy block has quickly proved popular. It stresses sketch and improv comedy over stand-up (it's co-owned by Gary Rideout of sketch troupe the Sketchersons). 945 Bloor St. W. ℰ **416/238-7337.** www.comedybar.ca. Cover: Free to C$12. Subway: Ossington.

The Rivoli ★   While the Riv is also known for its music performances, the Monday-night ALT.COMedy Lounge and Tuesday-night Sketch! Comedy Lounge are its biggest draws. The Riv features local and visiting stand-ups, and is best known as the place where the Kids in the Hall got their start. Shows take place in the intimate 125-seat back room. See p. 78 for a restaurant review. 332-334 Queen St. W. ℰ **416/597-0794.** www.altcomedylounge.com. Pay-what-you-can admission. Subway: Osgoode.

Second City ★   This was where Mike Myers received his formal—and improvisational—comic training. Over the years, the legendary Second City nurtured the likes of John Candy, Dan Aykroyd, Bill Murray, Martin Short, Andrea Martin, and Eugene Levy. It continues to turn out talented young actors. The shows are always funny and topical, though the outrageous post-show improvs usually get the biggest laughs. 51 Mercer St. ℰ **800/263-4485** or 416/343-0011. www.secondcity.com. Show only C$24-C$29; dinner & show C$39-C$56. Subway: St. Andrew.

Yuk Yuk's Toronto   Yuk Yuk's is Canada's original home of stand-up comedy. Comic Mark Breslin founded the place in 1976, inspired by New York's Catch a Rising Star and Los Angeles's Comedy Store. Famous alumni include Jim Carrey, Howie Mandel, and Norm MacDonald. Jerry Seinfeld, Robin Williams, Sandra Bernhard, and Bill Hicks have all headlined here. Tuesday is amateur night and correspondingly cheap. Another Yuk Yuk's is in Mississauga, not far from Pearson International Airport (5165 Dixie Rd.; ℰ **905/434-4985**). 224 Richmond St. W. ℰ **416/967-6425.** www.yukyuks. com. Show only C$12-C$20; dinner & show C$38-C$56. Subway: Osgoode.

Live Music Venues

The Drake Underground   In the basement of the Drake Hotel, this venue was designed with flexibility in mind. It's a good thing, too, because the performers who appear here range from local and visiting musical acts in a wide variety of genres to burlesque artists. At the Drake Hotel, 1150 Queen St. W. ℰ **416/531-5042.** Cover C$5-C$20. Subway: Osgoode, then a streetcar W to Beaconsfield Ave.

El Mocambo ★   This world-renowned rock-'n'-roll institution hosted an infamous Rolling Stones show in the '70s, while the likes of U2 and Elvis Costello graced its stage in their early years. Its famous neon sign blinked no more when the club closed for a few years, but the venue is now back. A top-to-toe renovation has resulted in quite a different look, and it now welcomes acts from genres as diverse as indie rock, hip-hop, and roots. 464 Spadina Ave. © **416/777-1777.** Cover C$5–C$20. Subway: Spadina, then a streetcar S to College St.

The Garrison Since opening in 2009, this club has quickly become a valued member of Toronto's live music scene. A mid-sized venue (capacity 350), it sports good sightlines and sound, and has a separate bar area up front if your ears need a break. It is co-owned and booked by scene veteran (Sneaky Dee's) and former rocker Shaun Bowring, and concentrates on local and visiting indie rock bands. 1197 Dundas St. W. © **416/519-9439.** Cover free to C$20. Subway: St. Patrick, then a streetcar W to Ossington Ave.

The Horseshoe Tavern Since 1947, this much-loved honky-tonk has played a crucial role in Toronto's music community. The country and blues sounds it showcased in the '60s and early '70s gave way to punk and New Wave, while its current booking policy primarily concentrates on modern rock and roots music styles. The Stones had a secret gig here in 1997, and the likes of Los Lobos, Wilco, and local heroes Blue Rodeo have also graced its stage. For 16 years, the free Nu Music Night every Tuesday has presented some real gems. The expanded room now holds 520, and a friendly and unpretentious atmosphere has remained constant. 368 Queen St. W. © **416/598-4753.** www.horseshoetavern.com. Cover free to C$25. Subway: Osgoode.

Hugh's Room Call this a folk supper club for baby boomers. Around since 2001, the 200-seat venue has good sound and sightlines (except at the bar) and decent food. The booking policy ranges from folk legends like Judy Collins and the Strawbs to emerging roots singer/songwriters. 2261 Dundas St. W. © **416/531-6604.** Cover C$10–C$50 Subway: Dundas West.

Lee's Palace Versailles this ain't, but ignore Lee's patina of grunge and focus instead on the excellent sightlines, high stage, and good sound. Such alternative-rock icons as Nirvana and Red Hot Chili Peppers have played the 600-capacity club, and indie rock is the primary focus these days. Alt-rock DJs spin in the upstairs room, the Dance Cave. 529 Bloor St. W. © **416/532-1598.** www.leespalace.com. Cover C$5–C$30. Subway: Bathurst.

The Melody Bar ★★ 🍸 This is Toronto's favorite karaoke bar, and sessions moderated by Peter Styles pack the place Friday and Saturday nights. During the rest of the week, you'll find local musicians (roots music is especially prominent), DJs, and open-mic events. Wednesday is queer night. At the Gladstone Hotel, 1214 Queen St. W. © **416/531-4635.** www.gladstonehotel.com. No cover. Subway: Osgoode, then a streetcar W to Gladstone Ave.

The Mod Club Theatre ★★ One of Toronto's best mid-sized live music venues, it's co-owned by Mark Holmes, former frontman of '80s rock faves Platinum Blonde. The Killers, Amy Winehouse, and Canadian favorites like Metric and Stars have all performed here; the concert hall morphs into a dance club later at night. 722 College St. © **416/588-4MOD (416/588-4663).** www.themodclub.com. Cover up to C$15; higher prices for major concerts. Subway: Queen's Park, then a streetcar W to Crawford St.

Phoenix Concert Theatre The Phoenix is an old-school rock venue—shows are standing-room-only—and it has a loyal local following. It has showcased such legends as the New York Dolls, Patti Smith, and Gang of Four, while newer stars such as Neko Case and the Raveonettes have also gigged here. On the weekends, it gets the crowds dancing with a mix of retro, Latin, alternative, and funk. 410 Sherbourne St. © **416/323-1251.** Tickets C$10–C$40. Subway: College, then any streetcar E to Sherbourne St.

literary TYPES ★

Harbourfront Centre is the hub of Toronto's literary scene. It hosts the world renowned **Authors at Harbourfront Centre** (AUTHORS) program, featuring a weekly reading series (Sept–June), as well as the annual **International Festival of Authors** (IFOA) held every October. Over the past 36 years, AUTHORS has welcomed more than 5,000 writers from over 100 countries, including 17 Nobel laureates. IFOA (created in 1980) is widely recognized as one of the most important writers' events in the world, drawing a virtual Who's Who of contemporary literature. Over 10 days, more than 100 authors from at least 20 countries present their work to Toronto audiences. For more information on both programs, visit www.readings.org.

Reservoir Lounge ★   This joint feels like a modern-day speakeasy. The cramped space—it seats only 100—is below street level, yet feels intimate rather than claustrophobic. Live jazz, whether Dixieland, vocal jazz, or swing, belts out 7 nights a week. Defunct elsewhere, the swing dance craze lives on here, as well-dressed hepcats show their moves. 52 Wellington St. E., lower level. ☏ **416/955-0887.** www.reservoirlounge. com. Cover Tues–Sat C$5–C$7; no cover Sun & Mon. Subway: King.

The Rex Hotel Jazz & Blues Bar ★   The busiest jazz club in the city, it presents two or even three different acts daily, 7 days a week. A casual watering hole lacking the pretensions of some jazz joints, it has been drawing jazz fans since it opened in 1951. The decor hasn't changed much since the old days, but the sounds here range from the traditional to the cutting edge. The Rex features the city's best players and sometimes attracts international talent. 194 Queen St. W. ☏ **416/598-2475.** www.therex.ca. Cover up to C$12. Subway: Osgoode.

The Rivoli ★   Not quite the mainstay of the local music scene it once was, the Riv's back room now hosts an eclectic mix of performances, including roots, rock, jazz, comedy, and poetry reading. Tori Amos and Norah Jones made their Toronto debuts here, and Toronto comedy legends the Kids in the Hall got their start here, too. Shows begin at 8pm and continue until 2am. Upstairs, there's a comfortable billiards room and a bar. 332-334 Queen St. W. ☏ **416/596-1908.** Cover pay-what-you-can admission to C$20. Subway: Osgoode.

Supermarket ★★   Kensington Market is famous for its food stores, so maybe it's appropriate that this new club is playing on the name. It offers a wide assortment of live jazz, soul, roots, and rock. Earlier in the evening, Supermarket is an affordable Asian fusion restaurant, and it occasionally hosts author readings and art events. 268 Augusta St. ☏ **416/840-0501.** www.supermarkettoronto.com. Cover C$5–C$12. Subway: Spadina, then a streetcar S to College St.

DANCE CLUBS

Dance clubs come and go at an alarming pace in Toronto, and most of the big-box clubs are in fact on the outskirts of town. Be sure to check out the club listings in the free weeklies *Now* (www.nowtoronto.com) and *The Grid* (www.thegridto.com), or at www.torontolife.com, to keep up with the currently cool (or hot) spots. Those listed below have survived the ultra-competitive scene by presenting a consistent music policy and lively atmosphere. Most clubs don't have rigid dress codes, though "no jeans" rules are not uncommon. And remember, it's always easier to get in earlier rather than later in the evening, when lines start to form. Several primarily gay and lesbian clubs attract a sizable hetero contingent; one notable destination is El Convento Rico (p. 202).

Crocodile Rock   There's something sweet about the fact that a club as untrendy and blue-collar as Crocodile Rock can survive in the heart of the entertainment district downtown. It caters to a slightly older crowd, for whom '80s pop will never die. 240 Adelaide St. W. ✆ **416/599-9751.** Cover C$5. Subway: St. Andrew.

Guvernment   A popular fixture on the Toronto dance club scene for almost a quarter-century now, thanks to its mandate of serving up something for just about everyone. Multiple rooms accommodate up to 3,000 club goers on always-crammed Saturday nights. Top-ranked DJs from around the world are often featured, and sounds range from house to trance, disco to hip-hop. 131 Queen's Quay E. ✆ **416/869-0045.** Cover C$10–C$15. Subway: Union.

Lula Lounge   Want to sip a well-mixed mojito or *caipirinha,* feast on fine Latin cuisine, and catch some great music without leaving your table? If so, make a date with Lula. Located on the outskirts of Little Portugal, this vibrant and spacious room is well worth the trek. It has the feel of a nightclub in pre-Castro Havana or New Orleans, while excellent sightlines and sound, and a capacity of 250, make it one of the city's best live music clubs. Latin sounds are a specialty, but a wide variety of world music is presented here. Country, jazz, rock, and classical artists have also performed here, including Norah Jones, Jonathan Richman, and Canadian rock heroes Sloan. 1585 Dundas St. W. ✆ **416/538-7405.** Cover free to C$30. Subway: St. Patrick, then a streetcar W to Dufferin St.

Sneaky Dee's ★   The antidote to the glut of posh clubs that have been proliferating in Toronto, this long-established oasis of dive-bar boasts pool tables, Mexican food, and alternative rock (from live bands or spun by a DJ) in the club upstairs until 2am. Downstairs, the bar is open until 3am on weekdays, 4:30am on weekends. 431 College St. ✆ **416/603-3090.** Cover up to C$10. Subway: Queen's Park, then any streetcar W to Bathurst St.

The Social   The first dance club to make a mark on the West Queen West strip, it continues to draw large crowds on the weekend. An eclectic mix of music styles is played, and a rotating cast of international star DJs is featured on Saturday nights. 1100 Queen St. W. ✆ **416/532-4474.** Cover from C$10. Subway: Osgoode, then a streetcar W to Dovercourt Ave.

This Is London ★   This club is more sophisticated and less frenzied than most of its peers—you might even manage a conversation. It is reminiscent of an old-fashioned gentlemen's club with its Oriental rugs and comfortable armchairs, though the dance floor is pretty hot. The music ranges from house to R&B to Top 40 and rock, and the dress code can be strict. The club's amazing ladies room features a makeup artist and hairstylist to help femmes fatales primp. 364 Richmond St. W. ✆ **416/351-1100.** Cover C$15-$20. Subway: Osgoode.

THE BAR SCENE

The current highly competitive night scene encompasses a flock of attractive bistros with diverse cuisine. You can enjoy cocktails, a reasonably priced meal, and in some, a game of pool in comfortable, aesthetically pleasing surroundings. Compared to dance clubs, the bars and lounges in Toronto are a pretty stable bunch.

Bars & Lounges

Barrio 🎁 The name is Spanish for neighborhood, and this charming and friendly lounge has been a popular fixture of the rapidly gentrifying Leslieville 'hood for almost a decade. It serves up a long list of microbrews and cocktails (try the Blueberry Hill, a mix of blueberry vodka, cranberry juice, and lime cordial). 896 Queen St. E. ℮ **416/572-0600.** Subway: Queen, then a streetcar E to Logan Ave.

The Communist's Daughter ★ 🎁 Not the easiest place to find (look for the Nazare Snack Bar sign), but well worth the quest. A tiny laid-back spot with Formica tables, it possesses one of the city's best jukeboxes. There's excellent live music on Saturday and Sunday afternoons (jazz and country, respectively). 1149 Dundas St. W. ℮ **647/435-0103.** Subway: St. Patrick, then a streetcar W to Ossington Ave.

The Drake Lounge ★ The bar at the Drake Hotel (see p. 54) is a perfect perch for sipping martinis and envisioning yourself in a glamorous bygone era. The Lounge is designed to evoke a mid-20th-century feel. It's dressed-up, grown-up fun, and it attracts a crowd of devoted locals and suburbanites. At the Drake Hotel, 1150 Queen St. W. ℮ **416/531-5042.** Subway: Osgoode, then a streetcar W to Beaconsfield Ave.

Foundation Room 🎁 Half the fun with subterranean clubs is knowing how to find them. But the Foundation Room has far more going for it than just that: The room is decked out in glorious Moroccan style, with plush lounges, hammered-brass chandeliers, and plenty of mirrors. The vibe is very sexy—and the pomegranate martinis are delicious. 19 Church St. ℮ **416/364-8368.** Subway: Union.

The Dakota Tavern 📷 This basement honky-tonk has quickly turned into a mecca for roots, bluegrass, and country rock in Toronto. High-profile singer/songwriters like Ron Sexsmith (a local resident), Serena Ryder, and John Doe (of X) have graced the small stage under the disco ball. Excellent Mexican and Southern-accented food is on offer, and the bar stools fashioned from wine barrels are a fun touch that pay homage to the Little Portugal locale. 249 Ossington Ave. ℮ **416/850-4579.** Subway: St. Patrick, then a streetcar W to Ossington Ave.

The Legendary Library Bar ★ This is one of the most romantic settings in town. This intimate, wood-paneled bar is the best place in the city to order a top-quality martini, served in a generous "fishbowl" glass. With its leopard-print couches and wingback chairs, it has an old-fashioned, almost colonial feel. At the Fairmont Royal York, 100 Front St. W. ℮ **416/863-6333.** Subway: Union.

Motel The recently opened Motel has quickly drawn hipsters into the heart of still-burgeoning Parkdale, just west of the Drake/Gladstone hub. Historic art pieces grace the wall, the Britpop and local content on the jukebox impresses, and the cozy place (capacity just 40) exudes a laid-back vibe. Guest bartenders and DJs will take care of your beverage and aural needs. Too bad you can't book a room. 1235 Queen St. W. ℮ **647/381-6246.** Subway: Osgoode, then a streetcar W to Gwynne Ave.

Reposado 🎁 The increased fashionableness of premium tequila is reflected in this chic little tequila bar on the scorching hot Ossington strip. It sports a relaxed vibe, the largest selection of tequilas in the city, and cool music from local combos and guest DJs on some nights. 136 Ossington Ave. ℮ **416/532-6474.** Subway: Osgoode, then a streetcar W to Ossington Ave.

The Roof ★★★ The late author and Montreal native Mordecai Richler called this the only civilized spot in Toronto. It's an old literary haunt perched on the 18th floor of the Park Hyatt, with comfortable couches in front of a fireplace. The walls sport caricatures of members of Canada's literary establishment. The James Bond martini—vodka with a drop of Lillet—is a popular choice. The south-facing view from the outdoor terrace is charming. At the Park Hyatt Toronto, 4 Avenue Rd.© **416/924-5471.** Subway: Museum or Bay.

Sutra Tiki Bar   Summer never ends at this sexy, intimate bar that's long been a Little Italy favorite. The drink list is composed of the usual hot-weather suspects (mojitos, *caipirinhas*) and lush champagne cocktails (try the house specialty, the Sutra). Sip to the strains of soul music. In warm weather, there's a patio out back with real sand. 612 College St.© **416/537-8755.** Subway: Queen's Park, then any streetcar W to Clinton St.

Sweaty Betty's ★   This low-key, unpretentious place won't be to everyone's taste—a good thing, since the seating capacity is limited to roughly 60 people (and that includes the patio). Famous for its snarky bartenders, this is a great spot for meeting others, since the close quarters means you'll hear everyone else's conversations. Absinthe is a trendy choice here, and the jukebox is superb. 13 Ossington Ave.© **416/535-6861.** Subway: Osgoode, then a streetcar W to Ossington Ave.

Watusi ★★ 👫   The popularity of *Mad Men* has been well-timed for Watusi, a swanky cocktail lounge exuding retro '60s cool. Located on now-hip Ossington Avenue, the place is littered with pop art, and as the clock ticks toward midnight, furniture is swept aside to make way for a long, lean dance floor. 11 Ossington Ave.© **416/533-1800.** Subway: Osgoode, then a streetcar W to Ossington Ave.

Pubs & Taverns

Allen's   Allen's sports a great bar that offers more than 150 beer selections and 278 single malts. Guinness is the drink of choice on Tuesday and Saturday nights, when folks reel and jig to the Celtic entertainment. 143 Danforth Ave.© **416/463-3086.** Subway: Broadview.

The Ben Wicks Restaurant and Pub 👫   Around since 1980, this is a much-loved fixture of the Cabbagetown neighborhood. It is named for and was opened by the late Ben Wicks, a popular local cartoonist whose artwork still adorns the walls. Reliable pub grub (think Guinness-battered fish and chips), a convivial atmosphere, and a revamped patio are other attractions. 424 Parliament St. © **416/961-9425.** Subway: College, then a streetcar E to Parliament St.

Brunswick House   Affectionately known as the Brunny, this cavernous historic tavern (it dates back to 1876) is a favorite of University of Toronto students, even after an extensive upgrade in 2005. It boasts 10 draughts on tap, and the joint is jumping on Thumpin' Thursdays, thanks to cut-price pitchers. "We dare you to party where your Dad did" is their clever tagline. Upstairs, the Champions lounge broadcasts live horse racing simulcasts and offers off-track betting. In its former life as Albert's Hall, it was the city's best blues club, featuring legendary gigs by the likes of Stevie Ray Vaughan and Jeff Buckley. 481 Bloor St. W.© **416/964-2242.** Subway: Spadina.

Ceili Cottage   World-famous oyster shucker Patrick McMurray has opened a pearl with his new Irish pub, located in Leslieville. He has transformed a former garage into a totally charming cottage, one with an authentic late 1800s look. A 5.1cm-thick (2-in.) Kilkenny limestone bar top shipped over from Ireland is the highlight of the bar area in which the owner can often be found shucking away. A separate dining room area and a pleasant patio complete the pretty picture. 1301 Queen St. E. © **416/406-1301.** Subway: Queen, then a streetcar E to Leslie St.

Dora Keogh Comfortable and friendly, with a decidedly authentic atmosphere, this is a good spot for a hearty meal and a pint. But the real reason to come is the music. Saturday afternoons feature top-notch jazz, while traditional Celtic melodies are served up on Thursdays at 9pm and Sundays at 5pm by some of the city's best players. The sessions are becoming legendary, especially since famous fiddler Natalie McMaster and members of the Chieftains have joined in. 141 Danforth Ave. © **416/778-1804.** Subway: Broadview.

Irish Embassy ★ Located in a stunning 1873 bank building in the Financial District, this pub fills up after the closing bell rings at the Toronto Stock Exchange. Guinness is just one of the many brews on tap, and there's an excellent pub-grub menu to tide you over. 49 Yonge St. © **416/866-8282.** Subway: King.

Madison Avenue Pub This is another favorite haunt of University of Toronto students, but older patrons will also feel welcomed. Beer is the beverage of choice here, with more than 150 varieties available on tap. The original pub at 14 Madison Ave. has gobbled up its neighbors at 16 and 18, and now this spot is a huge complex with six separate British-style pubs and a capacity nearing 2,000 people. 14 Madison Ave. © **416/927-1722.** Subway: Spadina.

Mill Street Brew Pub ★ Situated in the historic site of an old brewery, this pub features an award-winning array of beers brewed in small batches (some are available only seasonally). The Tankhouse Pale Ale is a constant, with its five malts blended for a particularly complex flavor. It's a top pick of local hipsters. In the Distillery District, 55 Mill St. © **416/681-0338.** Subway: King, then a streetcar E to Parliament St.

The Pilot This comfortable watering hole dates back to 1944, and it claims to be Toronto's longest continuously operating bar. Long-time regulars mingle with the suited after-work crowd, while local jazz fans love their Saturday and Sunday afternoon matinees in the Stealth Lounge. A lovely rooftop patio is another draw. 22 Cumberland St. © **416/923-5716.** Subway: Yonge/Bloor.

Wheat Sheaf Tavern Designated an historic landmark, this is the city's oldest tavern, in operation since 1849. It draws sports fans with 13 screens and fine chicken wings. The jukebox features 1,200 choices, and there are two pool tables and a popular outdoor patio. 667 King St. W. © **416/504-9912.** Subway: St. Andrew, then any streetcar W to Bathurst St.

THE GAY & LESBIAN SCENE

Toronto's gay and lesbian community is one of the largest of any city in North America, so the nightlife scene is diverse. It remains largely concentrated in the Gay Village, around Church and Wellesley streets, but popular new locales have recently opened in Parkdale. The free weekly newspaper *Xtra!* (www.xtra.ca) lists events, seminars, and performances, geared to the gay and lesbian community; also check out Gay Toronto (www.gaytoronto.com) for listings. Some mostly-straight nightspots, such as the Melody Bar (p. 196), have one night a week that's gay night.

The Beaver 🍴 The name probably tells you most of what you need to know. Located between the Gladstone and the Drake, and blessed with a great patio, this cozy watering hole is famous for its girl-on-girl Sunday parties. Good food and knowledgeable DJs are other attractions. 1192 Queen St. W. © **416/537-2768.** Subway: Osgoode, then a streetcar W to Gladstone Ave.

Crews, Tango, and the Zone ★ Located in two adjoining Victorian houses, this three-in-one club promises something for everyone. Crews is a gay bar for men, and it is known for its pubby atmosphere and its drag shows, which start at 11pm. The upstairs Tango bar draws a lesbian crowd to its dance floor and lounge. Then there's the Zone, which offers karaoke, drag queen and drag king shows, and dancing. 508 Church St. Subway: Wellesley.

El Convento Rico ★★ The Latin beat beckons one and all—straight, gay, and otherwise—to this lively club. It has welcomed a diverse crowd for nearly 20 years now. If you don't know how to salsa, meringue, or cha-cha, you can pick up the basics at the Friday-night dance lessons, but if you don't learn, no one on the jam-packed dance floor will notice. There's a substantial hetero contingent that comes out just to watch the fabulous drag queens—and don't be surprised if you encounter a bachelorette party in progress. Post-midnight shows, Friday and Saturday, are big draws. 750 College St. ☏ **416/588-7800.** www.elconventorico.com. Subway: Queen's Park, then a streetcar W to Shaw Ave.

Henhouse A new spot in Little Portugal, it's owned by two members of the Organ, a now-defunct Canadian New Wave rock band. Funky decor, a friendly atmosphere, cheap and cheerful food, and tasteful jukebox selections add up to a real success story. 1532 Dundas St. W. ☏ **416/534-5939.** Subway: St. Patrick, then a streetcar W to Dufferin St.

Pegasus Bar ★ This relaxed pub draws a gay and lesbian crowd with its four professional-size billiard tables, trivia nights, video games, pinball machines, and gigantic TV (tuned to gay dramas). The staff is warm and welcoming. 489B Church St. ☏ **416/927-8832.** Subway: Wellesley.

Sailor This bar is attached to Woody's (see below) but has a livelier atmosphere; unlike Woody's, you won't see many women here. Every Thursday, there's a Best Chest competition; every Friday, the prize is for Best Ass. In the evening, a DJ spins an assortment of dance and alternative tunes. 465 Church St. ☏ **416/972-0887.** Subway: Wellesley.

Slack's Formerly known as Slack Alice, it's the leading lesbian bar/restaurant in the village. It draws a more mixed crowd earlier in the week and occasionally hosts live jazz. The straightforward menu is well-executed. 562 Church St. ☏ **416/969-8742.** Subway: Wellesley.

Woody's ★ A local institution, immortalized in the television series *Queer As Folk.* Still the reigning men's bar in the village, it welcomes women and heteros. Best Chest contests, drag shows, and DJs are all featured on different nights. It's a popular meeting spot, especially for weekend brunch. 467 Church St. (S of Wellesley St.). ☏ **416/972-0887.** www.woodystoronto.com. Subway: Wellesley.

Zelda's Living Well ★ A long-time Gay Village favorite (known just as Zelda's), it recently moved to Yonge Street but still remains popular. Zelda's has great food; fun, tacky decor (including pink flamingos); and a great sense of humor. Ideally, you'll be there for one of the many theme nights, with Dirty Bingo, drag entertainment, and talent shows all served with a smile. 692 Yonge St. ☏ **416/922-2526.** Subway: Wellesley.

COFFEEHOUSES

Starbucks has certainly staked out plenty of territory in Toronto, but there are two Canadian chains that are just as popular: the **Second Cup,** which charges less for a latte, and the donut-and-coffee destination **Tim Horton's** (also known as Tim Ho's). Another chain with fewer locales is **Timothy's.** In addition to the late-night stops listed below, there's a growing barista movement in Toronto where the joe is strictly a daytime commodity—and often offers truly top brew (see p. 79).

Balzac's Coffee ★   If you're in the Distillery District (see p. 103), this is the place to stop for coffee. Not only is the setting dramatic (soaring ceilings, redbrick walls, and an elaborate chandelier), but the in-house roasted coffees are deservedly famous. There's also a location in Liberty Village. In the Distillery District, 55 Mill St. © **416/207-1709.** Subway: King, then a streetcar E to Parliament St.

Café Diplomatico ★ 🏮   You can come for the coffee, but it's not the main draw. Instead, crowds flock to this traditional cafe for the big patio and often for the beer on tap. It's a great hangout to watch the parade of passersby in Little Italy. 594 College St. © **416/534-4637.** Subway: Queen's Park, then a streetcar W to Clinton St.

Future Bakery   This rambling cafe attracts students and those looking for a good, cheap bowl of borscht alongside a decent mug of brew. There's also a good selection of breads, buns, and pastries. A neighborhood favorite. 483 Bloor St. W. © **416/922-5875.** Subway: Spadina or Bathurst.

Lettieri ★   The house rule at this small local chain is that after 7 minutes, a pot of coffee is no longer fresh. This place takes the bean seriously. In addition to the wide range of coffees, you can order focaccia sandwiches, tarts, cookies, and pastries. There are outposts at **441 Queen St.** (at Spadina Ave.; © **416/592-1360**) and at the corner of Bloor and Bathurst streets, tucked into the beloved **Honest Ed's** emporium (p. 168). 94 Cumberland St. © **416/515-8764.** www.lettiericafe.com. Subway: Bay.

Linux Caffe   Located near the University of Toronto campus and a short walk from College Street, this cool little cafe serves a fine brew using beans from local roaster Ideal Coffee and specializing in organic and fair-trade. There's also a fairly good simple menu. 326 Harbord St. © **416/534 2116.** Subway: Spadina, then walk S 3 blocks to Harbord St.

SIDE TRIPS FROM TORONTO

Toronto has plenty to offer visitors, but if you can afford to take the time to add a side trip, there are some excursions worth considering. Within just a 2-hour drive beyond the sprawling suburbs, you'll find pretty scenery, quaint towns, superb theater, one of the seven natural wonders of the world, and tempting culinary tourism destinations, including winery tours. Add another hour or so to your travel, and you'll be experiencing the wilderness of Algonquin Park.

This chapter describes four of the best-known destinations—the theater town of Stratford, the wine region of Niagara-on-the-Lake and the unparalleled Niagara Falls, the great outdoors of Muskoka Lakes and Algonquin Park, and the rich culinary bounty of Prince Edward County.

For information about the areas surrounding Toronto, contact Ontario Tourism (✆ 800/ONTARIO [800/668-2746]; www.ontariotravel.net) or visit its travel information center in the Atrium on Bay (street level) at 20 Dundas St. W.—it's just across Dundas Street from the Sears store at the northern edge of the Eaton Centre. It's open daily from 8:30am to 4:30pm; hours are extended during the summer, often to 8pm.

A note about Internet and Wi-Fi: Most accommodations in this chapter offer in-room or in-lobby Internet or Wi-Fi access. Some charge for it, some don't. For hotels that charge for Internet or Wi-Fi, the price ranges from C$15 to C$21 per day. When included in the room price, I've listed the services as "free."

STRATFORD ★

145km (90 miles) SW of Toronto

For those who care: This is the hometown of Justin Bieber. But its real claim to fame is the great Stratford Festival. Additionally, it's a charming and pretty place to amble before and after taking in a show.

The Festival has humble roots. The idea of a theater was launched in 1953, when director Tyrone Guthrie lured the great Sir Alec Guinness to the stage. Whether Sir Alec knew the "stage" was set up in a makeshift tent is another question, but his acclaimed performance gave the festival the push—and press—it needed to become an annual tradition. Since then, the Stratford Festival has grown to become one of the most famous

Side Trips from Toronto

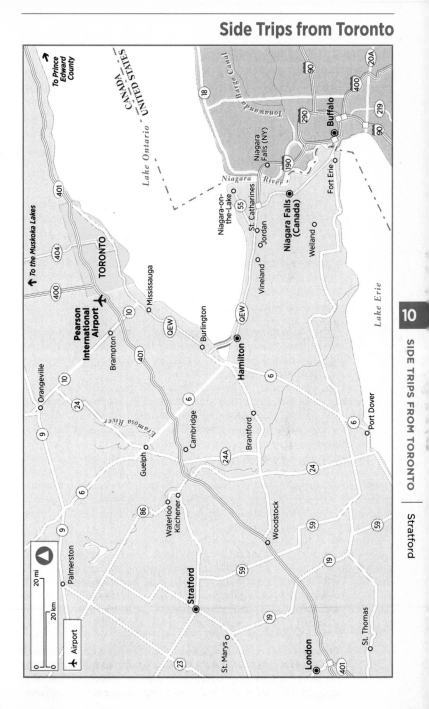

in North America, and its four theaters have put this scenic town on the cultural map. It has also triggered the development of fine restaurants, good hotels, and tours for everyone from theater-loving cyclists to history buffs.

Essentials

VISITOR INFORMATION   For first-rate visitor information, go to the **Visitors' Information Centre** by the river, on York Street at Erie Street. From May to early November, it's open Sunday through Wednesday 9am to 5pm and Thursday through Saturday 9am to 8pm. At other times, contact **Tourism Stratford** (✆ **800/561-SWAN** [800/561-7926] or 519/271-5140; www.welcometostratford.com).

GETTING THERE   Driving from Toronto, take Hwy. 401 west to I-278 at Kitchener. Follow Hwy. 8 west onto Hwy. 7/8 to Stratford. (Hwy. 7/8 turns into Ontario St., Stratford's main drag, once you enter city limits.)

For me, nothing beats the train, and Stratford is a small and very walkable town, so unless you're planning to tour the surrounding area, call **VIA Rail** (✆ **800/VIA-RAIL** [800/842-7245] or 416/366-8411; www.viarail.ca). Canada's national rail company operates several trains daily along the Toronto-Kitchener-Stratford route. The toll-free number works within North America; if you're traveling from overseas, you can book your rail travel in advance through one of VIA's general sales agents (there's a long list of local agents on www.viarail.ca).

10 The Stratford Festival ★★★

On July 13, 1953, *Richard III,* starring Sir Alec Guinness, was staged in a huge tent. From that modest start, Stratford's artistic directors have built on the radical, but faithfully classic, base established by Tyrone Guthrie to create a repertory theater with a glowing international reputation.

Stratford has four theaters. The **Festival Theatre** (55 Queen St.) has a dynamic thrust stage (a modern re-creation of an Elizabethan stage). The **Avon Theatre** (99 Downie St.) has a classic proscenium. The **Tom Patterson Theatre** (111 Lakeside Dr.) is an intimate 500-seat theater. The **Studio Theatre (**34 George St. E.) is a 278-seat space used for new and experimental works.

World-famous for its Shakespearean productions, the festival also offers classic and modern theatrical masterpieces. Recent productions have included *West Side Story, Cyrano de Bergerac,* and *Three Sisters;* from the Bard, there's an encyclopedia of productions, including *Macbeth* and *A Midsummer Night's Dream.* The bill always presents an impressive line-up that is designed to suit tastes from the contemporary to the historic, the comedic to the tragic.

The season usually begins in early May and continues through mid-November, with performances Tuesday through Sunday. Ticket prices range from C$25 to C$120, with special deals for students and seniors. For tickets, call ✆ **800/567-1600** or 519/273-1600, fax 519/273-3731, or visit **www.stratfordfestival.ca**. Tickets are also available in the United States and Canada at Ticketmaster outlets. The box office opens for the new season in mid-January.

Behind the Festival Curtain ★

The Stratford Festival offers several behind-the-scenes tours that will thrill theater buffs. There are **backstage tours of the Festival Theatre,** which take about an hour, and tours of the **costume and props warehouse** at 350 Douro St., which run roughly 45 minutes. Tours cost C$8 adults, C$6 seniors and students, and should be

Stratford

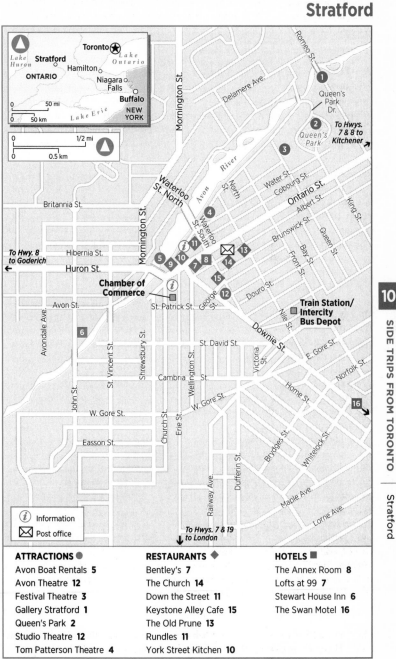

ATTRACTIONS ●
Avon Boat Rentals **5**
Avon Theatre **12**
Festival Theatre **3**
Gallery Stratford **1**
Queen's Park **2**
Studio Theatre **12**
Tom Patterson Theatre **4**

RESTAURANTS ◆
Bentley's **7**
The Church **14**
Down the Street **11**
Keystone Alley Cafe **15**
The Old Prune **13**
Rundles **11**
York Street Kitchen **10**

HOTELS ■
The Annex Room **8**
Lofts at 99 **7**
Stewart House Inn **6**
The Swan Motel **16**

Museums are grand, but who wants to spend a glorious summer day indoors? Thanks to the **Art in the Park** (www.art intheparkstratford.com), you can have both. On Wednesdays, Saturdays, and Sundays from June to September, regional artists gather at Lakeside Drive and Front Street, and put on a show from 9am to 5pm, weather permitting. The artists and artisans work in various media, so you'll find paintings, sculptures, ceramics, jewelry, and glass, among other things. While many of the works are for sale, this isn't just a market: The artists are selected through a juried process.

scheduled in advance by calling the box office at ✆ **800/567-1600** or 519/273-1600.

Some performances have **preshow lectures** or **post-performance discussions.** These are free of charge but need to be reserved in advance via the box office. There are also free "Meet the Festival" events with members of the acting company and a series of special lectures about the major plays of the season. For details, dates, and times, check out **www.stratfordfestival.ca**.

Exploring the Town

Stratford was founded in 1832, and much of its historic heart has been preserved. Wandering through its pristine residential street—lined with historic homes decorated with turrets, wraparound verandas, and stained-glass windows—is a little like stepping back in time. The Visitors' Information Centre by the Avon River has maps for self-guided tours. You can also download several free audio-tour podcasts about Stratford's gardens, landmarks, and downtown from **www.welcometostratford.com**.

Paddleboat, kayak, and canoe rentals are available at the **Boathouse,** behind the information center. In summer, it's open daily from 9am until dusk. Contact **Avon Boat Rentals** (40 York St.; ✆ **519/271-7739**). There's also a boat, the *Juliet III,* that offers scenic half-hour tours.

The **Shakespearean Gardens**—a pretty, formal English garden—is a great place to relax and contemplate the flowerbeds and tranquil river lagoon, and muse on a bust of Shakespeare by Toronto sculptor Cleeve Horne. For a picnic-friendly patch of green, visit **Queen's Park,** a stone's throw from the Festival Theatre.

And speaking of picnics, Stratford is in the heart of an agricultural belt, and the abundant food options reflect the city's pride in its regional culinary riches. There are farmers markets; big seasonal food fares such as Savour Stratford in September; loads of restaurant, farm, and dairy tours; and more. Check out www.welcometostratford. com/savour-stratford.php.

Stratford also has a good art museum, the **Gallery Stratford** (54 Romeo St.; ✆ **519/271-5271;** www.gallerystratford.on.ca). Located in an historic building on the fringes of Confederation Park, the museum exhibits contemporary and historical works by Canadian artists. Its hours change with the seasons, but mid-May through late September, it's open Tuesday through Sunday from 10am to 5pm (call ahead for hours Oct to mid-May).

A Couple of Excursions from Stratford

Only half an hour or so from Stratford, the twin cities of **Kitchener** and **Waterloo** have two drawing cards: the **Farmers' Market** and the famous 9-day **Oktoberfest** (✆ **888/294-HANS** [888/294-4267] or 519/570-HANS [519/570-4267]; www.oktoberfest.ca). The cities still have a large population of descendents of German settlers, and many are also Mennonites. On Saturday, starting at 6am, you can sample shoofly pie, apple butter, birch beer, summer sausage, and other Mennonite specialties at the market in the Market Square complex, at Duke and Frederick streets in Kitchener. For additional information, contact the **Kitchener-Waterloo Area Visitors and Convention Bureau** (2848 King St. E., Kitchener; ✆ **519/748-0800;** www.explorewaterlooregion.com). It's open in winter from 9am to 5pm weekdays only, daily in summer.

Eight kilometers (5 miles) north of Kitchener is the town of **St. Jacobs.** It has close to 100 shops in venues such as a converted mill, silo, and other factory buildings. The **Meetingplace** (33 King St.; ✆ **519/664-3518**) runs a short film about the Amish-Mennonite way of life (daily in summer, weekends only in winter). There's also the **St. Jacobs Outlet Mall** at 25 Benjamin Rd. E.; its offerings include Levi's, Lego, Reebok, CorningWare, Liz Claiborne, and Paderno. The mall is open Monday through Friday 9:30am to 9pm, Saturday 8:30am to 6pm, and Sunday noon to 5pm (closed Jan 1 and Dec 25). Call ✆ **519/888-0138** for more information.

Where to Stay

When you book your theater tickets, you can book your accommodations at no extra charge. Options range from guest homes for as little as C$75 to first-class hotels charging more than C$200. Call the **Stratford Tourism Alliance** at ✆ **800/561-7926** for information (note that some accommodations are open only to festival-goers, and these can be booked only through the Accommodation Bureau). You can also book a room via **Tourism Stratford's website** (www.welcometostratford.com); for extensive bed-and-breakfast listings, check out **www.bbcanada.com**. Rooms in Stratford are most expensive in June, July, and August; it's easier to get a discount from fall to spring. In winter, even the most opulent properties deeply discount their rates. Keep in mind that most accommodations here are smoke-free.

The Annex Room ★ This small, centrally located hotel is quaint, yet luxurious: Each room has a whirlpool tub and a fireplace. The rooms are airy and bright, and elegantly decorated. Because of the hotel's tiny size, you can count on personal, considerate service. The one drawback is that there is no elevator, so guests need to be able to climb stairs.

38 Albert St., Stratford, ON N5A 3K3. www.bentleys-annex.com. ✆ **800/361-5322** or 519/271-1407. Fax 519/272-1853. 6 units. C$225 double; off-season C$125 double. Additional adult C$25. AE, DC, MC, V. Free parking. **Amenities:** Restaurant. *In room:* A/C, TV, fridge, hair dryer, minibar, Wi-Fi (free).

Lofts at 99 ★★ For convenience, you can't beat this spot at the center of town formerly known as Bentley's (the on-site restaurant still goes by that name; see p. 212). Recent renovations have turned it into a modern, chic inn with a streamlined look. The rooms are elegant duplex suites with kitchenettes; five units have skylights. The split-level feature makes it great for families with young children. Like most Stratford accommodations, Lofts at 99 doesn't have an elevator. This is a smoke-free hotel.

I know, we're all here for the theater scene, but don't miss out on Stratford's excellent shopping options. If you were expecting touristy, overpriced, and kitschy, you're in for a pleasant surprise. Many of the stores downtown sell clothing and housewares that rival what you'll see in the best boutiques in Toronto. Prices tend to be quite reasonable. Here are some of my favorite spots.

o **Art: Gallery Indigena** (69 Ontario St.; ℂ **519/271-7881;** www.galleryindigena.com) is filled with wonderful finds. They specialize in works by the Inuit, Iroquois, Cree, Plains, Woodland, and North Pacific Coast peoples. In business for more than 3 decades, the gallery hosts several "Meet the Artist" events throughout the summer, and it ships artwork all over the world.

o **Books: Callan Books** (15 York St.; ℂ **519/273-5767**) is a charming spot with an eclectic collection that will particularly please history buffs. **Fundamentals** (52 Ontario St.; ℂ **519/273-6440**) is targeted at the small fry and has a particularly wonderful collection of illustrated storybooks.

o **Clothing: Elizabeth Noel** (26 Ontario St.; ℂ **519/273-4506**)

sells beautiful dresses and other ladylike pieces, many of which are by Canadian labels such as Sweet Chemise and Girl Friday. **The Green Room** (40 Ontario St.; ℂ **519/271-3240**) is actually several rooms, all jampacked with women's accessories. For men, there's **Gruv** ("groove"), at 10 Ontario St. (ℂ **519/273-1116**).

o **Gift Items:** The fair-trade company **Ten Thousand Villages** (14 Ontario St.; ℂ **519/272-0700**) sells crafts, jewelry, housewares, and toys from artisans in developing countries. **Rheo Thompson Candies** (55 Albert St.; ℂ **519/271-6910**) is a local institution that makes lovely chocolates, mints, jellies, and other candies.

o **Housewares:** You'll find both locally made cranberry glass and objects from Indonesia and Uzbekistan at **Watson's Chelsea Bazaar** (84 Ontario St.; ℂ **519/273-1790**). **White Oleander** (136 Ontario St.; ℂ **519/271-5616**) sells lovely linens, bedding, and tableware. The venerable **Bradshaws** (129 Ontario St.; ℂ **519/271-6283**) has been in business since 1895 selling crystal and china.

99 Ontario St., Stratford, ON N5A 3H1. www.bentleys-annex.com. ℂ **800/361-5322** or 519/271-1121. 12 units. From C$295 double. Additional adult C$25. Children 11 & under stay free in parent's room. AE, DC, MC, V. Free parking. **Amenities:** Restaurant. *In room:* A/C, TV, fridge, hair dryer, minibar, Wi-Fi (free).

Stewart House Inn ★ 🏠 This house was built in 1870, and the owners have decorated it with a suitably opulent Victorian style. There's also old-fashioned guest service: In the morning, coffee is delivered to your room; if you want to swim in the backyard saltwater pool, you'll be supplied with robes, towels, and tumblers for drinks. A full breakfast is served every morning between 8 and 10am in what used to be the ballroom. The guest rooms are nicely appointed, with each one themed to play up the romantic atmosphere. Still, the modern conveniences (flat-screen TVs, DVD players, and Wi-Fi) aren't spared. House policies are no smoking, no children, and no pets (there are, however, two small dogs in residence).

62 John St. N., Stratford, ON N5A 6K7. www.stewarthouseinn.com. © **866/826-7772** or 519/271-4576. Fax 519/273-1746. 7 units. From C$199 double. Rates include full breakfast. MC, V. Street parking. No children allowed. **Amenities:** Outdoor pool. *In room:* A/C, TV/DVD player, CD player, hair dryer, Wi-Fi (free).

The Swan Motel 🍴 The simple rooms here are typical, if high-end, motel fare, but the grounds are more like a small estate garden. Located 3km (1¾ miles) from downtown Stratford, the setting offers a tranquil escape. The property has been run by the same family for more than 40 years, and it has a warm, gracious atmosphere. The rooms are simple and clean. The grounds are the real drawing card, with a sweet Victorian gazebo, beds of perennial flowers, and an outdoor pool. This is a smoke-free hotel.

960 Downie St. S., Stratford, ON N5A 6S3. www.swanmotel.ca. © **519/271-6376.** Fax 519/271-0682. 24 units. From C$102 double. Additional adult C$15. Rates include continental breakfast. MC, V. Free parking. **Amenities:** Outdoor pool. *In room:* A/C, TV, fridge, hair dryer, Wi-Fi (free).

A NEARBY PLACE TO STAY & EAT

Langdon Hall ★★ Less than an hour's drive from Stratford, this elegant house stands at the head of a curving, tree-lined drive. Eugene Langdon Wilks, a great-grandson of John Jacob Astor, completed it in 1902. It remained in the family until 1987, when it was transformed into a beautiful country-house hotel. Today, Langdon Hall is a Relais & Châteaux property with Ontario's first restaurant to earn the much-vaunted Relais Gourmands status (a title held by the French Laundry and Fat Duck, among others). Its 81 hectares (200 acres) is a pleasing mix of manicured lawns, English gardens, and rustic woodlands. What's more, there's a balance of comfort and refinement that, combined with top-notch service, puts it on a par with Canada's truly great inns. You can choose to stay in the original house, in the converted stable suites, or in one of the rooms surrounding the cloister garden. There is an on-site spa, a small swimming pool, a network of cross-country ski trails, and a small billiards room. The generous public rooms are great gathering places, with wood-burning fires in winter and lush garden views in summer. Many come for the dining alone: Seasonal ingredients are turned into exquisite fare under the direction of chef Jonathan Gushue, and the wine list is extensive. Tea is served on the canopied veranda.

R.R. 3, Cambridge, ON N3H 4R8. www.langdonhall.ca. © **800/268-1898** or 519/740-2100. 52 units. From C$329 double. Rates include full breakfast. AE, DC, MC, V. Free parking. From Hwy. 401, take exit 275 S, turn right onto Blair Rd. & follow signs. Pets accepted at no additional cost. **Amenities:** Dining room; bar; babysitting; bike rental; concierge; health club; Jacuzzi; outdoor pool; room service; sauna; spa; tennis courts. *In room:* A/C, TV, CD player, hair dryer, Wi-Fi (free).

Where to Eat
EXPENSIVE

The Church ★★ FRENCH The Church is simply stunning. The organ pipes and the altar of the 1873 structure are intact, along with the vaulted roof, carved woodwork, and stained-glass windows. You can sit in the nave or the side aisles, and dine to appropriate music—usually Bach. Appetizers might include asparagus with black morels, white wine, and cream or sautéed foie gras with leeks and citron, mango, and ginger sauce. The menu is brief and to the point: classic meats with Canadian twists, such as caribou with port-and-blackberry sauce and cream-braised cabbage with shallots and glazed chestnuts; or lobster salad with green beans, new potatoes, and truffles scented with caraway. Desserts are equally dramatic. The upstairs Belfry, a more modest affair, is a popular pre- and post-theater gathering place and is open for lunch and dinner.

70 Brunswick St. (at Waterloo St.). ℰ **519/273-3424.** www.churchrestaurant.com. Reservations required. Main courses C$38–C$44. AE, DC, MC, V. The Church: Tues–Sat 5–8:30pm, Sun 11:30am–1:30pm & 5–8pm; off-season hours vary; closed Dec to mid-Apr. The Belfry: Tues–Sat 11:30am–midnight; off-season hours vary.

The Old Prune ★ CONTINENTAL Situated in a lovely Edwardian home, the Old Prune has three dining rooms and an enclosed garden patio. Former Montréalers, the proprietors demonstrate Québec flair in both decor and menu. The menu changes based on what's fresh and what's in season (much of the produce comes from the region's organic farms). Goods from local dairies, cheese makers, and other artisans are prominent on the menu. Among the main courses, you might find Perth County pork loin grilled with tamari and honey glaze, and served with shiitake mushrooms, pickled cucumbers, and sunflower sprouts; steamed bass in Napa cabbage with curry broth and lime leaves; or rack of Ontario lamb with smoky tomatillo-chipotle pepper sauce. Desserts, such as rhubarb strawberry Napoleon, are inspired.

151 Albert St. ℰ **519/271-5052.** www.oldprune.on.ca. Reservations required. 3-course prix-fixe menu C$66. AE, MC, V. Fri–Sun 11:30am–1pm, Tues–Sun 5–9pm; call for winter hours.

Rundles ★ 🔥 INTERNATIONAL Rundles provides a premier dining experience in a serene dining room overlooking the river. The prix-fixe dinner offers palate-pleasing flavor combinations. Appetizers might include shaved fennel, arugula, artichoke and Parmesan salad, or warm seared Québec foie gras. Typical main dishes include poached Atlantic salmon garnished with Jerusalem artichokes, wilted arugula, and yellow peppers in a light carrot sauce; or pink roast rib-eye of lamb with ratatouille and rosemary aioli. For dessert, try glazed lemon tart and orange sorbet, or hot mango tart with pineapple sorbet. In 2008, Rundles opened the Sophisto-Bistro, a more casual dining room, with a less-expensive (yet incredibly delicious) prix-fixe menu.

9 Cobourg St. ℰ **519/271-6442.** www.rundlesrestaurant.com. Reservations required. Rundles 3-course prix-fixe dinner C$80; Sophisto-Bistro 3-course prix-fixe menu C$50. AE, DC, MC, V. Apr–Oct Sat & Sun 11:30am–1:15pm; Tues & Sat 5–7pm, Wed–Fri 5–8:30pm. Closed Nov–Mar.

MODERATE

Bentley's CANADIAN/ENGLISH Located in the Lofts at 99 hotel (see p. 209), Bentley's is *the* local watering hole and a favorite theater-company gathering spot. In summer, you can sit on the garden terrace and enjoy the light fare—grilled shrimp, burgers, pizza, fish and chips, shepherd's pie, and pastas. The dinner menu features more substantial stuff, including lamb curry, sirloin steak, and salmon baked in white wine with peppercorn-dill butter. The bar offers 15 drafts on tap.

99 Ontario St. ℰ **519/271-1121.** www.bentleys-annex.com. Reservations not accepted. Main courses C$15–C$18. AE, DC, MC, V. Daily 11:30am–1am.

Down the Street ★ 🍴 INTERNATIONAL This charming bohemian spot is a welcome find, given Stratford's delicious but often pricey food scene. The menu offers selections from around the globe: Mexican guacamole and corn tortillas, Vietnamese-style pork chops in a spicy chili-honey glaze, French Dijon chicken supreme. The dessert list is short but good; try the bittersweet chocolate tart with raspberry sorbet.

30 Ontario St. ℰ **519/273-5886.** Reservations recommended. Main courses C$18–C$28. AE, DC, MC, V. Tues–Sat 11:30am–3pm & 5–9pm (bar open till 1am).

Keystone Alley Cafe ★ ASIAN/CONTINENTAL   The food here is better than at some pricier competitors. Lunch options may include a maple-grilled chicken-and-avocado club or a cornmeal-crusted Mediterranean tart. At dinner, entrees include breast of Muscovy duck with stir-fried Asian vegetables and egg noodles in honey-ginger sauce, as well as escallops of calf's liver with garlic potato purée and creamed Savoy cabbage with bacon. The short wine list is reasonably priced.

34 Brunswick St. 🕐 **519/271-5645.** Reservations recommended. Main courses C$15–C$27. AE, DC, MC, V. Mon–Sat 11:30am–2:30pm; Tues–Sat 5–9pm.

INEXPENSIVE

York Street Kitchen ECLECTIC   This small restaurant is a fun, funky spot that serves reasonably priced, high-quality food. It's a favorite with locals, especially the arts and media set. Grub is up all day, from breakfast burritos and other morning fare to build-your-own sandwiches at lunch and, in the evenings, good comfort foods such as meatloaf and mashed potatoes, or barbecued chicken and ribs.

41 York St. 🕐 **519/273-7041.** www.yorkstreetkitchen.com. Reservations not accepted. Main courses C$14–C$16. AE, V. Apr to early Oct daily 8am–8pm; early Oct to Mar daily 8am–3pm. Closed Dec 24 to Jan 5.

HAMILTON

Hamilton is a city that continues to transform itself. Located in southern Ontario on the western end of the Niagara Peninsula, the city wraps around the western part of Lake Ontario. It is the geographic center of the "Golden Horseshoe," at roughly the midway point between Toronto and Niagara Falls. Hamilton Harbour marks the northern limit of the city, and the Niagara Escarpment runs through its middle, bisecting the city into upper and lower parts. Once known for its steel mills and foundries, the city has become in recent years a center for higher education, medical services, and Internet technology. Through all the changes, its historic heart has remained unchanged.

History may well be the hallmark of Hamilton, and the range and number of the museums in the city are a testament to that fact. The jewel in the crown is Dundurn Castle, but there is also the historic estate of Whitehern, right next to city hall. A half-hour away is Westfield Heritage Village.

The Museum of Steam and Technology preserves the technology that powered the city 140 years ago, while the Canadian Warplane Heritage Museum has restored and displays aircraft from World War II, including the only operational Lancaster in North America. In nearby Ancaster, Griffin House preserves the story of Enerals Griffin, a Virginian slave who escaped to freedom and lived in this simple clapboard house, which is now a museum and an important cultural landmark of the Black Heritage Network.

Hamilton boasts two stunning waterfronts, each with its own stretch of new trails. The Beach Strip Trail is a 10km (6 miles) paved pathway along Lake Ontario that leads to the popular water park, Wild Waterworks. The west-end Hamilton Harbour Waterfront Trail, is another 10km magnet for walkers, joggers, and in-line skaters. Also here are Hamilton's popular Bayfront Park and Pier 4, home to boaters, dragon-boat races, family picnics, and summer festivals. Attractions here include the Hamilton Waterfront Trolley, cruises on the *Harbour Queen,* the new Pier 8 skate rink, and a William's Coffee Pub.

Robert Land, a United Empire Loyalist, was the first white settler in the Hamilton area, having fled from persecution in Pennsylvania, narrowly escaping execution. He settled at the head of the lake, believing his wife and children to be dead. His wife, Phebe, had managed to escape with her children to Nova Scotia, believing her husband was dead. When she journeyed to Niagara to claim farmland that was given to the loyalists, she heard rumors of a man called Land living in what would become Hamilton. She hired a boat, traveled to satisfy her curiosity, and discovered her long-lost husband.

The reunion, according to legend, was a joyous one, and the couple and their family, having been granted 405 hectares (1,000 acres) in the center of the future city of Hamilton, helped to build the community that would be home to generations of their descendants. Robert and Phebe are buried in the Hamilton Cemetery, alongside such characters as William Cook, a Canadian soldier who was killed with General Custer at the Battle of Little Big Horn, and Isabella Whyte, the secret half-sister of Queen Victoria. Tours of this Gothic cemetery are conducted regularly and offer a running commentary on the city's colorful past.

Events, exhibits, and programs commemorating and celebrating the Bicentennial of the War of 1812 will take place in 2012, 2013, and 2014, in the Hamilton area. Expect a peak in activities during 2013 to mark significant events like the 200th anniversary of the Battle of Stoney Creek, the sinking of warships the *Hamilton* and the *Scourge*, the encampment at Burlington Heights, and the Burlington Races.

It has been said that, for a city to be truly civilized, it must nurture its talent and create a home for that talent to blossom. Hamilton has excelled at both of these. The city is the hometown for comedians Red Green (aka Steve Smith), Martin Short, and Eugene Levy; singer Stan Rogers; architect Bruce Kuwabara; ballerina Karen Kain; and 2007 Canadian Idol winner Brian Melo.

Essentials

GETTING THERE By **car,** Hamilton is just a short detour from the QEW. Travelers from Buffalo, Fort Erie, and St. Catharines can take the QEW over the Skyway Bridge to Hwy. 403, which takes you to the center of the city. Those coming from Toronto will exit at Hwy. 403 in Burlington, before the Skyway Bridge. **Bus** lines offer regular service to Hamilton from many different locations. Via Rail brings **train** travelers from across Canada to the station in Aldershot, a short distance outside the city in neighboring Burlington. **By air,** you can get to Hamilton via John C. Munro Hamilton International Airport (it's both accessible and less stress-inducing than flying into Toronto's Pearson International Airport), which serves Southern Ontario well with direct WestJet service to cities like Calgary, Halifax, and Edmonton.

VISITOR INFORMATION Hamilton's Tourist Information Centre (© **800/263-8590** or 905/546-2666; www.tourismhamilton.com) is downtown at Jackson Square (2 King St. W.). The center is open Monday through Friday from 8:30am to 4:30pm. The Tourist Board also operates a staffed information center at Hamilton International Airport throughout the summer (May–Oct).

What to See & Do

African Lion Safari African Lion Safari is a popular local attraction where 1,000 animals roam free in this expansive drive-through reserve, while visitors remain "caged" in their cars. The family-owned business boasts successful breeding programs for many endangered and threatened species. Family-friendly activities include live animal shows, the popular "elephant swim," the "African Queen" boat cruise, "Nature Boy" scenic railway, and Misumu Bay Wet Play.

1386 Cooper Rd., R.R. 1, Cambridge, ON. ☎ **519/623-2620** or 800/461-WILD(9453). www.lionsafari. com. Admission C$30 adults; C$28 senior; C$25 children 3-12; children 2 and under free. Summer hours June 25–Sept 5 daily 9am–5:30pm; Sept 6–Oct 10 daily 9am–4pm.

Art Gallery of Hamilton ★★★ For the art lover, Hamilton is home to Ontario's third largest art gallery, the Art Gallery of Hamilton. After an C$18-million renovation and expansion designed by Hamilton-born architect Bruce Kuwabara, the AGH is now a beautiful exhibition space, and home to the Joey and Toby Tanenbaum collection of 19th-century European art. One of the best bargains in town is the "First Fridays" initiative, where visitors have free entrance to the gallery from 5 to 9pm on every first Friday of the month. Combine a tour of the gallery with a light meal in the gallery cafe and you've got a great evening on a shoestring. Special exhibitions occur regularly. And don't miss the work-in-progress, Bruegel-Bosch Bus by Kim Adams.

123 King St. W., Hamilton, ON. ☎ **905/527-6610.** www.artgalleryofhamilton.com. Admission C$10 adults, C$8 seniors and students, C$4 children 6-17, children 5 and under free. Tues-Wed noon-7pm; Thurs-Fri noon-9pm; Sat-Sun noon-5pm.

Battlefield House Museum and Park Like Dundurn and Whitehern, Battlefield is a National Historic Site. It is home to the annual re-enactment of the Battle of Stoney Creek, a pivotal battle in the War of 1812. In addition to the weekend-long event held every June, Battlefield House is a "living history" museum offering visitors year-round tours by period-costumed guides.

77 King St. W., Stoney Creek, ON. ☎ **905/662-8458.** www.battlefieldhouse.ca. Admission adults C$6.50, seniors C$5.50, students 13-17 C$5.50, children 6-12 C$4.50, children 5 and under free, families C$17. July to early Sept Tues–Sun 11am–4pm; Sept–June Tues–Sun 1–4pm.

Canadian Warplane Heritage Museum ★ ☺ The Canadian Warplane Heritage Museum showcases the aircraft used by Canadians or Canada's military from the beginning of World War II up to the present. The collection includes aircraft that really fly and several that remain on static display. Visitors can climb into the cockpit of a real World War II trainer or a real jet fighter. There are interactive flight combat simulators, interactive video displays, movies, photographs, and memorabilia from Canadian history. Its prized possession is probably the most famous Allied bomber of World War II, the Avro Lancaster, the only operational one in North America and one of only two air-worthy Lancasters in the world. It is also the only one you can buy a flight on for special occasions, although the cost is very steep (starting at C$2,500 for 1 hr.). The Hamilton International Air Show returned in 2011 and has been a great success. See http://airshow.warplane.com/hamilton-airshow-2011.aspx for details.

9280 Airport Rd., Mount Hope. ☎ **905/679-4183.** www.warplane.com. Admission C$10 adults, C$9 seniors and students 13-17, C$6 children 6-12, children 5 and under free. Daily 9am–5pm.

Dundurn Castle ★★ Dundurn is a classic mid-19th-century Regency-style villa. Costumed guides give visitors a glimpse into the life of a prominent 1850s Victorian family and their servants. The gardens have been extensively restored, notably the kitchen garden. The plantings are all heritage varieties that would have been harvested here in the 1850s. The gift shop features Canadian handmade crafts, souvenirs, and special gifts. You can also visit the Hamilton Military Museum, all inside Dundurn Park.

610 York Blvd., Hamilton. © **905/546-2872.** www.dundurncastle.com. Admission C$11 adults, C$9 seniors and students 13-17, C$5.50 children 6-12, children 5 and under free. July 1 to Labour Day daily 10am-4pm; Labour Day to June 30 Tues-Sun noon-4pm.

Griffin House   Griffin House is a reminder of the bravery and determination of black men and women who journeyed to freedom in southern Ontario via the Underground Railroad. Griffin House offers tours and black history–related programs as part of the Black Heritage Network. The site is located on top of a hill overlooking the Dundas Valley and is managed as a joint project.

733 Mineral Springs Rd., Ancaster. © **905/546-2424.** griffinhouse@hamilton.ca. Admission C$2, children 5 and under free. Open on public holidays from Victoria Day to Thanksgiving 1-4pm.

James Street North Art Crawl   Part of Hamilton's emerging arts scene, the historic downtown street is becoming an arts hub with artists and young professionals moving into the area's affordable historic homes and downtown lofts and studios. The *National Post* newspaper called the area the "New Brooklyn," referring to artists and young people flocking to the area after being priced out of Toronto. The art crawl happens every second Friday of the month. Stores, restaurants, and galleries extend their hours and open their doors to the street, transforming the strip into a wonderful, art-loving street party, welcoming to young and old alike.

James St. North Art District, from King William St. to Strachan St. www.jamesstreetnorth.ca. Every 2nd Fri year-round 6pm-midnight.

The Harbourfront and HMS *Haida*   Families will enjoy a visit to HMCS *Haida,* where you can walk the decks of Canada's most famous warship. The *Haida* saw service in World War II and the Korean War and is the last Tribal Class destroyer in the world.

Pier 9, 658 Catharine St., Hamilton. © **905/526-0911.** Admission C$3.90 adults, C$3.60 seniors, C$1.90 children 17 and under. May–Sept daily 10am-5pm.

The Museum of Steam and Technology   This example of 19th-century public works architecture preserves two 14m-high (45-ft.), 64-metric-ton (70-ton) steam engines, which pumped the first clean water to the city over 140 years ago. One engine operates as a demonstration every day. The only surviving facility of its time in North America, the museum is a National Historic Site and a Civil and Power Engineering Landmark. The museum offers various permanent and changing exhibits, as well as a wide range of special family-oriented events.

900 Woodward Ave., Hamilton. © **905/546-4797.** steammuseum@hamilton.ca. Admission C$6.50 adults, C$5 seniors and students 13-17, C$4.50 children 6-12, children 5 and under free. July 1 to Labour Day daily 11am-4pm; Labour Day to June 30 Tues-Sun noon-4pm.

Royal Botanical Gardens ★★   The RBG is Canada's most famous gardens, with the largest lilac collection in the world. An exhilarating trip the RBG takes you through five gardens, a 30km (19-mile) trail system, and four nature sanctuaries. A cafe and two teahouses are on the grounds.

680 Plains Rd., Burlington. © **905/527-1158.** www.rbg.ca. Adult C$13; senior (65+) C$10; student/youth C$10; children 5-12 C$7.50, children 4 and under free; family (2 adults, 2 children 17 and under) C$34. Daily 10am-dusk.

Westfield Heritage Village ★ A restored 19th-century village, with over 30 buildings, including a schoolhouse and a blacksmith shop, this village brings history to life. It's quite common to see artists painting the old houses and shops. The buildings are all carefully restored and staffed with costumed interpreters, re-creating the spirit of early Canadian culture. Much of the village is handicapped accessible.

1049 Regional Rd. 552 (Kirkwall Rd.), Rockton. ⓒ **800/883-0104** or 519/621-8851. www. westfieldheritage.ca. Admission C$8.50 adults, C$6.50 seniors and students 13–17, C$5.50 children 6–12, children 5 and under free. Apr–Oct daily 12:30–4pm.

Whitehern ★★ Almost hidden gardens surround this home, which is part Georgian, part Edwardian, and part Victorian. The McQuesten family lived here from 1852 to 1968, and were instrumental in establishing the Royal Botanical Gardens McMaster University, and the Queen Elizabeth Way. In the 1930s, Misses Hilda and Mary McQuesten would hold a June tea for the Woman's Missionary Society. Whitehern has revived the affair with its own version, featuring music, lemonade, tea, and homemade ice cream, as part of its warm-weather program, "Picnic in the Park," which runs throughout the summer. Even without the tea, this is an inviting garden to visit. Lovingly restored to the design created in the early 1930s by landscape architect and founder of Sheridan Nurseries, Howard Dunnington-Grub, it is a green surprise in the center of the city. Costumed guides conduct tours.

41 Jackson St. W., Hamilton. ⓒ **905/546-2018.** www.whitehern.ca. Admission C$6.50 adults, C$5.50 seniors and students 13–17, C$4.50 children 6–12, children 5 and under free. July 1 to Labour Day daily 11am–4pm; Labour Day to June 30 Tues–Sun noon–4pm.

Shopping

One of the little-known pleasures of Hamilton is the shopping, from the great bargains of Ottawa Street to the art finds of James North. It's one of the enduring charms of the city, where each neighborhood has a distinctly different character, and each offers the intrepid shopper an exceptional experience. Even if you don't buy, the walk through these small, distinct neighborhoods will be worth it.

There is no place in the country like Hamilton's **Ottawa Street.** It is the textile bargain capital of Canada. The street is lined with stores that specialize in everything you need to sew clothing or make draperies or upholster furniture. There are stores that specialize in buttons and trims, and those that provide curtain rods and rings. You can find authentic Chanel wool gabardine by the yard and Versace silk for a fraction of their value. Restaurants like Café Limoncello and Logans echo the relaxed European flavors of the neighborhood and are a great place to recuperate from shopping with a cappuccino or a plate of pierogi. And now, with rents in other parts of the city inching ever upward, galleries and artists' studios are appearing. This is now the place to browse for antiques and art. Add to that an excellent and authentic Farmers' Market on Saturday mornings, and it's clear that Ottawa Street is a very cool place.

In the little shops on **Locke Street,** you can discover great bargains on antiques and collectibles, designer clothes, and specialty items for the kitchen. Everything from a carved Victorian settee to vintage clothing can be found here, at incredible prices. A transit gallery displays work from contemporary artists from the area and from across the country. The Beach Road Butcher Shop, also on Locke Street, is famous for its lean spicy kielbasa, and Christina, the proprietor's daughter, makes a thousand delicious cabbage rolls a week. The Earth to Table Bread Bar is the perfect stop for coffee and freshly baked bread.

The James Street North neighborhood bubbles with an artsy avant garde style. Here you can discover the works of tomorrow's noteworthy artists while they are still affordable. Galleries, art supply stores, and a history museum, as well as artists' studios and little cafes, make this a great place to spend an afternoon shopping.

Where to Eat

Ancaster Mill ★★★ REGIONAL   If you have drifted up to Ancaster to visit the Griffin House, be sure to stop at the Old Mill. It has one of the prettiest settings of any restaurant in town, and serves excellent fresh and local cuisine along with a view of the waterfall. The Sunday brunch here is famous and Chef Jeff Crump ensures that ingredients are fresh, local, and top quality.

548 Old Dundas Rd., Ancaster. ☏ **905/648-1827.** www.ancasteroldmill.com. Main courses C$22-C$40. Sun brunch, C$41 adults, C$20 children. AE, MC, V. Tues-Sat 11:30am-10pm; Sun 9:30am-2:30pm, and 5-9pm.

Café Limoncello ITALIAN   At this busy casual Italian restaurant, good solid Italian dishes are served. Bruschetta, pasta, veal parmigiana, and calamari are customer favorites.

226 Ottawa St., Hamilton. ☏ **905/549-3556.** www.cafelimoncello.com. Main courses C$14-$C20. AE, MC, V. Sun-Wed 9am-9pm, Thurs-Sat 9am-11pm.

The Earth to Table Bread Bar BAKERY/CAFE   An artisanal bread bar by day and a superb pizzeria by night, this comfortable cafe is an inviting place any time of day. Bettina Schormann, the wizard of bread and pastry, turns out magical loaves and irresistible sweets. The cafe serves wine and beer as well as fair-trade coffee. One of my favorite places in the city.

258 Locke St. S., Hamilton. ☏ **905/522-2999.** www.breadbar.ca. Pizzas C$11-C$14. AE, MC, V. Daily 8am-11:30pm.

Il Fiasco Café and Wine Bar ITALIAN   Picture this: In front of you is a chilled glass of sauvignon blanc and a plate of fresh crab cakes. Around you are blue walls with a lighthearted hand-painted mural. Just outside the large window, people are browsing through antiques shops, buying fresh bread in the little bakery, and sipping espresso in outdoor cafes. This could be a small Parisian street scene, or perhaps a street in a trendy Toronto neighborhood. But no. The restaurant is a tiny Italian-style gem, and is fast becoming the vibrant heart of bohemian cafe culture. It's a great place for lunch or dinner.

182 Locke St. S., Hamilton. ☏ **905/522-8549.** www.ilfiasco.ca. Main courses C$11-C$25. AE, MC, V. Tues-Wed 11:30am-3pm and 5-9pm; Thurs-Fri 11:30am-3pm and 5-10pm; Sat 11:30am-10pm; closed Sun-Mon.

Quatrefoile Restaurant REGIONAL/INTERNATIONAL   This restaurant is as beautiful to look at as it is delicious to dine in, with white leather chairs, silver accents, and fresh flowers. It was chosen as one of the 10 best restaurants in Canada by *EnRoute* magazine. Chef Fraser Macfarlane produces French classics with a modern and local accent, and the service is gently attentive without being intrusive. Definitely worth the drive to Dundas.

16 Sydenham St., Dundas, ON. ☏ **905/628-7800.** www.quatrefoilerestaurant.com. Main courses C$32-C$44. AE, MC ,V. Tues-Sat 12-3pm, 5pm-closing.

Williams Coffee Pub CAFE   This attractive coffee shop has a large patio with views of the harbor, good casual food, coffee, tea, and soft drinks, as well as free wireless Internet.

47 Discovery Dr., at the foot of James St. N., Hamilton. ☏ **905/522-5886.** Paninis and wraps C$6-C$7. AE, MC, V. Daily 8am-10pm.

NIAGARA-ON-THE-LAKE & NIAGARA FALLS

130km (81 miles) SE of Toronto

Never mind that Oscar Wilde called it "a bride's second great disappointment," the honeymoon capital of Niagara Falls is worth the 2-hour drive from Toronto just to witness the majesty of the falls themselves. The tacky shops, motels, attractions—it's an unabashed tourist trap—can either be ignored or enjoyed, depending on your sensibility. Then take a scenic drive about a half-hour back toward Toronto, along the **Niagara Parkway** (p. 225), to Niagara-on-the-Lake, a quiet and pretty 19th-century village that offers a welcome retreat after the carnival atmosphere of Niagara Falls. Many travelers prefer to stay at NOTL, where the food and wine offerings go well beyond the fast-food chains of the Falls and can be quite sophisticated for a tourist region. (You're now in the heart of Niagara wine country.) This is also home to the **Shaw Festival,** a theater event on par with Stratford's festival and another reason to visit, or even stay for a day or two.

Essentials

VISITOR INFORMATION The **Niagara-on-the-Lake Chamber of Commerce** (26 Queen St., Niagara-on-the-Lake; ✆ 905/468-1950; www.niagaraonthelake.com) provides information and can help you find accommodations. Open daily from 9am to 7:30pm from April through October, and from 10am to 5pm during the rest of the year.

For Niagara Falls travel information, contact **Niagara Falls Tourism** (5515 Stanley Ave., Niagara Falls; ✆ 800/56-FALLS [800/563-2557] or 519/356-6061; www.niagarafallstourism.com) or the **Niagara Parks Commission** (✆ 877/NIA-PARK [877/642-7275]; www.niagaraparks.com).

GETTING THERE Niagara-on-the-Lake is best seen by **car.** From Toronto, take the Queen Elizabeth Way (signs read QEW) to Niagara via the cities of Hamilton and St. Catharine's, and exit at Hwy. 55. The trip takes about 1½ hours.

Amtrak and **VIA** (✆ 416/366-8411) operate **trains** between Toronto and New York, but they stop only in Niagara Falls and St. Catharine's, not in Niagara-on-the-Lake. Call ✆ 800/361-1235 in Canada or **800/USA-RAIL** (800/872-7245) in the United States. From either place, you'll need to rent a car. Rental outlets in St. Catharine's include **Hertz** (350 Ontario St.; ✆ 905/682-8695). In Niagara Falls, **Avis** is at 5734 Valley Way (✆ 905/357-2847).

The Shaw Festival

Founded in 1962, the Shaw was known for many years for presenting the dramatic and comedic works of George Bernard Shaw and his contemporaries. However, since Jackie Maxwell became artistic director, the mandate has changed: the Shaw now features forgotten plays from Shaw's era (often penned by women writers), as well as classics and new works by Canadian playwrights. As impressive a destination for theater-goers as Stratford, it runs from April until the first weekend of November and plays in the historic **Court House Theatre,** the exquisite **Shaw Festival Theatre,** the **Royal George Theatre,** and the **Studio Theatre.** Recent performances have included *Born Yesterday, Star Chamber,* and Shaw's *In Good King Charles's Golden Days.*

Driving through Niagara-on-the-Lake by car is a delight, but many would argue that the region is best viewed by bicycle. VIA Rail offers the **Toronto-Niagara Greenbelt Express** for cyclists. These passenger trains have a bike cargo car, and you can hop aboard—for C$62 per person round trip—and get to Niagara Falls in less than 2 hours. From there, you can bike to your hotel (if you're a light traveler) or arrange for pick-up for an extra fee. Call ✆ 888/619-5984 or visit **www.bike train.ca** for more details.

Free chamber concerts take place at various locales Sunday at 11am. Chats introduce performances on Friday evenings in July and August, and question-and-answer sessions follow Tuesday-evening performances.

The Shaw announces its festival program in mid-January. Prices range from C$30 to C$110; there are some "special matinees" that offer tickets for C$40 seniors and C$25 students. For more information, contact the **Shaw Festival** (✆ **800/511-7429** or 905/468-2172; www.shawfest.com).

Exploring the Town

Niagara-on-the-Lake is small, and most of its attractions are along one main street, making it easy to explore on foot. In 1792, it briefly served as the capital of Upper Canada (though the town was then called Newark). The town was burned down during the War of 1812 but quickly rebuilt afterwards.

SIGHTS

Fort George National Historic Site ★ ☺   The fort played a central role in the War of 1812: It was headquarters for the British Army's Centre Division. The division comprised British regulars, local militia, Runchey's corps of former slaves, and aboriginal forces. The fort was destroyed by American artillery fire in May 1813. After the war, it was partially rebuilt, but it was abandoned in 1828 and not reconstructed until the 1930s. You can view the guardroom (with its hard plank beds), the officers' quarters, the enlisted men's quarters, and the sentry posts. The self-guided tour includes interpretive films. The fort is one of Ontario's favorite "haunted" sites (ghost-hunting tours are available throughout the summer and in October).

26 Queen St., Niagara Pkwy. ✆ **905/468-4257.** www.parkscanada.ca or www.friendsoffortgeorge.ca. C$12 adults, C$10 seniors, C$6 children 6-16, free for children 5 & under. Apr-Oct daily 10am-5pm; Nov-Mar Sat & Sun 10am-5pm.

Niagara Historical Society Museum   For history buffs, this museum has more than 8,000 artifacts pertaining to local history. The collection includes possessions of United Empire Loyalists who first settled the area at the end of the American Revolution. So, if branding irons, portraits, maps, and other artifacts are your thing, take a few hours to peruse the museum.

43 Castlereagh St. (at Davy St.). ✆ **905/468-3912.** C$5 adults, C$3 seniors, C$2 students (w/ID), C$1 children 5-12, free for children 4 & under. May-Oct daily 10am-5pm; Nov-Apr daily 1-5pm.

A SHOPPING STROLL

It's a pleasant pastime to stroll along the town's main artery, Queen Street, and check out some entertaining, albeit touristy, shops. The **Niagara Apothecary,** at no. 5

Niagara-on-the-Lake

Niagara River

Niagara Parkway

Lake Ontario

Melville St.

Ball St.

Delater St.

Ricardo St.

Wellington St.

Byron St.

Picton St.

Davy St.

Platoff St.

Castlereagh St.

Nelles St.

King St.

Regent St.

Victoria St.

Gate St.

Front St.

Prideaux St.

Queen St.

Johnson St.

Gage St.

Centre St.

Anne St.

John St.

Simcoe St.

Mississauga St.

William St.

Mary St.

Butler St.

Dorchester St.

Lake Ontario

Inset map
Lake Ontario
TORONTO
Niagara-on-the-Lake
USA
CANADA
Hamilton
Niagara Falls
20 mi
20 km

1/4 mi
0.25 km

10

SIDE TRIPS FROM TORONTO | Niagara-on-the-Lake & Niagara Falls

ATTRACTIONS & SHOPPING ●
Court House Theatre **12**
Shaw Festival Theatre **21**
Fort George National
Historic Site **22**
Greaves Jam **9**
Irish Design **7**
Maple Leaf Fudge **17**
Niagara Apothecary **18**
Niagara Historical
Society Museum **16**
The Owl & the Pussycat **13**
Royal George Theatre **4**
Scottish Loft **14**
Shaw Shop **6**
Studio Theatre **21**

RESTAURANTS ◆
Angel Inn **11**
Epicurean **5**
Niagara Home Bakery **8**
Shaw Café and Wine Bar **3**
Stagecoach Family Restaurant **10**

HOTELS ■
Harbour House **15**
Moffat Inn **20**
Oban Inn **1**
The Old Bank House **2**
Prince of Wales **19**

221

Ooh, Scary

For those who believe in ghosts, Fort George is one of Ontario's favorite "haunted" sites. Reported "sightings" include a soldier patrolling its perimeter and a young damsel who appears in an 18th-century mirror. Whether you're a believer or a skeptic, the Ghost Tours are fun for the family. They run evenings from May through September, with bonus dates around Halloween. The cost is C$12 adults and children 12 and up, and C$5 children 11 and under. Contact the **Friends of Fort George** at *℃* **905/468-6621**, or visit **www.friends offortgeorge.ca** for a schedule and for more details.

(*℃* **905/468-3845**), dates to 1866 and is a store and also a bit of a museum, with the original, gold-leaf and black-walnut counters, and glass and ceramic apothecary ware, on display. At no. 13 is the **Scottish Loft** (*℃* **905/468-0965**), which is filled with tartans, Celtic memorabilia, candy, books, and other assorted Scottish-themed notions. **Maple Leaf Fudge** (no. 14; *℃* **905/468-2211**) is a tooth-aching stop: You can watch as the aproned staff makes 20-plus flavors on marble slabs. At no. 16 is a charming toy store, the **Owl and the Pussycat** (*℃* **905/468-3081**). At no. 35 is **Greaves Jam** (*℃* **905/468-7331**), run by fourth-generation jam makers—truly good stuff. **Irish Design,** at no. 38 (*℃* **905/468-7233**), sells hand-knit sweaters, traditional gold and silver jewelry, and other treasures from the Emerald Isle. The **Shaw Shop** (*℃* **800/511-7429**), no. 79, next to the Royal George Theatre, carries GBS memorabilia and more. A Dansk outlet and several galleries selling contemporary Canadian and ethnic crafts round-out the mix.

JET-BOATING THRILLS

Jet-boat excursions leave from the dock across from 61 Melville St., at the King George III Inn. Don a rain suit, poncho, and life jacket, and climb aboard. The boat takes you out onto the Niagara River for a trip along the stonewalled canyon to the whirlpool downriver. The ride starts slow but gets into turbulent water. Trips, which operate from May to October, last an hour and cost C$57 adults and C$48 children 13 and under. Reservations are required, and if you make your booking online, you'll get a discount of C$5 per ticket. Call the **Whirlpool Jet Boat Company** at *℃* **888/438-4444** or 905/468-4800, or visit **www.whirlpooljet.com**.

Where to Stay

In summer, hotel space is in high demand. If you're having trouble nailing down a room, contact the **Niagara-on-the-Lake Chamber of Commerce** (*℃* **905/468-1950;** www.niagaraonthelake.com), which provides information about accommodations, from luxurious hotels to charming bed-and-breakfasts. B&Bs can also be located and booked via **www.bbcanada.com**. The prices listed below are for the peak summer season; deep discounts are available at all of these properties in early spring, late fall, and winter.

IN TOWN

Harbour House ★★★ Tucked away on a quiet street that's close to the marina, this hotel offers serenity and tranquillity from the moment you step through the front door. The focus is on comfort with understated luxury, from the Frette robes to the flickering fireplaces. The beds are particularly cozy, with king-sized mattresses topped by a layer of hypoallergenic duck feathers. (For those with allergies, alternative bedding is available.) Service is thoughtful and efficient, and guests are treated to lavish breakfasts and late afternoon wine-and-cheese receptions. The hotel is entirely nonsmoking.

85 Melville St., Niagara-on-the-Lake, ON L0S 1J0. www.harbourhousehotel.ca. ✆ **866/277-6677** or 905/468-4683. Fax 905/468-0366. 31 units. From C$299 double. Rates include breakfast. AE, DC, MC, V. Free parking. **Amenities:** Bike rental; concierge; room service. *In room:* A/C, TV/DVD player, CD player, hair dryer, minibar, Wi-Fi (free).

Moffat Inn 🗲 This is a fine budget-conscious choice in a convenient location. Most rooms have brass-framed beds, and eight have fireplaces. Guests tend to congregate on the patio, which is set in a beautiful flower garden. But if you have trouble climbing stairs, this hotel is not a good choice since most of the guest rooms are on the second floor, and there's no elevator and no porter to handle luggage.

60 Picton St. (at Queen St.), Niagara-on-the-Lake, ON L0S 1J0. www.moffatinn.com. ✆ **905/468-4116.** 24 units. From C$125 double. AE, MC, V. Free parking. **Amenities:** Restaurant. *In room:* A/C, TV, hair dryer, Wi-Fi (free).

Oban Inn ★ In a prime location overlooking the lake, the Oban Inn is a lovely place to stay. The town's first real country inn, it's in a charming, sizeable white Victorian house with a large veranda. The gorgeous gardens provide the fragrant bouquets throughout the house. A complete renovation updated the pretty rooms with modern amenities, including LCD plasma televisions, Bose sound systems, and individual temperature controls in all rooms. The spa is also a popular attraction.

160 Front St. (at Gate St.), Niagara-on-the-Lake, ON L0S 1J0. www.obaninn.ca. ✆ **866/359-6226** or 905/468-2165. 26 units. From C$260 double. AE, DC, DISC, MC, V. Free parking. **Amenities:** Restaurant; lounge; babysitting; bike rental; concierge; room service; spa. *In room:* A/C, TV, CD player, hair dryer, Internet ($10 per day).

The Old Bank House ★ Beautifully situated down by the river, this two-story Georgian was built in 1817 as the first branch of the Bank of Canada. In 1902, it hosted the Prince and Princess of Wales, and today, it's a charming bed-and-breakfast inn. Several tastefully decorated units have private entrances, and one also has a private trellised deck. If you're planning a romantic weekend away, you'll love the Rose Suite, with its cathedral ceiling and private balcony.

10 Front St., Niagara-on-the-Lake, ON L0S 1J0. www.oldbankhouse.com. ✆ **877/468-7136** or 905/468-7136. 9 units. From C$189 double. Rates include breakfast. AE, MC, V. Free parking. **Amenities:** Restaurant (in high season); Jacuzzi. *In room:* A/C, TV, Wi-Fi (free).

Prince of Wales ★★ This is one of Niagara-on-the-Lake's most luxurious hotels, and you could say it has it all: a central location across from the lovely gardens of Simcoe Park; recreational facilities, including an indoor pool; a full-service spa; lounges, bars, and restaurants; and conference facilities. If you're adverse to floral fabrics and overstuffed furniture, this is not the place for you. However, if you're looking to be seriously pampered in a faux-Victorian setting, it's a good bet. Also, it's one of the rare hotels in town with a wheelchair-accessible room. Pets are welcome. This is a smoke-free hotel.

6 Picton St., Niagara-on-the-Lake, ON L0S 1J0. www.vintage-hotels.com. ✆ **888/669-5566** or 905/468-3246. 110 units. From C$275 double. AE, DC, DISC, MC, V. Free parking. Small pets accepted ($35 per pet). **Amenities:** Dining room; cafe; bar; lounge; bike rental; concierge; health club; Jacuzzi; indoor pool; room service; spa. *In room:* A/C, TV, CD player, hair dryer, Wi-Fi ($10 per day).

ALONG THE WINE ROUTE

Inn on the Twenty and the Vintage House ★ Cave Spring Cellars, one of Niagara's best-known wineries, offers modern, well-equipped, and generous suites. Each one has an elegantly furnished living room with a fireplace and a Jacuzzi in the bathroom. Seven are duplexes—one of them, the deluxe loft, has two double beds on the second level—and five are single-level suites with high ceilings. All of the suites are nonsmoking. The inn's eatery, On the Twenty Restaurant & Wine Bar (below), is across the street and is a great place to dine. The inn's spa offers a full range of services for men and women, and has special packages for couples. Next door is the **Vintage House,** an 1840 Georgian mansion with three suites, all with private entrances. All rooms are nonsmoking.

3845 Main St., Jordan, ON L0R 1S0. www.innonthetwenty.com. © **800/701-8074** or 905/562-5336. 30 units. From C$259 suite. MC, V. Free parking. From QEW, take the Jordan Rd. exit S; at the 1st intersection, turn right onto 4th Ave., then right onto Main St. **Amenities:** Restaurant; concierge; nearby golf course; health club; spa. *In room:* A/C, TV, hair dryer, Internet (free).

Where to Eat

IN TOWN

The stylish **Shaw Cafe and Wine Bar** (92 Queen St.; © **905/468-4772**) serves lunch and light meals, and has a patio. The **Epicurean** (84 Queen St.; © **905/468-3408**) offers hearty soups, quiches, sandwiches, and other fine dishes in a sunny, Provence-inspired dining room. Service is cafeteria style. Half a block off Queen Street, the **Angel Inn** (224 Regent St.; © **905/468-3411**) is a delightfully authentic English pub. For an inexpensive down-home breakfast, go to the **Stagecoach Family Restaurant** (45 Queen St.; © **905/468-3133**). It also serves basic family fare, such as burgers, fries, and meatloaf, but it doesn't accept credit cards. **Niagara Home Bakery** (66 Queen St.; © **905/468-3431**) is the place to stop for sweet treats like chocolate-date squares and pastries, and savories such as individual quiches.

ALONG THE WINE ROAD

Hillebrand Estates Winery Restaurant ★ CANADIAN/CONTINENTAL This dining room is light and airy, and its floor-to-ceiling windows offer sweeping views over the vineyards to the distant Niagara Escarpment and more intimate peeks into wine cellars that bulge with oak barrels. The seasonal menus feature such dishes as poached Arctic char with shellfish ragout; or prosciutto-wrapped pheasant breast atop linguine tossed with mushrooms, roasted eggplant, and shallot. The starters are equally luxurious. In case the food isn't enticing enough (and it should be), the restaurant also hosts special events throughout the year, many featuring jazz musicians.

1249 Niagara Stone Rd., btw. Niagara-on-the-Lake & Virgil. © **905/468-7123**. www.hillebrand.com. Reservations strongly recommended. Main courses C$36–C$40. AE, MC, V. Daily spring–fall noon–11pm (closes earlier in winter).

On the Twenty Restaurant & Wine Bar ★ CANADIAN This warm and friendly restaurant is a favorite among foodies for good service and a small but well-chosen selection of Ontario wines (with a few international additions)—but mostly for the cuisine that features ingredients from many local producers. There's the added advantage that the food is created with wine pairings in mind; especially rich desserts

touring NIAGARA-ON-THE-LAKE WINERIES

Visiting a local winery is one of the most delicious ways to pass an hour or two in this region. You'll also see some of the best in new and innovative wine design, architecture, and viticulture. As with any major wine region, there are the big, commercial enterprises and the small, artisan ones. Lately, celebrities have joined the club (here, as elsewhere), so you can try wines with names such as Mike Weir, Wayne Gretzky, or Dan Aykroyd; mostly for the novelty, not the nose. Look for the VQA label: It identifies wines made with locally grown grapes. For maps of the area and information about vintners, contact the **Wine Council of Ontario** (✆ **905/684-8070;** www.wines ofontario.org). The wineries listed below are close to the town of Niagara-on-the-Lake. Tours are free. Prices for tastings vary with the winery and the wine you're sampling, but are usually about C$10.

If you turn off Hwy. 55 and go down York Road, you'll reach **Château des Charmes,** west of the town of St. David's (✆ **905/262-4219;** www.chateaudes charmes.com). The winery was built to resemble a French manor house, and its architecture is unique in the region. One-hour tours are given daily. It's open from 10am to 6pm year-round.

To reach **Stratus** (2059 Niagara Stone Rd.; ✆ **905/468-1806;** www. konzelmann.ca), one of the region's more cutting-edge wineries with a focus on sustainable practices and eco-design, take Niagara Stone Road out of Niagara-on-the-Lake. This vintner is famous for its award-winning blends. Reservations are not required for tastings, but if you're traveling in a group of six or more, it's best to call in advance. Tours of the modern winery are by appointment only.

are made to enjoy with ice wines and late-harvest wines. On the Twenty Restaurant is associated with **Inn on the Twenty** (p. 224), across the street.

At Cave Spring Cellars, 3836 Main St., Jordan. ✆ **905/562-7313.** www.innonthetwenty.com. Reservations recommended. Main courses C$22–C$35. MC, V. Daily 11:30am–3pm & 5–10pm.

The Restaurant at Vineland Estates ★★★ CANADIAN/CONTINENTAL Situated in a renovated 1845 farmhouse with a sprawling patio that offers beautiful views, this restaurant serves some of the most innovative food along the wine trail. Start with a plate of mussels in a ginger broth. Follow with Canadian Angus tenderloin with a risotto of truffles and morel mushrooms; or pan-seared sweetbreads with a celeriac and potato mash, and comfit of mushrooms glazed with ice wine. For dessert, try the tasting plate of Canadian farm cheeses, including Abbey St. Benoit blue Ermite; sweet-tooths can indulge in the maple-walnut cheesecake in a biscotti crust.

3620 Moyer Rd., Vineland. ✆ **888/846-3526** or 905/562-7088. www.vineland.com. Reservations strongly recommended. Main courses C$32–C$38. AE, MC, V. Daily noon–2:30pm & 5–9pm.

Along the Niagara Parkway ★★

The Niagara Parkway, on the Canadian side of the falls, is a lovely, scenic drive. Unlike the American side, there is plenty of natural beauty, including vast tracks of parkland. You can drive along the 56km (35-mile) parkway all the way from Niagara-on-the-Lake to Niagara Falls, taking in attractions en route. Here are the major ones, listed in the order in which you'll encounter them:

- **The White Water Walk** (4330 River Rd.; ℂ **905/374-1221**): The boardwalk runs beside the raging white waters of the Great Gorge Rapids. Stroll along and wonder at your leisure how it must feel to challenge this mighty torrent, where the river rushes through the narrow channel at an average speed of 35kmph (22 mph). Admission is C$8.75 adults, C$5.15 children 6 to 12, free for children 5 and under. Open daily from 9am to 5pm (closes at 7 or 8pm from mid-May till Labour Day).
- **The Whirlpool Aero Car** (ℂ **905/354-5711**): This red-and-yellow cable-car contraption whisks you on a 1,097m (3,599-ft.) jaunt between two points on the Canadian side of the falls. High above the Niagara Whirlpool, you'll enjoy excellent views of the surrounding landscape. Admission is C$12 adults, C$6.80 children 6 to 12, free for kids 5 and under. Open daily May to the third Sunday in October. Hours are from 10am to 5pm (closes at 7 or 8pm from mid-May till Labour Day).
- **The Niagara Parks Botanical Gardens and School of Horticulture** (ℂ **905/356-8119**): Stop here for a free view of the vast gardens and a look at the 12m-diameter (39-ft.) **Floral Clock,** made up of 25,000 plants. The gorgeous **Butterfly Conservatory** is also in the gardens. In this lush tropical setting, more than 2,000 butterflies (50 international species) float and flutter among such nectar-producing flowers as lantanas and *pentas.* The large, bright-blue, luminescent Morpho butterflies from Central and South America are particularly gorgeous. Interpretive programs and other presentations take place in the auditorium and two smaller theaters. The native butterfly garden outside attracts the more common swallowtails, fritillaries, and painted ladies. Visitors are encouraged to wear brightly colored clothing to attract the butterflies. Admission is C$12 adults, C$6.80 children 6 to 12, free for children 5 and under. Open daily September to June 9am to 5pm, July and August 9am to 7pm.
- **Queenston Heights Park:** This is the site of a famous War of 1812 battle, and you can take a walking tour of the battlefield. Picnic or play tennis in the shaded arbor before moving to the **Laura Secord Homestead** (Partition St., Queenston; ℂ **905/262-4851**). This heroic woman threaded enemy lines to alert British authorities to a surprise attack by American soldiers during the War of 1812. Her home contains a fine collection of Upper Canada furniture from the period, plus artifacts recovered from an archaeological dig. Stop at the candy shop and ice-cream parlor. Tours run every half-hour. Admission is C$4.75 adults, C$3.65 children 6 to 12, free for children age 5 and under. It's open summer daily 11am to 5pm, fall to spring Wednesday to Sunday 11am to 5pm.
- **Fruit Farms and Wineries:** This is home to some of Canada's best stone fruit and other orchards, so you'll find peaches, apples, pears, nectarines, cherries, plums, and strawberries at **Kurtz Orchards** (ℂ **905/468-2937**) and elsewhere; you can tour the 32 hectares (79 acres) at Kurtz on a tractor-pulled tram. **Inniskillin Winery** (Line 3, Service Rd. 66; ℂ **905/468-3554** or 905/468-2187), the pioneering winery behind Canada's famous ice wine, is open June to October daily from 10am to 6pm, November through May Monday through Saturday from 10am to 5pm. The self-guided free tour has 20 stops that explain the winemaking process. A free guided tour, offered daily in summer and Saturdays only in winter, begins at 2:30pm.
- **Old Fort Erie** (350 Lakeshore Rd., Fort Erie; ℂ **905/871-0540**): It's a reconstruction of the fort that was seized by the Americans in July 1814, besieged later by the British, and finally blown up as the Americans retreated across the river to

Buffalo. Guards in period costume stand sentry duty, fire the cannons, and demonstrate drill and musket practice. Open from the first Saturday in May to mid-September daily from 10am to 5pm, and weekends only mid-September to Canadian Thanksgiving (U.S. Columbus Day). Admission is C$9.25 adults, C$5.15 children 6 to 12, free for children 5 and under.

Seeing Niagara Falls

You simply cannot come this far and not see the Falls, which are one of the seven *natural* wonders of the world. When you arrive, step up to the low railing that runs along the road and take in the spectacular view over Horseshoe Falls. Then consider climbing aboard the *Maid of the Mist* ★★ (5920 River Rd.; © **905/358-5781;** www.maidofthemist.com). The sturdy boat takes you right in to the basin—through the turbulent waters around the American Falls; past the Rock of Ages; and to the foot of the Horseshoe Falls, where 159 million L (42 million gal.) of water tumble over the 54m-high (177-ft.) cataract each minute. You'll get wet, and your glasses will mist—but that just adds to the thrill. Boats leave from the dock on the parkway just down from the Rainbow Bridge. Trips operate daily from mid-May to mid-October. Fares are C$15 adults, C$8.90 children 6 to 12, free for children 5 and under.

Go down under the falls using the elevator at the **Table Rock Centre,** which drops you 46m (151 ft.) through solid rock to the tunnels and viewing portals of the **Journey Behind the Falls** (© **905/354-1551**). You'll receive—and appreciate—a rain poncho. Admission is C$13 adults, C$7.50 children 6 to 12, free for children 5 and under. Another attraction at the Table Rock Centre (which has just completed a C$32-million renovation) is **Niagara's Fury.** Visitors "experience" the creation of the falls in a chamber that swirls visual images over a 360-degree screen. It's a sense-surround ride, complete with shaking ground underfoot, an enveloping blizzard, and a temperature drop in the room from 75° to 40°F degrees (24°–4°C) in 3 seconds. It's an intense experience, and not appropriate for young children. Fares are C$15 adults, C$9 children 6 to 12, free for children 5 and under. (*Warning:* The operators advise that Niagara's Fury may not be appropriate for children 6 and under, as they might find it too scary. Also, adults with a history of heart disease or back/neck injuries may want to pass on this attraction.) Open daily 9am to 9pm.

If you can't get enough of the falls, ride the external glass-fronted elevators 159m (522 ft.) to the top of the **Skylon Tower Observation Deck** (5200 Robinson St.; © **905/356-2651;** www.skylon.com). The observation deck is open from June to

The Honeymoon Capital of the World

Seeing Niagara Falls as it is today—in all of its loud, neon, tacky glory—you might wonder how anyone would have thought it a romantic destination for a honeymoon. But back in 1801, when the Falls was simply a natural wonder of the highest order, Aaron Burr's daughter, Theodosia, chose it as the perfect place for her honeymoon. Napoleon's brother Jerome Bonaparte followed in her footsteps with his bride a few years later, and then suddenly everybody thought Niagara Falls was *the* place for newlyweds. Well, not *everybody*. Oscar Wilde visited Niagara Falls in 1881 and then quipped: "Every American bride is taken there, and the sight of the stupendous waterfall must be one of the earliest if not the keenest disappointments in American married life."

A FAMILY adventure

Niagara Falls has plenty of family attractions. A popular choice is **Marineland ★** (7657 Portage Rd.; ℂ **905/356-9565;** www.marinelandcanada.com). Its multiple aquariums have a walrus mascot, dolphins, sea lions, and freshwater fish. Friendship Cove, a 17-million-L (4.5-million-gal.) breeding and observation tank, lets the little ones see killer whales up close.

Marineland also has rides, including a Tivoli wheel (a fancy Ferris wheel), Dragon Boat rides, and Dragon Mountain, a roller coaster that loops, double-loops, and spirals through 305m (1,001 ft.) of tunnels. Admission is C$40 adults and children 10 and over, C$33 children 5 to 9, free for children 4 and under. It's open daily mid-May to June and September to mid-October 10am to 5pm, July and August 9am to 6pm; it's closed mid-October through mid-May.

Another popular family attraction at the falls is Canada's first **Great Wolf Lodge** (3950 Victoria Ave.; ℂ **905/354-4888** or 800/605-9653). Part of an American chain of family resorts known for the quality of services, rooms, and activities, Great Wolf is probably best known for its massive indoor water park. But wait, there's more, including a four-story interactive tree-house water fort.

Labour Day daily from 8am to midnight; hours vary the rest of the year, so call ahead. Adults pay C$13, children 12 and under C$7.55. It's pricey for an elevator ride.

The Falls are equally dramatic in winter, when ice formations add a certain beauty to it all and the crowds of high summer are wonderfully absent.

WHERE TO STAY & DINE NEAR THE FALLS

Niagara Falls isn't Vegas—a good thing, for the most part—but it is showing signs of appreciating the demand for high-end hospitality. If you enjoy the bright lights—and the casino scene—of Niagara Falls after dark, one luxe hotel choice is the **Niagara Fallsview Casino Resort** (6380 Fallsview Blvd.; ℂ **888/325-5788;** www.falls viewcasinoresort.com), which opened in 2004. It has its own 18,580-sq.-m (199,993-sq.-ft.) casino, a performing-arts theater, a spa, and 10 dining spots. Another good hotel bet is the **Sheraton on the Falls** Hotel (5875 Falls Ave.; ℂ **888/234-8410** or 905/374-4445), which offers rooms with a truly gorgeous view of the Falls; many have balconies. There's also the **Skyline Inn** (5685 Falls Ave.; ℂ **800/263-7135** or 905/374-4444), which is right by Casino Niagara.

Restaurants here grill top steaks, steam expensive lobster, and plate overpriced pasta—much like other tourist destinations. More interesting are the delights that come with two new arrivals. First, beloved Toronto chef Jamie Kennedy (Gilead Café, see p. 74) has expanded to the 14th floor of the Sheraton with views of the Falls at **Jamie Kennedy on the Falls** (ℂ **905/374-4444**). Kennedy partners with revered wine columnist and Niagara-wine expert Tony Aspler to bring a new taste to town: local, seasonal fare. Next up is another Toronto chef, Massimo Capra (Mistura), who has also taken an interest in Niagara. **The Rainbow Room by Massimo Capra** at the Crowne Plaza Niagara Falls (ℂ **905/374-4447**) features fine Italian fare, also complemented by Aspler's viticulture selections. Other Niagara dining options include the **Pinnacle Restaurant** (6732 Fallsview Blvd.; ℂ **905/356-1501**), with a continental menu and a remarkable view from the top of the Konica Minolta Tower. **The Keg** (5950 Victoria Ave.; ℂ **905/353-4022**) is a steakhouse chain. Over at

Niagara Falls

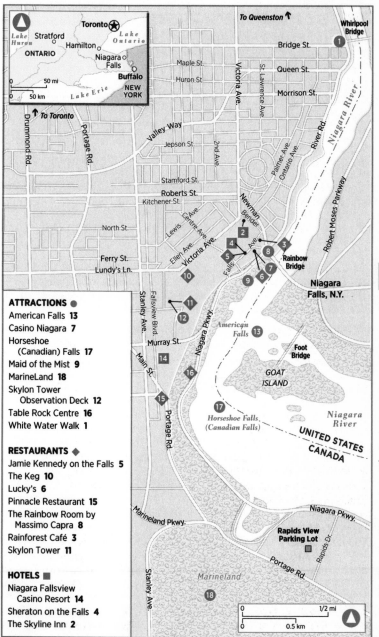

ATTRACTIONS ●

American Falls **13**
Casino Niagara **7**
Horseshoe
  (Canadian) Falls **17**
Maid of the Mist **9**
MarineLand **18**
Skylon Tower
  Observation Deck **12**
Table Rock Centre **16**
White Water Walk **1**

RESTAURANTS ◆

Jamie Kennedy on the Falls **5**
The Keg **10**
Lucky's **6**
Pinnacle Restaurant **15**
The Rainbow Room by
  Massimo Capra **8**
Rainforest Café **3**
Skylon Tower **11**

HOTELS ■

Niagara Fallview
  Casino Resort **14**
Sheraton on the Falls **4**
The Skyline Inn **2**

Casino Niagara, **Lucky's** (5705 Falls Ave.; ℂ **888/946-3255**) serves up hearty portions of prime rib, as well as burgers and pizza. The **Rainforest Café** (5875 Falls Ave.; ℂ **905/374-2233**) is a family favorite with its animatronic gorillas and serpents, and its tried-and-true menu of pizzas, burgers, and sandwiches. The **Skylon Tower** (ℂ **905/356-2651**) revolving restaurant is an old-timer at 236m (774 ft.) above the ground and overlooking the Falls, with menus featuring Caesar salads, filet mignon, lobster tails, and more fancy classics.

FROM COLLINGWOOD TO TOBERMORY

Nestled at the base of Blue Mountain, **Collingwood** is the town closest to Ontario's biggest skiing area. Collingwood first achieved prosperity as a Great Lakes port and shipbuilding town. Many mansions and the Victorian main street are reminders of the glory days. And just east of Blue Mountain sweep 14km (8¾ miles) of golden sands at **Wasaga Beach.**

North beyond Collingwood stretches the **Bruce Peninsula National Park,** known for its limestone cliffs, wetlands, and forest. From **Tobermory,** you can visit an underwater national park.

Essentials

GETTING THERE If you head west from Barrie, northwest from Toronto, you'll go along the west Georgian Bay coast from Collingwood up to the Bruce Peninsula. Driving from Toronto, take Highway 400 to Highway 26 West.

VISITOR INFORMATION For information, contact the **Georgian Triangle Tourist Association** (ℂ **888/227-8667** or 705/445-7722; www.visitsouthgeorgianbay.ca).

Blue Mountain Ski Trails, Slides, Rides & More

In winter, skiers flock to **Blue Mountain Resort,** at R.R. 3, Collingwood (ℂ **705/445-0231;** www.bluemountain.ca). Ontario's largest resort has 15 lifts, 98% snowmaking coverage on 36 trails, and three base lodges. In addition, there are three repair, rental, and ski shops, a ski school, and day care. Lift rates start at C$34 per day.

In summer, you can take advantage of the so-called "Green Season" attractions. These include tennis, golfing, and mountain biking; there's also a private beach on the shores of Georgian Bay that's a 10-minute ride by shuttle from the resort. Blue Mountain offers many programs for kids, ranging from tennis camp to weekend scavenger hunts on the beach.

A popular spot in Collingwood is the **Scenic Caves Nature Adventures** (260 Scenic Caves Rd., Collingwood; ℂ **705/446-0256;** www.sceniccaves.com). The area was carved out by glaciers during the Ice Age and today is a UNESCO World Biosphere Reserve. The caves are set into limestone cliffs and offer unique sights—including the "chilling" Ice Cave, a natural refrigerator that boasts icicles, even on the hottest days of summer.

Bruce Peninsula National Park

Bruce Peninsula National Park (P.O. Box 189, Tobermory; ℂ **519/596-2233** or 519/596-2263; www.pc.gc.ca) features limestone cliffs, abundant wetlands, quiet beaches, and forest sheltering many species of orchids, ferns, and several insectivorous plants. About 100 species of bird also inhabit the park. Three campgrounds (one trailer, two tent) offer 242 campsites (no electricity).

The **Bruce Trail** winds along the Georgian Bay Coastline, while Highway 6 cuts across the peninsula; both end in Tobermory. The Bruce Trail is one of Ontario's best-known trails, stretching 885km (550 miles) from Queenston in Niagara Falls to Tobermory. The most rugged part of the trail passes through the park along the Georgian Bay shoreline. **Cypress Lake trails,** from the north end of the Cyprus Lake campground, provide access to the Bruce Trail and lead to cliffs overlooking the bay. You can use canoes and manpowered craft on Cyprus Lake. The best swimming is at **Singing Sands Beach** and **Dorcas Bay,** both on Lake Huron on the west side of the peninsula. Winter activities include cross-country skiing, snowshoeing, and snowmobiling.

An Underwater National Park

From Tobermory, you can visit the underwater national park. The **Fathom Five National Marine Park** (P.O. Box 189, Tobermory; ℭ **519/596-2233;** www.pc.gc. ca) features a good 20 shipwrecks that lie in wait for divers who want to explore the 19-odd islands in the park. The most accessible is **Flowerpot Island,** which you can visit by tour boat to view the weird and wonderful rock pillar formations. Go for a few hours to hike and picnic. Six campsites are available on the island on a first-come, first-served basis. Boats leave from Tobermory harbor.

Where to Stay

Beild House Country Inn & Spa ★ *Beild* is the Scottish word for shelter, but this charming inn is anything but basic. The stately Edwardian house dates from 1909. The public rooms are warmed by two wood-burning fireplaces and decorated with folk art, quill boxes from Manitoulin, and sculptures. Guest rooms are individually furnished with elegant pieces (one contains a bed once owned by the duke and duchess of Windsor). The five third-floor rooms have canopied beds and fireplaces. The hotel offers a generous breakfast. There's also a fine five-course dinner, with such dishes as Georgian Bay trout on spinach with herbed beurre blanc, and pork tenderloin with grilled apples and a port wine glaze.

64 3rd St., Collingwood, ON L9Y 1K5. ℭ **888/322-3453** or 705/444-1522. Fax 705/444-2394. www. beildhouse.com. 11 units. From C$280 double. Rates include breakfast. AE, MC, V. **Amenities:** Restaurant; spa. *In room:* A/C.

Blue Mountain Resort ★ ☺ Stay here, right at the mountain base, and you can beat the winter lift lines. In summer, the resort offers access to a private beach, which is 10 minutes away by shuttle. The real reason to stay at Blue Mountain is the wealth of activities—it's impossible to be bored here. Guest rooms are on the smallish side and are simply furnished in a country style. You can also rent one- to three-bedroom condos, either slope-side or overlooking the fairway. This is an excellent choice for families—Blue Mountain has a great deal to offer kids.

R.R. 3, Collingwood, ON L9Y 3Z2. ℭ **705/445-0231.** www.bluemountain.ca. 95 units. From C$149 double; from C$179 suite. Special packages available. AE, MC, V. **Amenities:** Dining room; 2 lounges; mountain-bike rental; children's programs; fitness center; 18-hole golf course; outdoor & indoor pools; spa; 12 tennis courts; squash courts; kayak rental. *In room:* A/C, TV.

Where to Dine

Alphorn Restaurant ☺ SWISS Bratwurst, Wiener schnitzel, chicken Ticino, and cheese fondue are just some of the favorites served at this casual, Alpine-style restaurant. It's popular with families. Best to go early, as the place is crowded winter and summer. Save room for the Swiss crepes with chocolate and almonds.

Hwy. 26 W., Collingwood. (C) **705/445-8882.** Reservations not accepted. Main courses C$14–C$22. AE, MC, V. Year-round Mon–Fri 4–10pm, Sat & Sun 4–10:30pm; summer also daily 11:30am–3pm.

Spike & Spoon Bistro & Gallery ★ CONTINENTAL   This longtime favorite is under new management, and the few changes are an improvement. The Spike & Spoon's menu is shorter than it used to be, and an art gallery has been added to the second floor (a charming addition). The setting is still grand—the restaurant is in an elegant mid–19th-century redbrick house that once belonged to a Chicago millionaire—and seasonal dishes are prepared with fresh ingredients and garnished herbs grown out back in the restaurant garden.

637 Hurontario St. (C) **705/446-1629.** Reservations recommended. Main courses C$16–C$26. MC, V. Tues–Sat noon–2:30pm; Tues–Sun 6–10pm.

ALONG GEORGIAN BAY: MIDLAND & PARRY SOUND

Midland

Midland is the center for cruising through the thousands of beautifully scenic Georgian Islands, and **30,000 Island Cruises** (C) **705/549-7795;** www.georgianbaycruises.com) offers 3-hour cruises following the route of Brele, Champlain, and La Salle up through the inside passage to Georgian Bay. May to Canadian Thanksgiving (U.S. Columbus Day), boats usually leave the town dock twice a day. Fares are C$18 adults, C$16 seniors, C$8 children ages 5 to 14, and free for children 4 and under.

Midland lies 53km (33 miles) east of Barrie and 145km (90 miles) north of Toronto. If you're driving from Barrie, take Highway 400 to Highway 12 West to Midland.

EXPLORING THE AREA

See the box below for details on **Sainte-Marie Among the Hurons.** Across from the Martyrs' Shrine, the **Wye Marsh Wildlife Centre** (C) **705/526-7809;** www.wyemarsh.com) is a 60-hectare (148-acre) wetland/woodland site offering wildlife viewing, guided and self-guided walks, and canoe excursions in the marsh. A floating boardwalk cuts through the marsh, fields, and woods, where trumpeter swans have been reintroduced into the environment and now number 40 strong. Reservations are needed for the canoe trips (call the number above) offered in July and August and occasionally September. In winter, cross-country skiing and snowshoeing are available. For information, visit the website. Admission is C$11 adults; C$8.50 students, seniors, and children 6 to 12; and free for children 5 and under. The center is open daily 9am to 5pm, but is closed on December 25.

In town, **Freda's,** in an elegant home at 342 King St. ((C) **705/526-4851**), serves excellent Continental cuisine. Just down the street at 249 King St. is **Riv Bistro** ((C) **705/526-9432**), which offers Mediterranean cooking and plenty of seafood.

EN ROUTE TO THE MUSKOKA LAKES: ORILLIA

Traveling to the Muskoka Lakeland region, you'll probably pass through **Orillia** (from Barrie, take Hwy. 11). Here, you can visit Canadian author/humorist **Stephen**

THE tragic tale OF SAINTE-MARIE AMONG THE HURONS

Midland's history dates from 1639, when Jesuits established a fortified mission, **Sainte-Marie Among the Hurons,** to bring Christianity to the Huron tribe. However, the mission retreat lasted only a decade, for the Iroquois, jealous of the Huron-French trading relationship, stepped up their attacks in the area. By the late 1640s, the Iroquois had killed thousands of Hurons and several priests, and had destroyed two villages within 10km (6¼ miles) of Sainte-Marie. Ultimately, the Jesuits burned down their own mission and fled with the Hurons to Christian Island, about 32km (20 miles) away. But the winter of 1649 was harsh, and thousands of Hurons died. In the end, only a few Jesuits and 300 Hurons were able to make the journey back to the relative safety of Québec. The Jesuits' mission had ended in martyrdom and murder. It was 100 years before the Native Canadians in the region saw Europeans again, and those newcomers spoke a different language.

Today, local history is recaptured at the **mission** (✆ **705/526-7838**), 8km (5 miles) east of Midland on Highway 12 (follow the HURONIA HERITAGE signs). The

blacksmith stokes his forge, the carpenter squares a beam with a broadaxe, and the ringing church bell calls the missionaries to prayer, while a canoe enters the fortified water gate. A film depicts the life of the missionaries. Special programs given in July and August include candlelight tours and a 1½-hour canoeing trip (at extra cost). Admission is C$11 adults, C$9.75 seniors and students, C$8.50 children 6-12, and free for children 5 and under (all prices are slightly discounted in early May and in the fall after Labour Day). From April 30 to November 2, it's open daily 10am to 5pm.

Just east of Midland on Highway 12 rise the twin spires of the **Martyrs' Shrine** (✆ **705-526-3788**), a memorial to the eight North American martyr saints. As six were missionaries at Sainte-Marie, this imposing church was built on the hill overlooking the mission, and thousands make pilgrimages here each year. The bronzed outdoor stations of the cross were imported from France. Admission is C$3 adults, free for children 9 and under.

Leacock's summer home (50 Museum Dr.; ✆ 705/329-1908; www.leacockmuseum.com), a green-and-white mansard-roofed and turreted structure with a central balcony overlooking the beautiful lawns and garden sweeping down to the lake. The interior is filled with heavy Victorian furniture and mementos of this Canadian Mark Twain, author of 35 volumes of humor, including *Sunshine Sketches of a Little Town* (New Canadian Library), which caricatured many of the residents of Mariposa, a barely fictionalized version of Orillia. Admission is C$5 adults, C$4 seniors, C$3 students, and C$2 children ages 3 to 12. It's open weekdays from 9am to 5pm; closed on legal holidays.

GEORGIAN BAY ISLANDS NATIONAL PARK

The park consists of 59 islands in Georgian Bay and can be reached by water taxi from Honey Harbour, a town north of Midland right on the shore. (As you're taking Hwy. 400 north, branch off to the west at Port Severn to reach Honey Harbour.) Hiking, swimming, fishing, and boating are the name of the game in the park. In summer, and on weekends and holidays, the boaters really do take over—but it's a quiet retreat weekdays, late August, and off-season. The park's center is on the largest island, **Beausoleil,** with camping and other facilities. For more information, contact **Georgian Bay Islands National Park** (☏ **705/756-2415;** www.pc.gc.ca).

The Parry Sound Area

Only 225km (140 miles) north of Toronto and 161km (100 miles) south of Sudbury, the Parry Sound area is the place for active vacations. For details, contact the **Parry Sound Area Chamber of Commerce** (70 Church St.; ☏ **705/746-4213;** www.parrysoundchamber.ca), which is open daily from 10am to 4pm.

There's excellent canoeing and kayaking; if you need an outfitter, contact **White Squall Paddling Centre** (53 Carling Bay Rd., Nobel; ☏ **705/342-5324;** www.whitesquall.com), which offers both day trips and multiday excursions. Run by **30,000 Island Cruise Lines** (9 Bay St., Parry Sound; ☏ **705/549-3388;** www.georgianbaycruises.com), the *Island Queen* cruises through the 30,000 islands for 3 hours. It leaves the town dock once or twice a day; fares are C$18 adults, C$16 seniors, C$8 children ages 5 to 14, and free for children 4 and under.

And there are many winter diversions, as well—loads of cross-country ski trails and more than 1,000km (621 miles) of well-groomed snowmobiling trails. For details on cross-country skiing, contact the **Georgian Nordic Ski and Canoe Club** (☏ **888/866-4447** or 705/746-5067; www.georgiannordic.com), which permits day use of their ski trails.

Nature lovers will head for **Killbear Provincial Park** (☏ **705/342-5492,** or 705/342-5227 for reservations), farther north up Highway 69; it offers 1,600 hectares (3,954 acres) set in the middle of 30,000 islands. There are plenty of watersports—swimming at a 3km (1¾-mile) beach on Georgian Bay, snorkeling or diving off Harold Point, and fishing for lake trout, walleye, perch, pike, and bass. The climate is moderated by the bay, which explains why trillium, wild leek, and hepatica bloom. Among the more unusual fauna are the Blandings and Map turtles that inhabit the bogs, swamps, and marshes.

There are three **hiking trails,** including 3.5km (2.2-mile) Lookout Point, leading to a commanding view over Blind Bay to Parry Sound; and the Lighthouse Point Trail, crossing rocks and pebble beaches to the lighthouse at the peninsula's southern tip. There's also **camping** at 883 sites in seven campgrounds.

WHERE TO STAY

Since the recent closure of the stunning and long-established Inn at Manitou, the area is short on destination resorts. Still, this remains a great place to explore for the remarkable landscapes and abundant outdoor activities. For where to lay your head, there are a handful of small inns and B&Bs like the charming and clean **Little Lake Inn** (669 Yonge St., Midland; ✆ **888/297-6130**; www.littlelakeinn.com; C$119-C$169) and the newly refurbished and upscale **Glenn Burney Lodge** (49 Glenn Burney Rd., Seguin; ✆ **705/746-5943**; www.glennburneylodge.ca; C$129-C$199) that fully reopened in 2010. Alternatively, it's a safe bet to choose from one of the many chains that operate here, like the **Best Western** in Midland (924 King St.; ✆ **705/526-9307**; www.bestwestern.com; C$109-C$139) or the **Comfort Inn** in Parry Sound (120 Bowes St.; ✆ 705/746-6221; www.comfortinn. com; C$79-C$114). The **Microtel Inn** (292 Louisa St.; ✆ **705/746-2700**; www. microtelinn.com; C$89-C$119) in Parry Sound is popular for its affordability, good service, and basic comforts.

THE MUSKOKA LAKES

Just a 90-minute drive north of Toronto, the Muskoka region has been a magnet for visitors since the 19th century. Though the area proved futile for farming (it's located on the Canadian Shield, where you need dig only a foot or two in some places to come up against sheets of granite), the 1,600 lakes, pretty terrain, and laid-back attitude combine to make it an excellent place for a retreat. In the past decade, Muskoka's charms have expanded to include excellent golf courses, soothing spas, great burger joints, and some fine dining. The region is most popular in summer, when families congregate lakeside and Hollywood celebrities such as Goldie Hawn and Tom Hanks lounge at their "cottages." But autumn can be stunning for color peepers and winter good for cold-climate sports.

Once accessible only by water, Muskoka remains a boater's dream. The region also has several towns of note: Gravenhurst, Bracebridge, Port Carling, Huntsville, and Bala. It's well worth devoting a day or two to explore the area, the quaint towns, and most of all, the dazzling waterways. This is not the Great White North, but a fashionable cottage country that, particularly in summer and on holidays, is busy with crowds. If you're looking for wide open wilderness, you have to travel further north to Algonquin Park or to some of the more remote stretches of Georgian Bay.

Essentials

GETTING THERE You can drive from the south via Hwy. 400 to Hwy. 11, from the east via hwys. 12 and 169 to Hwy. 11, and from the north via Hwy. 11. It's about 160km (99 miles) from Toronto to Gravenhurst, 15km (9¼ miles) from Gravenhurst to Bracebridge, 25km (16 miles) from Bracebridge to Port Carling, and 34km (21 miles) from Bracebridge to Huntsville. **VIA Rail** (✆ **416/366-8411;** www.viarail. ca) services Gravenhurst, Bracebridge, and Huntsville from Toronto's Union Station. An airport about 18km (11 miles) from Gravenhurst is used mainly for small aircraft. Several other landing strips and a helicopter landing pad are at the Deerhurst Resort in Huntsville.

VISITOR INFORMATION For information on the region, contact **Muskoka Tourism** (✆ **800/267-9700** or 705/689-0660; www.discovermuskoka.ca).

GETTING AROUND While you won't need a car if you plan to stay close to your resort while you're here (an entirely reasonable proposition), you will need a car if you're planning to do a lot of sightseeing in the area. You could take the train to Bracebridge and then rent a car at **Budget** (1 Robert Dollar Dr.; ✆ **705/645-2755**).

Huntsville has an **Enterprise** car rental center at 197 Main St. W. (✆ **705/789-1834**).

Exploring the Towns

Gravenhurst and Huntsville are scenic, and they also have enough shops, restaurants, parks, and public squares to make them worth a visit. Unless you have kids and plan to visit Santa's Village (see below), there's not much of a reason to linger in Bracebridge.

GRAVENHURST

Gravenhurst is Muskoka's first town—the first you reach if you're driving from Toronto and the first to achieve town status.

Sailing is one of Muskoka's greatest summer pastimes. Gravenhurst is home to the Muskoka Fleet, which includes a lovingly restored coal-powered 1887 steamship, the **RMS** *Segwun.* There are many options for cruising, such as a 1-hour tour; a 2½-hour lunch cruise; and a 4-hour late-afternoon tour of **Millionaire's Row,** where the real estate is as dazzling as the natural beauty. Reservations are required for all tours; call ✆ **866/687-6667** or 705/687-6667, or visit **www.realmuskoka.com** for more information. Tour prices start at C$18 adults, C$11 children 12 and under.

Year-round, there are theater performances at the **Gravenhurst Opera House** (✆ **705/687-5550**), which celebrated its 109th anniversary in 2010. In summer, there are shows at the **Port Carling Community Hall** (✆ **705/765-5221**).

BRACEBRIDGE: SANTA'S WORKSHOP

Halfway between the equator and the North Pole, **Bracebridge** bills itself as Santa's summer home, and **Santa's Village** (✆ **705/645-2512**; www.santasvillage.ca) is a fantasyland full of kiddie delights: pedal boats and bumper boats on the lagoon, a roller-coaster sleigh ride, a Candy Cane Express, a carousel, and a Ferris wheel. Mid-June through Labour Day, it's open daily from 10am to 6pm. Admission is C$27 children 5 and over, C$22 seniors and children 2 to 4, and free for children under 2.

HUNTSVILLE

Starting in the late 1800s, lumber was the name of the game in Huntsville, which today is Muskoka's biggest town. You can see some of the region's early history at the **Muskoka Heritage Place,** which includes **Muskoka Pioneer Village** (88 Brunel Rd., Huntsville; ✆ **705/789-7576**; www.muskokaheritageplace.org). It's open from mid-May to mid-October daily from 11am to 4pm. Admission is C$10 adults, C$7 children 3 to 12, free for children 2 and under. Muskoka Heritage Place also features the **Portage Flyer Steam Train.** Once part of the world's smallest commercial railway (running from 1904–58), it's been reborn as a tourist attraction and reopened in 2010 after a thorough renovation.

Robinson's General Store on Main Street in Dorset (✆ **705/766-2415**) is so popular, it was voted Canada's best country store. Wood stoves, dry goods, hardware, pine goods, and moccasins—you name it, it's here.

Where to Stay

Muskoka is famous for its lakes, and also for its resorts. Bed-and-breakfast and country-inn choices also abound. Contact **Muskoka Tourism** (✆ **800/267-9700** or 705/689-0660; www.discovermuskoka.ca). The prices listed below are for the peak summer season; deep discounts are available in early spring, late fall, and winter.

The Muskoka Lakes Region

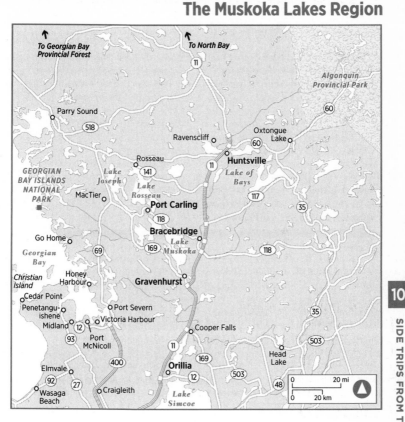

To Georgian Bay
Provincial Forest

To North Bay

11

Algonquin
Provincial Park

60

Parry Sound
518

Ravenscliff

Oxtongue
60 Lake

GEORGIAN
BAY ISLANDS
NATIONAL
PARK

Rosseau
141

Huntsville

11

Lake of
Bays

Lake
Joseph

Lake
Rosseau

117

35

MacTier

Port Carling
118

Bracebridge

Georgian
Bay

Go Home

69

169

Lake
Muskoka

118

Christian
Island

Honey
Harbour

Gravenhurst

Cedar Point

Penetangu-
ishene
Midland 12

Port Severn
Victoria Harbour

35

Cooper Falls

503

93

Port
McNicoll

11
169

Head
Lake

Elmvale
92

400

Orillia

27

12

503

48

Craigleith

Wasaga
Beach

Lake
Simcoe

0   20 mi
0   20 km

RESORTS

Deerhurst Resort ★★★ ☺   The Deerhurst is a perfect spot for a family vacation. This stunning resort complex rambles over 320 hectares (791 acres) and offers everything from two 18-hole golf courses (part of the Muskoka Golf Trail) to a golf academy; a full-service Aveda spa; endless nature trails for hiking (or snowmobiling or cross-country skiing in winter); canoeing, kayaking, and all manner of watersports; an ambitious musical revue that runs all summer; and horseback riding. The accommodations here are spread out among several buildings on the property and range from high-ceilinged hotel rooms in the Terrace and Bayshore buildings to fully appointed one-, two-, or three-bedroom suites, many with fireplaces and/or whirlpools.

1235 Deerhurst Dr., Huntsville, ON P1H 2E8. www.deerhurstresort.com. ✆ **800/461-4393** or 705/789-6411. Fax 705/789-2431. 388 units. From C$197 double. AE, DC, DISC, MC, V. Free parking. Take Canal Rd. off Hwy. 60 to Deerhurst Rd. **Amenities:** 2 restaurants; 2 bars; children's programs; concierge; 2 18-hole golf courses; indoor sports complex; 11 Jacuzzis; 5 pools (2 indoor, 3 outdoor); room service; sauna; spa; tennis courts. *In room:* A/C, TV, hair dryer, Internet (free), minibar.

Delta Grandview Resort ★ ☺   This small resort retains the natural beauty and contours of the original farmstead while providing the latest resort facilities. Eighty

THE ROCKY ROAD FOR golfers

Muskoka attracts golfers by the droves. Many of the region's resorts offer pro-designed courses, created by the likes of Nick Faldo, Mike Weir, and Mark O'Meara. The greens here truly are different. Muskoka is located on the **Canadian Shield,** a bedrock layer just a few feet below the surface, that makes an excellent setting for golfers. The landscape is rugged with natural rock outcroppings. Not only does the locale make for a stunning landscape, it heightens the challenge.

The Muskoka Tourism website (**www.discovermuskoka.ca**) has information about great local golf courses. Another good resource is **www.teeingitup.com/ontario**. You'll also find information on resort websites: **Taboo** (below) has a course that's considered one of the best in Canada; the **Delta Grandview** (p. 237) has the first course designed by Mark O'Meara; and Deerhurst (p. 237) has two 18-hole courses, including the famous **Deerhurst Highlands.** Another big draw is the **Rock** (www.therockgolf.com), a course designed by Nick Faldo on the shores of Lake Rosseau.

accommodations are traditional hotel-style rooms, but most units are suites in a series of buildings, some down by the lake and others up on the hill with a lake view. The main dining room, the Rosewood Inn, is located in one of the resort's original buildings and overlooks Fairy Lake. In the summer, snacks are served at the Dockside Restaurant right on the shores of the lake, and the free Kidzone program provides supervision—and plenty of fun—for kids 4 to 12 from 8am to 4pm.

939 Hwy. 60, Grandview Drive, Huntsville, ON P1H 1Z4. www.deltahotels.com. (C) **888/472-6388** or 705/789-4417. 123 units. From C$230 double. AE, DC, DISC, MC, V. Free parking. **Amenities:** 2 restaurants; babysitting; children's programs; 2 golf courses (18-hole & 9-hole); health club; indoor & outdoor pools; 3 tennis courts. *In room:* A/C, TV, Internet ($12 per day).

Taboo Resort ★★★ ☺ Near Gravenhurst in the southern Muskoka region, Taboo stands out for sleek sophistication in a leafy setting. Known until May 2003 as Muskoka Sands, the resort's new name may suggest a hedonistic adults-only retreat. The truth is anything but: Taboo is a family-friendly zone, with a kids' club that schedules activities every day during the high season in summer. And the fact that the resort is so willing to take care of the children means that many adults can soak up spa treatments or dine at one of the on-site restaurants without a second thought. One of my favorite things here is that every room, large and small alike, has its own deck or balcony. While all of the sophisticated offerings at the resort are excellent, nothing beats taking in the utterly serene setting it enjoys. The hotel is entirely nonsmoking.

1209 Muskoka Beach Rd., Gravenhurst, ON P1P 1R1. www.tabooresort.com. (C) **800/461-0236** or 705/687-2233. 157 units. From C$229 double. AE, DC, MC, V. Free parking. **Amenities:** 2 restaurants; bar; children's programs; concierge; 2 golf courses (18-hole & 9-hole); health club; Jacuzzi; 4 pools (3 outdoor, 1 indoor); room service; sauna; spa; 5 tennis courts. *In room:* A/C, TV, fridge, hair dryer, Wi-Fi (free).

Windermere House Resort ★ This traditional lakeside resort was destroyed by fire in 1996 but was rebuilt according to the original 1870s design. Well-manicured lawns sweep down to the lovely Lake Rosseau, while a broad veranda furnished with Adirondack chairs sets the leisurely mood. You can take in the water sports or just kick back with a book and a beverage. Renovations added modern conveniences (including air-conditioning) while retaining old-fashioned charm. Most of the rooms have gorgeous views (the best ones overlook the lake), and a few have balconies or decks. This is a smoke-free hotel and seasonal, open from May through October only.

2508 Windermere Rd., off Muskoka Rte. 4 (P.O. Box 68), Windermere, ON P0B 1P0. www.windermere house.com. © **888/946-3376** or 705/769-3611. Fax 705/769-2168. 70 units. From C$220 double. Rates include breakfast. Weekly rates also available. AE, MC, V. Free parking. **Amenities:** Restaurant; lounge; children's programs; golf course; outdoor pool; room service; tennis courts. In room: A/C, TV, Internet (free), minibar.

A COUNTRY INN

Inn at the Falls ★ 🏨 This attractive "inn" is actually a group of seven Victorian houses on a quiet cul-de-sac overlooking Bracebridge Falls and the Muskoka River. Inviting floral gardens surround an outdoor heated pool, patios, and lawns for relaxing. Some units have fireplaces, Jacuzzis, and balconies; others have views of the Falls. The Fox & Hounds is a popular local gathering place. In winter, the fire crackles and snaps; in summer, the terrace is filled with umbrella-shaded tables. The more elegant Carriage Room serves upscale continental fare. Quite the perfect get-away-from-it-all spot, and easy on the budget, too. This is a smoke-free hotel.

1 Dominion St. (P.O. Box 1139), Bracebridge, ON P1L 1V3. www.innatthefalls.net. © **877/645-9212** or 705/645-2245. 39 units. From C$155 double. Rates include breakfast. Additional adult C$16. AE, DC, MC, V. Free parking. **Amenities:** 2 restaurants; nearby golf course; outdoor pool; Wi-Fi (free). In room: TV.

Where to Eat

EXPENSIVE

Eclipse ★★ CANADIAN/INTERNATIONAL The spacious dining room with a soaring ceiling of Douglas fir beams offers an expansive view over hills and lakes. The lengthy dinner menu has plenty of vegetarian options and fare for carnivores, too. A favorite appetizer is the baked phyllo pastry filled with forest mushrooms and goat cheese. The Sizzle—the signature dish—is tiger shrimp sautéed in garlic, dried chilies, and white wine, and baked under mozzarella. Filling stuff. Entrees include breast of pheasant filled with wild rice and cranberries, and a rack of lamb rubbed with fresh herbs and served with an apple-maple compote. The wine list, with 300-plus selections, offers plenty of pairings.

1235 Deerhurst Dr. (at the Deerhurst Resort), Huntsville, ON P1H 2E8. © **705/789-6411.** www.deerhurst resort.com. Reservations recommended. Main courses C$24–C$45. AE, DC, MC, V. Daily 5–11pm.

3 Guys and a Stove ★★ ☺ INTERNATIONAL This is a family restaurant with a special menu for kids. But don't let the unpretentious atmosphere and the casual name fool you—the cooking is *very* fine. The curried pumpkin-and-sweet potato soup is an absolute must when it's on the menu; the spicy chicken stew is another winner. This restaurant is also a terrific choice for vegetarians: The list of pasta and rice main-course dishes is substantial.

143 Hwy. 60, Huntsville. © **705/789-1815.** www.3guysandastove.com. Main courses C$20–C$38. AE, MC, V. Daily 11am–9:30pm.

MODERATE

Blondie's ★ 🏨 COMFORT FOOD/DELI/SEAFOOD This family-run restaurant is a rare find in Muskoka: a mix of the area's typical comfort foods—fish and chips, prime rib, eggs Benedict, smoked-meat sandwiches—plus more exotic fare, such as sushi. Blondie's is also the official caterer to the Gravenhurst Opera House.

The setting is like a country kitchen, with round wooden tables and cheery decorations, and the service is just as warm.

151 Brock St., Gravenhurst. ℭ **705/687-7756.** Reservations recommended for dinner. Main courses C$12–C$21. MC, V. Mon & Tues 9:30am–3pm; Wed–Sat 9:30am–8pm.

ALGONQUIN PARK

Algonquin Park is one of Canada's largest provincial parks with more than 2,000 lakes. Established as a wildlife sanctuary in 1893, it's famous for its natural beauty. It's familiar beyond its borders for the landscape's profound influence on the Group of Seven artists who came here to find inspiration; they recorded their impressions in timeless works of art that hang in galleries the world over, especially in the AGO in Toronto. (There's also an unsolved mystery known to fans of the famous troupe of pioneering painters: Tom Thomson drowned in these waters as a young man. Foul play is widely considered since he was an expert canoeist.)

The interior of Algonquin Park can be accessed by foot or by canoe. There are three backpacking trails in the park covering more than 140km (87 miles) of ground. Canoe route variations are almost infinite; routes extend for 2,100km (1,305 miles) in a network that crisscrosses the whole of the park. Go for 1 night or 10, or take a season, if you can.

Call it a cliché if you must, but paddling a canoe here is truly one of the most entrancing things to experience. There is an embracing calm and relaxation that come with being far-removed from any bustle; imagine silence at sunset broken only by the splash of a fish jumping on a still lake.

The park is open year-round, and you're free to make the trip as invigorating as you like: Experience the pure exhilaration from hiking the network of trails, paddle whitewater canoes, or simply dive from one of the many rugged cliffs into bracing, clear lakes. But deciding the right time and place to go can be the difference between remembering beautiful sun-dappled days on the water . . . or fleeing storms of hungry black flies. As the old Boy Scouts motto goes: Be prepared.

Camping Gear Checklist

Small first-aid kit, including gauze pads and antiseptic

Tent with waterproof fly

Sleeping bag (a thick one in autumn)

Therm-a-Rest or foam mattress

Groundsheet and extra tarp (for a dinner area, to cover your pack in the canoe, and to use as a makeshift sail if you're feeling really lazy)

Extra garbage bags and zip-lock bags for waterproofing

Hiking shoes and water shoes or sandals

Rain gear

Sun hat and sun block

Lightweight stove and fuel

Cooking utensils (pots, bowls, cups, cutlery, scouring pad)

Toilet paper (and zip-lock bags to pack out your used paper)

Biodegradable hand soap and dish detergent

Toiletries (toothbrush, toothpaste, etc.)

Insect repellent

10m (33-ft.) nylon rope for food hanging and clothesline

Matches in waterproof container

Pocket flashlight and pocket knife

Water bottle(s) and iodine tablets or water-purification system

Backpack (for hikers, backpacks should have an internal or external aluminum frame and waist belt to help distribute the weight)

ALGONQUIN'S best PICKS

- **Best Picnic Spots: Tea Lake Dam Picnic Ground** is located 8km (5 miles) from the west gate on the Oxtongue River. This quiet, sheltered picnic area has stone barbecue pits and views of the river below. Post-lunch swimming is also an option.

- **Best Place to Swim:** Although located right off the highway at Km 34, **Lake of Two Rivers Picnic Ground** has one of the largest beaches in the park and gets plenty of sun during the day.

- **Best Day Hikes:** The short **Barron Canyon Trail** (1.5km; .9 mile) skirts the steepest section of the spectacular Barron Canyon, and it's the definitive way to view the 100m (328-ft.) canyon walls from above.

- **Best Day Canoe Routes: Costello Creek,** located off gigantic Opeongo Lake, offers a meditative paddle at the south end of the lake and is easily accessed from the Parkway Corridor. Great for animal-spotting, too.

- **Best Historic Spot: The Logging Museum,** a fascinating walk through Algonquin Park's logging history, has a dozen or so relics from that bygone era arranged along an easy 1.3km (.8-mile) trail. A small theater plays thematic archival film footage.

- **Best Park Activity for Kids:** Kids love the naturalist-led evenings at the **East Beach Outdoor Theatre.** The free hour-and-a-half program starts just after sundown and consists of a short film, a slide show, and an audience discussion.

Essentials

VISITOR INFORMATION There's an excellent Visitor Centre on Hwy. 60 (② **705/633-5572;** www.algonquinpark.on.ca), at Km 0.0, that features exhibits about the park's history, a bookstore, a restaurant, and a gallery of Algonquin art. Also on offer are staff-led expeditions to hear the timber wolves howling at night.

GETTING THERE The southern border of Algonquin Park is about 300km (186 miles) north of Toronto, about 2½ hours by car. To get there, take Hwy. 400 north to Barrie, then take Hwy. 11 north to Huntsville, and finally travel east along Hwy. 60 to the west gate of the park. Hwy. 60, the park's only major highway (open year-round and also known as the Parkway Corridor), runs through the south end of park. The east gate is located just west of the town of Whitney, Ontario. The west gate is located just east of the town of Dwight, Ontario. There are many other access points to the park that run off Hwy. 17 to the north of the park. Other access points run off Hwy. 11 to the west, and still others off Hwy. 60 to the east.

    Ontario Northland Rail and Coach (② **705/472-4500** or 800/363-7512 ext. 0; www.ontarionorthland.ca) services Gravenhurst, Bracebridge, and Huntsville from Toronto's Union Station. **Muskoka Airport** (② **705/687-2194**), about 18km (11 miles) from Gravenhurst, is used mainly for small aircraft. Several landing strips and a helicopter landing pad are also available at the Deerhurst Resort in Huntsville (see above).

GETTING AROUND The park spans 7,725 square kilometers (2,983 square miles) of land, so planning is essential. To get an overview of your options, get a copy of *Canoe Routes of Algonquin Park* – you can order it online at www.ontarioparks.com/english/algo-canoeing.html or at the park visitor centre, order it ahead, or download it online. You can choose to go it alone or use an outfitter to set up your route and itinerary. All canoe trips depart from one of the 29 numbered access point offices, and all hiking trips depart from one of four trail heads. Before you head into the wilds, you must register with a park warden and pick up your interior camping permits *at least 3 hours before sunset*. Averaging 4 to 6 hours of paddling per day, you can expect to cover 15km to 25km (9¼ miles–16 miles), including portages.

What to See & Do

Among the most popular hiking trails is the 2.4km (1.5-mile) self-guided trail to the 100m-deep (328-ft.) Barron Canyon on the park's east side. People looking for an extended backpacking trip should try the Highland Trail, which extends from Pewee Lake to Head, Harness, and Mosquito lakes for a round-trip of 35km (22 miles). For a more ambitious route, the Western Uplands Hiking Trail combines three loops for a total of 169km (105 miles), beginning at the Oxtongue River Picnic Grounds on Hwy. 60. It will take upwards of 2 weeks to hike, by which time, you'll be something of an expert on the pleasures of this pristine park.

Overnight camping trips—especially long ones in a canoe—are serious business and should be undertaken only with someone experienced in tow. You have to be totally self-sufficient, with all your food and equipment on your back or in your canoe.

Interior sites can be booked up to 5 months in advance by calling **Ontario Parks** toll-free between 7am and 11pm (© **888/668-7275,** or © **519/826-5290** for outside Canada and the U.S.) or by booking through the website at www.ontario parks.com. Reservations can be made using Visa, MasterCard, check, or money order. Fees are roughly C$40, but may vary by site.

Before you call Ontario Parks to make your reservation, you must first know your exact route, and that means you need a copy of your map in front of you. Remember, the people who work at the reservation service are not trip counselors; if you have any questions about your prospective route, then call the Algonquin Park Information Office (© **705/633-5572**) before making your reservation. The staff there will be happy to review individual trips and make helpful suggestions.

Where to Stay & Eat

If you're not interested in camping, these two lodges are the park's top offerings. The restaurants are open to non-guests with advance reservations.

Arowhon Pines ★★★ This high-end resort is in a class by itself. It features an impressive dining room with a wraparound porch looking out onto Little Joe Lake. The grounds are heavily wooded and located so far from the highway that moose and other wildlife make regular appearances next to the comfortable cabins. Rooms are simple yet tasteful and comfortable. Shared cabins include en suite bathrooms and shared lounges, while private cabins offer their own decks and fireplaces. The grandeur of the great outdoors is reproduced in the Arowhon dining experience: Dramatic dining room, high ceilings, dark lake, and excellent food (think: chilled fruit soup, summer trout or roast venison, ample and excellent desserts, and local cheeses).

Algonquin Park, P.O. Box 10001, Ontario P1H 2G5. www.arowhonpines.ca. © **705/633-5661** in summer, 416/483-4393 or 866/633-5661 in winter. 50 bedrooms in 13 cabins. From C$400 double. Rates include 3 meals daily. DC, MC, V. **Amenities:** Restaurant; sauna; tennis courts; canoes; kayaks. *In-room:* Hairdryer.

Bartlett Lodge ★★★ Beautiful log cabins and artists' studios, a commitment to sustainable tourism, and a great dining room, to boot. This resort, a collection of just 12 cabins and 2 studios, plus a main lodge with lounge and restaurant, is a bit of paradise in the park. What's more, it's on an island; to reach it, you have to take a boat from a landing on Cache Lake. It also has nearly a century of history, opening in 1917, just 24 years after the park opened. One of the cabins is off-grid: solar-powered with a wood stove for heat. Other cabins range from cozy one-bedrooms to luxurious three-bedroom accommodations. The food is made to match, a rotating selection of gourmet specialties always cooked to perfection, such as delicious grilled salmon or duck confit. The Lodge also offers tent platform rentals.

Algonquin Park, P.O. Box 10004, Huntsville, ON P1H 2G8. ✆ **705/633-5543** or 866/614-5355. www. bartlettlodge.com. 12 cabins & 2 studios. From C$310 double. Rates include 3 meals daily. DC, MC, V. **Amenities:** Restaurant; canoes; kayaks. *In room:* Fridge.

PRINCE EDWARD COUNTY

75km (47 miles) SW of Toronto

Culinary tourism is on the rise everywhere, and Ontario is definitely in on the game. Traveling to eat has turned Prince Edward County (PEC), a once-remote island on Lake Ontario a couple of hours' drive east of Toronto, into a very hot spot.

The United Empire Loyalists moved into the area known as "the County", originally settled by Mohawk Indians, and soon turned it into a wealthy region rich in barley. As demand for beer grew across North America, so did the County's barleybaron mansions. Today, a handful of these beauties have been transformed into luxury inns. For most of the past century, PEC was a quiet, sometimes poor, agricultural area with just one small town, the struggling Picton. It still has one main town, but now Picton is thriving. And a number of smaller towns and villages, such as Bloomfield, Wellington, Milford, and Waupoos, have distinguished themselves with food-related attractions such as a craft brewery, a stellar ice-cream shop, or a unique cheese dairy.

A couple of decades ago, a back-to-the-land movement started attracting painters, artisans, glass blowers, and organic-minded farmers. Aspiring vintners came next, then chefs, bakers, even gourmet hot-dog makers. Now, the place is a hot culinary spot, especially for Torontonians. Given the pristine sand dunes, inland lakes, the Sandbanks Provincial Park, and a mysterious lake that sits perched 62m (203 ft.) up above Lake Ontario, the County is worth a day or two to take in the sights and senses. Keep in mind that this area is best explored during warm months, from spring through fall. A number of shops, galleries, and restaurants close, or seriously cut back hours, during the winter months.

Essentials

VISITOR INFORMATION **Prince Edward County Chamber of Tourism & Commerce** is at 116 Main St., Picton (✆ **800/640-4717;** or 613/476-2421; www. pecchamber.com). It has a wealth of information about what to see and do, as well as where to dine and sleep. Hours change with the seasons, but it's generally open 9am to 5pm, with some added hours in summer and through autumn.

To help you choose from the range of culinary vacations, visit the **Savour Ontario** website (www.savourontario.ca; the site is a bit obtuse—start by clicking "Find a Restaurant," and you're on your way). There's also the **Ontario Culinary Tourism Alliance** website (www.ontarioculinary.com); although the organization serves the trade, the site has a lot of useful information for tourists.

🎁 sipping SPOTS

Barley Days Brewery With a nod to the County's barley-rich past, this craft brewery is an entirely modern enterprise. Stop by for a taste and a tour.

13730 Loyalist Parkway, Picton. ℭ **613/476-7468**. www.barleydaysbrewery.com.

Norman Hardie Wines This small estate makes excellent wines from grapes grown in the area and in Niagara. The acclaimed results are putting the County on the wine map. Stop by for a tasting: There are a handful of vintages to choose from and always someone on hand to guide you through the experience. A little taste of Burgundy in Ontario.

1152 Greer Rd., Wellington. ℭ **613/399-5297**.

GETTING THERE Prince Edward County is easy to reach by car. From Toronto, take Hwy. 401 east to exit 525 (before Trenton), then take Hwy. 33 to Picton. The drive takes about 2½ hours.

What to See & Do

The County is best explored by car, although it's also a great place to bike once you've arrived. You can visit wineries and restaurants on cycling tours or map your own itinerary. In fact, most of the tours in the region, from art to wine, are self-directed. It's in keeping with the region's independent, off-the-beaten-path character.

Arts Trail The County is a busy community of artists, in addition to food and wine pros, and this initiative equips visitors with the information and routes they need to discover more than 30 artists, artisans, and galleries. You can expect to find beautiful paintings, sculpture, contemporary photography, pottery, blown glass, handcrafted jewelry, and more. There are eight galleries that represent multiple artists, as well; the Oeno is particularly cutting edge. Like most things in the County, this is a seasonal program; the 2011 kick-off was spring and ran through autumn.

ℭ **866/845-664**. www.artstrail.ca.

Lake on the Mountain It's a small, sometimes turquoise-hued lake perched 62m (203 ft.) above the great Lake Ontario and a local legend because its source remains a mystery to this day. Surrounded by a pretty park, a popular pub, some lovely country homes, and a small inn, the lake offers a grand view across the Bay of Quinte. Bring a picnic lunch and watch the ferries below as they cross the 1km (½-mile) channel to the mainland. It's a great place to bid farewell to the County before hopping aboard the car ferry below at Glenora.

C.R. 7 (off Hwy. 33, near Glenora). (ℭ **613/476-2421**). www.ontarioparks.com/english/lakem.html. Daily vehicle permit C$10–$18. Daily 9:30am–dusk. From Hwy. 401, take Hwy. 49 S to Picton.

Sandbanks National Park ★ It's a short drive to this spectacular provincial park that includes the West Lake formation, claimed to be the largest freshwater bay-mouth sand-dune system in the world. In other words: It's an amazing beach. The water is shallow, the sand clean, and the dunes—many between 12m (39 ft.) and 25m (82 ft.) high—provide a bit of topography that's good for hiking and also for sheltered picnic areas on blistering days. In fact, this camping ground and natural water-park features plenty of picnic areas and day-use programs like campfires and other activities. So, you can come for the day or stay overnight—but the latter only if you've planned well ahead since these campground sites are booked months in advance.

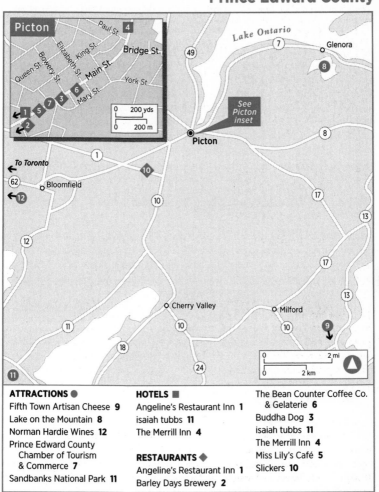

ATTRACTIONS ●

Fifth Town Artisan Cheese **9**
Lake on the Mountain **8**
Norman Hardie Wines **12**
Prince Edward County
  Chamber of Tourism
  & Commerce **7**
Sandbanks National Park **11**

HOTELS ■

Angeline's Restaurant Inn **1**
isaiah tubbs **11**
The Merrill Inn **4**

RESTAURANTS ◆

Angeline's Restaurant Inn **1**
Barley Days Brewery **2**

The Bean Counter Coffee Co.
  & Gelaterie **6**
Buddha Dog **3**
isaiah tubbs **11**
The Merrill Inn **4**
Miss Lily's Café **5**
Slickers **10**

R.R. 1, Picton. ☎ **613/393-3319.** www.ontarioparks.com/english/sand.html. Daily vehicle permit C$10–$18. Daily 9:30am–dusk.

Taste Trail If you're interested in exploring wineries, cafes, restaurants, breweries, and more, this self-guided route through the County has a lot to offer. There's a free booklet that lists 31 participating businesses, as well as route maps and brief listings on each destination. Once on the road, you'll find there are signs identifying the Taste Trail, too. Along the way, there are plenty of tastings and tours to consider. Take your time; this is slow food—anything but fast.

☎ **866/845-6644.** www.tastetrail.ca.

Where to Stay

There are many good options for staying a night or two, from homey B&Bs to lakeside self-catering cottages to very pretty inns. The County's inns are some of the best choices if you're looking for good dining and lodging all in one locale.

Angéline's Restaurant Inn ★★★ ☺ The heart of this modest but pretty property is the original Victorian house, where the dining room serves up local ingredients with sophisticated flare under the guidance of chef Sebastien Schwab. There are three dining areas, including the Victorian Room for small private parties. The cozy rooms are mostly situated in a separate building; a new suite has been added to the main house. There are gardens and public rooms for all to enjoy, too. Angéline's is known also for its workshops, which range from on-site pottery classes to well-being seminars (think: feng shui and numerology).

433 Main St. (Hwy. 33), Bloomfield, ON K0K 1G0. www.angelinesrestaurantinn.com. ✆ **877/391-3301.** or 613/393-3301. 10 units. C$80–C$135 double. AE, DC, DISC, MC, V. Free parking. Take Hwy. 401 E to exit 522; proceed S on Wooler Rd. to Hwy. 33 S (Loyalist Pkwy.), turn left on C.R. 1 (Prince Edward Rd. 1), then turn right on Hwy. 62 S & drive directly to Bloomfield. **Amenities:** Restaurant; cafe. *In room:* TV, DVD player, Wi-Fi (free).

isaiah tubbs This is the biggest resort around these parts, with acres of gardens and woodlands very close to Sandbanks Park. The rooms range from simple ones in the restored 1820s home to more spacious suites in outlying lodges; best of all are the Beach House Suites, which give you a taste of the exceptional location. The food is pretty standard but better than many family-style resorts.

1642 County Rd. 12, Picton. www.isaiahtubbs.com. ✆ **800/724-2393.** 88 units. From C$169 double. AE, DC, MC, V. Take Hwy. 401 E to exit 522 (Wooler Rd.), then go S on Wooler Rd. to Hwy. 33; turn right onto Hwy. 33, turn right at County Rd. 32 in Bloomfield, then turn right onto County Rd. 12 & follow it for approximately 9km (5½ miles). **Amenities:** 2 restaurants; bar; fitness center; heated pool (seasonal); sauna; tennis courts. *In room:* A/C, TV, fridge, hair dryer, Wi-Fi (free).

Merrill Inn ★ Simply one of the nicest inns in the area, the Merrill has a great location in the center of Picton. Housed in an impressive Victorian manse, the rooms are elegant yet comfortable, and attention to detail is evident throughout, from the good linens to tasteful antique decorations and pretty bathrooms. The food is another top draw, whether you're staying the night or not. The stellar dining room led by chef Michael Sullivan (who has a passion for local and fresh ingredients) is a leader in regional cuisine. There's also a good wine bar and a sunny patio. In between hot breakfasts with homemade breads, a picnic lunch, and a three-course a la carte dinner, there's time for one of the Merrill's 1-hour walking tours of Picton. Choose

More Cheese, Please

Fifth Town Artisan Cheese (4309 County Rd. 8, Picton; ✆ 613/476-5755; www.fifthtown.ca) is the world's first LEED-certified dairy, meaning it has outstanding eco-practices. It's worth a visit and tour just to see the process, which includes recycling clean water for the property's wetlands, and to check out the ultra-modern building design. All very new. More importantly, the cheeses are works of art—and definitely good enough to eat. They also offer wine and cheese tastings from June to September. Call ahead to check on hours and tours.

between the "Graveyards and Gallows" tour or the less grim option of the town's historic architecture. Either way, a good way to get a little exercise in between meals.

343 Main St., Picton. www.merrillinn.com. ✆ **866/567-5969** or 613/476-7451. 13 units. From C$179 double. Rates include breakfast. AE, MC, V. Free parking. **Amenities:** Restaurant; wine bar; spa. *In room:* A/C, TV, Wi-Fi (free).

Where to Eat

Food is a major attraction here, so unless you stay and stay, there are more places to feast than your belt can comfortably accommodate. Road trips around the region will lead you to discoveries like a beautiful little winery, or you can opt for staying in Picton, where you can choose from the many cafes, restaurants, pubs, and specialty shops. For a more complete list of what's on offer, visit http://prince-edward-county.com.

The Bean Counter Coffee Co. & Gelaterie LIGHT FARE/ICE CREAM One

of the many good choices on Picton's main street, this open and airy cafe serves fair-trade coffee, homemade cakes, light lunch fare, and more than 20 flavors of ice cream made in-house. A perfect spot for refueling after a day on the dunes.

172 Main St., Unit 101, Picton. ✆ **613/476-1718.** www.beancountercafe.com. Sandwiches from C$5. AE, DC, MC, V. Mon–Fri 8am–9pm; Sat & Sun 9am–9pm.

Buddha Dog LIGHT FARE Healthy hot dogs: The concept might be hard to

swallow, but in fact, these tasty little dogs—more like sausages, really—are made using local, small-scale farm goods. Since starting out in the County, the owners have also opened shops in Toronto. Expect to eat at least two. There are a number of excellent sauces to pile on, too.

172 Main St., Picton. ✆ **613/476-3814.** www.buddhafoodha.com. Hot dogs from C$2.50. AE, DC, MC V. Mon–Fri 11am–4pm; Sat & Sun 11am–5pm.

Miss Lily's Café CAFE Situated in Books & Company, the charming Picton book-

store on the town's main strip, this is a local hang-out and a great place to relax over a cup of coffee, light breakfast, or lunch.

289 Main St., Picton. ✆ **613/476-9289.** Main courses from C$5.50. AE, MC, V. Mon–Fri 7am–9pm; Sat 8am–9pm; Sun 9am–5pm.

Slickers ICE CREAM The County is known for a healthy sense of pride in local

foods, and even the ice-cream shops are in on the trend. This small spot with a pretty patio in Bloomfield serves up an eclectic collection of flavors, each one inspired by what's in season. Flavors include rhubarb ginger, local cantaloupe, apple pie, and even a maple walnut made with local syrup. They're all delicious. Open in summer only.

271 Main St., Bloomfield. No phone. www.slickersicecream.com. Single scoop from C$3. No credit cards. Daily 11am–9pm.

10

SIDE TRIPS FROM TORONTO

Prince Edward County

PLANNING YOUR TRIP TO TORONTO

Toronto is an easy place to go for a spur-of-the-moment visit. Still, whether you're traveling on a whim or charting your course months in advance, some planning will help you make the most of your trip. This chapter will help you prepare.

GETTING THERE

By Plane

Pearson International Airport (YYZ) is the busiest airport in Canada, and its terminals are massive (particularly Terminal 1). Almost all flights into Toronto arrive here. Expect a long walk to the Immigration and Customs area, which you will have to clear in Toronto, even if you're flying on to another Canadian destination. (There are maps of both terminals online at www.gtaa.com.) There are tourism information booths at both terminals.

Canada's only national airline, **Air Canada** (© 888/247-2262; www.aircanada.ca), operates direct flights to Toronto from most major American cities and many smaller ones. It also flies from major cities around the world and operates connecting flights from other U.S. cities. It is based in Pearson's Terminal 1. **WestJet** (© 888/937-8538; www.westjet.com), based in Calgary, has become an increasingly popular choice for anyone coming to Toronto from the United States, as well as some locations in the Caribbean and Mexico.

Upstart **Porter Airlines** (© 888/619-8622 or 416/619-8622; www.flyporter.com) has gained a great reputation for service and flies to **Toronto City Centre Airport** from four U.S. locations—Newark, Chicago, Boston, and Myrtle Beach—as well as a rapidly increasing number of Canadian cities, including Halifax, Montréal, Québec City, St. John's, and Ottawa. Porter, along with a handful of commuter flight services, is the only airline that flies to the Toronto City Centre Airport, which is located on the western side of the Toronto Islands.

To find out which airlines travel to Toronto, see "Airline Websites," p. 263.

GETTING INTO TOWN FROM THE AIRPORT

To get from the airport to downtown, take Hwy. 427 south to the Gardiner Expressway East. A **taxi** costs about C$50 if you're going downtown (it's higher if you're heading to north or east Toronto).

The convenient **Airport Express bus** (© **905/564-6333;** www.torontoairport express.com) travels between the airport, the bus terminal, and major downtown hotels—the Westin Harbour Castle, Fairmont Royal York, Sheraton Centre Toronto, and Delta Chelsea—every 20 to 30 minutes, from 4:55am to 12:55am. The fare is C$20 one-way, C$33 round-trip.

The cheapest way to go is by **bus and subway,** which takes about an hour. During the day, you have three options: the no. 192 "Airport Rocket" bus to Kipling station, the no. 58A bus to Lawrence West station, or the no. 307 bus to Eglinton West station. In the middle of the night, you can take the no. 300A bus to Yonge and Bloor streets. The fare of C$2.75 includes free transfer to the subway (which is available till 1:30am). All buses make stops at both airport terminals 1 and 3. It doesn't matter which bus you use; they all take roughly the same amount of time. (The Airport Rocket reaches the subway fastest, but the subway ride to downtown is twice as long as from the other stations.) For more information, call the **Toronto Transit Commission,** or TTC (© **416/393-4636;** www3.ttc.ca).

By Car

Crossing the border between Canada and the U.S. by car gives you a lot of options—the U.S. highway system leads directly into Canada at 13 points. If you're driving from Michigan, you'll enter at Detroit-Windsor (I-75 and the Ambassador Bridge) or Port Huron–Sarnia (I-94 and the Bluewater Bridge). If you're coming from New York, you have more options. On I-190, you can enter at Buffalo–Fort Erie; Niagara Falls, New York–Niagara Falls, Ontario; or Niagara Falls, New York–Lewiston. On I-81, you'll cross the Canadian border at Hill Island; on Rte. 37, you'll enter at either Ogdensburg-Johnstown or Rooseveltown-Cornwall.

From the United States, you are most likely to enter Toronto from the west on Hwy. 401 or Hwy. 2 and the Queen Elizabeth Way. If you come from the east, via Montréal, you'll also use hwys. 401 and 2.

Here are approximate driving distances to Toronto: from Boston, 911km (566 miles); Buffalo, 155km (96 miles); Chicago, 859km (534 miles); Cincinnati, 806km (501 miles); Detroit, 379km (235 miles); Minneapolis, 1,564km (972 miles); Montréal, 545km (339 miles); New York, 797km (495 miles); Ottawa, 453km (281 miles); and Québec City, 790km (491 miles).

Be sure you have your driver's license and car registration if you plan to drive your own vehicle into Canada. It isn't a bad idea to carry proof of automobile liability insurance, too.

If you are a member of the American Automobile Association (AAA), the **Canadian Automobile Association (CAA),** Central Ontario Branch, in Toronto (© **416/221-4300;** www.caa.ca), provides emergency road service.

I don't recommend driving in Toronto, but if you're planning to make side trips outside of the city, you may wish to rent a car in Toronto or at Pearson International Airport. If you pay with credit card, you might get automatic coverage (check with your credit card issuer before you go). Be sure to read the fine print of the rental agreement—some companies add conditions that will boost your bill if you don't fulfill certain obligations, such as filling the gas tank before returning the car.

By Train

Amtrak's (☎ **800/USA-RAIL** [800/872-7245]; www.amtrak.com) "Maple Leaf" service links New York City and Toronto via Albany, Buffalo, and Niagara Falls. It departs daily from Penn Station. The journey takes 12½ hours. Note that the lengthy schedule allows for extended stops at Customs and Immigration checkpoints at the border. VIA Rail Canada (☎ **888/VIA-RAIL** [888/842-7245]; www.viarail.ca) is the nation's top rail line and offers many routes and generally pleasant service. Trains arrive in Toronto at Union Station on Front Street, 1 block west of Yonge Street, opposite the Fairmont Royal York Hotel (see p. 54). The station has direct access to the subway.

By Bus

Greyhound (☎ **800/231-2222;** www.greyhound.com) is the best-known bus company that crosses the U.S. border. You can travel from almost anywhere in the United States and Canada. You'll arrive at the Metro Coach Terminal downtown at 610 Bay St., near the corner of Dundas Street. Another option is **Coach Canada** (www.coachcanada.com), which travels from many places in the United States, as well as from Québec, to Ontario.

The bus may be faster and cheaper than the train, and its routes may be more flexible if you want to stop along the way. Bear in mind that it's more cramped, toilet facilities are meager, and meals are taken at fast-food rest stops.

Depending on where you are coming from, check into Greyhound's special unlimited-travel passes and discount fares. It's hard to provide sample fares because bus companies, like airlines, are adopting yield-management strategies, causing prices to change from day to day.

GETTING AROUND

By Public Transportation

The **Toronto Transit Commission,** or TTC (☎ **416/393-4636** for 24-hr. information, recordings available in 18 languages; www3.ttc.ca), operates the subway, bus, streetcar, and light rapid transit (LRT) system.

Fares, including transfers to buses or streetcars, are C$3 or 5 tickets or tokens for C$12.50 for adults. Seniors and students ages 13 to 19 with valid ID pay C$2, or 10 tickets for C$17; children 12 and under pay C$0.75, or 10 tickets for C$5.50. You can buy a special day pass for C$10 that's good for unlimited travel for one adult on weekdays and for up to two adults and four children on weekends.

For surface transportation, you need a token, a ticket (for seniors or kids), or exact change. You can buy tokens and tickets at subway entrances and at authorized stores that display the sign TTC TICKETS MAY BE PURCHASED HERE. Bus drivers do not sell tickets, nor will they make change. Always obtain a free transfer where you board the train or bus, in case you need it. In the subways, use the push-button machine just inside the entrance. On streetcars and buses, ask the driver for a transfer.

THE SUBWAY The TTC faced some serious public-relations issues in 2010, including a drunken bus driver, but it nonetheless remains fast (especially compared with snarled surface traffic), clean, and very simple to use. There are two major lines—Bloor-Danforth and Yonge-University-Spadina—and one smaller line, Sheppard, in the northern part of the city. The Bloor Street east-west line runs from

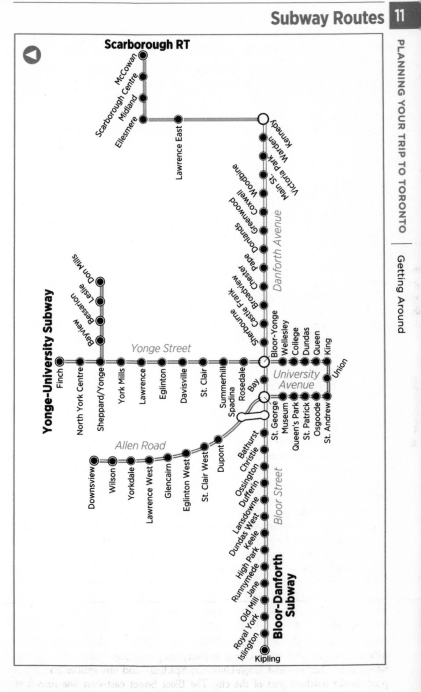

Scarborough RT

McCowan
Scarborough Centre
Midland
Ellesmere
Lawrence East
Kennedy
Warden
Victoria Park
Main St.
Woodbine
Coxwell
Greenwood
Donlands
Pape
Chester
Broadview
Castle Frank
Sherbourne

Danforth Avenue

Yonge-University Subway

Don Mills
Leslie
Bessarion
Bayview

Yonge Street

Finch
North York Centre
Sheppard/Yonge
York Mills
Lawrence
Eglinton
Davisville
St. Clair
Summerhill
Spadina
Rosedale
Bay
Bloor-Yonge
Wellesley
College
Dundas
Queen
King
Union

University Avenue

St. George
Museum
Queen's Park
St. Patrick
Osgoode
St. Andrew

Allen Road

Downsview
Wilson
Yorkdale
Lawrence West
Glencairn
Eglinton West
St. Clair West
Dupont
Bathurst
Christie
Ossington
Dufferin
Lansdowne
Dundas West
Keele
High Park
Runnymede
Jane
Old Mill
Royal York
Islington
Kipling

Bloor Street

Bloor-Danforth Subway

Kipling Avenue in the west to Kennedy Road in the east (where it connects with Scarborough Rapid Transit to Scarborough Centre and McCowan Rd.). The Yonge Street north-south line runs from Finch Avenue in the north to Union Station (Front St.) in the south. From there, it loops north along University Avenue and connects with the Bloor line at the St. George station. A Spadina extension runs north from St. George to Downsview station at Sheppard Avenue. The Sheppard line connects only with the Yonge line at Sheppard station and runs east through north Toronto for just 6km (3¾ miles).

The LRT system connects downtown to Harbourfront. The fare is one ticket or token. It runs from Union Station along Queens Quay to Spadina Avenue, with stops at Queens Quay ferry docks, York Street, Simcoe Street, and Rees Street; then it continues up Spadina Avenue to the Spadina subway station. The transfer from the subway to the LRT (and vice versa) at Union Station is free.

The subway operates Monday to Saturday from 6am to 1:30am and Sunday from 9am to 1:30am. From 1am to 5:30am, the Blue Night Network operates on basic surface routes. It runs about every 30 minutes. For route information, pick up a *Ride Guide* at subway entrances or call ☎ **416/393-4636.** Multilingual information is available.

BUSES & STREETCARS Where the subway leaves off, buses and streetcars take over. They run east-west and north-south along the city's arteries. When you pay your fare (on bus, streetcar, or subway), always pick up a transfer so that you won't have to pay again if you want to transfer to another mode of transportation.

TAXIS In many cities, taxis are an expensive mode of transportation, but this is especially true of Toronto. In 2008, rates were raised (again) because of the high cost of fuel. It's C$4 the minute you step in and C$0.25 for each additional 155m (509 ft.). Fares can quickly mount up. You can hail a cab on the street, find one in line in front of a big hotel, or call one of the major companies—**Diamond** (☎ **416/366-6868**), **Royal** (☎ **416/777-9222**), or **Metro** (☎ **416/504-8294**). If you experience problems with cab service, call the **Metro Licensing Commission** (☎ **416/392-3082**).

FERRY SERVICE Toronto Parks and Recreation operates ferries that travel to the Toronto Islands. Call ☎ **416/392-8193** for schedules and information. Round-trip fares are C$6.50 adults, C$4 seniors and children 15 to 19, C$3 children under 15.

By Car

Toronto is a rambling city, but that doesn't mean the best way to get around is by car. There are long traffic jams, especially during morning and afternoon rush hours. A reputation for "two seasons: winter and construction" means the warmer months are especially busy with road work. And to make matters worse, there is an escalating turf war between the numerous cyclists and motorists sharing the road.

Parking can be very expensive, too, and the city's meter maids are notoriously aggressive in issuing pricey parking tickets at any opportunity.

RENTAL CARS If you decide to rent a car, try to make arrangements in advance. Companies with outlets at Pearson International Airport include **Thrifty, Budget, Avis, Hertz, National,** and **Enterprise** . The rental fee depends on the type of vehicle, but do keep in mind that the quoted price does not include an added sales tax. It also does not include insurance; if you pay with a particular credit card, you might get automatic coverage (check with your credit card issuer before you go). *Note:* If you're under 25, check with the company—many will rent on a cash-only basis, some only with a credit card, and others will not rent to you at all. Also, keep in mind that you must be 21 or older to rent a car.

Car-rental insurance probably does not cover liability if you cause an accident. Check your own auto insurance policy, the rental company policy, and your credit card coverage for the extent of coverage: Is your destination covered? Are other drivers covered? How much liability is covered if a passenger is injured? (If you rely on your credit card for coverage, you may want to bring a second credit card with you, as damages may be charged to your card and you may find yourself stranded with no money.)

PARKING It can be a hassle to find parking in downtown Toronto, and parking lots have a wide range of fees. Generally speaking, the city-owned lots, marked with a big green "ᴘ," are the most affordable. They charge about C$2 per half-hour. After 6pm and on Sunday, there is usually a maximum rate of C$12. Observe the parking restrictions—otherwise, the city will tow your car away, and it'll cost more than C$100 to get it back.

DRIVING RULES A right turn at a red light is legal after coming to a full stop, unless posted otherwise. Passengers must wear seat belts; if you're caught not wearing one, the fine is substantial. The speed limit in the city is 50kmph (31 mph). You must stop at pedestrian crosswalks. If you are following a streetcar and it stops, you must stop well back from the rear doors so passengers can exit easily and safely. (Where there are concrete safety islands in the middle of the street for streetcar stops, this rule does not apply, but exercise care, nonetheless.) Radar detectors are illegal.

FAST FACTS: TORONTO

Area Codes Toronto's area codes are **416** and **647;** outside the city, the code is **905** or **289.** You must dial all 10 digits for all local phone numbers.

Business Hours Banks are generally open Monday through Thursday from 10am to 3pm, Friday 10am to 6pm. Most stores are open Monday through Wednesday from 10am to 6pm, and Saturday and Sunday from 10am to 5pm, with extended hours (until 8 or 9:30pm) on Thursday and often on Friday.

Cellphones See "Mobile Phones," below.

Crime See "Safety," below.

Customs

What You Can Bring into Canada Generally speaking, Canadian Customs regulations are generous, but they get complicated when it comes to firearms, plants, meat, and pets. Visitors can bring rifles into Canada during hunting season; handguns and automatic rifles are not permitted. Fishing tackle poses no problem (provided the lures are not made of restricted materials—specific feathers, for example), but the bearer must possess a nonresident license for the province or territory where he or she plans to use it. You can bring in, free of duty, up to 50 cigars, 200 cigarettes, and 200g (7 oz.) of tobacco, provided you're at least 18 years of age. You are also allowed 1.2L (41 oz.) of liquor or 1.5L (51 oz.) of wine, as long as you're of age in the province you're visiting (19 in Ontario). There are no restrictions on what you can take out (but if you're thinking of bringing Cuban cigars back to the United States, beware—they can be confiscated, and you could face a fine). In terms of pets, visitors from the U.S., the U.K., Ireland, Australia, and New Zealand can bring a cat or dog without quarantine. For more information (and for updates on these policies), check with the **Canada Border Services Agency** (✆ **204/983-3500** or 506/636-5064; www.cbsa.gc.ca).

What You Can Take Home from Canada   For information on what you're allowed to bring home, contact one of the following agencies:

U.S. Citizens: U.S. Customs & Border Protection (CBP), 1300 Pennsylvania Ave., NW, Washington, DC 20229 (✆ **877/287-8667;** www.cbp.gov).

U.K. Citizens: HM Customs & Excise at ✆ **0845/010-9000** (from outside the U.K., 020/8929-0152), or consult their website at **www.hmce.gov.uk**.

Australian Citizens: Australian Customs Service at ✆ **1300/363-263** or **www.customs. gov.au**.

New Zealand Citizens: New Zealand Customs, the Customhouse, 17–21 Whitmore St., Box 2218, Wellington (✆ **04/473-6099** or 0800/428-786; www.customs.govt.nz).

Disabled Travelers   Most disabilities shouldn't stop anyone from traveling. There are more options and resources out there than ever before.

Toronto is a very accessible city. Curb cuts are well made and common throughout the downtown area; special parking privileges are extended to people with disabilities who have special plates or a pass that allows parking in no-parking zones. The subway and trolleys are not accessible, but the city operates **Wheel-Trans,** a special service for those with disabilities. Visitors can register for this service. For information, call ✆ **416/393-4111** or visit **http://www3.ttc.ca/TTC_Accessibility/index.jsp**.

Community Information Toronto (425 Adelaide St. W., at Spadina Ave.; ✆ **416/397-4636**) may be able to provide limited information and assistance about social-service organizations in the city. It does not have specific accessibility information on tourism or hotels, though. It's open daily from 8am to 10pm.

Organizations that offer a vast range of resources and assistance to travelers with disabilities include **MossRehab** (✆ **800/CALL-MOSS** [800/225-5667]; www.mossresource net.org); the **Canadian National Institute for the Blind** (**CNIB;** ✆ **416/486-2500;** www. cnib.ca) or the **American Foundation for the Blind** (**AFB;** ✆ **800/232-5463;** www.afb. org); and **SATH** (Society for Accessible Travel & Hospitality; ✆ **212/447-7284;** www.sath. org). **AirAmbulanceCard.com** is now partnered with SATH and allows you to preselect top-notch hospitals in case of an emergency. **Flying with Disability** (www.flying-with-disability.org) is a comprehensive information source on airplane travel.

Doctors   The staff or concierge at your hotel should be able to help you locate a doctor. You can also call the **College of Physicians and Surgeons of Ontario** (80 College St.; ✆ **416/967-2626**) for a referral from 8am to 5pm Monday through Friday.

Drinking Laws   The legal age for purchase and consumption of alcoholic beverages is 19 throughout Ontario; proof of age is required and often requested at bars, nightclubs, and restaurants, so it's always a good idea to bring ID when you go out.

Bars are usually open until 2am in Toronto, except during special events like the Toronto International Film Festival, when many venues are open later. A government monopoly runs liquor sales: **Liquor Control Board of Ontario (LCBO)** stores sell liquor, wine, and some beers. Most are open daily from 10am to 6pm (some have extended evening hours). The nicest shop is the **LCBO Summerhill** (10 Scrivener Sq.; ✆ **416/922-0403;** subway: Summerhill). Built in a former train station, this outpost hosts cooking classes, wine and spirit tastings, and party-planning seminars. Another good branch is at the **Manulife Centre** (55 Bloor St. W.; ✆ **416/925-5266**). See **www.lcbo.com** for information about products and special in-store events.

Do not carry open containers of alcohol in your car or any public area that isn't zoned for alcohol consumption. The police can fine you on the spot.

Driving Rules See "Getting There" and "Getting Around," earlier in this chapter.

Electricity Like the United States, Canada uses 110 to 120 volts AC (60 cycles), compared to 220 to 240 volts AC (50 cycles) in most of Europe, Australia, and New Zealand. Downward converters that change 220 to 240 volts to 110 to 120 volts are difficult to find in Canada, so bring one with you if you need it.

Embassies & Consulates All embassies are in Ottawa, the national capital. They include the **Australian High Commission** (50 O'Connor St., Ste. 710, Ottawa, ON K1P 6L2; ☎ **613/236-0841**), the **British High Commission** (80 Elgin St., Ottawa, ON K1P 5K7; ☎ **613/237-1530**), the **Embassy of Ireland** (130 Albert St., Ottawa, ON K1P 5G4; ☎ **613/233-6281**), the **New Zealand High Commission** (727–99 Bank St., Ottawa, ON K1P 6G3; ☎ **613/238-5991**), the **South African High Commission** (15 Sussex Dr., Ottawa, ON K1M 1M8; ☎ **613/744-0330**), and the **Embassy of the United States of America** (490 Sussex Dr., Ottawa, ON K1N 1G8; ☎ **613/238-5335**).

Consulates in Toronto include the **Australian Consulate-General** (175 Bloor St. E., Ste. 314, at Church St.; ☎ **416/323-1155**), the **British Consulate-General** (777 Bay St., Ste. 2800, at College St.; ☎ **416/593-1290**), and the **U.S. Consulate** (360 University Ave.; ☎ **416/595-1700**).

Emergencies Call ☎ **911** for fire, police, or ambulance.

For emergency dental services from 8am till midnight, call the **Dental Emergency Service** (☎ **416/485-7121**). After midnight, your best bet is the **University Health Network,** which manages three downtown hospitals (☎ **416/340-3111**). Otherwise, ask the front-desk staff or concierge at your hotel.

Family Travel Toronto is a kid-friendly town. There are plenty of great attractions, such as the water park at Ontario Place; the idiosyncratic Ontario Science Centre; Paramount Canada's Wonderland, a conventional theme park on the outskirts of town noted for its super roller coasters; the artsy Harbourfront centre; and the Toronto Zoo, which rivals the great zoos of the world.

For more suggestions on family and kid-oriented entertainment in Toronto, see "Especially for Kids," in chapter 6. If you're already in town, pick up a copy of *Toronto Families,* a free magazine produced by the publishers of *Today's Parent Toronto* (an award-winning national magazine). You can also check it out online at **www.torontofamilies.ca**.

Helpful features in this guide include "Family-Friendly Hotels" (p. 60).

Recommended family travel websites include **Help! We've Got Kids** (www.helpwevegotkids.com); **Family Travel Forum** (www.familytravelforum.com); **Family Travel Network** (www.familytravelnetwork.com); and **TravelWithYourKids.com**.

To locate accommodations, restaurants, and attractions that are particularly kid-friendly, look for the "Kids" icon throughout this guide.

Gasoline (Petrol) Gasoline is sold by the liter, and taxes are already included in the printed price (unlike most products in Canada). Fill-up locations are known as gas stations or service stations.

Hospitals In the downtown core, the **University Health Network** (UHN) manages three hospitals: **Toronto General,** at 200 Elizabeth St.; **Princess Margaret,** at 610 University Ave.; and **Toronto Western,** at 399 Bathurst St. The UHN has a central switchboard for all three (☎ **416/340-3111**). Other hospitals include **St. Michael's** (30 Bond St.; ☎ **416/360-4000**) and **Mount Sinai** (600 University Ave.; ☎ **416/596-4200**). Also downtown is the **Hospital for Sick Children** (555 University Ave.; ☎ **416/813-1500**). Uptown, there's **Sunnybrook Hospital** (2075 Bayview Ave., north of Eglinton Ave. E.; ☎ **416/480-6100**). In the eastern part of the city, go to **Toronto East General Hospital** (825 Coxwell Ave.; ☎ **416/461-8272**).

Hotlines   There are many services, including the **Poison Information Centre** (℡ 800/267-1373), **Distress Centre** suicide-prevention line (℡ 416/408-4357), **Toronto Rape Crisis Centre** (℡ 416/597-8808), **Assaulted Women's Helpline** (℡ 416/863-0511), and **AIDS & Sexual Health InfoLine** (℡ 416/392-2437). For kids or teens in distress, there's **Kids Help Phone** (℡ 800/668-6868).

Health   Toronto has excellent hospitals and doctors—though hopefully you won't have any occasion to need these services. Bring any prescriptions you might require with you. Decongestants, cough and cold remedies, and allergy medications are available without prescription in pharmacies. Two major chains dominate. **Pharma Plus** has many locations around town, including at one at 63 Wellesley St., at Church Street (℡ **416/924-7760**), that's open daily from 8am to midnight. Other Pharma Plus branches are in College Park, Manulife Centre, Commerce Court, and First Canadian Place. **Shopper's Drug Mart** is also everywhere. The only 24-hour drugstore near downtown is the **Shopper's Drug Mart** at 700 Bay St., at Gerrard Street West (℡ **416/979-2424**).

Insurance   Even though Canada is just a short drive or flight away for many Americans, U.S. health plans (including Medicare and Medicaid) do not provide coverage here, and the ones that do often require you to pay for services up front and reimburse you only after you return home. As a safety net, you may want to buy travel medical insurance. Travelers from the U.K. should carry their European Health Insurance Card (EHIC), which replaced the E111 form as proof of entitlement to free/reduced cost medical treatment abroad (℡ **0845/606-2030;** www.ehic.org.uk). Note, however, that the EHIC covers only "necessary medical treatment," and for repatriation costs, lost money, baggage, or cancellation, travel insurance from a reputable company should always be sought (www.travelinsuranceweb.com).

For information on traveler's insurance, trip cancellation insurance, and medical insurance while traveling, please visit **www.frommers.com/planning**.

Internet & Wi-Fi   Even budget hotels in Toronto now provide Internet access—and often Wi-Fi access. If you don't have a computer with you, there's **Insomnia** (563 Bloor St. W.; ℡ **416/588-3907**). Another option is **FedEx Kinko's.** There are several in the city, but one sure bet is the location at 505 University Ave., at Dundas Street West (℡ **416/970-8447**).

There's also a not-for-profit group called **Wireless Toronto** that's dedicated to providing hotspots. You'll need to register online at **http://wirelesstoronto.ca**; after that, you'll be able to get 20 minutes of free Wi-Fi at places such as Harbourfront's York Quay (p. 106) and Yonge-Dundas Square (p. 190). A complete list of hotpots is available on the website.

Legal Aid   If you are pulled over for a minor infraction (such as speeding), you'll be given a ticket that you pay at a later date. Pay fines by mail or directly into the hands of the clerk of the court. If accused of a more serious offense, say and do nothing before consulting a lawyer. Here, the burden is on the state to prove a person's guilt beyond a reasonable doubt, and everyone has the right to remain silent, whether he or she is suspected of a crime or actually arrested. Once arrested, a person can make one telephone call to a party of his or her choice. International visitors should call their embassy or consulate. If you need to get a lawyer while in Toronto, contact the **Law Society of Upper Canada** (℡ **800/668-7380** or 416/947-3300; www.lsuc.on.ca).

LGBT Travelers   After same-sex marriage became legal in Ontario in 2003, gay and lesbian couples flocked to Toronto to marry. Although in July 2006, the Civil Marriage Act legalized same-sex marriage across Canada, pioneer Toronto remains one of the most in-demand wedding destinations for same-sex couples.

If you want to get married in Toronto, it's pretty simple: Go with your partner to the Registrar General's office at 900 Bay St. (at Wellesley), bring ID (including your passport and birth certificate), pay a small fee, and the marriage license will be yours; there's no residency requirement. See www.toronto.ca for details and an application form that you can download. For help organizing a wedding beyond the confines of city hall, check out the wedding-planner pages at www.toronto.com. One company that specializes in planning same-sex weddings is **I Do in Toronto** (☏ **888/418-1188;** www.idointoronto.com). While many wedding ceremonies are conducted at the **Toronto Civic Wedding Chambers** (100 Queen St. W.; ☏ **416/363-0316**), couples are increasingly choosing to wed elsewhere. One popular place is the **Metropolitan Community Church of Toronto** (☏ **416/406-6228;** www.mcctoronto.com), which has been very active in the battle for same-sex marriage rights.

Mail Postage for letter mail (up to 30g/1 oz.) to the United States costs C$1.03; overseas, it's C$2.06. Mailing letters within Canada costs C59¢. Note that there is no discounted rate for mailing postcards. For more information, go to **www.canadapost.ca**.

Postal services are available at some drugstores. Almost all drugstores sell stamps, and many have a separate counter where you can ship packages from 8:30am to 5pm. Look for a sign in the window indicating such services. There are also post-office windows in **Atrium on Bay** (☏ **416/506-0911**), in **Commerce Court** (☏ **416/956-7452**), and at the **TD Centre** (☏ **416/360-7105**).

Mobile Phones Most U.S. cellphone carriers have roaming agreements with Canadian cellphone carriers. Before leaving home, check with your carrier for rates and availability. You can rent a cellphone in Toronto from **Hello Anywhere** (☏ **888/729-4355** or 416/367-4355; www.helloanywhere.com). Also, cellphone rentals are available through many of Toronto's more upscale hotels, including the **Park Hyatt Toronto,** the **Metropolitan Hotel,** and the **Sutton Place Hotel.**

Money & Costs

THE VALUE OF THE CANADIAN DOLLAR VS. OTHER POPULAR CURRENCIES

Can$	US$	UK£	Euro (€)	Aus$	NZ$
C$1	US$1.00	65p	0.74€	A$1	NZ$1.20

Frommer's lists exact prices in the local currency. The currency conversions quoted above were correct at press time. However, rates fluctuate, so before departing, consult a currency exchange website, such as **www.oanda.com/currency/converter**, to check up-to-the-minute rates.

Toronto is one of Canada's most expensive cities (along with Vancouver), but compared with other major world cities, such as New York, London, and Tokyo, it's very affordable. There are some exceptions, like the above-mentioned high taxi fares, pricey museum admissions (especially compared with the recent, progressive programs in places like London that draw crowds with discounted or free admissions), high sales taxes, and thanks to the government monopoly on alcohol, inflated prices for wine, beer, and cocktails.

Currency Canadians use **dollars** and **cents:** Paper currency comes in C$5, C$10, C$20, C$50, and C$100 denominations. Coins come in 1-, 5-, 10-, and 25-cent, and 1- and 2-dollar denominations. The gold-colored C$1 coin is a "loonie"—it sports a loon on its "tails" side—and the large gold-and-silver-colored C$2 coin is a "toonie." If you find these names somewhat . . . ah, colorful, just remember that there's no swifter way to reveal that you're a tourist than to say "one-dollar coin."

WHAT THINGS COST IN TORONTO	C$
Taxi from the airport to downtown	60.00
Subway ride	3.00
Round-trip ticket for the Toronto Island Ferry	6.50
Local telephone call	0.50
Double at the Delta Chelsea Hotel (moderate)	189.00
Soup, sandwich, and frites lunch at Gilead Café (moderate)*	23.00
Three-course dinner for one at Grano (moderate)*	50.00
Pint of beer at Mill Street Brew Pub	7.00
Coca-Cola (355mL/12-oz. can)	1.50
Cup of coffee (black, not latte)	2.00
Admission to the Art Gallery of Ontario	18.00
Movie ticket	12.99
Ticket for the Canadian Opera Company	20.00–317.53
Show at the Second City comedy club	30.00
375mL (12.7-oz.) bottle of Inniskillin Vidal ice wine (LCBO)	79.00
*Includes tax and tip, but not wine	

Ideally, you should exchange enough petty cash to cover airport incidentals, tipping, and transportation to your hotel before you leave home; however, it's very easy to withdraw money upon arrival at an ATM at Pearson airport. Check with your local American Express or Thomas Cook office, or with your bank. American Express cardholders can order foreign currency over the phone at ☎ 800/807-6233.

It's best to exchange currency or traveler's checks at a bank, not a currency exchange, hotel, or shop. Get up-to-the-minute exchange rates online before you go at **www.oanda.com/currency/converter** or **www.xe.com/ucc**.

ATMs   The easiest and best way to get cash away from home is from an ATM (automated teller machine), sometimes referred to as a "cash machine," or a "cashpoint." The **Cirrus** (☎ 800/424-7787; www.mastercard.com) and **PLUS** (☎ 800/843-7587; www.visa.com) networks span the globe. Go to your bank card's website to find ATM locations at your destination. Be sure you know your daily withdrawal limit before you depart. *Note:* Many banks impose a fee every time you use a card at another bank's ATM, and that fee can be higher for international transactions than for domestic ones. In addition, the bank from which you withdraw cash may charge its own fee. For international withdrawal fees, ask your bank. Banks that are members of the **Global ATM Alliance** charge no transaction fees for cash withdrawals at other Alliance member ATMs; these include Bank of America, Scotiabank (Canada, Caribbean, and Mexico), Barclays (U.K. and parts of Africa), Deutsche Bank (Germany, Poland, Spain, and Italy), and BNP Paribas (France).

Credit Cards   MasterCard and Visa are almost universally accepted in Toronto; American Express has become more common, but many independent boutiques and small restaurants still don't accept it. Overall, credit cards are a smart way to "carry" money. They also provide a convenient record of all your expenses, and they generally offer relatively good exchange rates. You can withdraw cash advances from your credit cards at banks or ATMs, but high fees make credit card cash advances a pricey way to get cash. Keep in mind that you'll pay interest from the moment of your withdrawal, even if you pay your monthly bills on time. Also, note that many banks now assess a 1% to 3% "transaction fee" on *all* charges you incur abroad (whether you're using the local currency or your native currency).

Traveler's Checks   Traveler's checks are something of an anachronism in Toronto, since ATMs have made getting cash accessible at any time. However, traveler's checks are still widely accepted—and unlike cash, can be replaced if lost or stolen.

You can buy traveler's checks at most banks. They are offered in denominations of $20, $50, $100, $500, and sometimes $1,000. Generally, you'll pay a service charge ranging from 1% to 4%.

The most popular traveler's checks are offered by **American Express** (© **800/807-6233,** or © 800/221-7282 for card holders—this number accepts collect calls, offers service in several foreign languages, and exempts Amex gold and platinum cardholders from the 1% fee); **Visa** (© **800/732-1322**); and **MasterCard** (© **800/223-9920**).

Be sure to keep a record of the traveler's checks serial numbers separate from your checks, in the event that they are stolen or lost. You'll get a refund faster if you know the numbers.

Another option is the new prepaid traveler's check cards, reloadable cards that work much like debit cards but aren't linked to your checking account. The **American Express Travelers Cheque Card,** for example, requires a minimum deposit, sets a maximum balance, and has a one-time issuance fee of $15. You can withdraw money from an ATM (for a fee of $2.50 per transaction, not including bank fees), and the funds can be purchased in dollars, euros, or pounds. If you lose the card, your available funds will be refunded within 24 hours.

Medical Conditions   If you have a medical condition that requires **syringe-administered medications,** carry a valid signed prescription from your physician; syringes in carry-on baggage will be inspected. Insulin in any form should have the proper pharmaceutical documentation. If you have a disease that requires treatment with **narcotics,** you should also carry documented proof with you—smuggling narcotics aboard a plane carries severe penalties.

For **HIV-positive visitors,** Canada does not require testing to enter the country on a tourist visa. However, a traveler can be denied entry to Canada if they are assessed as requiring health services during their stay. (Canada does not cover medical costs incurred by travelers.)

Newspapers & Magazines   The four daily newspapers are the *Globe and Mail,* the *National Post,* the *Toronto Star,* and the *Toronto Sun. Eye* and *Now* are free arts-and-entertainment weeklies. *Xtra!* is a free weekly targeted at the gay and lesbian community. In addition, many English-language ethnic newspapers serve Toronto's Portuguese, Hungarian, Italian, East Indian, Korean, Chinese, and Caribbean communities. *Toronto Life* is the major monthly city magazine. *Where Toronto* magazine is usually free at hotels and some Theater District restaurants.

Petrol   Please see "Gasoline," earlier in this section.

Passports   See **www.frommers.com/planning** for information on how to obtain a passport. See "Embassies & Consulates," above, for whom to contact if you lose yours while traveling in Canada. For other information, please contact the following agencies:

For Residents of Australia   Contact the Australian Passport Information Service at © **131-232** or visit the government website at www.passports.gov.au.

For Residents of Ireland   Contact the **Passport Office** (Setanta Centre, Molesworth Street, Dublin 2; © **01/671-1633;** www.irlgov.ie/iveagh).

For Residents of New Zealand   Contact the Passports Office at ✆ **0800/225-050** in New Zealand or 04/474-8100, or log on to www.passports.govt.nz.

For Residents of the United Kingdom   Visit your nearest passport office, major post office, or travel agency, or contact the **United Kingdom Passport Service** at ✆ **0870/521-0410** or search its website at **www.ukpa.gov.uk.**

For Residents of the United States   To find your regional passport office, either check the U.S. Department of State website www.state.gov or call the **National Passport Information Center** toll-free number (✆ **877/487-2778**) for automated information.

Police   In a life-threatening emergency, call ✆ **911.** For all other matters, contact the **Toronto Police Service** (40 College St.; ✆ **416/808-2222**).

Safety   Toronto enjoys an unusually safe reputation as far as big cities go, although a steady supply of guns coming across the border from the U.S. is damaging the now worn-out reputation of "Toronto the Good." But keep in mind that it is a big city, with all of the difficulties that implies. While lovely parks such as Allan Gardens and Trinity Bell-woods have been cleaned up in recent years, it's best to avoid all big parks after dark unless you're attending a special event such as a theatre performance. During the day, keep your valuables close and your eyes peeled for pickpockets. This is important to keep in mind when you're at a major tourist attraction, on a crowded shopping strip such as Yonge Dundas Square, and on the subway or streetcar.

More about safety on Toronto's public transit system: If it's late and you're alone on an almost-empty platform, wait for the train by the big "DWA" sign (it stands for **"Designated Waiting Area,"** and it has an intercom and a closed-circuit TV camera trained on it). There is a DWA area at every TTC station. If there is an incident on a subway car, press the alarm—the yellow strip is very visible—and note that it is silent. If you are traveling by bus, there is a **"Request Stop"** program in effect between 9pm and 5am, in which female passengers traveling alone can disembark at streets in between regular TTC bus stops. For information about these safety features, visit **http://www3.ttc.ca/Riding_the_TTC/Safety_and_Security/index.jsp**.

Senior Travel   The term "seniors" is proving to be more elastic than most face-lifts. Boomers in the above-50 group should check out the local magazine *Zoomer,* which is connected to **CARP** (Canadian Association of Retired Persons; ✆ **416/363-8748;** www.carp.ca). Members of **CARP** or **AARP** (the American analog; ✆ **888/687-2277;** www.aarp.org) can get discounts on hotels, airfares, and car rentals. Otherwise, seniors can expect to receive discounts on the TTC (subway and bus), and on many (but not all) admissions to attractions. Keep in mind that it is usually necessary to show photo identification when purchasing discounted tickets or admissions.

Smoking   The Smoke-Free Ontario Act, which came into effect in 2006, is one of the most stringent in North America. It bans smoking in all workplaces and in all enclosed public spaces. There are no smoking areas in restaurants or bars, and covered patios are also smoke-free. Some patios and rooftops have smoking sections.

Taxes   As of July 1, 2010, the Ontario government implemented a "harmonized" tax system, with a 13% sales tax on virtually everything for sale. (Previously, the federal GST was 5% and the Ontario sales tax was 8%, but the Ontario sales tax was not applied to purchases such as fast-food meals.) Taxes are added when you purchase an item, rather than being included in the original price, as is common in much of Europe. The Canadian government suspended the GST Visitors' Rebate Program in 2007.

Within the city of Toronto, there is a new bylaw, introduced in 2009, that obliges retailers to charge a minimum of 5¢ per plastic bag. There are no exceptions to this rule. (The funds collected are not really a tax, since they go into the store's coffers and not the city's, but some people consider this a tax on shoppers.)

Telephones **To call Toronto from the U.S.:** Canada and the U.S. use the same area-code system. Simply dial 1, the Toronto area code (416 or 647), and the number.

To call Toronto from other countries:

1. Dial the international access code: 00 from the U.K., Ireland, or New Zealand; or 0011 from Australia.
2. Dial the country code 1.
3. Dial the city code 416 or 647, and then the number.

To make international calls To make international calls from Toronto, first dial 00, and then the country code (U.K. 44, Ireland 353, Australia 61, New Zealand 64). Next, dial the area code and number. However, if you are calling the U.S. from Toronto, you need only to dial 1 and then the area code and phone number.

For directory assistance Dial 🕾 **411** if you're looking for a phone number; online, visit **www.canada411.com**.

For operator assistance If you need operator assistance in making a call, dial 🕾 **0** (zero).

Toll-free numbers Numbers beginning with 800 or 866 are toll-free within Canada and the U.S. However, calling an 800 number from other countries is not toll-free. In fact, it costs the same as an overseas call.

Many convenience stores and packaging services sell **prepaid calling cards** in denominations up to C$50; for international visitors, these can be the least expensive way to call home. It's hard to find public pay phones; those at airports now accept American Express, MasterCard, and Visa credit cards. Local calls made from pay phones in most locales cost C50¢ (no pennies). Most long-distance and international calls can be dialed directly from any phone. **For calls within Canada and to the United States,** dial 1 followed by the area code and the seven-digit number. **For other international calls,** dial 011 followed by the country code, city code, and the number you are calling.

Calls to area codes **800, 888, 877,** and **866** are toll-free. However, calls to area codes **700** and **900** (chat lines, bulletin boards, "dating" services, and so on) can be very expensive—usually a charge of C95¢ to C$3 or more per minute, and they sometimes have minimum charges that can run as high as C$15 or more.

For **reversed-charge or collect calls,** and for person-to-person calls, dial the number 0, then the area code and number; an operator will come on the line, and you should specify whether you are calling collect, person-to-person, or both. If your operator-assisted call is international, ask for the overseas operator.

For **local directory assistance** ("information"), dial 🕾 **411;** for long-distance information, dial 1, then the appropriate area code, and 555-1212.

Time Toronto is on Eastern Standard Time. When it's noon in Toronto, it's 9am in Los Angeles (PST), it's 7am in Honolulu (HST), 10am in Denver (MST), 11am in Chicago (CST), noon in New York City (also on EST), 5pm in London (GMT), and 2am the next day in Sydney (UTC + 9).

Daylight Saving Time is in effect from 1am on the second Sunday in March to 1am on the first Sunday in November. Daylight Saving Time moves the clock 1 hour ahead of standard time.

Tipping Tips are a very important part of certain workers' income, and gratuities are the standard way of showing appreciation for services provided. (Tipping is certainly not compulsory if the service is poor!) In hotels, tip **bellhops** at least C$1 per bag (C$2–C$3 if you have a lot of luggage) and tip the **chamber staff** C$1 to C$2 per day (more if you've left a disaster area for him or her to clean up). Tip the **doorman** or **concierge** $2 or more only if he or she has provided you with some specific service (for example, calling a cab for you or obtaining difficult-to-get theater tickets). Tip the **valet-parking attendant** C$1 or more every time you get your car.

In restaurants, bars, and nightclubs, tip **service staff** 15% to 20% of the check, tip **bartenders** 10% to 15%, tip **checkroom attendants** C$1 per garment, and tip **valet-parking attendants** C$1 per vehicle.

As for other service personnel, tip **cab drivers** 15% of the fare; tip **skycaps** at airports at least C$1 per bag (C$2–C$3 if you have a lot of luggage); and tip **hairdressers** and **barbers** 15% to 20%.

Toilets   You won't find public toilets or "restrooms" on the streets in Toronto, but they can be found in hotel lobbies, bars, restaurants, museums, department stores, railway and bus stations, and service stations. Public parks also offer restrooms, although they may be closed and/or not very clean. Large hotels and fast-food restaurants are often the best bet for clean facilities. Restaurants and bars in resorts or heavily visited areas may reserve their restrooms for patrons. There are also restrooms throughout the underground PATH system near the various food courts. There are restrooms at major subway stations, such as Yonge-Bloor, which are best used in the daytime when the subways are busy.

VAT   See "Taxes," above.

Visas   For citizens of many countries, including the U.S., U.K., Ireland, Australia, and New Zealand, only a passport is required to visit Canada for up to 90 days; no visas or proof of vaccinations are necessary. For the most up-to-date list of visitor visa exemptions, visit **Citizenship and Immigration Canada** at **www.cic.gc.ca**.

Visitor Information   The best source for Toronto-specific information is **Tourism Toronto** (© 800/499-2514 from North America or 416/203-2600; www.seetorontonow. com). The website includes sections on accommodations, sights, shopping, and dining, plus up-to-the-minute events information. There's also a "Special Offers" section, which has package deals for hotels, and attractions or shows.

For information about traveling in the province of Ontario, contact **Tourism Ontario** (© 800/ONTARIO [800/668-2746]; www.ontariotravel.net). While in Toronto, visit its information center in the **Atrium on Bay** (street level) at 20 Dundas St. W.—it's just across Dundas Street from the Sears store at the northern edge of the Eaton Centre. It's open daily from 8:30am to 4:30pm; hours are extended during the summer, often to 8pm.

Toronto.com (www.toronto.com), operated by the *Toronto Star,* offers extensive restaurant reviews, events listings, and feature articles. A couple of other great sources for local goings-on and news: the **Torontoist** blog (www.torontoist.com) and **blogTO** (www. blogto.com). If you love to shop, check out **SweetSpot** (www.sweetspot.ca) for its extensive Toronto coverage of local designers and boutiques. www.toronto.com also offers plenty of up-to-date reviews of hotels, nightclubs, restaurants, bars, and shows around town.

BlogTO produces some of my favorite local maps: You can pick them up for free at shops and restaurants around town. At press time, they have produced maps for West Queen West, Leslieville, Parkdale, and Little Italy. *Where Toronto* also prints good neighborhood maps in the magazine. Online, take a look at **Google Maps** (http://maps.google. com) for details on getting from Point A to Point B.

Water   Toronto's tap water is safe to drink, and it is tested continuously to guarantee public safety. For details, visit the City of Toronto's water information page at **www. toronto.ca/water**. However, while you'll see many locals swimming in Lake Ontario, this is not a good idea if you want to stay healthy; the lake contains high levels of *E. coli,* which causes nasty bacterial infections.

Wi-Fi   See "Internet & Wi-Fi," earlier in this section.

Women Travelers   Toronto is an easy place to be for solo travelers, male or female. At night, take note of the TTC's "Request Stop" program for women traveling on buses (see "Safety," above). Check out the award-winning website **Journeywoman** (www.journeywoman.com), a "real-life" women's travel-information network, where you can sign up for a free e-mail newsletter and get advice on everything from etiquette and dress to safety. The travel guide *Safety and Security for Women Who Travel,* **2nd Edition,** by Sheila Swan and Peter Laufer (Travelers' Tales), offers common-sense tips on safe travel. For general travel resources for women, go to Frommers.com.

AIRLINE WEBSITES

Canadian Airlines

Air Canada
www.aircanada.com

Porter Airlines
www.flyporter.com

WestJet
www.westjet.com

Major Airlines

Aeroméxico
www.aeromexico.com

Air Canada
www.aircanada.com

Air France
www.airfrance.com

Air India
www.airindia.com

Air Jamaica
www.airjamaica.com

Air New Zealand
www.airnewzealand.com

Alitalia
www.alitalia.com

American Airlines
www.aa.com

British Airways
www.british-airways.com

Caribbean Airlines (formerly BWIA)
www.caribbean-airlines.com

China Airlines
www.china-airlines.com

Continental Airlines
www.continental.com

Cubana
www.cubana.cu

Delta Air Lines
www.delta.com

El Al Airlines
www.elal.co.il

Emirates Airlines
www.emirates.com

globespan
www.flyglobespan.ca

Hawaiian Airlines
www.hawaiianair.com

Iberia Airlines
www.iberia.com

Lan Airlines
www.lan.com

Lufthansa
www.lufthansa.com

Qantas Airways
www.qantas.com

TACA
www.taca.com

United Airlines
www.united.com

US Airways
www.usairways.com

Virgin Atlantic Airways
www.virgin-atlantic.com

Index

Accommodations

Restaurants